An Introduction to Machine Translation

An Introduction to Machine Translation

W. John Hutchins
The Library,
University of East Anglia,
Norwich, UK

and

Harold L. Somers
Centre for Computational Linguistics,
University of Manchester Institute of
Science and Technology,
Manchester, UK

ACADEMIC PRESS

Harcourt Brace Jovanovich, Publishers

LONDON   SAN DIEGO   NEW YORK   BOSTON
SYDNEY   TOKYO   TORONTO

This book is printed on acid-free paper

ACADEMIC PRESS LIMITED
24–28 Oval Road
LONDON NW1 7DX

United States Edition published by
ACADEMIC PRESS INC.
San Diego, CA 92101

Copyright © 1992 by
ACADEMIC PRESS LIMITED

A catalogue record for this book is
available from the British Library

ISBN 0-12-362830-X

Printed in Great Britain at the University Press, Cambridge

Contents

Foreword

Machine translation was a matter of serious speculation long before there were computers to apply to it; it was one of the first major problems to which digital computers were turned; and it has been a subject of lively, sometimes acrimonious, debate every since. Machine translation has claimed attention from some of the keenest minds in linguistics, philosophy, computer science, and mathematics. At the same time it has always attracted the lunatic fringe, and continues to do so today.

The fascination with machine translation doubtless has many sources. No one who reads the King James Bible, or FitzGerald's *Rubaiyat of Omar Khayyam*, or any of the dozen or so translations that are made every month of *Scientific American* or *Geo* magazine, or the facing pages of the magazines the Canadian airlines give their clients, can retain any doubt that translation is one of the highest accomplishments of human art. It is comparable in many ways to the creation of an original literary work. To capture it in a machine would therefore be to capture some essential part of the human spirit, thereby coming to understand its mysteries. But just because there is so much of the human spirit in translation, many reject out of hand any possibility that it could ever be done by a machine. There is nothing that a person could know, or feel, or dream, that could not be crucial for getting a good translation of some text or other. To be a translator, therefore, one cannot just have some parts of humanity; one must be a complete human being.

Many scientists believe that there is insight to be gained from studying machine translation even when it is applied to very pedestrian kinds of text with the expectation of producing results of a quite pedestrian kind. This is because translation is a task that obviously exercises every kind of linguistic ability, except those involved with the production and perception of speech, without requiring any other contact with the world. For example, a scientist interested in how people collect words to make up sentences, and sentences to make up texts, might seek to test his theories in a computer program that produced sentences and texts. Such a scientist would face the problem of how to provide his program with something that it wanted to say. Programs do not generally have needs or desires that they might expect to fulfill by talking, or perceptions of the world that might strike them as worthy of comment. The investigator would therefore be faced with the logically prior problem of how to provide his machine with an urge to talk. One way to do this that avoids the problems of perception, and most of the problems of motivation, is to have the program simply say what it is told to say. This proposal clearly runs the risk of trivializing the problem. The solution is to provide the stimulus in a different language from the one in which the response must be given.

Much of the motivation for studying machine translation has been very different, coming from the perceived need to produce more translations, to produce them faster, and to produce them at lower cost. More and more of the world's commerce is conducted across national, and therefore linguistic, boundaries so that letters, agreements, contracts, manuals, and so forth, must be produced in several languages. Modern technology develops and changes faster than ever before, and the accompanying texts must therefore be replaced correspondingly sooner. Futhermore, advanced technology, such as cars, computers, and household appliances, is no longer available only to people with advanced education, so that the texts that are needed to operate and maintain these products can no longer be produced only in English. In the countries of the European Communities, in Canada, in many developing countries, and doubtless soon in the Soviet Union, translations are required for legal or nationalistic reasons even when a single version might fill the primary need.

In recent years, this perceived need for more translations than human translators can produce has led to a great increase in activity in the field, especially in Europe and Japan. To be sure, the aims of this work do not encompass anything comparable to the King James Bible or the *Rubaiyat of Omar Khayyam*. They do not even include the *Scientific American* or even advertising copy. In the near term, practical machine translation is intended to be applied to two kinds of material. The first is material that covers such a narrow subject matter, and in such a routine fashion, as to require little on the part of the translator that could really count as understanding. The second is material that will be read by people seeking only a rough idea of what is being said, so that an extremely rough translation will be adequate. Maintenance manuals for machines belong in the first category and the second finds its customers in companies with major competitors abroad and in government agencies with unlisted addresses.

Only under very special circumstances are the readers of translated texts allowed to see what emerges from the translation machine and, if they did they would surely be surprised at how different it is from what they actually get. This is because it has almost invariably undergone a process called 'post-editing' by a human translator. This, the defenders of the machine are quick to point out, is no different from what happens when translations are made in the traditional manner; an initial translation is checked by a 'reviser', who often changes the first version quite extensively. But critics of machine translation, of whom there are many, are more inclined to credit the translation to the post-editor, and only some occasional hints to the machine. Certainly, even when applied to texts on very limited subjects by authors with no literary pretentions, machine translation still generally produces results that would not be acceptable from a human translator under any circumstances. Just what would improve the quality of the result, and even whether any substantial improvement is possible, are open questions. Indeed, it is an open question whether the great investment that has been made in the enterprise since the first systems were put to use in the 1960s has resulted in any real improvement.

As an observer of machine translation, John Hutchins has, in several other publications, provided many readers with their first introduction to the subject. Harold Somers has stimulated the interest of generations of students in it at the University of Manchester Institute of Science and Technology which, largely as a result of his endeavours, has also become one of the world's foremost centres for research in machine translation. They clearly both have opinions on the open questions of machine translation, but they are not the subject of this book. The reader who seeks insight into the open questions, however, will do well to begin here. This is a technical book, in the sense of explaining the parts of machine translation systems, the principles behind the parts, and such relevant theory as is available from linguistics and computer science. It is a non-technical book in that it assumes no prior knowledge of these matters on the part of its readers. The first part of the book gives all the background necessary for the remarkably detailed and insightful descriptions of several representative systems that make up the second part. There must be few people, even among those who are professionally engaged in this work, who would not find information in this second part that was new and surprising to them.

Martin Kay

Preface

It has been estimated that the demand for translations is growing at a rate well beyond the present or foreseeable capacity of the translation profession. The application of computers to this task was first proposed over forty years ago. The idea had an immediate impact on the public, but interest fell away when no working systems appeared. In recent years, however, interest has grown markedly with the commercial development of crude but reasonably cost-effective computer-based aids for translators. It has focused attention again on the research in Machine Translation (MT) which had continued largely unnoticed. There is now a demand for basic introductions to the subject, from translators and other potential users of systems and from scientists in related fields of research.

The primary aim of this book is to serve the need felt by many teachers in further and higher education for a students' introduction to MT. It is anticipated that it could form the basis for courses attended by students of linguistics or computer science, perhaps as components of courses on computational linguistics or artificial intelligence. As a textbook it will probably be most suitable for students who have already attended seminars on linguistics or computer science, although we have provided two background chapters for those readers who feel they lack knowledge in either of these areas. Familiarity with computational linguistics or artificial intelligence is not assumed.

A second category of reader is the researcher in some related sphere of natural language processing who is looking for an introductory overview of the problems encountered and the methods and techniques applied in MT. There is growing regard by many active in artificial intelligence, cognitive science, information retrieval, computer science, and the 'language industries' in general for what research in MT has to offer. There is also increasing awareness among theoretical linguists that programs for MT (and other areas of computational linguistics) may provide realistic 'testbeds' of their hypotheses about how language functions.

As a third category of reader, we may anticipate the interested layperson, someone whose curiosity has been aroused by the prospects of automating translation and who would like to find out more. We hope that there will be nothing too abstruse to deter such readers from reading the whole text, although some of the chapters in the second part may be somewhat demanding.

Our aim in this book is to introduce what may legitimately be regarded as the well-established core of methods and approaches in MT. It is concerned with the problems and difficulties of programming computers to translate, with what has been achieved and with what remains to be done; it is not concerned primarily with practical aspects of operating systems, although we have included chapters on the kinds of systems which are available and on how systems may be evaluated. It is not, however, in any sense a guide for translators and others who want a comparative survey of the capabilities and limitations of currently marketed systems or who want accounts of successful (or unsuccessful) implementations of systems in working environments. That would be quite a different book, although undoubtedly one which would be welcomed.

The book is in two parts. In the first part we describe the basic processes, problems and methods. Chapter 1 is a general introduction, with a brief history. Chapters 2 and 3 give the linguistic and computational backgrounds respectively, which might be omitted by those very familiar with these two areas. In Chapter 4 we introduce the basic strategies of system design. Chapters 5, 6 and 7 represent the core chapters, covering respectively the three basic translation processes of analysis, transfer and generation. Chapter 8 describes the ways in which systems operate in practice, and Chapter 9 outlines approaches to the evaluation of systems.

In the second part we describe in detail some actual systems, chosen to illustrate particular features. Here readers will find that the relatively clear-cut distinctions made in the first half do not always apply strictly when discussing individual systems. They will note that in almost every case these are systems in evolution; it is often impossible to give detailed descriptions of the current status of projects, and readers should also be aware that our accounts do not necessarily represent the views of project researchers now or in the past.

Chapter 10 is devoted to Systran, the best known 'direct' system and the most widely used mainframe MT system at the present time. Chapter 11 is on Susy, an example of a standard 'transfer' design. Chapter 12 describes the archetypal sublanguage system Météo, in daily use since the mid 1970s. Chapter 13 covers Ariane, regarded as one of the most important research projects for many years. Chapter 14 is devoted to the well-known multilingual Eurotra project supported by the European Communities. Chapter 15 covers Metal, the most advanced commercial system, based on many years of research at the University of Texas. Chapter 16 describes the innovative Rosetta project, exploring a compositional isomorphic approach inspired by Montague grammar. Chapter 17 gives an account of the DLT project, notable for its use of Esperanto as an interlingua. The final chapter deals briefly with some other projects and systems including a knowledge-based system, the example-based approach, a statistics-based system, and systems for monolinguals; it covers also controlled language and sublanguage systems and systems aimed at telephone speech translation; and it concludes with comments on possible future directions.

We have, of course, not intended to be comprehensive in our coverage of MT systems. There are two obvious omissions: readers will find no detailed descriptions of the numerous Japanese systems, nor accounts of the commercial systems now on the market. Their absence in this introductory text does not reflect any judgement whatever by the authors of the value or significance of the systems concerned. Indeed, we have both written elsewhere at length on these systems, and in this book references will be found for interested readers. Our criteria for including systems for detailed treatment were that systems should be good representatives of important MT approaches or techniques, should illustrate well developments which have been significant, and which are well documented for students and others to follow up, particularly English-language documentation. They are systems which, in our opinion, any future MT researchers ought to be familiar with.

During the writing of this book we have leaned on many colleagues in the field, and especially at the Centre for Computational Linguistics at UMIST, where staff and students on the Computational Linguistics and Machine Translation courses have been a constant inspiration. The University of East Anglia is also to be thanked for granting study leave to WJH, without which this book might still only be nearing completion. Deserving special thanks are Iris Arad, Claude Bédard, Paul Bennett, Jeremy Carroll, Jacques Durand, Martin Earl, Rod Johnson, Martin Kay, Jock McNaught, Jeanette Pugh and Nick Somers. In addition, we would like to mention Liz Diggle who transcribed the lectures on which some of these chapters are based, and Jane Wooders who helped prepare the camera-ready copy of the end result. Finally, thanks to our wives for their tolerance while this book has been in the making.

W. John Hutchins

Harold L. Somers

List of abbreviations and symbols

Listed here are abbreviations found in the text which are not always explained wherever they occur. Not included are everyday abbreviations as given in *Everyman's Dictionary of Abbreviations*.

acc — accusative

adj — adjective

adjgrp — adjective group

AdjP — adjectival phrase

adv — adverb

AI — Artificial Intelligence

AGT — agent

ALPAC — Automated Language Processing Advisory Committee

art — article

ARTD article (definite)

ASCII — American Standard Code for Information Interchange

ATN — Augmented Transition Network

ATR — Advanceded Telecommunications Research

attr — attribute

aux — auxiliary

BKB — Bilingual Knowledge Bank

BSO — *Bureau voor Systeemontwikkeling*

BT — British Telecom

C — condition

CAT — Computer-Aided (or Assisted) Translation

CAT, <C,A>,T — <Constructor, Atom>, Translator

cat — category

CCRIT — *Centre Canadien de Recherche sur l'Informatisation du Travail*

CD — compact disk

CEC — Commission of the European Communities

CETA — *Centre d'Etudes pour la Traduction Automatique*

CFG — context free grammar

CLG — Constraint Logic Grammar

CLRU — Cambridge Language Research Unit

Cmod — condition modifier

CMU — Carnegie Mellon University

compl — complement

COND — condition

conjug — conjugation

CONSTR — construct

DCG — Definite Clause Grammar

def — definiteness

demp — demonstrative pronoun

deriv — derivation

des — *désinence* [inflection]

det — determiner

detp — determiner phrase

DLT — Distributed Language Translation

d-obj — direct object

dtr — daughter

EBMT — Example-Based Machine Translation

ECS — Eurotra constituent structure

EMS — Eurotra morphological structure

ENT — Eurotra normalized text

ERS — Eurotra relational structure

ETS — Eurotra text structure

exper — experiencer

f — feminine

FAHQT — Fully Automatic High Quality Translation

fun — function

gen — gender, genitive

gend — gender

GETA — *Groupe d'Etudes pour la Traduction Automatique*

gov — governor

GADJ — *groupe adjectival* [=AdjP]

GB — Government and Binding

GN — *groupe nominal* [=NP]

GPSG — Generalized Phrase Structure Grammar

HAMT — Human-Aided (or Assisted) Machine Translation

IBM — International Business Machines

indic-pres — indicative present

inf-compl — infinitival complement

inst — instrument

i-obj — indirect object

IS — interface structure

ISSCO — *Istituto per gli Studi Semantichi e Cognitivi*

KBMT — Knowledge-Based Machine Translation

L — location

lex — lexeme, lexical

LFG — Lexical Functional Grammar

LKB — Linguistic Knowledge Bank

LOC, loc — locative

LR — logical role, logical relation

LRC — Linguistics Research Center

LU — lexical unit

m — masculine

MAHT — Machine-Aided (or Assisted) Human Translation

masc — masculine

Mips — millions of instructions per second

MIR — METAL Interface Representation

MIT — Massachussetts Institute of Technology

mod — modifier

MT — Machine Translation

n — noun

nbr — number

NC — noun (common)

ncomp — noun complement

NEC — Nippon Electric Company

neut — neuter

nom — nominative

NP — noun phrase

num — number

OCR — optical character recognition, reader

obj — object

p — preposition

PAHO — Pan-American Health Organization

pastpart — past participle

pat — patient

pers — person

PHVB — *phrase verbale* [=VP]

pkt — punctuation

pl, plur — plural

PP — prepositional phrase

pospron — possessive pronoun

pred — predicate

prep — preposition

pres — present

pron — pronoun

prop-n — proper noun

qtf, quant — quantifier

ref — reference

ROM — read-only memory

S — sentence

SComp — sentential complement

sem — semantic

SF — syntactic function

SFB — *Sonderforschungsbereich*

sg, sing — singular

subj, SUJ— subject, *sujet*

T — time

TAUM — *Traduction Automatique de l'Université de Montréal*

TG — Transformational Generative (grammar)

tns — tense

UMIST — University of Manchester Institute of Science and Technology

USAF — United States Air Force

v, VB — verb

VDU — visual display unit

verbfunc — verb function

VP — verb phrase

Vpass — verb (passive)

VST — verb stem

vwl — vowel

WTC — World Translation Center

∀ universal quantifier 'all'

∃ existential quantifier 'exists'

∪ set union

→ rewrites as

⇒ is transformed into

↑ metavariable 'up', or 'mother'

↓ metavariable 'down', or 'self'

/ 'slash' indicating missing element (GPSG) or rightwards combination (Categorial)

\ 'back-slash' leftwards combination

< linearly precedes

△ (in diagrams) details omitted

* ungrammatical, unacceptable or anomalous

1
General introduction and brief history

The mechanization of translation has been one of humanity's oldest dreams. In the twentieth century it has become a reality, in the form of computer programs capable of translating a wide variety of texts from one natural language into another. But, as ever, reality is not perfect. There are no 'translating machines' which, at the touch of a few buttons, can take any text in any language and produce a perfect translation in any other language without human intervention or assistance. That is an ideal for the distant future, if it is even achievable in principle, which many doubt.

What has been achieved is the development of programs which can produce 'raw' translations of texts in relatively well-defined subject domains, which can be revised to give good-quality translated texts at an economically viable rate or which in their unedited state can be read and understood by specialists in the subject for information purposes. In some cases, with appropriate controls on the language of the input texts, translations can be produced automatically that are of higher quality needing little or no revision.

These are solid achievements by what is now traditionally called Machine Translation (henceforth in this book, MT), but they have often been obscured and misunderstood. The public perception of MT is distorted by two extreme positions. On the one hand, there are those who are unconvinced that there is anything difficult about analysing language, since even young children are able to learn languages so easily; and who are convinced that anyone who knows a foreign language must be able to translate with ease. Hence, they are unable to appreciate the difficulties of the task or how much has been achieved. On the other hand, there are those who believe that because automatic translation of Shakespeare, Goethe, Tolstoy and lesser literary authors is not feasible there is no role for any kind of computer-based translation. They are unable to evaluate the contribution which less than perfect translation could make either in their own work or in the general improvement of international communication.

1.1 The aims of MT

Most translation in the world is not of texts which have high literary and cultural status. The great majority of professional translators are employed to satisfy the huge and growing demand for translations of scientific and technical documents, commercial and business transactions, administrative memoranda, legal documentation, instruction manuals, agricultural and medical text books, industrial patents, publicity leaflets, newspaper reports, etc. Some of this work is challenging and difficult. But much of it is tedious and repetitive, while at the same time requiring accuracy and consistency. The demand for such translations is increasing at a rate far beyond the capacity of the translation profession. The assistance of a computer has clear and immediate attractions. The practical usefulness of an MT system is determined ultimately by the quality of its output. But what counts as a 'good' translation, whether produced by human or machine, is an extremely difficult concept to define precisely. Much depends on the particular circumstances in which it is made and the particular recipient for whom it is intended. Fidelity, accuracy, intelligibility, appropriate style and register are all criteria which can be applied, but they remain subjective judgements. What matters in practice, as far as MT is concerned, is how much has to be changed in order to bring output up to a standard acceptable to a human translator or reader. With such a slippery concept as translation, researchers and developers of MT systems can ultimately aspire only to producing translations which are 'useful' in particular situations — which obliges them to define clear research objectives — or, alternatively, they seek suitable applications of the 'translations' which in fact they are able to produce.

Nevertheless, there remains the higher ideal of equalling the best human translation. MT is part of a wider sphere of 'pure research' in computer-based natural language processing in Computational Linguistics and Artificial Intelligence, which explore the basic mechanisms of language and mind by modelling and simulation in computer programs. Research on MT is closely related to these efforts, adopting and applying both theoretical perspectives and operational techniques to translation processes, and in turn offering insights and solutions from its particular problems. In addition, MT can provide a 'test-bed' on a larger scale for theories and techniques developed by small-scale experiments in computational linguistics and artificial intelligence.

The major obstacles to translating by computer are, as they have always been, not computational but linguistic. They are the problems of lexical ambiguity, of syntactic complexity, of vocabulary differences between languages, of elliptical and 'ungrammatical' constructions, of, in brief, extracting the 'meaning' of sentences and texts from analysis of written signs and producing sentences and texts in another set of linguistic symbols with an equivalent meaning. Consequently, MT should expect to rely heavily on advances in linguistic research, particularly those branches exhibiting high degrees of formalization, and indeed it has and will continue to do so. But MT cannot apply linguistic theories directly: linguists are concerned with explanations of the underlying 'mechanisms' of language production and comprehension, they concentrate on crucial features and do not attempt to describe or explain everything. MT systems, by contrast, must deal with actual texts. They must confront the full range of linguistic phenomena, the complexities of terminology, misspellings, neologisms, aspects of 'performance' which are not always the concern of abstract theoretical linguistics.

In brief, MT is not in itself an independent field of 'pure' research. It takes from linguistics, computer science, artificial intelligence, translation theory, any ideas, methods and techniques which may serve the development of improved systems. It is essentially 'applied' research, but a field which nevertheless has built up a substantial body of techniques and concepts which can, in turn, be applied in other areas of computer-based language processing.

1.2 Some preliminary definitions

The term **Machine Translation** (MT) is the now traditional and standard name for computerised systems responsible for the production of translations from one natural language into another, with or without human assistance. Earlier names such as 'mechanical translation' and 'automatic translation' are now rarely used in English; but their equivalents in other languages are still common (e.g. French *traduction automatique*, Russian *avtomatičeskii perevod*). The term does not include computer-based translation tools which support translators by providing access to dictionaries and remote terminology databases, facilitating the transmission and reception of machine-readable texts, or interacting with word processing, text editing or printing equipment. It does, however, include systems in which translators or other users assist computers in the production of translations, including various combinations of text preparation, on-line interactions and subsequent revisions of output. The boundaries between **Machine-Aided Human Translation** (MAHT) and **Human-Aided Machine Translation** (HAMT) are often uncertain and the term Computer-Aided (or Computer-Assisted) Translation (both CAT) can sometimes cover both. But the central core of MT itself is the automation of the full translation process.

Although the ideal may be to produce high-quality translations, in practice the output of most MT systems is revised (**post-edited**). In this respect, MT output is treated no differently than the output of most human translators which is normally revised by another translator before dissemination. However, the types of errors produced by MT systems do differ from those of human translators. While post-editing is the norm, there are certain circumstances when MT output may be left unedited (as a **raw** translation) or only lightly corrected, e.g. if it is intended only for specialists familiar with the subject of the text. Output may also serve as a rough draft for a human translator, as a **pre-translation**.

The translation quality of MT systems may be improved — not only, of course, by developing better methods — by imposing certain restrictions on the input. The system may be designed, for example, to deal with texts limited to the **sublanguage** (vocabulary and grammar) of a particular subject field (e.g. polymer chemistry) and/or document type (e.g. patents). Alternatively, input texts may be written in a **controlled language**, which reduces potential ambiguities and restricts the complexity of sentence structures. This option is often referred to as **pre-editing**, but the term can also be used for the marking of input texts to indicate proper names, word divisions, prefixes, suffixes, phrase boundaries, etc. Finally the system itself may refer problems of ambiguity and selection to human operators (usually translators, though some systems are designed for use by the original authors) for resolution during the processes of translation itself, i.e. in an **interactive** mode.

Systems are designed either for one particular pair of languages (**bilingual** systems) or for more than two languages (**multilingual** systems), either in one direction only (**uni-directional** systems) or in both directions (**bi-directional** systems). In overall system design, there are three basic types. The first (and also historically oldest) is generally referred to as the **direct translation** approach: the MT system is designed in all details specifically for one particular pair of languages in one direction, e.g. Russian as the language of the original texts, the **source language**, and English as the language of the translated texts, the **target language**. Source texts are analysed no more than necessary for generating texts in the other language. The second basic type is the **interlingua** approach, which assumes the possibility of converting texts to and from 'meaning' representations common to more than one language. Translation is thus in two stages: from the source language to the interlingua, and from the interlingua into the target language. Programs for analysis are independent from programs for generation; in a multilingual configuration, any analysis program can be linked to any generation program. The third type is the less ambitious **transfer** approach. Rather than operating in two stages through a single interlingual meaning representation, there are three stages involving, usually, syntactic representations for both source and target texts. The first stage converts texts into intermediate representations in which ambiguities have been resolved irrespective of any other language. In the second stage these are converted into equivalent representations of the target language; and in the third stage, the final target texts are generated. Analysis and generation programs are specific for particular languages and independent of each other. Differences between languages, in vocabulary and structure, are handled in the intermediary transfer program.

Within the stages of analysis and generation, most MT system exhibit clearly separated components dealing with different levels of linguistic description: morphology, syntax, semantics. Hence, **analysis** may be divided into morphological analysis (e.g. identification of word endings), syntactic analysis (identification of phrase structures, etc.) and semantic analysis (resolution of lexical and structural ambiguities). Likewise, **generation** (or synthesis) may pass through levels of semantic, syntactic and morphological generation. In transfer systems, there may be separate components dealing with **lexical transfer** (selection of vocabulary equivalents) and **structural transfer** (transformation of source text structures into equivalent target text ones).

In many older systems (particularly those of the direct translation type), rules for analysis, transfer and generation were not always clearly separated. Some also mixed linguistic data (dictionaries and grammars) and computer processing rules and routines. Later systems exhibit various degrees of **modularity**, so that system components, data and programs can be adapted and changed independently of each other.

1.3 Brief history of MT

The use of mechanical dictionaries to overcome barriers of language was first suggested in the 17th century. Both Descartes and Leibniz speculated on the creation of dictionaries based on universal numerical codes. Actual examples were published in the middle of the century by Cave Beck, Athanasius Kircher and Johann Becher. The inspiration was the 'universal language' movement, the idea of creating an unambiguous language based on logical principles and iconic symbols (as the Chinese characters were believed to be), with which all humanity could communicate without fear of misunderstanding. Most familiar is the interlingua elaborated by John Wilkins in his 'Essay towards a Real Character and a Philosophical Language' (1668).

In subsequent centuries there were many more proposals for international languages (with Esperanto as the best known), but few attempts to mechanize translation until the middle of this century. In 1933 two patents appeared independently in France and Russia. A French-Armenian, George Artsouni, had designed a storage device on paper tape which could be used to find the equivalent of any word in another language; a prototype was apparently demonstrated in 1937. The proposal by the Russian, Petr Smirnov-Troyanskii, was in retrospect more significant. He envisaged three stages of mechanical translation: first, an editor knowing only the source language was to undertake the 'logical' analysis of words into their base forms and syntactic functions; secondly, a machine was to transform sequences of base forms and functions into equivalent sequences in the target language; finally, another editor knowing only the target language was to convert this output into the normal forms of that language. Although his patent referred only to the machine which would undertake the second stage, Troyanskii believed that "the process of logical analysis could itself be mechanised".

Troyanskii was ahead of his time and was unknown outside Russia when, within a few years of their invention, the possibility of using computers for translation was first discussed by Warren Weaver of the Rockefeller Foundation and Andrew D. Booth, a British crystallographer. On his return to Birkbeck College (London) Booth explored the mechanization of a bilingual dictionary and began collaboration with Richard H. Richens (Cambridge), who had independently been using punched cards to produce crude word-for-word translations of scientific abstracts. However, it was a memorandum from Weaver in July 1949 which brought the idea of MT to general notice and suggested methods: the use of war-time cryptography techniques, statistical analysis, Shannon's information theory, and exploration of the underlying logic and universal features of language. Within a few years research had begun at a number of US centres, and in 1951 the first full-time researcher in MT was appointed: Yehoshua Bar-Hillel at MIT. A year later he convened the first MT conference, where the outlines of future research were already becoming clear. There were proposals for dealing with syntax, suggestions that texts should be written in controlled languages, arguments for the construction of sublanguage systems, and recognition of the need for human assistance (pre- and post-editing) until fully automatic translation could be achieved. For some, the first requirement was to demonstrate the technical feasibility of MT. Accordingly, at Georgetown University Leon Dostert collaborated with IBM on a project which resulted in the first public demonstration of a MT system in January 1954. A carefully selected sample of 49 Russian sentences was translated into English, using a very restricted vocabulary of 250 words and just six grammar rules. Although it had little scientific value, it was sufficiently impressive to stimulate the large-scale funding of MT research in the United States and to inspire the initiation of MT projects elsewhere in the world, notably in the Soviet Union.

For the next decade many groups were active: some adopting empirical trial-and-error approaches, often statistics-based, with immediate working systems as the goal; others took theoretical approaches, involving fundamental linguistic research, aiming for long-term solutions. The contrasting methods were usually described at the time as 'brute-force' and 'perfectionist' respectively. Examples of the former were the lexicographic approach at the University of Washington (Seattle), later continued by IBM in a Russian–English system completed for the US Air Force, the statistical 'engineering' approach at the RAND Corporation, and the methods adopted at the Institute of Precision Mechanics in the Soviet Union, and the National Physical Laboratory in Great Britain. Largest of all was the group at Georgetown University, whose successful Russian–English system is now regarded as typical of this 'first generation' of MT research. Centres of theoretical research were at MIT, Harvard University, the University of Texas, the University of California at Berkeley, at the Institute of Linguistics in Moscow and the University of Leningrad, at the Cambridge Language Research Unit (CLRU), and at the universities of Milan and Grenoble. In contrast to the more pragmatically oriented groups where the 'direct translation' approach was the norm, some of the theoretical projects experimented with early versions of interlingua and transfer systems (e.g. CLRU and MIT, respectively).

Much of the research of this period was of lasting importance, not only for MT but also for computational linguistics and artificial intelligence — in particular, the development of automated dictionaries and of techniques for syntactic analysis — and many theoretical groups made significant contributions to linguistic theory. However, the basic objective of building systems capable of producing good translations was not achieved. Optimism had been high, there were many predictions of imminent breakthroughs, but disillusionment grew as the complexity of the linguistic problems became more and more apparent. In a 1960 review of MT progress, Bar-Hillel criticized the prevailing assumption that the goal of MT research should be the creation of **fully automatic high-**

quality translation (FAHQT) systems producing results indistinguishable from those of human translators. He argued that the 'semantic barriers' to MT could in principle only be overcome by the inclusion of vast amounts of encyclopaedic knowledge about the 'real world'. His recommendation was that MT should adopt less ambitious goals, it should build systems which made cost-effective use of human–machine interaction.

In 1964 the government sponsors of MT in the United States formed the Automatic Language Processing Advisory Committee (ALPAC) to examine the prospects. In its influential 1966 report it concluded that MT was slower, less accurate and twice as expensive as human translation and stated that "there is no immediate or predictable prospect of useful Machine Translation". It saw no need for further investment in MT research; instead it recommended the development of machine aids for translators, such as automatic dictionaries, and continued support of basic research in computational linguistics. The ALPAC report was widely condemned as narrow, biased and shortsighted — it was certainly wrong to criticize MT because output had to be post-edited, and it misjudged the economic factors — but large-scale financial support of current approaches could not continue. Its influence was profound, bringing a virtual end to MT research in the United States for over a decade and damaging the public perception of MT for many years afterwards.

In the following decade MT research took place largely outside the United States, in Canada and in Western Europe, and virtually ignored by the scientific community. American activity had concentrated on English translations of Russian scientific and technical materials. In Canada and Europe the needs were quite different: the Canadian bicultural policy created a demand for English–French (and to a less extent French–English) translation beyond the capacity of the market, and the European Economic Community (as it was then known) was demanding translations of scientific, technical, administrative and legal documentation from and into all the Community languages.

A research group was established at Montreal which, though ultimately unsuccessful in building a large English–French system for translating aircraft manuals, is now renowned for the creation in 1976 of the archetypal 'sublanguage' system Météo (Chapter 12) for translating weather reports for daily public broadcasting. In 1976 the Commission of the European Communities decided to install an English–French system called Systran, which had previously been developed by Peter Toma (once a member of the Georgetown team) for Russian–English translation for the US Air Force, and had been in operation since 1970 (see Chapter 10). In subsequent years, further systems for French–English, English–Italian, English–German and other pairs have been developed for the Commission. In the late 1970s, it was also decided to fund an ambitious research project to develop a multilingual system for all the Community languages, based on the latest advances in MT and in computational linguistics. This is the Eurotra project, which involves research groups in all member states (see Chapter 14).

For its basic design, Eurotra owes much to research at Grenoble and at Saarbrücken. During the 1960s the French group had built an 'interlingua' system for Russian–French translation (not purely interlingual as lexical transfer was still bilingual); however, the results were disappointing and in the 1970s it began to develop the influential transfer-based Ariane system (Chapter 13). The Saarbrücken group had also been building its multilingual 'transfer' system SUSY since the late 1960s (Chapter 11). It was now the general consensus in the MT research community that the best prospects for significant advances lay in the development of transfer-based systems. The researchers at the Linguistics Research Center (LRC) at Austin, Texas (one of the few to continue after ALPAC) had come to similar conclusions after experimenting with an interlingua system and was now developing its transfer-based METAL system (Chapter 15); and in Japan work had begun at Kyoto University on the Mu transfer system for Japanese-English translation. The Eurotra group adopted the same basic approach, although it found subsequently that the demands of large-scale multilinguality led to the incorporation of many interlingual features.

However, during the 1980s the transfer-based design has been joined by new approaches to the interlingua idea. Most prominent is the research on knowledge-based systems, notably at Carnegie Mellon University, Pittsburgh (see section 18.1), which are founded on developments of natural language understanding systems within the Artificial Intelligence (AI) community. The argument is that MT must go beyond purely linguistic information (syntax and semantics); translation involves 'understanding' the content of texts and must refer to knowledge of the 'real world'. Such an approach implies translation via intermediate representations based on (extra-linguistic) 'universal' elements. Essentially non-AI-oriented interlingua approaches have also appeared in two Dutch projects: the DLT system at Utrecht based on a modification of Esperanto (Chapter 17) and the Rosetta system at Phillips (Eindhoven) which is experimenting with Montague semantics as the basis for an interlingua (Chapter 16)

More recently, yet other alternatives have emerged. For many years, automatic translation of speech was considered utopian, but advances in speech recognition and speech production have encouraged the foundation of projects in Great Britain (British Telecom) and in Japan (Advanced Telecommunications Research, ATR): see section 18.6. The sophistication of the statistical techniques developed by speech research has revived interest in the application of such methods in MT systems; the principal group at present is at the IBM laboratories at Yorktown Heights, NY (see section 18.3)

The most significant development of the last decade, however, is the appearance of commercial MT systems. The American products from ALPSystems, Weidner and Logos were joined by many Japanese systems from computer companies (Fujitsu, Hitachi, Mitsubishi, NEC, Oki, Sanyo, Sharp, Toshiba), and in the later 1980s by Globalink, PC-Translator, Tovna and the METAL system developed by Siemens from earlier research at Austin, Texas. Many of these systems, particularly those for microcomputers, are fairly crude in the linguistic quality of their output but are capable of cost-effective operation in appropriate circumstances (see Chapter 9). As well as these commercial systems, there have been a number of in-house systems, e.g. the Spanish and English systems developed at the Pan-American Health Organization (Washington, DC), and the systems designed by the Smart Corporation for Citicorp, Ford, and the Canadian Department of Employment and Immigration. Many of the Systran installations are tailor-made for particular organisations (Aérospatiale, Dornier, NATO, General Motors).

Nearly all these operational systems depend heavily on post-editing to produce acceptable translations. But pre-editing is also widespread: in some systems, for instance, operators are required, when inputting text, to mark word boundaries or even indicate the scope of phrases and clauses. At Xerox, texts for translation by Systran are composed in a controlled English vocabulary and syntax; and a major feature of the Smart systems is the pre-translation editor of English input.

The revival of MT research in the 1980s and the emergence of MT systems in the marketplace have led to growing public awareness of the importance of translation tools. There may still be many misconceptions about what has been achieved and what may be possible in the future, but the healthy state of MT is reflected in the multiplicity of system types and of research designs which are now being explored, many undreamt of when MT was first proposed in the 1940s. Further advances in computer technology, in Artificial Intelligence and in theoretical linguistics suggest possible future lines of investigation (see Chapter 18), while different MT user profiles (e.g. the writer who wants to compose a text in an unknown language) lead to new designs. But the most fundamental problems of computer-based translation are concerned not with technology but with language, meaning, understanding, and the social and cultural differences of human communication.

1.4 Further reading

The history of MT is covered by Hutchins (1986), updated by Hutchins (1988). Basic sources for the early period are Locke and Booth (1955) — which reproduces Weaver's memorandum — Booth (1967) and Bruderer (1982). For the period after ALPAC (1966) there are good descriptions of the major MT systems in King (1987), Nirenburg (1987a) and Slocum (1988), while Vasconcellos (1988) and the ongoing Aslib conference series *Translating and the Computer* (published under various editors) provide the wider perspectives of commercial developments and translators' experiences.

2
Linguistic background

This chapter introduces some of the terminology, ideas and methods of those aspects of linguistics which are most relevant to MT. Readers who have a good background in linguistics might like to skip parts of this chapter, or read it quickly so as to see our own, perhaps idiosyncratic, approach to familiar material. The first part of the chapter (sections 2.1 to 2.7) introduces some basic terminology and concepts; the second describes briefly some of the formal apparatus of linguistic description (section 2.8), the linguistic theories which have influenced much MT research (section 2.9), and some recent developments which are beginning to influence MT research in various ways (section 2.10). Some knowledge of the content of sections 2.1 to 2.8 is essential for the understanding of all chapters. The information in the last two sections should be regarded as supplementary, for reference when the need arises.

2.1 The study of language

The study of language takes many forms. It can concentrate on historical aspects, language change and evolution, older forms of a language, the origin of language. It can concentrate on social aspects: how language is used to communicate, to influence opinions, to persuade others, how it differs between the sexes and classes, from region to region, from one social context to another. It can concentrate on psychological aspects: language acquisition by children, second language learning by adults, the language of the mentally handicapped or mentally ill, the creative use of language, etc. It can concentrate on political and geographical aspects:

problems of language spread and death, bilingualism, dialects and their status, national languages, standardization and normalization of technical terminology. Finally, and in the opinion of many the most central concern, it can concentrate on the 'nature' of language, on the underlying 'system' of language and languages.

There is a long and successful tradition in Western linguistics that language systems can be studied in isolation in a worthwhile way. It has always been routine for writers of grammars to abstract away from the heterogeneity of actual speech communities and to present some kind of community norm. Linguists do not attempt to account for the full range of observable phenomena but rather concentrate on aspects which they believe can be handled satisfactorily in a systematic fashion. The basic assumption is that language users do not constantly refer to a vast store or memory of previously observed utterances but have available a set of abstract formulae and rules enabling them to construct and understand expressions which have never occurred before.

This tacit and unconscious 'knowledge' of the system of rules and principles is said to represent the **competence** of native speakers. It is contrasted with their actual **performance**, the use and comprehension of language on particular occasions, the directly observed spoken utterances and written texts, including any hesitations, slips of the tongue and misspellings. Although performance is founded on, and ultimately explained by, the competence of speakers, it directly reflects competence only in ideal circumstances. Actual communication is determined as much by external factors as by the 'internalised' grammar, e.g. by memory limitations, lack of concentration, nervousness, inebriation, prejudice and social constraints.

Consequently, linguistics must go beyond observation and description: it must also explain the judgements, intuitions and introspections of speakers. For example, how can ambiguity and synonymy be 'observed'? How else other than by asking directly can we discover that (1a) can sometimes be equivalent to (1b) and sometimes to (1c)?

(1a) Visiting relatives can be boring.

(1b) It can be boring to visit relatives.

(1c) Relatives who visit can be boring.

And how can observation help to discover that the similar sentence (2a) is not ambiguous, why it can be equivalent only to (2b) and why (2c) is anomalous? (Following the well-established practice in linguistics, unacceptable or anomalous sentences are marked with an asterisk here and throughout this book.)

(2a) Visiting hospitals can be boring.

(2b) It can be boring to visit hospitals.

(2c) *Hospitals which visit can be boring.

2.2 Grammar

It is assumed that the basic task of linguistics is to study the competence of the 'ideal' speaker-hearer, which is represented by the **grammar** of rules and principles underlying the potential ability of any native speaker to utter and comprehend any legitimate expression in the language. Theoretical linguistics is therefore concerned primarily with the rigorous and precise (i.e. formal) description of grammars, which (as is now widely accepted by most linguists) should satisfy the following basic requirements. Grammars should be **observationally adequate**, by being capable of demonstrating whether a particular string of words is or is not well-formed. They should be **descriptively adequate**, by assigning structural descriptions to strings of well-formed sentences in order to explain native speakers' judgments about relationships between utterances. And they should be **explanatorily adequate**, by representing the best available descriptively adequate grammar in the light of a general theory of what kinds of grammars are possible for human languages. The latter requirement leads linguistics to consider the principles and constraints on language as such, and hence to investigations of **universal grammar**, i.e. a description of the resources available for constructing the grammars of individual languages. The more powerful the theory of universal grammar, the less comprehensive individual grammars need to be, because the specific rule-systems of particular languages will be consequences of the general properties of universal grammar.

There are arguments about the autonomy of formal linguistics. On the one hand, some linguists maintain that 'language systems' must be described independently of particular usages of languages, and universal grammar must be studied independently of particular grammars of individual languages, just as physics describes the principles of motion independently of the particular movements of objects in particular situations. On the other hand, some linguists believe that theoretical constructs must have some psychological 'reality', in order that theories can be 'tested' against actual linguistic performance. To some extent, these arguments can be disregarded in fields of 'applied' linguistics such as computational linguistics: what matters is whether the results have practical value in suggesting methods and approaches of greater power and generality in more rigorous, internally consistent, and perhaps universally valid frameworks.

2.3 Phonology and orthography

Although almost all MT systems at present deal with (written) text input and output, research in speech MT is taking place and will no doubt increase in the near future. In this respect, phonetics and phonology obviously play an important role. Phonetics is concerned with the description of the sound units of languages in general; **phonology** is concerned with the description of the sound units (**phonemes**) available in a particular language and the way they combine with each other. For speech MT, analysis of the input sound, and generation of synthetic speech in the target language are the two problems in this area. Of these, the former is significantly the more difficult. While our writing system tends to identify individual speech sounds that make up a word (roughly one letter per sound), in reality the exact acoustic properties of the individual phonemes vary greatly depending on the surrounding context (as well as varying from speaker to speaker, and even from one occasion to another with the same speaker). For example the [t] sounds in *top*, *stop*, *bottle*, *pot* and *scotch* are all acoustically quite dissimilar, although sharing certain acoustic features which however are also found in other phonemes (for example [d], [s], [th]). It is the combination of distinctive acoustic features which enables the brain — or a speech recognition device — to interpret them as representing the [t] sound. Analysis of speech input by computer is usually based on statistical probability: each element in a sequence of sounds is open to various interpretations, but usually only one combination of these interpretations is statistically likely. This is where phonology, describing what combinations of sounds are permitted, plays a role.

By contrast, synthesising speech is a problem that is well on its way to being solved: much synthetic speech is almost indistinguishable from the real thing (for example the standard messages sometimes heard on the telephone are often synthesised, and are not recordings of human speech). Nevertheless, problems with **suprasegmental** features such as pitch, stress and tone remain: robot speech in TV and cinema science fiction is often portrayed as lacking these features (an accurate reflection of the state of the art in the late 1980s!).

For most MT systems, such problems are irrelevant, since they deal with written input and output. As such, the **orthography** (or spelling) is usually given *a priori*, though a system which was designed to deal with **ill-formed input** would need to know about **orthotactics** — what sequences of letters are legal in a given language — to be able to handle and correct misspellings. For example, English allows words to begin with the sequences *spr-, spl-, str-, skr-, kl-, sl-*, but not **stl-, *skl-* or **sr-*; the initial sequence *zmrzl-* is possible in Czech (*zmrzlina* 'ice cream') but not in English. However, many orthotactically possible words do not actually occur in a language, e.g. in English we have *split, slit, lit, slid* and *lid*, but not **splid*; and we have *gull, dull* and *dud*, but not **gud*. The knowledge of possible combinations of letters can be used to suggest corrections of misspelled words.

Orthography also covers paralinguistic problems such as the use of different type styles and punctuation, a little-studied but nevertheless important issue in multilingual tasks like translation. For example, in English, an italic type-face (or underlining) is often used to indicate emphasis, while in German the convention is to space out the words l i k e t h i s. In Japanese, emphasis is more usually indicated by a change of word order, or by a special suffix. Similarly, punctuation conventions differ. In English, we distinguish restrictive and descriptive relative clauses with the use or not of a separating comma, as in (3), whereas in German the comma is required irrespective of the type of relative clause:

(3a) Books which are imported from Japan are expensive.

(3b) Futons, which are Japanese-style beds, are very comfortable.

In other cases, English uses commas liberally for emphasis (4a), where German uses none (4b).

(4a) This year, the man, however, and his wife, too, will go on holiday.

(4b) Dieses Jahr werden jedoch der Mann und auch seine Frau
Urlaub machen.

Other conventions differing from language to language are those regarding quote marks (e.g. the use in French of « and »), use of capital letters (e.g. German nouns) or not (e.g. nationality adjectives in French), question marks with indirect questions, and much more.

2.4 Morphology and the lexicon

Morphology is concerned with the ways in which words are formed from basic sequences of phonemes. Two types are distinguished: inflectional morphology and derivational morphology. Words in many languages differ in form according to different functions, e.g. nouns in singular and plural (*table* and *tables*), verbs in present and past tenses (*likes* and *liked*). **Inflectional morphology** is the system defining the possible variations on a root (or base) form, which in traditional grammars were given as 'paradigms' such as the Latin *dominus, dominum, domini, domino*, etc. Here the root *domin-* is combined with various endings (*-us, -um, -i, -o*, etc.), which may also occur with other forms: *equus, servus*, etc. English is relatively poor in inflectional variation: most verbs have only *-s, -ed* and *-ing* available; languages such as Russian are much richer, cf. the verb *delat'* with present tense forms *delayu, delae*, *delaet, delaem, delaete, delayut*, and past tense forms *delal, delala, delalo, delali*. Languages can be classified according to the extent to which they use inflectional morphology. At one end of the scale are so-called **isolating** languages, like Chinese, which have almost no inflectional morphology; at the other end are **polysynthetic** languages, of which Eskimo is said to be an example, where most of the grammatical meaning of a sentence is expressed by inflections on verbs and nouns. In between are **agglutinative** languages, of which Turkish is the standard example, where inflectional suffixes can be added one after the other to a root, and inflecting languages like Latin, where simple affixes convey complex meanings: for example, the *-o* ending in Latin *amo* ('I love') indicates person (1st), number (singular), tense (present), voice (active) and mood (indicative).

Derivational morphology is concerned with the formation of root (inflectable) forms from other roots, often of different grammatical categories (see below). Thus, from the English noun *nation* may be formed the adjective *national*; the further addition of *-ise* gives a verb *nationalise*, adding the suffix *-ism* instead gives the noun *nationalism*, or adding *-ist* gives an agentive noun *nationalist*. And by yet further suffixation we can have *nationalisation* and *nationalistic*, or by adding prefixes *renationalise, denationalisation*, etc.

Often included under the heading of morphology is **compounding**, where whole words are combined into new forms. The meanings of compounds are sometimes obvious from their components (*blackberry*), sometimes slightly different (a *blackboard* is a special type of board, typically but not necessarily black), and sometimes completely opaque (a *blackleg* is a traitor or strike breaker). What makes compounding a problem in morphology is that in some languages (though not usually in English), compounds are formed by simply writing the two words together, without a space or hyphen between them. This is a problem when new or novel compounds are formed, and so do not appear in the dictionary (e.g. in German *Lufthansafrachtflüge* 'Lufthansa cargo flights').

The **lexicon** of a language lists the lexical items occurring in that language. In a typical traditional dictionary, entries are identified by a base (or 'canonical') form of the word. This sometimes corresponds to the uninflected root (as in English), though not always. In French dictionaries for example, verbs are listed under one of their inflected forms (the infinitive): *manger*. In Latin dictionaries, nouns are given in the nominative singular (*equus*), and verbs in the 1st person singular present tense active voice (*habeo*). Traditional dictionary entries indicate pronunciations, give grammatical categories, provide definitions and (often) supply some etymological and stylistic information.

The lexicon in an MT system and generally in linguistics is slightly different. Some MT systems have only **full-form lexicons**, i.e. lists of the words as they actually occur, with their corresponding grammatical information. So for example the lexicon might list separately the words *walks*, *walking* and *walked*. This option is less attractive for highly inflecting languages, where each lexical item may have ten or twenty different forms, and so the lexicon will list a root form, and there will be an interaction with a morphology component to analyse or generate the appropriate forms (see further in sections 5.1 and 7.2.1).

The MT lexicon will give the information needed for syntactic and semantic processing (see below): grammatical category (noun, verb, etc.), **subcategorisation features** (i.e. what 'subcategory' the word belongs to, e.g. transitive or intransitive verb, masculine or feminine noun), and semantic information (animate noun, verb requiring human subject). Often these last two types of information are used in conjunction with each other, as when a subcategory is defined in terms of **selection restrictions** on the words it can occur with. So for example, the verb *laugh* has a selection restriction on its subject, namely that it be animate.

An MT system must obviously also include data on correspondences between lexical items in different languages. Because this is often quite complex, many systems separate the information required for analysing or producing texts in one particular language and the information about lexical correspondences in two languages. The former is contained in **monolingual** lexicons and the latter in **bilingual** (or transfer) lexicons. As well as word-pair equivalents, MT lexicons often indicate the conditions under which equivalences can be assumed: different grammatical categories (*feed*: verb or noun), semantic categories (*board*: flat surface or group of people), or syntactic environment (*know* a fact or how to do something) and so on.

2.5 Syntax

Syntax comprises the rules or principles by which words (lexical items) may combine to form sentences. Rules apply to the **grammatical categories**. It is common to distinguish between the grammatical categories of individual lexical items such as noun, determiner (article), adjective, verb, adverb, preposition, etc., and the **constituents** indicating groupings of items, e.g. noun phrase, subordinate clause, sentence. Syntactic description also recognises **subcategories** or grammatically significant subdivisions of the categories, as mentioned in the previous section.

Linguists find it useful to distinguish major and minor categories. The **major categories** are the ones with large membership: nouns, verbs, adjectives. These are sometimes called **open class categories**, because new members are continually being added to the set (by making new derivations or compounds). The **minor** or **closed class categories** are the grammatical or function words like prepositions, conjunctions and determiners: these form small and finite sets which are rarely or never added to. This distinction is significant for MT in three ways: first, users of MT systems are normally permitted to add new words to the lexicon in the major categories, but not in the minor categories; second, the syntactic behaviour of minor category words is often more idiosyncratic, whereas the behaviour of open class words is easier to generalise; and third, an 'unknown word' in a text being processed by an MT system can (and must) be assumed to belong to one of the major categories.

Following the usual practice, grammatical categories are abbreviated in this book as 'n' for noun, 'v' for verb, 'adj' for adjective, 'det' for determiner, 'adv' for adverb, 'prep' for preposition, 'NP' for noun phrase, 'PP' for prepositional phrase, 'VP' for verb phrase, 'S' for sentence.

Syntactic descriptions are concerned with three basic types of relationships in sentences: **sequence**, e.g. in English adjectives normally precede the nouns they modify, whereas in French they normally follow; **dependency**, i.e. relations between categories, e.g. prepositions may determine the morphological form (or case) of the nouns which depend on them in many languages, and verbs often determine the syntactic form of some of the other elements in a sentence —see below); and **constituency**, for example a noun phrase may consist of a determiner, an adjective and a noun.

2.5.1 Syntactic features and functions

Relations between constituent or dependent items are sometimes indicated by the sharing of **syntactic features**. The difference between (5a) and (5b) lies in the fact that in (5a) the noun and the verb are both 'singular' and in (5b) they are both 'plural'. The extent of such kinds of agreement can be greater in other languages, as in the French example (6), where each word is marked as 'plural' and in addition the noun *rues* and the adjectives *grandes* and *embouteillées* are all 'feminine'. In the Russian examples in (7), the verb in each case agrees with its subject in both number and gender.

(5a) The boy runs.

(5b) The boys run.

(6) *Les grandes rues sont embouteillées.*
'The main roads are jammed'

(7a) *Čelovek kuril.*
'The man was smoking'

(7b) *Ženščina kurila.*
'The woman was smoking'

(7c) *Lyudi kurili.*
'The people were smoking'

The sources of agreement relations lie in the **governor** in a dependency relation or in the **head** of a phrase structure. The governor or head is the element or item which is obligatory in a structure: the verb in a sentence or verb phrase, the noun in a noun phrase, the preposition in a prepositional phrase, etc. These heads or governors determine the forms of dependent (or governed) elements: adjectives agree with nouns, prepositions 'govern' particular noun endings, etc.

The **grammatical functions** of words in sentences are related to syntactic roles. In many European languages, the noun (or noun phrase) in the nominative (if applicable) which agrees in number with a following verb is referred to as the grammatical 'subject' of the sentences (*the boy* in (5a) for example). Other functions include those of 'direct object' and 'indirect object', for example *the book* and *(to) the girl* respectively in both (8a) and (8b).

(8a) The man gave the book to the girl.

(8b) The man gave the girl the book.

Other sentential functions include 'prepositional object' (*on his deputy* in (9)), 'sentential complement' (*that he would come* in (10)) and 'adverbials' which (in English for example) are typically adverbs or prepositional phrases (*soon* in (11a) and *in a few minutes* in (11b)).

(9) The President relies on his deputy.

(10) He promised that he would come.

(11a) He will arrive soon.

(11b) He will arrive in a few moments.

Within the noun phrase typical functions are 'determiner' (*the*, *a* and so on), 'quantifier' (*all*, *some*, numbers) and 'modifier' (adjectives, relative clauses).

2.5.2 Deep and surface structure

Syntactic functions such as 'subject' and 'object' refer to the functions of the elements in the sentence largely irrespective of meaning. So for example, although *the man* is subject of (8a) and (8b), in related sentences (12a) and (12b), the subject is *the book* and *the girl* respectively.

(12a) The book was given to the man by the girl.

(12b) The girl was a given the book by the man.

However, linguists commonly make a distinction between a **surface structure** and an underlying **deep structure**, and consider passive forms like (12a) and (12b), as well as nominalisations as in (13a) to have the same underlying forms as (8a) and (13b) respectively. The syntactic functions of the elements in these hypothetical underlying forms can be recognised as 'deep subject' and 'deep object'. Therefore, in (12a) *the book* is simultaneously surface subject and deep object.

(13a) the destruction of the city by the enemy...

(13b) The enemy destroyed the city.

Linguists differ as to whether the underlying form actually is the same as the most neutral surface form (for example, the active declarative sentence), or is some abstract **canonical form** from which active, passive, nominalisation and so on are all derived in some way. We will return to this question below. However the distinction between deep and surface syntactic functions is one which is generally accepted and understood.

2.5.3 Predicate–argument structure

Syntactic relationships within sentences may also be described in terms of **predicate–argument structures**. This term refers to the traditional division of propositions in logic into **predicates** and **arguments**. A sentence such as (5a) above corresponds to the proposition *run (boy)*, where the predicate *run* has a single argument *boy*; a sentence such as (8a) corresponds to *gave (man, book, girl)*, a proposition with three arguments. The predicate usually corresponds to the main verb in the syntactic structure, and the arguments are its dependents. A representation which focuses on this aspect of sentence structure is called a 'dependency representation', see 2.8.1 below. The assignment of different functions or roles to the arguments is part of the grammatical theories of Valency and Case, both widely used in MT, and which are discussed in sections 2.9.5 and 2.9.6 below.

2.6 Semantics

Semantics is the study of the ways in which individual words (lexical items) have meaning, either in isolation or in the context of other words, and the ways in which phrases and sentences express meanings. A common assumption is that word meanings involve **semantic features**. Words such as *man, woman, boy, girl* share a common feature 'human' in contrast to animals, and share with animals a feature 'animate' which distinguishes them both from inanimate physical objects (*rock, table, chair*) or from abstract notions (*beauty, honesty*). Furthermore, a feature such as 'male' distinguishes *man* and *boy* from *woman* and *girl*, and a feature 'young' distinguishes *boy* and *girl* from *man* and *woman*. Such features indicate not only the potential range of extra-linguistic objects to which they may refer (i.e. assuming a matching of semantic features and real-world attributes), but also the appropriate conjunction of words in texts (sentences), e.g. *girl* and *dress*, *chair* and *sit*. Such features are often organised into a **semantic feature hierarchy**: for example, 'humans' along with animals, birds, reptiles and insects are all 'animate'; animate things along with plants are 'living'; living beings along with artefacts are all 'physical objects'. Generalisations can be made at various different points in such a hierarchy: for example, any animate thing can be the subject of the verb *walk*, but only humans (normally) can *talk*. Such generalisations can be captured by supposing the hierarchy to be an **inheritance hierarchy**, so that it is sufficient to say that the word *teacher* has the feature 'human' to know that it is also 'animate', 'living', and so on. Inasmuch as semantic features tend to reflect the realities of the world around us, semantic feature hierarchies are rarely as simple these examples suggest, and semantic features are more usually arranged in 'polyhierarchies' or **semantic networks** with lots of interwoven inheritance hierarchies.

It is common to study relationships between lexical items within a **semantic field** or 'semantic system'. The vocabulary of kinship is one example: *father, mother, son, daughter, uncle, brother, grandfather, cousin*, etc. Another could be the verbs of motion: *walk, ride, drive, swim, run*, etc. In many cases the analysis of a semantic field or system can be formulated in terms of semantic features.

Words in the same semantic field often have similar or comparable SYNTACTIC behaviour: for example, most verbs of motion are intransitive and take a locative prepositional phrase as a prepositional object.

Along with semantic features are **semantic functions**, also known as 'case roles': here, the semantic relationship between the predicate and its arguments is captured. This notion is at the centre of the theory of Case grammar and is discussed in more detail below (section 2.9.6).

Whether a particular word or expression is appropriate to refer to some entity or event is determined not only by the semantic features which constitute its **denotation**, but also by less easily formalised aspects of **connotation**. Among these may be included differences of **register**: a *friend* may be called *pal*, *mate* or *guy* in colloquial usages, the informal *lavatory* or *loo* is likely to be referred to as a *public convenience* in official statements, etc. Differences of subject **domain** affect semantic usage: for the physicist the term *field* means something quite different from the farmer's *field*, and terms such as *force* and *energy* are defined in ways which common usage is unaware of.

2.7 Text relations

Links between and within sentences are conveyed by the use of pronouns, definite articles, nominalisations, etc. Consider a sentence like (14)

(14) An old soldier bought a pair of trousers.

In a subsequent sentence the old soldier may be referred to by an appropriate pronoun (e.g. *he* for male persons). Or the same kind of reference may be conveyed by a definite expression (*the man*), or by a nominalisation of his action (*the purchaser*). The term **anaphoric** reference is widely used to cover these usages. Within sentences, such reference may be expressed by reflexive pronouns (15).

(15) The man bought himself a shirt.

However, it should be noted that pronouns and definite expressions may also refer to entities not previously mentioned in a text or discourse; they may refer to persons or objects already known or easily inferable from the situation —this is **deictic** (or 'pointing') reference. For example, in the brief text in (16a), the pronoun *it* refers not to the restaurant, but to the unmentioned but inferable meal eaten there; similarly, in (16b), the *it* refers to the sea implied by the mention of a ferry boat.

(16a) We went to a restaurant last night. It was delicious.

(16b) We took the ferry from Liverpool to Dublin. It was very rough.

Less frequently, anaphoric or deictic reference points forward rather than backwards. For example, (16b) can easily be rephrased as in (17a). Yet there are some restrictions on forward anaphora, or **cataphora** as it is sometimes called. Sentence (17b) seems acceptable, with the cataphoric reference of *it* to *car*, but in (17c) we cannot be sure if *he* refers to *the old man* or to some other person.

(17a) It was very rough when we took the ferry from Liverpool to Dublin.

(17b) You can put it in the garage if you come by car.

(17c) He looked relieved when the old man heard he didn't have to
pay tax.

In general, the sequence of words and ideas in sentences is determined by text relationships. The start of a sentence typically makes a link to previous sentences; the initial words refer to elements already mentioned or presumed to be already known — either by anaphoric reference or by presupposition. The remainder of the sentence conveys something new about these 'known' or 'given' elements. The first part of the sentence is what it is 'about', and is called its **theme**. What follows, the new information, is the **rheme**. In an alternative terminology, these are **topic and comment** respectively. The processes involved in the selection of theme elements is frequently referred to as **thematisation**: in English and other European languages, passivisation is one common means of changing the theme of a sentence.

In English, the distinction between old and new information is expressed primarily by the use of definite or indefinite expressions, but in languages such as Russian where there are no articles, the distinction is conveyed by word order (18). Initial (thematic) elements are assumed to have been already known to the listener or reader, and later (rhematic) elements are perhaps being mentioned for the first time in the present context.

(18a) *Ženščina vyšla iz domu.*
WOMAN-nom CAME OUT HOUSE-gen
'The woman came out of the house'

(18b) *Iz domu vyšla ženščina.*
'A woman came out of the house'

In (18a) *ženščina* is an old (thematic) noun, where the definite article is appropriate in English; in (18b) it is a new (rhematic) noun, where English requires an indefinite article..

2.8 Representations

A major focus of formal linguistics is the definition of **structural representations** of natural language texts, and the definition of formal **grammars** which define the range of well-formed representations. Earlier, we mentioned three types of syntactic relationship found in linguistic descriptions: sequence, dependency and constituency. Two basic types of representation are in common use, emphasising one or other of dependency or constituency; sequence is optionally indicated on both types of representation.

2.8.1 Dependency

A traditional method of representing the dependency relations in a sentence is by a **dependency tree** where the dependents of each governor are portrayed as stemming from them on branches. In (19a) and (19b) we give a sentence and its corresponding dependency tree structure.

(19a) A very tall professor with grey hair wrote this boring book.

(19b)

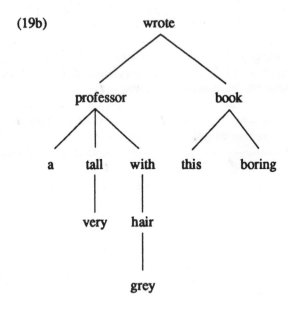

The adjective *tall* is modified by the adverb *very*, and so governs it; determiners (*a, this*) and adjectives (*boring, tall, grey*) are governed by nouns (*professor, book, hair*); nouns are dependent on prepositions (*with*) or on the verb (*wrote*). The head or 'governor' of the whole sentence is the main verb.

We can indicate sequence in a dependency tree by convention: either by attaching significance to the ordering of branches or by labelling the branches with information from which the sequence can be derived. The first approach is illustrated in (19b) where the branches are ordered left-to-right in a sequence which corresponds to English word order. However, in this case we need also some general and specific rules to know where the governor fits in the sequence. In English for example, the governor generally goes in the middle: if the governor is a noun it comes after a determiner and any adjective(s) but before a prepositional modifier. Likewise the verb comes after a subject but before an object.

Predicate–argument structure (2.5.3 above) may thus be seen as an example of ordered dependency structure; in the proposition *gave(man,book,girl)* the governor is *gave* and its relationships to its dependents is given by their order, *man* before *book* before *girl*.

If we were now to ignore the left-to-right ordering of branches (and make the necessary lexical alterations), the dependency tree in (19b) could also serve equally well for an equivalent Welsh sentence (20a), where the governor typically precedes (nearly) all its dependents, or for an equivalent Japanese sentence (20b), where the governor always comes last.

(20a) *Ysgrifennodd athro tal iawn a gwallt llwyd ganddo y llyfr undonnog hwm.*

WROTE PROFESSOR TALL VERY & HAIR GREY TO-HIM THE BOOK BORING THIS

(20b) *Ichi-ban takai shiraga-de-no sensei-wa kono omoshirokunai hon-wo kaita.*

VERY TALL GREYHAIRED PROFESSOR THIS BORING BOOK WROTE.

If in a dependency tree no significance is to be attached to the order of branches, then branches have to be labelled in some way if the sequence of elements is to be recorded. We could, for example, label one branch as subject and another as object while specifying no ordering of branches. In English the general rule would be for subjects to precede verbs (their governors) and for objects to follow; in Welsh the governor would precede subjects and objects, and in Japanese the governor would come last.

This kind of dependency representation is often used in connection with Valency or Case grammar, which we will discuss below (sections 2.9.5 and 2.9.6).

2.8.2 Phrase structure

The traditional method of representing the structural constituency of a sentences is the **phrase structure tree**, e.g. for the same sentence (19a) the tree in (21).

(21)

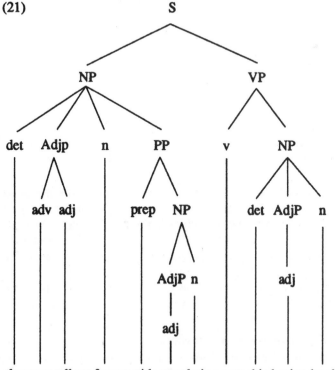

the very tall professor with grey hair wrote this boring book

This represents a typical analysis (though not necessarily one which would be adopted by all linguists). It shows that *this boring book* is a noun phrase (NP) containing a determiner (*this*), an adjectival phrase (AdjP) consisting of the adjective (*boring*) and a noun (*book*); that the prepositional phrase (PP) *with grey hair* is a constituent of the larger noun phrase *the very tall professor with grey hair*; that the verb *wrote* and the NP *this boring book* constitute a verb phrase (VP); and that the sentence (S) as a whole is basically in two parts: a noun phrase (*the very tall professor with grey hair*) and a verb phrase (*wrote this boring book*).

An alternative and equivalent representation of a phrase structure is a bracketed string of categories and elements (22):

(22) S(NP(det(the),
          AdjP(adv(very), adj(tall))),
          n(professor),
          PP(prep(with),NP(AdjP(adj(grey)),n(hair))))),
      VP(v(wrote),
         NP(det(this),
            AdjP(adj(boring)),
            n(book))))

To derive the tree (21) or its equivalent bracketed string (22), we have the rules in (23) and (24).

(23a) S → NP VP

(23b) NP → (det) (AdjP) n (PP)

(23c) AdjP → (adv) adj

(23d) VP → v NP

(23e) PP → prep NP

(24a) det → {*the, this*}

(24b) n → {*professor, hair, book*}

(24c) adv → *very*

(24d) adj → {*tall, grey, boring*}

(24e) prep → *with*

(24f) v → *wrote*

In each rule in (23) the category on the left can be replaced by the sequence of categories on the right, where those categories enclosed in brackets are optional. These rules are known as **phrase structure rules.** Following convention, we indicate terminal symbols in lower case. Terminal symbols are categories which do not appear on the left-hand-side of phrase structure rules, but appear in rules such as those in (24), where the surface strings are shown: curly brackets indicate alternatives. Clearly, in reality such rules would involve long lists of alternatives, so the formalism shown in (24) is rarely used: rather, terminal symbols are matched to categories listed in the lexicon.

A phrase structure grammar is said to generate a tree such as (21). The reader should be careful to distinguish two uses of the term 'generate': the use here — which comes from mathematics — defines a static relationship between a grammar and a representation or tree structure; there is another use of the term, which we shall use elsewhere in this book, referring to one of the procedures involved in producing a translation of a text. We shall return to this in the section 2.9.1.

Phrase structure rules capture various other grammatical relationships: **dominance** (category S dominates NP and VP in rule (23a), category VP dominates v and NP in rule (23c)) and **precedence** (NP precedes VP in rule (23a), and AdjP precedes n in rule (23b)). Linguists often use the terminology of genealogical trees to describe relationships between nodes: a **mother** node is a node which dominates another (so S is the mother of NP and VP in our example); conversely, NP and VP are the **daughters** of S; nodes which share a common mother are, of course, **sisters**. Conventionally, only female kinship terms are used.

Dominance, or motherhood, should not be confused with governorship in a dependency grammar, since the dominating category is made up of the elements it dominates, whereas in dependency, the governor is just one of the elements that make up the sentence. In fact, the dependency notion of governorship can be incorporated into a phrase structure grammar by singling out in each rule one of the daughters as being the governor. (However, since it must be a terminal symbol, the gramar in (23) would have to be adjusted if we wanted to do this.) The precedence relationship obviously corresponds to the idea of sequence mentioned earlier.

In a phrase structure grammar, syntactic functions can be defined in terms of dominance and precedence. For example, 'subject' might be defined as being the NP dominated by S and preceding a VP, while 'object' is an NP dominated by VP and preceded by a verb.

2.8.3 Feature-based representations

In several sections above we have mentioned additional features — syntactic and semantic — which play a part in linguistic representation. In general, features can be represented as **attributes** with corresponding **values**, and as such are often called 'attribute–value pairs'. Features can be used to represent almost everything we have discussed so far: 'category' can be an attribute with values such as 'noun', 'verb', 'noun phrase', etc; grammatical features such as 'gender', 'number', 'tense' are all possible attributes, with the expected range of values; 'surface function' might have values such as 'subject', 'modifier' and so on, while there might be a parallel attribute 'deep function', with the same range of values. Thus, the nodes of our tree representations can be labelled not with single values, but with features in the form of attribute–value pairs. Sets of such features are usually called **feature bundles**.

Linguistic theories which use feature-based representations often include a **feature theory** which, for example, defines the lists of attributes and their possible values, but also might include rules about which features can or must be combined. For example, the feature theory might say that if the value of the 'category' attribute is 'noun', then the 'gender' feature is relevant, while if it is 'verb', then 'tense' must have a value. There might also be a system of default values, for example we could assume that the value of 'number' for a noun is 'singular' if it is not otherwise specified.

The values of attributes need not be generally restricted to single atomic units. In the case of 'semantic feature' for example, we might want to stipulate a whole set of values, e.g. '{human, male, young}' for *boy*. In some theories, the value of an attribute can itself be a feature bundle. In this way, an entire tree structure can be replaced by a complex **feature structure**. Traditionally, feature structures are enclosed in square brackets. Sets of values (which might also be feature bundles) are shown in curly brackets. For example, we could represent (21) above as the feature structure (25), where the constituents or daughters ('dtr') at each level are listed as an ordered set.

(25) [cat:sentence
        dtr:{[cat:np,function:subj,num:sing,
            dtr:{[cat:det,function:det,num:sing,lex:a],
                [cat:adjp,function:mod,
                dtr:{[cat:adv,function:mod,lex:very],
                    [cat:adj,function:head,lex:tall]}],
                [cat:n,function:head,num:sing,lex:professor,
                 sem:{human}],
                [cat:pp,function:mod,
                dtr:{[cat:prep,function:head,lex:with],
                    [cat:np,function:obj,
                    dtr:{[cat:adjp,function:mod,
                        dtr:{[cat:adj,function:head,lex:grey]},
                        [cat:n,function:head,num:sing,lex:hair,
                         sem:{bodypart}]}}}],
            [cat:vp,function:pred,
            dtr:{[cat:v,function:head,tense:past,lex:write,string:wrote],
                [cat:np,function:obj,num:sing,
                dtr:{[cat:det,function:det,num:sing,lex:this],
                    [cat:adjp,function:mod,
                    dtr:{[cat:adj,function:head,lex:boring]}],
                    [cat:n,function:head,num:sing,
                     lex:book,sem:{ ETC}]}}}]}]

It is also possible on the other hand to use feature structures to represent dependency trees, such as (19b), which is shown as (26). In this example, we treat syntactic function as the main feature on which to base the structure, rather than constituency ('subj', 'obj', 'mod' etc.) as in (25).

(26) [cat:v,tense:past,lex:write,string:wrote,
    subj:[cat:n,num:sing,lex:professor,sem:{human},
      det:[cat:det,num:sing,lex:a],
      mod:{[cat:adj,lex:tall,
          mod:[cat:adv,lex:very]],
        [cat:prep,lex:with,
         obj:[cat:n,num:sing,lex:hair,sem:{bodypart},
         mod:[cat:adj,lex:grey]]]}
    obj:[cat:n,num:sing,lex:book,sem:{ ETC},
      det:[cat:det,num:sing,lex:this],
      mod:[cat:adj,lex:boring]]]

2.8.4 Canonical and logical form

Linguists often talk about **canonical form**, meaning a form of neutral representation. We have already seen this idea in section 2.4, where we talked about canonical form for lexical items, which can be the uninflected root, a conventional inflected form (e.g. infinitive of the verb in French and Spanish) or even some hypothetical or hybrid form, which might be a stem, even though this never normally occurs alone (e.g. Latin *equ-* 'horse'), or else some other made-up identifier. Although this last type of canonical representation is not usually found in dictionaries, it is quite common in other sorts of linguistic representation, where we want to talk about a word without drawing attention to its specific surface form. For example we might want a convenient way to refer to the verb *be* in all its forms (*being, been, am, are, was, were*). Lexical canonical forms may be given also for multi-word or discontinuous lexical items (e.g. *aircraft carrier, give ... a hand*): a device often used is to replace the space with an underline character '_', e.g. *aircraft_carrier*.

Canonical form is also — perhaps more often — used to describe in a neutral way a construct rather than a single lexical item. For example, just as we wish to relate the different inflected forms of a word to a single canonical lexical item, so too we might wish to have a way of referring to various closely related sentences or sentence parts (e.g. irrespective of tense, passivization, etc.). This notion of 'canonical form' is very close to the idea of deep structure, seen in 2.5.2, while a predicate–argument representation as in 2.5.3 is also sometimes used for this purpose. Often, canonical syntactic form is taken to correspond to the surface form of the least marked structure, e.g. an active declarative sentence with no special thematization effects. If this seems counter-intuitive in the light of the discussion of deep structure, it should be born in mind that in his earliest formulation of the concept, Chomsky believed that surface structures were derived from deep structures by transformations (see 2.9.2 below). It is not impossible to imagine that one possible surface structure is the one derived from deep structure without any transformations, and is thus identical to it. Since the transformations embody deviations from the most neutral form of a proposition, e.g. by introducing passive voice, then this equation of deep structure, canonical form, and 'unmarked' surface structure is quite plausible.

A further candidate for canonical form might be **logical form**, which is a representation used to make explicit the meaning of an utterance in terms of the truth conditions it implies. This is a representation found in formal logic, in which notably the introduction and distinction of participants in the event being described is made explicit. Of particular interest to logicians is the issue of **quantifier scope**, which logical form representations make explicit. For example, a sentence such as (27a) would be represented as (27b), with the interpretation (27c).

(27a) Cats like fish.

(27b) $\forall x \, \text{cat}(x) \, \forall y \, \text{fish}(y) \, \text{like}(x, y)$

(27c) Whenever something (x) is a cat, then for whatever things which are fish (y), x likes y.

Logical form representations make explicit **quantifier scope ambiguities** such as the classical (28a) which might be represented as (28b) and which is to be read as (28c), or which might be represented as (28d), with the interpretation (28e).

(28a) Every man loves a woman.

(28b) $\exists y \, \text{woman}(y) \, (\forall x \, \text{man}(x) \, \text{love}(x, y))$

(28c) There is a woman whom all men love.

(28d) $\forall x \, \text{man}(x) \, (\exists y \, \text{woman}(y) \, \text{love}(x, y))$

(28e) For every man there is a woman whom he loves.

Although the second reading is pragmatically more plausible in this case, it is not always so obvious. Determining and indicating the correct quantifier scope is important because, as the following examples show, the two readings are not always equivalent, and important consequences might follow, e.g. if in some language the two readings receive different translations, or if, for some reason, we want to passivize the sentence, as in (29).

(29a) All the teachers in this room speak two languages.

(29b) Two languages are spoken by all the teachers in this room.

Only in (29b) can we be sure that there are two specific languages in question, whereas (29a) is simply a statement about multilingualism in general. Clearly, quantifier scope is closely related to differences of theme and rheme (section 2.7 above): (29a) is a statement about teachers and (29b) is about two (particular) languages.

2.9 Formal grammar and linguistic theory

2.9.1 Context free grammars and rewrite rules

The grammar in (23) is an example of a **context free grammar** (CFG). A CFG consists of a set of **rewrite rules** of the form A → α, where A belongs to a set of **non-terminal symbols** and α is a sequence of non-terminal and/or terminal symbols. The application of a sequence of rewrite rules is said to generate a representation of a sentence, and a grammar consisting of such rewrite rules is called a **generative grammar**. As we said above, we must be aware of the special meaning of the term 'generate' in this context. What a CFG grammar does is to define a formal relationship between a set of possible texts and their representations. This is actually a static definition, and the grammar is quite independent of the use to which it is put. The starting point can be either a text or the grammar. In the first case, the grammar is used to find out what the representation of the text should be; in the second case, the grammar is used to produce acceptable texts. It is reversible in this respect. The static 'declarative' nature of CFGs is somewhat obscured by the perhaps misleading — but now firmly established — use of the arrow symbol '→' and the term 'generate'. CFG rules are not instructions (or 'procedures') to be followed, but descriptions or definitions; the rules are in a certain sense quite reversible. (For more on the distinction between 'declarative' and 'procedural' see section 3.2.)

CFGs have some very interesting properties when it comes to their implementation as computational devices (see Chapter 3). However, it has been recognised that the simple formalism seen in (23) is inadequate in several respects for describing and explaining certain natural language structures. For example, in order to account for a passive verb form, as in sentence (30) it would be necessary to add further phrase structure rules (31).

(30) This book was written by the old professor.

(31a) VP → Vpass (PP)

(31b) Vpass → aux pastpart

where Vpass represents a passive verb form, consisting typically of an auxiliary (*was*) and a past participle (*written*). But by having apparently independent sets of rules, it is difficult to make explicit the special relationship between active sentences and their passive counterparts.

In another respect, the rules in (23) are too tolerant: there is nothing to prevent a transitive verb appearing in an intransitive structure (32a) or an intransitive one in a transitive structure (32b).

(32a) *The man put.

(32b) *The man went the book.

One solution is to invoke **subcategorization features** (as mentioned above, section 2.4), which express the appropriate restrictions on the context in which a certain word may occur. So for example, we can stipulate that the v in rule (23c) must have a lexical entry specified as transitive, i.e. that it can occur followed by an NP: the lexical entry might include a subcategorization feature something like (33); the notation '[transitive]' is sometimes written as '[— NP]', where the bar indicates the position of the element in question.

(33) v[transitive] → *wrote*

Rule (23c) above must now be rewritten to indicate that the subcategory 'v[transitive]' is needed, as in (34).

(34) VP → v[transitive] NP

The distinction between categories like v and subcategories like 'v[transitive]' means that generalizations which apply to all v's (irrespective of subcategorization

feature) can easily be stated. Furthermore, categories are often subdivided according to various different criteria, for different purposes: these subcategorizations
appear as features in the lexicon (cf. section 2.8.3), which can be evoked as
necessary by different rules. For example, the pastpart in (31) can be replaced by
a v with the appropriate subcategorization feature 'past-participle'.

One problem not readily addressed by simple phrase structure grammars
concerns relationships between sentences such as the following, which differ
according to whether the direct object is a full noun, as in (35a), or it is a
'*wh*-interrogative' (*who, what*, etc.), as in (35b).

(35a) Mary put the book on the table.

(35b) What did Mary put on the table?

2.9.2 Transformational rules

It was in an attempt to overcome such difficulties that the formal distinction
was introduced between representations of surface structure and deep structure (cf.
section 2.5.2 above). Both (35a) and the related (35b) are said to have similar deep
structures (36) (the triangle notation in the tree structure indicates by convention
that the details of this part of the tree are not of interest at the moment).

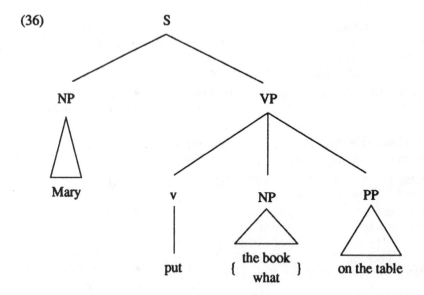

The surface form of (35a) is directly related to this deep form, but the surface
form of (35b) is derived by **transformational rules** which move the NP *what* to
the beginning and insert the auxiliary *did* between it and the subject NP *Mary* to
give the surface structure tree (37).

(37)

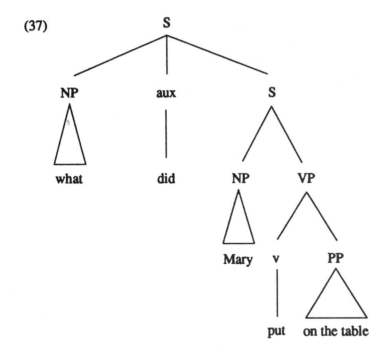

Transformational rules are formulated in terms of pairs of structural descriptions. The change in structure between (36) and (37) can be captured by the rule (38).

(38) X NP v wh Y ⇒ X wh *did* NP v Y

where X and Y indicate optional unspecified structures that are unaffected by the rule. (Readers should note that this example is for illustrative purposes only; in fact this formulation would now be rejected by most linguists.)

Grammars including rules such as (38) have different and more complex properties (especially from the point of view of computational implementation) than CFGs. In particular, it is more difficult to be certain of the reversibility of such rules, since they are able to add and delete elements freely, as well as to move them around. The example (38) showed a fairly simple rule where the elements being manipulated are all single constituents, but the formalism of transformational rules can equally be used with more complex trees. In later chapters we shall see many examples of similar rules for manipulating trees in preparation for translating between languages with different sentence structures, e.g. between English and Welsh (examples (19a) and (20a) above). In this context, the process is generally referred to as **tree transduction** (see Chapter 6 in particular.)

One major function of deep structure analysis is to illuminate relationships which are implicit in surface forms. Compare, for example the two sentences in (39).

(39a) John persuaded Mary to visit his father.

(39b) John promised Mary to visit his father.

We know that in (39a) the person who is (or was) to visit John's father is not John but Mary, whereas in (39b) it is not Mary but John. The deep structure for (39a) would be (40).

(40)

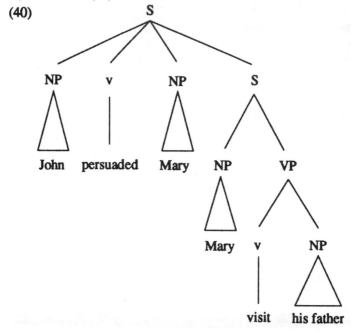

The derivation of the surface form (39a) from the deep structure in (40) involves the deletion of the NP *Mary* in the complement S, and the transformation of the finite verb (*visit*) into an infinitive. A similar deep structure for (39b) — with *promised* instead of *persuaded* and *John* instead of the second *Mary* — would involve the same rules to generate a surface form. Running the procedure in the opposite direction gives us the appropriate interpretation of the embedded sentence (which might be needed for translation into a language which makes the subject of the embedded sentence explicit or where knowing what the subject would be is needed for gender or number agreement): the lexical entries for *promise* and *persuade* tell us whether to copy the surface subject or to copy the surface object into the subject position in the embedded sentence.

As another example, consider the sentence (41a). It is clear that the deep subject of *like* must be *John* and that *seems* expresses the speaker's attitude to the proposition (41b). Consequently, a deep structure is proposed which corresponds roughly to the 'equivalent' expression (41c), where the sentence (41b) is the complement of *seems* in the whole structure. (Differences in meaning between (41a) and (41c) are attributable to differences of theme and rheme: cf. section 2.7 above.)

(41a) John seems to like easy solutions.

(41b) John likes easy solutions.

(41c) It seems that John likes easy solutions.

The generation of (41a) from such a deep structure involves the **raising** of the NP *John* from the embedded sentence to be the grammatical subject of *seem* in the sentence as a whole. Similar transformational rules involving the raising of elements occur in sentences such as (42)

(42) Mary is believed to be a good cook.

where *Mary* is the subject of *be a good cook* and the entire phrase *Mary is a good cook* is the complement of *believe*. Verbs that have this syntactic behaviour are often called 'raising verbs'.

The addition of transformational rules to the phrase structure rules gave the **transformational-generative** (TG) grammars associated with Chomsky, the first substantial attempt to overcome the limitations of simple phrase structure rules such as those in (23) and to develop a grammar with some descriptive adequacy. In this model there is a 'base component' containing a lexicon and phrase structure rules, and generating deep structures, a 'semantic component' which interprets deep structures, a 'transformational component' consisting of transformational rules which convert deep structures into surface structures, and a 'phonological component' which produces phonetic representations of sentences from surface structures. The core notion is that of abstract 'deep structure' representations, in which surface ambiguities are eliminated, implicit relationships are made explicit, and synonymous sentences have the same representation. From a multilingual point of view, the idea that translationally equivalent sentences share a common deep representation, but have different surface structures due to different transformational and phonological components, had some appeal.

However, in the course of time the deficiencies of the TG model emerged. Briefly, two such deficiencies are, first, the excessive 'power' of transformational rules: in theory it is possible to devise a rule to do almost anything with a phrase structure which makes it virtually impossible for a parser (section 3.8) to recognise which particular transformational rule has applied; and, second, the recognition that semantic interpretation could not be restricted to deep structures and has to include information from surface structures, such as the scope of quantifiers (cf. 2.8.4 above). In the last twenty years various models of generative grammar have been developed in response to such difficulties, mainly by exploiting the full power of phrase structure rules and/or by restricting or eliminating transformational rules (sections 2.10.1 to 2.10.4 below). Nevertheless, although the theory itself is now superseded, the concepts of 'deep structure' and of 'transformation' are frequently referred to in many discussions of linguistic representations, and have influenced the design of many MT systems.

Certain concepts and formalisations are common to most of the models of generative grammar that have been developed since Chomsky's original formulation. Among them are the use of subcategorisation features (already discussed above), the treatment of traces and gaps, the $\overline{X}$ notation and the notion of valency and case (or thematic) roles. These concepts are discussed in the next three sections.

2.9.3 Traces and gaps

The notion of a **trace** may be illustra.. d by (43), a modification of (37) above.

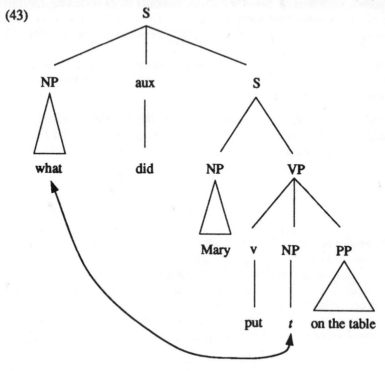

(43)

Whereas in (37) the movement of *what* from a direct object NP position to an initial position left no object for *put* in the surface form, we now have a trace (*t*) of the NP. By this means, the subcategorisation requirements for *put* are intact and the semantic relationship between the verb and *what* can be read directly from the surface structure (43), thus eliminating the need to refer to deep structure in this respect. However, there are various limitations on the types of structural configurations in which a lexical element can be legitimately related (**bound**) to a trace element, and these have been discussed at length in the linguistics literature.

In contrast to a trace, a **gap** in a phrase structure represents lexical items or strings which have been completely deleted (and not just moved elsewhere). For example, in (44a) a second occurrence of *likes* has been omitted, and in (44b) the fragment *gone swimming* has been elided. The 'reconstruction' of such ellipses presents considerable problems both for theoretical linguistics and for computational analysis.

(44a) John likes fish, and Bill meat.

(44b) John has gone swimming and Bill has too.

2.9.4 $\overline{\overline{X}}$ theory

The formalism known as $\overline{\overline{X}}$ **theory** ('$\overline{X}$' is pronounced — and sometimes written — as 'X-bar') developed from the recognition of similarities in the phrase structures of nominalisations and of sentences. Compare the structures in (46) for (45a-b).

(45a) The student solved the problem.

(45b) the solution of the problem

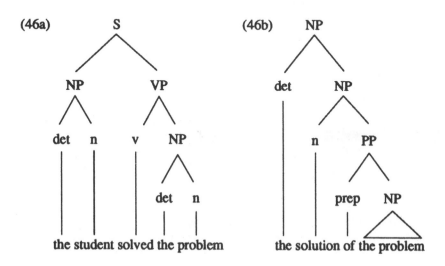

In particular, (46b) contains a hierarchy of head categories: n (*solution*) is embedded as head item in an NP (*solution of the problem*), and this NP is in turn the head of the whole NP (*the solution of the problem*). To express such hierarchies of categories the bar notation was developed: an NP is thus a higher order n: $\overline{N}$, and a higher order NP is $\overline{\overline{N}}$ (pronounced 'N double bar'). The further generalisation of the notation and its extention to other configurations resulted in a uniform $\overline{\overline{X}}$ structure:

(47)

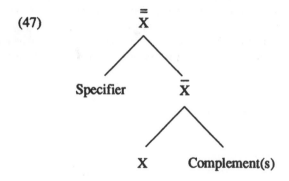

The X can represent any category (noun, verb, adjective); the specifier can be filled by any appropriate preceding modifier (determiner, adverb); and the complement(s) by any succeeding modifier (noun phrase, verb phrase, prepositional phrase). The following are examples of structures dominated by $\overline{\overline{N}}$, $\overline{\overline{Adj}}$, and $\overline{\overline{Prep}}$, respectively:

(48a) this objection to the theory

(48b) too hot to handle

(48c) away from her problems

The specifiers are *this* (48a), *too* (48b) and *away* (48c). The $\overline{X}$ categories correspond to the dominating categories: in (48a) it is the NP (i.e. $\overline{N}$) *objection to the theory*, in (48b) it is an AdjP (i.e. $\overline{Adj}$) *hot to handle*, and in (48c) it is a PP (i.e. $\overline{Prep}$) *from her problems*. The complements are thus a PP (*to the theory*) in (48a), a VP (*to handle*) in (48b), and an NP (*her problems*) in (48c).

The basic idea of $\overline{X}$ theory is found in a number of current linguistic theories and appears also in computational linguistics, although direct applications of the notation in MT are rare and relatively recent (for one example see the representation in example (9) in Chapter 14).

2.9.5 Valency grammar

In section 2.8.1 we introduced the notion of a dependency representation, which differs from a phrase-structure representation in focusing on governor–dependent relations, corresponding to the predicate–argument structure mentioned in section 2.5.3.

In such a structure, a distinction is often made between **complements** or arguments which are closely associated with the verb, inasmuch as their syntactic form and function is predictable from the verb, and **adjuncts** which act as sentential modifiers. The number and nature of the complements which a given verb takes are given by its valency. Typically, verbs have a valency value between 1 and 3 (though verbs like *rain*, with a dummy subject, might be said to have a valency of 0). Monovalent verbs are intransitives like *fall* taking a single argument, the subject; divalent verbs take two arguments and may be transitive, taking a subject and object, or a subject and a prepositional phrase (e.g. *look* which has a prepositional complement with *at*); trivalent verbs include verbs taking a subject, direct and indirect object (e.g. *give*), or subject, object and prepositional complement (e.g. *supply someone with something*), or even two prepositional complements (e.g. *rely on someone for something*). Complements may also take the form of clauses introduced by *that* (e.g. *say that...*), infinitival clauses introduced by *to* (e.g. *expect to...*) or participial clauses (e.g. *like going*).

While the complements can be predicted by (or are controlled by) the verb, adjuncts are less predictable and can occur more freely with almost any verbs. The predicate and its complements express the central core of a sentence, while the adjuncts express the circumstances of time, location, reason, purpose, and so on, which accompany the central proposition.

Besides describing the syntactic form of its arguments, a valency description might also express semantic feature restrictions on the arguments. For example, the entry for *supply* might stipulate that the subject and object should be human or have human connections (e.g. an institution), while the *with*-complement must be a commodity.

Valency grammar is useful in translation in two ways: first, although corresponding verbs in different language often have different syntactic structures, their numerical valency is usually the same. By juxtaposing valency information, the correspondences can be identified. For example, while *look* takes a prepositional complement with *at*, the corresponding French verb *regarder* takes a direct object. An extreme example of this is *like* and *plaire*: compare (46).

(46a) The audience liked the film.

(46b) *Le film a plu aux spectateurs.*

The subject of *like* corresponds to the indirect object of *plaire*, while the direct object becomes the subject in the French.

The second benefit of Valency grammar is in the translation of prepositions: those marking complements are rarely translated directly, unless by coincidence the valency patterns coincide (e.g. *count on* and *compter sur*): more commonly there is an arbitrary correspondence of prepositions, if indeed both verbs take prepositional complements (cf. *look at / regarder*). Table 2.1 shows a range of German and English verb pairs and the corresponding prepositional complements, and indicates the wide range of possibilities: for example, although *mit* usually translates as *with*, *rechnen mit* is *count ON*, *prahlen mit* is *boast OF* and so on.

	at	in	of	on	to
an	*arbeiten* work	*glauben* believe	*denken* think	*stecken* stick	*gewöhnen* accustom
auf	*blicken* look	*trauen* trust	*zutreffen* be true	*rechnen* count	*weisen* point
für		*s.interessieren* be interested	*zutreffen* be true		*sorgen* see
in	*ankommen* arrive	*kleiden* dress		*einsteigen* get	*einwilligen* agree
mit		*handeln* trade	*prahlen* boast	*rechnen* count	*geschehen* happen
zu			*gehören* be part	*gratulieren* congratulate	*führen* lead

Table 2.1 Prepositional complements in English and German

If a prepositional phrase is a complement, we must look to the verb to see how to translate it. On the other hand, adjunct prepositional phrases can usually be translated independently of the verb.

Valency does not only apply to verbs and their arguments. Adjectives too have valency patterns, especially when they are used predicatively (e.g. *proud OF*, *interested IN*, *concerned WITH*). Within noun phrases too, valency patterns can be predicted: where the noun is derived from a verb, or is semantically cognate, the complement structure is often derived in parallel: cf. (13) above and (47)-(50).

(47) The people are fighting for freedom.
the people's fight for freedom...

(48) The boy gave his brother a book.
the boy's gift of a book to his brother...

(49) The government raised £10m by indirect taxation.
the raising by the government of £10m by indirect taxation...

(50) Coventry dramatically beat Spurs by 3-2 after extra-time in the Final at Wembley in 1987 for the first time ever.
Coventry's dramatic first-ever extra-time 3-2 victory against Spurs in the Final at Wembley in 1987...

For other types of nouns the type of modification can also be predicted, and hence they can be said to have a valency structure. For example a *book* is often *of* some type of material, *by* someone, *about* something, and so on.

2.9.6 Case grammar

An elaboration of dependency, valency, and predicate-argument structure is found in **Case grammar**, in which the **semantic functions** of the complements (and in some versions, the adjuncts) are given. The nature of the relationship of a dependent noun or noun phrase (argument) to its governing verb (predicate) in a sentence may be expressed in terms of roles such as 'agent' (instigator of an action), 'patient' (entity affected), 'instrument' (means of achieving action), etc. Across languages, these semantic functions remain constant while the syntactic functions (subject, object and so on) differ. The semantic function label is thus a convenient point of contact for the syntactic representations for the corresponding sentences. The name 'Case grammar' derives from the term 'deep case', an unfortunate term intended to underline the distinction between surface syntactic functions (or 'surface cases' like nominative, accusative, dative) and deeper semantic functions. Other terms indicating roughly the same concept include 'semantic role', 'thematic role' and so on.

It is postulated that the range of possible semantic functions is relatively small: typically Case grammarians have identified a set of about ten. As well as those mentioned above, they include 'experiencer' (entity undergoing a non-physical action), 'recipient', 'source' (initial state or cause of action), 'goal' (aim or result of action), 'location' and (a few) others. So for example in (51) the case roles might be agent (*the teacher*), patient (*the children*), recipient (*to their parents*), instrument (*minibus*), and time (*on Thursday*).

(51) The teacher brought the children back to their parents by minibus on Thursday.

A major problem in Case theory is precisely the identification of an appropriate set of roles. In addition, it is sometimes not clear whether or not each role can occur more than once in a given sentence: the Valency distinction between complements and adjuncts is useful here, since a sentence involving a verb which takes, for example, a locative complement (e.g. *park*) might also have a locative adjunct, as in (52).

(52) In the village, you can park your car on any street.
      locative adjunct   locative complement

It should be noted that, like Valency, Case relations are not necessarily confined to sentences with finite verbs: they may also be applied in noun phrases to label modifiers of nouns derived from verbs. For example (53) has patient (*water*), instrument (*by pesticides*) and location (*in Europe*).

(53) pollution of water by pesticides in Europe

Semantic functions or Case roles are linked to semantic features (see section 2.6) in that certain functions are usually filled by elements bearing certain features. This can either be general (e.g. agents are usually animate, locations are usually places), or specific to verbs or verb classes (e.g. *eat* requires its patient to be edible, verbs of giving require the recipient to be animate). This link is used to describe both the syntactic and semantic behaviour of words in a sentence, and to make choices between alternative interpretations of individual words. For example, *enter* requires an enclosed space as its direct object: because of this we are able to assume in (54) that the interpretation of *bank* is the building rather than the edge of a river.

(54) The man entered the bank.

2.9.7 Unification grammar

Unification grammar is the name for a number of linguistic approaches which have recently emerged, including GPSG, LFG and Categorial grammar, all of which are discussed below. What they have in common is the use of feature representations (cf. 2.8.3. above), and the formal device of **feature unification**. The basic idea is that feature structures can be merged if the values of the features are compatible. In this way, structures are built up until representations such as those illustrated in (25) and (26) above emerge. Two feature structures are defined as being compatible either where the two structures have no feature attributes in common, as in (55a) and (55b); or where those feature attributes which are common to both structures share the same values, as in (56a) and (56b). (Unification is symbolized by the logical 'set union' operator ∪.)

(55a) [def=yes] ∪ [num=plur,sem=animate] =
        the   *mice*

     [def=yes,num=plur,sem=animate]
          the mice

(55b) [def=yes,num=sing] ∪ [sem=animate] =
          this   *sheep*

     [def=yes,num=sing,sem=animate]
          this sheep

(56a) [def=yes,num=plur] ∪ [num=plur,sem=animate] =
  those   *cats*

[def=yes,num=plur,sem=animate]
  those cats

(56b) [def=no,num=sing,gen=masc] ∪ [num=sing,gen=masc] =
  un   *homme*

[def=no,num=sing,gen=masc]
  un homme

The formalism allows grammars to construct higher-order constituents, for example by merging the structures, as by a rule such as (57a). This rule permits unification in the case of (57b), i.e. the structure is accepted as well-formed; but in (57c) unification is blocked, since the values of 'num' are in conflict, i.e. the structure is considered ungrammatical.

(57a) NP[def=X,gov=Y,num=Z] → det[def=X,num=Z] n[lex=Y,num=Z]

(57b)

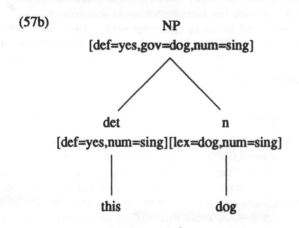

(57c)

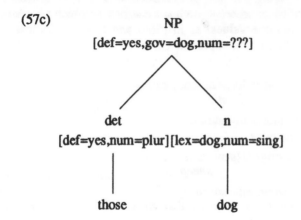

It should be noted that 'unification' as understood by linguists is slightly different from the concept of unification found in certain programming styles (see section 3.9). However, unification-based programming languages are highly suitable for implementing (linguistic) unification-based grammars. The main difference is that in linguistic unification, the exact order of attribute–value pairs may be ignored. Other differences are less important.

2.10 Influential theories and formalisms

We conclude this chapter with brief outlines of some linguistic theories which have influenced some MT researchers and may be expected to influence future research in various ways.

2.10.1 Lexical Functional Grammar

Lexical Functional Grammar (LFG) offers a formalism for expressing exactly the kind of feature structure building outlined in the previous section. In LFG there is a sequence of representations: constituent-structure (c-structure), which closely resembles the standard phrase structure representation, and feature-structure (f-structure) which is a feature-based dependency structure representation. The c-structure is given by a standard Phrase Structure Grammar (section 2.8.2 above), except that the rules also stipulate feature equations which must be applied. The application of these equations serves to build up the f-structure. It is achieved by the use of two 'metavariables': '↑' (pronounced 'up') and '↓' (pronounced 'down'). ↑ refers to the feature structure of the mother node in the tree, while ↓ refers to the daughter node to which it is attached, i.e. to itself. An example of a rule may help to clarify.

$$
\text{(58)} \quad \text{NP} \rightarrow
\begin{array}{ccc}
\text{det} & & \\
(\uparrow \text{det} = \downarrow & \text{adj} & \text{n} \\
\uparrow \text{def} = \downarrow \text{def} & (\uparrow \text{mod} = \downarrow) & (\uparrow = \downarrow) \\
\uparrow \text{num} = \downarrow \text{num}) & &
\end{array}
$$

This rule states that when building the f-structure for the NP, the values for the features 'det', 'def' and 'num' are taken from the det, and the values for 'mod' from the adj. The annotation ($\uparrow = \downarrow$) attached to n means that the entire structure is copied into NP. Notice that the values for 'det' and 'mod' will themselves be entire feature structures. In constructing the f-structure, a major part is played by the unification of features (as described above): for example, on the assumption that we have lexical entries such as (59), the value for 'num' is given both by the feature structure of the det and by the feature structure of the n.

(59) n → *dog* (↑pred=dog ↑num=sing)
    det → *this* (↑def=yes ↑pred=this ↑num=sing)
    adj → *hungry* (↑pred=hungry)

If the equations resulting from the instantiation of the metavariables ↑ and ↓ can be unified then the f-structure for the NP can be built. The structure for the NP *this hungry dog* is shown in (60). Notice that all the information we really

(60)   NP

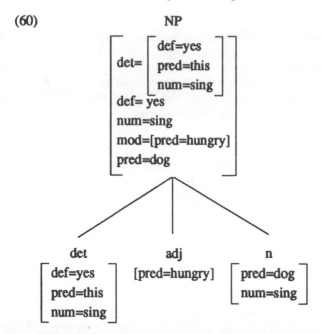

want has found its way up to the mother node, so that the substructures (for det, adj and n) can effectively be discarded.

The LFG formalism for mapping from c-structure to f-structure, coupled with the mechanism of feature unification, has proved a very powerful tool. The facility to build dependency structures from phrase-structure rules appears to give the LFG formalism the best of both approaches, and it has proved very popular for experimental MT systems.

2.10.2 Categorial grammar

An alternative to the constituency representation of category groups (section 2.8.2) is provided by the formalism of **categorial grammar**. In a categorial grammar there are just two or three fundamental categories, e.g. sentence S and nominal N or S, NP and VP; and there are just two functor symbols, a slash '/' and a back-slash '\' indicating what is expected to the right and left respectively. Other grammatical categories (adjective, adverb, etc.) are thus defined in terms of their potential to combine with one another or with one of the fundamental categories in constituency structures. Thus a transitive verb might be defined as 'VP/NP' because it combines with a noun phrase (to its right) to form a verb phrase; and an adjective might be defined as 'NP/NP' because in combination with a noun phrase to its right it forms a (higher order) noun phrase ($\overline{\overline{N}}$, in $\overline{X}$ theory). In other words, category symbols themselves define how they are to combine with other categories. Combinatory rules are those of simple 'cancellation' (or 'application') and 'composition', as in (61).

(61a) A/B B $\Rightarrow$ A

(61b) B B\A $\Rightarrow$ A

(61c) A/B B/C ⇒A/C

(61d) C\B B\A ⇒C\A

Categorial grammar was proposed in the early days of MT research for the treatment of syntactic structures. In recent years it has been revived, in part because of parallels with other approaches (e.g. $\overline{X}$ theory), its compatibility with unification-based formalisms and with principles of semantic compositionality (section 2.10.6 below.)

2.10.3 Government and Binding

The initial response to the problems of the excessive 'power' of transformational grammar (section 2.9.2) was to impose conditions on the application of rules, e.g. by constraints on transformations, subcategorisation features, selection restrictions, etc. This was the approach in the model known as the **Extended Standard Theory**. The alternative was to develop a theory of conditions on the forms of structures themselves, i.e. a theory of the general principles underlying the construction of grammatical representations. This is the basic approach of what is known as **Government and Binding theory** (GB theory).

GB theory is concerned less with the elaboration of rules for particular languages than with establishing the abstract principles of language itself, with the constraints on individual languages deriving from a **universal grammar**. There is now just one basic transformational rule, expressed as 'Move α'. Its operation in a particular language depends on the specific values attached to α in that language. The particular syntactic structures of a language depend on the values or parameters attached to various 'subtheories' of the model. These subtheories include (very briefly): the $\overline{X}$ theory sketched above (section 2.9.4); a theory for assigning 'thematic roles' (cf. section 2.9.6), θ-theory; a Case theory for assigning surface case roles (e.g. nominative, genitive) regulated essentially by government and agreement restrictions; a Binding theory concerning the co-reference conditions for NPs, i.e. involving anaphora, pronominalisation, etc. (sections 2.7 and 2.9.3 above); a Bounding theory defining limitations placed on the movement rule; a Control theory for dealing with the indexing of empty categories and traces (cf. section 2.9.3 above); a Government theory defining the sets of items which may be governed by a category (cf. section 2.8.1 above).

The attraction of GB theory for some MT researchers lies in the postulation of universal principles which could provide the framework for MT systems and it has been the basis for some small-scale projects.

2.10.4 Generalized Phrase Structure Grammar

As its name suggests, this model is an attempt to provide descriptively adequate grammars without using transformational rules of any kind, i.e. be 'strongly equivalent' to a context-free grammar. Since there are computationally effective parsers for context-free grammars (section 3.8), the model of **Generalized Phrase Structure Grammar** (GPSG) has a considerable attraction for computational linguistics.

The characteristic features of the model may be briefly summarised. GPSG makes a formal distinction between dominance and precedence relations; instead of a single rule, such as (62a), there is one rule specifying constituency only (62b), (where the items are unordered) and a general rule for precedence (62c) (where H indicates any head category).

    (62a) VP → V NP PP

    (62b) VP = V, NP, PP

    (62c) H < NP < PP

In this way the parallelism in the category orders of sentences, noun phrases, verb phrases, etc. (cf. the motivation for $\overline{X}$ theory, section 2.9.4.) is captured in a single generalisation. In GPSG there are general procedures for moving categories and features up, down and across trees, and for ensuring various types of agreement between governors and dependents; these are the 'Head Feature Convention', the 'Foot Feature Principle', and the 'Control Agreement Principle'. Instead of transformational rules GPSG provides metarules to define relations between sets of rules (e.g. those producing active structures and corresponding passive structures), and a 'slash' feature to account for gapping and preposing of *wh* elements (cf. 2.9.3 above), e.g. the formalism X/Y refers to a category X lacking feature (or category) Y, thus VP/NP refers to a VP lacking an expected direct object NP, cf. Categorial grammar (above). Finally, for semantic interpretation the model integrates a version of Montague grammar (see next section) rather than deriving a Logical Form representation as in transformational grammar and GB theory.

2.10.5 Semantic compositionality

The attraction of the semantic theory put forward by Richard Montague has been that it provides a means for integrating syntactic theories and well-established methods of formal logic. The basic principle is that of semantic **compositionality**, i.e. that the meanings of complex expressions (e.g. sentences) are functions of the meanings of their component basic expressions (e.g. words). It is a principle which has now been adopted in a number of linguistic formalisms and theories. A brief outline will indicate the general idea; fuller details are found in Chapter 16 on the Rosetta project, the most significant application of Montague grammar in MT research.

A **Montague grammar** specifies a set of basic expressions (meaningful units. e.g. words) and a set of syntactic rules prescribing the construction of larger expressions (e.g. sentences) from basic expressions. Expressions are assigned semantic interpretations in relation to the semantic domain of a 'possible world': each basic expression has a basic meaning (a direct association with an 'object' in the domain), and each syntactic rule has a meaning function reflecting the logical (truth) value of the combination concerned. The meanings of expressions (sentences) can thus be related to propositions of an intensional logic formalism and given an interpretation with respect to a 'model' of possible states of affairs, i.e. determining the conditions for a given sentence to be true. Montague grammar assumes that semantic interpretation can be based on relatively simple 'surface' structural information, and this obvious attraction has given it almost paradigm status in contemporary formal semantic theory.

Nevertheless, Montague semantics has been criticised for inadequacies in the treatment of certain linguistic phenomena, notably interrogatives and imperatives, and a number of innovations have appeared in recent years. One of these is **Situation Semantics**, which introduces formal mechanisms for taking discourse and speaker environments into account for semantic interpretation and for providing richer representations of content going beyond truth conditions.

2.11 Further reading

General introductions to linguistics are numerous, from among which we would recommend Lyons (1981a). There are also standard text books dealing with most of the individual topics mentioned here.

For morphology and the lexicon see Bauer (1988), and for morphology and syntax see Allerton (1979). For a general treatment of semantics, see Lyons (1981b), and for text relations, anaphora, etc. Halliday and Hasan (1976).

Dependency grammar is discussed in Herbst *et al.* (1979:32-46), while Schubert (1987) goes into more detail, and is specifically concerned with its application to MT.

For a general and comparative introduction to the various syntactic theories, see Sells (1985) or Horrocks (1987) on LFG, GB and GPSG, and Radford (1988) on TG, GB and $\overline{X}$ theory.

A detailed treatment of Valency and Case with particular reference to Computational Linguistics is given by Somers (1987a). This is the source of Table 2.1.

For an introduction to unification-based grammar formalisms, see Shieber (1986).

The standard reference for LFG is Bresnan (1982), for GB Chomsky (1982), and for GPSG Gazdar *et al.* (1985), though readers may find the secondary references cited above more accessible. Categorial grammar has its origins in the work of mathematical logic; it was first proposed in the MT context by Bar-Hillel (1953); for a recent substantial treatment see Oehrle *et al.* (1988).

For Montague grammar the basic introduction is Dowty *et al.* (1981); its application in MT is described in Chapter 16. For Situation Semantics see Barwise and Perry (1983); its potential for MT has been outlined by Rupp (1989).

3
Computational aspects

In this chapter we present some background concerning the essential computational aspects of MT system design. We will assume in the reader a basic but not in-depth knowledge and awareness of computers. For this reason, readers who come from a computer science background may find that some of the material in this chapter, especially in the first five sections, rather familiar to them, and such readers might like to skip those parts which do not address new issues.

The chapter is in two parts: the first (sections 3.1 to 3.4) concerns some rudiments of computer science, while the second (section 3.5 onwards) turns to the aspects of **computational linguistics** which are particularly relevant to MT. Computational linguistics in general is concerned with developing computational tools for linguistic problem solving, and most of the techniques described in the second part of this chapter also feature in many applications other than MT.

3.1 Data and programs

In essence the computer is simply an electronic machine which can process large amounts of data quickly and accurately (in the sense that it will always produce identical results if asked to repeat the same task more than once). The physical units which comprise a computer system, its **hardware**, include a central processor (which performs the basic operations), an internal storage space, or **memory**, and various **input** and **output** devices which allow the computer to communicate with the outside world. Among these are keyboards, printers and screens (visual display units or VDUs), typically used directly by humans for exchanging information with the computer; but other 'input/output' devices include disk drives, magnetic tape readers and so on, which allow data to be stored externally, and to be read in and used as necessary. One particularly important type of data is the **software**, which tells the computer what to do. Software generally consists of **programs** (the American spelling is always used for this term in computer science, even in British English) which are sets of instructions telling the computer to read some data, perform some calculation, output some message, and so on.

Programs are written in **programming** languages, of which there are many different varieties. Programming languages enable the human programmer to write instructions clearly and concisely without worrying too much about the details of how the computer will actually go about implementing the instructions. They also enable programs written for one computer to be used on another computer, as long as the programming language in question is available on both the computers. The variety of tasks that a computer can be programmed to perform is of course vast, and different programming languages are typically aimed at making certain types of tasks more or less easy. Very general-purpose programming languages which slightly facilitate a broad selection of tasks are called low-level programming languages, while programming languages aimed at greatly facilitating much more specific tasks are called **high-level** languages, and accordingly have a much narrower range of applications. As we will see later, some MT systems are written in low-level languages, while some are written in high-level languages. The former have the advantage of being **portable** from one machine to the other, but they have the disadvantage of being more difficult for the human observer to understand, because so much of the program code has to do with mundane, non-linguistic aspects of the translation task.

Programs are typically **stored** somewhere in the computer memory or, more often, on some external device like a diskette, and then loaded when they are to be used. In this sense, program **code** is just an example of data. Indeed, there are special programs — usually written in very low-level languages — whose job it is to convert programs written in some higher-level language into a form that the computer can understand. Sometimes the process might be repeated so that what the higher-level program actually does is to interpret yet another program written in an even higher-level programming language. This happens quite often in computational linguistics.

3.2 Separation of algorithms and data

There is in general a very important distinction between programs and other sorts of data. A program is essentially a set of instructions (an algorithm) saying how to solve some problem or achieve some goal. The best programs express these solutions in the most general terms, so that they can be used for solving a whole set of similar problems in the same way. Imagine for example a program which was able to add 3 and 5 and give the answer 8. This program has some use, but it is rather limited. In particular, it does not help us add 7 and 3, for example. Now consider a program which will add ANY two numbers: this is a much more useful program. The only problem is that we have to tell it, each time we run it, WHICH numbers to add. The program itself says HOW to add, but it is the data which must be supplied separately that tell it WHAT to add. This idea of separating the data from the programs is very important in computational linguistics and MT. As a simple example, consider a program which looks up words in a dictionary. This program will be much more useful if we can use it for different dictionaries (as long as they have the same format).

This notion of separation (sometimes called 'decoupling') of algorithms and data has many consequences in computational linguistics. It means for example that MT systems can be designed to a certain extent independently of the particular languages concerned; the algorithms will determine how the computer goes about translating, while the data will capture the linguistic details. This means that, in the ideal world at least, computer scientists can work on the algorithms, while linguists work on the data. In reality it is not so simple, but there are certainly examples of MT systems consisting of translation software which operates in a similar manner for different sets of data, e.g. dictionaries and grammar rules.

A further advantage of separation is that it helps to distinguish two essentially different types of error that may occur in large computational systems, namely errors arising from an incorrect algorithm, and errors in the data. The often-quoted example of someone receiving a gas bill for £0 is an example (presumably) of an algorithm error: the program algorithm should include instructions about how to deal with the special case of a zero bill. On the other hand, someone receiving a bill for £10,000 is probably the victim of a data error: the wrong meter readings have been given to the computer. In MT too we can distinguish between mistranslations resulting from the program algorithm doing things in the wrong order, for example, and mistranslations resulting from the wrong information, e.g. a typographical error in the dictionary or a missing rule in the grammar.

Another issue connected to the distinction between algorithms and data is the question of 'declarative' and 'procedural' information. Declarative information is data which consist essentially of facts or definitions of objects and relationships; procedural information concerns what we want to do with those facts. A simple example will clarify: we can imagine the fact that the verb *eats* is the 3rd person singular present tense form of the verb *eat* is stored somehow in a 'lexical database' (see below). The relationship between *eats* and *eat*, and also the association of 'singular' and 'present tense' (etc.) to *eats* is declarative knowledge. There may be several different 'procedures' which use this knowledge in different ways. For example, there may be a procedure for discovering whether or not a certain word or phrase is a plausible subject of the verb *eats* (e.g. by testing if it is 3rd person singular): this would be an 'analysis' procedure (cf. section 1.2 and Chapter 5); deciding that *eats* translates into French as *mange* (because *mange* is the 3rd person singular present tense form of the verb *manger* just as *eats* is of *eat*) is another (used in 'transfer', cf. section 1.2 and Chapter 6); and finally finding out what the appropriate form of the verb *eat* should be if the tense is present and the subject is 3rd person singular is yet another procedure (used in 'generation', cf. section 1.2 and Chapter 7). In its simplest form, the distinction procedural vs. declarative corresponds exactly to algorithm vs. data. But it should be understood that in many MT systems, the procedural information is coded in a special formalism which must be then interpreted by the computer using a standard programming language: so the procedural information coded in the formalism is still data, but of a different kind from the declarative data which the procedures make reference to. The possibility of distinguishing information which is neutral and can be used in different ways by different parts of the system is obviously advantageous: often, in MT systems, the linguistic information is mainly declarative in nature, while the computational side of the MT process represents procedural information.

3.3 Modularity

So far we have talked in terms of programs or algorithms for solving some problem without really considering what it means to solve a problem. In particular, some problems might be harder or bigger than others, and parts of the solution to one problem might be useful for the solution of another. For these two reasons, it is usual in designing algorithms to introduce an element of **modularity** into the design, that is, to divide the problem to be solved into sub-problems, and to divide those sub-problems further, until there is a collection of small, self-contained, relatively simple problems with correspondingly simple algorithms. Furthermore, it is to be hoped that these mini-programs can be used as building blocks, or **modules**, in the construction of other programs solving related but slightly different problems.

Modular programming has an additional advantage of making it easier to locate and correct algorithmic errors. If the computation is divided up into small, manageable blocks, each representing a specific and easily identifiable process, it is easier to see exactly where in the larger process something is going wrong. Furthermore, in the best cases, the modules can be developed and tested separately. This is an obvious engineering principle found in many spheres of life, and in computing no less than anywhere else.

In computational linguistics and MT, it is generally held that the modularisation should be linguistically rather than simply computationally motivated. It is considered desirable, for example, that the modules represent sub-tasks that linguists recognise as self-contained, rather than tasks which happen to be convenient for a computer program to treat at the same time or in the same way. When a system gets very large, it is important to be able to keep track of what each part of the system is intended to do; and it is helpful if the computational design of the system in some way reflects an intuitive linguistic approach to the problem. Furthermore, *ad hoc* solutions are avoided: the computational convenience of combining sub-problems may be vetoed by the linguistically motivated modularity requirement. The apparent advantages of combining notionally distinct sub-problems in one module may be forgotten or no longer understood at later stages when a system grows more complex.

Another important aspect of modularity is the relative independence of the modules. This is essential if they are to be tested separately. But equally, when the time comes, it must be possible to fit the modules together smoothly. An essential part of modularity is, therefore, the design of the interfaces between the modules, and here is where the important question of data structures comes in. This is true in general in computing, although we shall chiefly be interested in the kind of data structures that are especially useful for computational linguistics and MT (sections 3.6 and 3.8).

3.4 System design

Before considering more specifically the field of computational linguistics, there is an issue which does not always get the attention it deserves. This is the question of **robustness** in system design. What is often neglected when designing a computational system is how wrong decisions or unsatisfactory implementations are to be put right.

There are two approaches. One is to incorporate into the design some sophisticated **debugging tools** ('bugs' are errors in the program) that help system designers to get 'inside' the system when it goes wrong, to see what is happening, perhaps by working through the program step by step until the problem is revealed. The second, which is not necessarily an alternative, but may go together with the first, is the idea of incremental system design involving **rapid prototyping**. An outline system is built up in short, self-contained stages, keeping at each stage those parts that are basically right, but throwing away those which turn out to be obviously incorrect. The prototype program gives a framework for subsequent elaboration and avoids the risk of building a whole system in detail which has to be abandoned and started again.

3.5 Problems of input and output

Earlier, we pointed out that the computer communicates with the outside world via various input/output devices. In this section we consider briefly the nature of this communication, with specific reference to the problems that occur in computational linguistics and MT.

In general, input/output can take two forms. On the one hand, we have the loading of data such as programs, dictionaries and grammars, and the manipulation of data structures. This is data handling of a computational nature, and clearly we can expect such data handling to be designed and developed in a 'computer-friendly' way. On the other hand, we have the input of the texts to be translated and the output of the result, at least one of which will be in a 'foreign' language; in addition, in certain types of system, there is communication with a human operator at the time of the computation, in what are called interactive systems. It is these two latter types of problem that we shall address here.

3.5.1 Interactive systems

We consider first the notion of interaction. A major development in computer architecture was the introduction of facilities to write a program which would stop what it was doing, send a message to some output device (usually a VDU screen), wait for the human user to respond (by typing something in), and then continue processing using the new data provided by the user. It means that computer programs can be **interactive** in the sense that they can rely on real-time communication from the outside world to tell them how to proceed next. In fact, the majority of present-day computer programs are interactive, in some sense, when the computer offers a list (or menu) of possible things to do next, and waits for the user to choose. In more sophisticated systems, the information provided by the human might be more significant, and might be used in much more complicated ways. Typically in MT, interactions are used to supplement the data that the system already has in its dictionaries and grammars, e.g. by asking for some information about a word in the text which is not in the dictionary (is it misspelled? is it a proper name? is it a noun or a verb? and so on). Other types of interaction in MT might result from the fact that the system has computed alternative solutions to some problem, and asks the human to decide which is the right one.

A major task of research in this connection is to make such interactions user-friendly, which means ensuring that users understand quickly what they are supposed to do, are able to do it without too much difficulty, and, of course, give the right sort of answer. For example, consider a program which enables a dictionary to be built interactively by adding new words to it as they occur in texts. To do this, users might be asked whether a new word is a noun or a verb, and if it is a verb, whether it is transitive or intransitive. Two problems immediately arise: does the "noun or verb?" question apply to the word as used in this particular text, or does it apply to all possible uses of this word in general? Many words (in English at least) can be either nouns or verbs depending on the context. Secondly, the user may not understand the terms 'transitive' and 'intransitive' and may not be relied upon to give a 'correct' answer.

3.5.2 'Foreign' languages

Computer technology has been mostly developed in the USA, one of the most thoroughly monolingual societies in the world. For this reason, problems arising from the use of the computer with languages other than English did not at first receive much attention, and even today this is seen as a special ('abnormal') problem. Many languages of the world use either a completely different writing system from English, or else a slightly different variant of the English writing system, involving in particular special characters (German 'ß', Icelandic 'ð'), combinations of characters (Spanish *ll*, Welsh *ch*), or — most commonly — characters modified with accents or diacritics. Each of these deviations from the comfortable norm assumed by American computer pioneers leads to problems at various stages in the computational process.

Let us begin with the case of languages using the Roman alphabet with extensions. Apart from the obvious problem of finding a user-friendly way of permitting special characters or accented characters to be typed in, and adapting screens and printers so that they can be output (and these two tasks alone are not insignificant), there are problems involving the handling of such data within the computer.

The simple representation of all the different characters is not so difficult. Obviously, computers can handle more than 26 letters: on a computer keyboard there are many additional characters besides the 26 lower and upper case letters of the alphabet: there are the numerals 0 to 9, some punctuation marks, '$', '%',

'*' and so on. In fact, the typical computer can handle 64, 128 or 256 different characters easily (the numbers are powers of 2, and come from the fact that computers represent characters internally as binary numbers with 6, 7 or 8 bits), so there is generally enough 'space' for all the characters — at least for alphabetical writing systems (see below). Input and output is handled by low-level programs which convert the character codes into something that a human will recognise (e.g. for most computers, the character with the binary code 01000111 (i.e. 71 decimally) looks like this: G).

However, human users expect their character sets to have certain properties; in particular as having a certain in-built order, which is used, e.g., when consulting dictionaries. But it should be noticed that the order can differ slightly from language to language. For a Welsh speaker, *d* is the fifth, not the fourth, letter of the alphabet; for a French speaker, there are five different letters (*e, é, è, ê* and *ë*) which however count as the 'same' when sorting words into alphabetical order. In the Scandinavian languages, the letters *æ, å, ø,* and *ö* come at the end of the alphabet, making the consultation of dictionaries confusing for those unfamiliar with the practice. All these differences are problems for which computational solutions must be found.

For languages which use alphabetic scripts other than Roman (Greek and Russian are obvious examples), a whole new set of code-to-character correspondences must be defined, together with their in-built order. (It should be noted that we cannot just transcribe the Greek or Russian into the Roman alphabet; often, Greek and Russian texts contain words written in Roman characters: there has to be some way of indicating within the text when the character set changes!) For widely used languages there will already be suitable programs, but for some languages — notably where there has previously been no great economic incentive to design a computer character set — an MT system will have to find some other solution. Furthermore, not all languages with alphabetic scripts are written left-to-right, e.g. Arabic and Hebrew, so any input/output devices making this assumption will be useless for such languages.

Some languages do not even use alphabetical writing systems. The best known examples are Japanese and Chinese, with character sets of about 3,000 or 6,000 respectively (or even more for erudite texts). The special problems that these languages pose for computational linguistics have occupied researchers, especially in Japan and China, for many years. Devising codes for all the characters is not the primary problem, nor even designing printers and VDUs that can display them. Much more problematic has been the question of input: clearly, a keyboard with upwards of 3,000 keys is barely practical, so other approaches had to be explored. In fact, solutions have been found, and it is even arguable that in solving these problems, the Japanese in particular have learned more about non-numeric problem solving than their Western counterparts, and may now be ahead of them in many fields related to language processing.

3.6 Lexical databases

Turning now to more linguistic matters, we consider some of the computational aspects of handling language data. The first of these concerns dictionaries. Obviously, a major part of any MT system is going to be its lexical resources, that is to say, the information associated with individual words. The field of **computational lexicography** is concerned with creating and maintaining computerized dictionaries, whether oriented towards making conventional types of dictionaries accessible on-line to computer users, or whether oriented towards compiling dictionaries for use by natural language processing systems. In the case of MT, this latter activity is made all the more complex by the fact that we are dealing with more than one language, with bilingual and multilingual lexical data.

Lexical databases can be very large. It is difficult to say accurately how many words there are in a language, but current commercial MT systems typically claim to have general-language dictionaries containing upwards of 15,000 entries, and to have technical dictionaries of similar sizes. Although with such claims there is often uncertainty about exactly what counts as a 'word', these figures are a good indication of the order of magnitude for the dictionary of a working MT system.

The fact that the dictionary is very large means that designers of MT systems must pay particularly close attention to questions of storage, access and maintenance. Even with clever **compaction** routines for encoding data in compressed formats, dictionaries are still too big for storage in the central memories of computer systems. This means that MT systems have to find ways of partitioning the data and reading it in as and when necessary in a convenient manner. In practice, MT systems often have several different dictionaries, some containing frequently accessed entries, others containing rarer or more specialised vocabulary. Because dictionary access can be slow and complex, it is often preferable to do it just once at an early stage in the translation process. Whereas human translators will consult dictionaries at many various stages of translation, many MT systems have a single **dictionary look-up** phase, when all the relevant information associated with the particular words in the source text is read into a temporary area of memory, where it can be accessed quickly during the later translation processes.

A second consequence of the size of MT dictionaries is that their compilation demands great efforts. As we shall see, the content of a dictionary for use by an MT system is quite unlike the content of a dictionary for humans use. Therefore, although there are now many commercially available on-line dictionaries and word lists, they always have to be worked on to make them suitable for incorporation in an MT system — and for many languages MT system developers still do not have the benefit of on-line word lists to start with. To reinforce this distinction, computational linguists often prefer to use the term lexicon to refer to the dictionary part of a system.

It is particularly important to ensure consistency within an MT lexicon, so computational lexicographers do not normally work alphabetically through a vocabulary but typically concentrate on some linguistically homogeneous set of words, e.g. transitive verbs, abstract nouns or the terminology of a subject field. Furthermore, the lexicographers have to assume that the linguistic information to be encoded has been agreed upon and stabilized. The grammar writers might want to change the way a particular linguistic phenomenon is handled, but it could imply changing 2,000 or 3,000 dictionary entries! For this reason, many computational linguists believe that it is a good investment to develop computational tools which aid lexicographers to build new entries. Consistency and completeness can be facilitated by providing menus or templates for entering the lexical data which is required, e.g. the gender of a noun, whether it has an irregular plural, whether it is 'mass' or 'count', whether its case endings are similar to other nouns of a certain pattern, and so on.

As already mentioned, the lexicons used in computational linguistics and MT are quite different from what humans understand by 'dictionary'. A monolingual dictionary for the human user usually contains information about parts of speech, irregular inflected forms, a definition of meaning in some form, and (often) some indication of the history of the word. In bilingual dictionaries, we find lists of translation equivalents, often loosely subdivided, usually on semantic grounds, and, in the case of 'idioms', an example sentence from which the reader is expected to infer correct usage. In particular, if some grammatical feature of the source word happens to be also true of the target word, it is taken to be understood. For example, the English word *grass* is usually a mass noun and has no plural; however, we do find the form *grasses* when the implied meaning of the singular form is 'type of grass'. The same is true of the French word *herbe*, but this will not be stated explicitly. Dictionaries for human users avoid stating the obvious: it is assumed that we know that the object of the verb *eat* is normally something edible, and that if it is not, then the verb is being used in some 'metaphorical' sense.

By contrast the lexicons used in MT systems must contain the obvious: all information required by programs must be available. MT lexicons include information about parts of speech but in a much more explicit form, as we have shown already in Chapter 2 and as later examples will amply illustrate. Likewise, meanings — if they are coded at all — must be in a form which the computer can use, e.g. in terms of semantic features or selection restrictions (as also shown in Chapter 2); the kinds of definitions found in dictionaries for human use are not practical. Similarly, the bilingual lexicons for MT must express precisely the conditions under which one word can be translated by another, whether grammatical, semantic or stylistic, and in each case, the circumstances which license one or other translation have to be coded explicitly.

These differences will become apparent in the following sections on parsing and especially in later chapters when we discuss the linguistic problems of MT.

3.7 Computational techniques in early systems

It is appropriate at this stage to look briefly at the computational techniques used by the 'first generation' MT systems. As mentioned in section 1.3, it is often said that a relatively unsophisticated approach to the computational side of the problem of translation was one of the reasons for the comparative failure of the earliest MT systems. We shall look briefly at a typical example and its shortcomings.

Figure 3.1 shows an explanation of a procedure (actually coded in a low-level programming language) for translating *much* and *many* into Russian. The procedure is effectively a flow-chart, since each step includes an indication of which step to go to next, depending on whether the task at that step succeeds or fails. For example, the first step is to check whether the word before *many* is *how*: if so, go to step 2, otherwise go to step 3. Step 2 indicates the appropriate Russian word (with some additional grammatical information), and the 'go to 0' shows that this is the end of the procedure. Step 3 is a similar test, with 4 following if successful and with 5 following if not; and so on for the subsequent steps.

1(2,3)	Is preceding word *how*?
2(0)	*skol'ko* (numeral, invariable)
3(4,5)	Is preceding word *as*?
4(0)	*stol'ko že* (numeral, variable)
5(7,9)	Is current word *much*?
6(0)	Not to be translated (adverb)
7(6,11)	Is preceding word *very*?
8(0)	*mnogii* (adjective, hard stem, with sibilant)
9(8,12)	Is preceding word a preposition, and following word a noun?
10(0)	*mnogo* (adverb)
11(12,10)	Is following word a noun?
12(0)	*mnogo* (adverb)

Figure 3.1 Translation of *much* and *many* into Russian

Readers who have some familiarity with the BASIC programming language available on many microcomputers will immediately recognize this style of programming where you have to 'jump around' in the program. This makes it quite difficult to find out what is happening, and makes debugging (troubleshooting) particularly difficult. But notice, in particular, that there is no easily discernible underlying linguistic theory: it is difficult to tell from looking at this program what the linguistic analysis of *much* is. Nor can the procedure be easily generalised for translating other, perhaps similar, words or sequences.

This style of MT programming was, of course, almost inevitable given the lack of high-level programming languages at the time. In the next sections, we consider the kinds of techniques that are now available and which overcome the weaknesses of these early attempts.

3.8 Parsing

A major component of computational linguistics in general, and hence a feature of the computational aspect of MT, comes under the general heading of **parsing**. This word refers to computer programs which take as data a grammar and a lexicon, as input a text (e.g. a sentence) and produce as output an analysis of the structure of the text. In discussing parsing, it must be understood that several familiar words have a special meaning. By **grammar**, we understand a set of **rules** which describe what combinations and sequences of words are acceptable, i.e. whether a given input is 'grammatical'. Grammar rules are usually expressed in terms of the **categories** (or parts of speech) of the words, though the rules may also refer to **features** associated with words and phrases (see also sections 2.5.1 and 2.8.3). The information about what categories and features are associated with individual words is stored in the lexicon. Usually, too, the rules imply a **structured** analysis, where certain sequences of categories are recognised as forming mutually substitutable **constituents** or groups of words, which in turn combine to form bigger units (cf. section 2.8.2).

As an introduction to what this means in practice, consider a very simple grammar for (a subset of) English. As we saw in Chapter 2 the usual way to write grammars is as sets of **rewrite rules**:

(1a) NP → det (adj) n

(1b) NP → pron

(1c) S → NP VP

(1d) VP → v NP

Rule (1a) states that a noun phrase (NP) can consist of a det[erminer], an optional adj[ective] (as indicated by the brackets) and a noun (n). Rule (1b) is another rule for a noun phrase, indicating that an NP can consist of just a pron[oun]. The rules in (1c) and (1d) are for the recognition of other constituents, S[entence] and VP (verb phrase), where the latter consists of a v[erb] and an NP.

Rules of this nature are familiar to linguists (Chapter 2), but in the context of this chapter, we illustrate briefly how computer programs can be developed to take these rules and apply them to texts. Here only a flavour of some of the techniques can be given; a full account of all the possibilities would fill a book on its own (see section 3.10 below).

3.8.1 Top-down and bottom-up

In parsing techniques a basic distinction is made between top-down approaches and bottom-up approaches. In top-down parsing, the parser starts at the most abstract level and attempts to flesh out the structure by building downwards towards the lowest level, i.e. to the words themselves. In the case of our example above, this would mean that parsing starts with the node S and rule (1c). For this rule to apply, the parser must find an NP which is followed by a VP. But the NP requirement means that rule (1a) or rule (1b) apply, and they mean in turn that either a pronoun or a determiner followed by an optional adjective and a noun have to be present in the input. Likewise in order to satisfy the VP requirement there must be a verb followed by another noun phrase (again as defined by rules 1a or 1b). In bottom-up parsing on the other hand, the parsing starts with the words and attempts to build upwards. For example, take the input sentence:

(2) He loves the women.

The string of categories attached to the words is 'pron v det n'. The parser looks for rules that allow the combination of some of these categories into higher-level abstractions, applying rules perhaps in the sequence shown in (3).

(3) pron v det n
    NP v det n   using rule (1b)
    NP v NP   using rule (1a)
    NP VP   using rule (1d)
    S   using rule (1c)

For the simple grammar above, the difference of approach may not seem important. It becomes significant, however, when there are large grammars and many potentially ambiguous sentences. Suppose we enlarge our grammar as follows (4) in order to account for prepositional phrases (PP) and to deal with other possible types of noun phrases (NP):

(4a) S → NP VP PP
(4b) S → NP VP
(4c) VP → v NP
(4d) NP → det n
(4e) NP → det adj n
(4f) NP → det n PP
(4g) NP → det adj n PP
(4h) NP → pron
(4i) PP → prep NP

We now see that there are effectively two different types of S (with or without the PP), and five basically different types of NP, two of which involve a PP, which in turn involves an NP. Because this grammar contains such **recursive rules**, it predicts an infinite variety of possible structures. When parsing in a top-down mode, there are immediately two alternative predictions about what the S will be, and both start with an NP, for which there are in turn five possibilities. Even before anything is consulted in the lexicon there are ten possible analyses, any number of which could turn out to be completable.

3.8.2 Backtracking

In both top-down and bottom-up parsing, it is not always the case that the first decision taken is the right one. If we consider using the grammar in (4) to parse (2) in a top-down manner, applying the rules in the order they are given, we can see that rule (4a) entails a 'false start': it will not lead to a sucessful parse because there is no PP in (2). Similarly all (4d–g) will lead to failure since the first NP in (2) corresponds to the structure given by (4h). Even with this simple example it can be seen that the computer has to be able to revise any 'decisions' it may have taken. This is called **backtracking**. To illustrate the need to backtrack in the case of a bottom-up parser, consider an input string which is **structurally ambiguous**, such as (5). By 'structural ambiguity' is meant that the rules allow two alternative solutions depending, in this example, on where the PP (*with a telescope*) fits into the structure.

(5) He saw the girl with a telescope.

In one case, the NP consists of just *the girl* (i.e. rule 4d is applied) and the VP is *saw the girl* (rule 4c); as a result, the parser recognises that the PP is part of an S of the type NP VP PP (rule 4a). In the other case, the PP is taken to be part of the NP (*the girl with a telescope*) by applying rule 4f; the resulting NP is part of a VP (rule 4c again) and the parser will recognise an S of the NP VP type, by rule 4b. Again if the rules are applied in the order in which they are given (this time looking at the right-hand-side to see if the rule is satisfied), the first solution reached will be the one predicted by (4a). This will be because in processing *the girl* ..., the NP defined by rule (4d) will be successfully identified before recognition of the NP defined by (4f). In order to obtain both solutions, the process will have to backtrack to the point at which rule (4d) applied and test whether any other rules might also be applicable.

There are essentially two ways of causing a parser to consider all possible solutions, depending on the strategy adopted each time a choice of alternatives is encountered. On the one hand, the parser can take one possible solution to its ultimate conclusion (successful parse or 'false trail') and then return to the last choice point and try the alternatives, until each of these is exhausted. In each case, successful paths must be somehow 'remembered'. This approach is called **depth-first** parsing. The alternative is a strategy where all options are explored in parallel, so that both false and true trails are kept 'alive' until the last possible moment. This **breadth-first** approach means that there is no need for backtracking as such.

3.8.3 Feature notations

On the basis of the kinds of rules in (4), parsing alone cannot decide whether an analysis is plausible or not; all possible combinations of categories and groupings are attempted whatever the context (cf. also section 2.9.1 on context-free grammars). A parser applying the rules in (4) would find both sentences in (6) acceptable, even though they contain what we (as English speakers) recognise as simple grammatical errors.

(6a) They loves the women.

(6b) The man love the women.

One way of making parsing more subtle is to introduce **feature notations** on rules. For example we might further specify that the NP which is the first constituent of an S (the subject) must agree in number with the VP, thereby accounting for the acceptability of (2) as against (6a) and (6b). In order to do this, we need to use 'variables' in the rules. A **variable** (used here in the programming sense) is something which stands for or represents a real object: it is a slot waiting for a value to be assigned to it. An obvious example of the use of variables comes from algebra, where the *x*s and *y*s in equations are variables which stand for numbers. In programming languages, variables are effectively locations in the computer's memory area where values can be stored temporarily, for the purpose of some calculation. For example, when we say "Think of a number; now double it...'', this is equivalent in computational terms to assigning a numerical value to a variable — *x*, say — and then calculating the value of $2 \times x$.

In computational linguistics, we often use variables to stand for words, or grammatical categories, or features; in the case of the grammar in (1), the specification of number agreement between subject and verb can be stated as in (7a); the number feature of the NP comes from its n (7c) or pron (7d), while the number feature of the VP comes from its v (7b).

(7a) S → NP[num=$X] VP[num=$X]

(7b) VP[num=$Y] → v[num=$Y] NP[num=?]

(7c) NP[num=$Z] → det (adj) n[num=$Z]

(7d) NP[num=$Z] → pron[num=$Z]

It is always important to distinguish variables from real values, and different programming languages or rule-writing formalisms have different conventions for doing this. A common convention is to preface variables with a special symbol such as '$' (as we have done here), or '_'. In some formalisms the use of capital or lower case letters is distinctive. The important point is that once a value has been assigned to a variable, it keeps that value for the rest of the rule; because similarly-named variables in different rules will not necessarily have the same value, it is often good programming practice to use different variable names in neighbouring rules, so as to avoid confusion.

To illustrate how the rules in (7) operate, consider a sentence such as (8).

(8) The women like him.

We see that the value of $X in (7a) must be the same for the NP *the women*, and for the verb *like*. In a top-down mode, the value for 'num' will be set by the completion of rule (7c), where it is the word *women* that tells us the NP is plural. Now the processor will be looking for a plural VP, and will find it in *like him*, by dint of *like* being plural (7b). Notice that the value of 'num' for the object NP *him* in (7b) is not relevant here, even though it has been calculated by the NP rule (7d). In a bottom-up parser, the feature constraints act as an additional filter on the rules. So for example in *a man like a bear*, although *a man* is an NP, and *like a bear* is a possible VP, they do not agree in number, so (7b) fails, and, presumably, some other rule identifies the whole thing as an NP, with *like* functioning as a conjunction.

As we shall see, MT systems often use formalisms which are even more complex than this, though the details need not concern us for the moment.

3.8.4 Trees

In these examples of parsing, the end results are not very informative: the sentence is or is not grammatical, is or is not syntactically ambiguous. For MT we need more information than that: specifically, we need to know what the internal structure of the sentence is. To do this, it is necessary, while parsing, to make a record of which rules were used, and in which order. This is the purpose of the tree structures familiar to linguists (cf. section 2.8.2). If we take again our ambiguous example (6), there are two parse trees associated with this sentence as in (9).

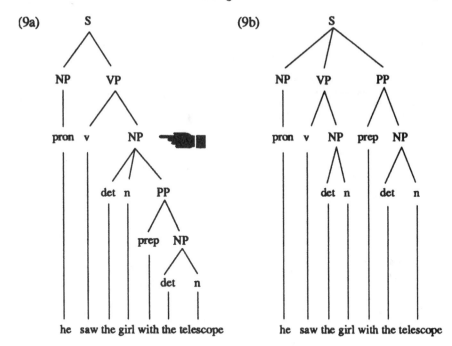

(9a)

(9b)

he saw the girl with the telescope

These two trees capture the fact that in (9a) the NP rule (4f) has been used which includes a PP to build the right-most constituent at the level marked with a pointer, whereas in (9b) the PP is 'attached' at a higher level using rules (4d) for the NP and (4a) for the S. These two trees represent the two different analyses in the sense of recording two different 'parse histories'. In linguistic terms, they correspond to the two readings of the sentence: one in which the PP is part of the NP (i.e. the girl has the telescope), and the other where the PP is at the same level as the subject (i.e. the man has the telescope). As we shall see in later chapters, these two competing analyses may lead to different translations.

For convenience, a **bracketed notation** for trees is sometimes used: the equivalents for the trees in (9a) and (9b) are shown in (10a) and (10b) respectively.

    (10a) S(NP(pron(he)),
           VP(v(saw),NP(det(the),
                      n(girl),
                      PP(prep(with),NP(det(the),n(telescope))))))

    (10b) S(NP(pron(he)),
           VP(v(saw),NP(det(the),n(girl))),
           PP(prep(with),NP(det(the),n(telescope)))))

The tree structures required may of course be much more complex, not only in the sense of having more levels, or more branches at any given level, but also in that the labelling of the **nodes** (i.e. the ends of the branches) may be more informative. This might be the case where feature annotations are included, e.g. adding information about the grammatical nature of the constituents — singular or plural, gender, etc., as illustrated in (7) above. Quite often, we also need to indicate relations between branches of the tree, e.g. to show that *he* is the subject of the verb in examples (5) and (6) above, that a verb and a particle really belong together (e.g. *pick* and *up* in *pick the book up*), or that a pronoun is referring to another noun phrase in the same sentence (e.g. *John* and *he* in *John said he would come*). In order to do this, the tree structure must become more complex, with 'pointers' leading from one branch to another (11), or with 'co-indexed' branches, perhaps with arbitrary numerical values (12).

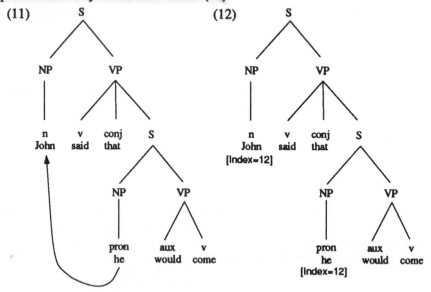

Tree structures are widely used in computational linguistics and MT, not only for showing the results of parsing, but also for other representations of texts. In particular, it is quite common for the tree structure resulting from a syntactic parse to be manipulated by further rules into a tree structure suitable for generation in the target language. The procedure is reminiscent of the transformation rules familiar to linguists (section 2.9.2), and requires very powerful rule formalisms which define **tree-to-tree mappings** (often referred to as 'tree-transduction'), i.e. which define the circumstances under which one tree structure can be transformed into, or mapped onto, another. Examples of such rules are given particularly in Chapter 6.

3.8.5 Charts

Trees are not the only data structures used in computational linguistics or in MT systems. A particularly useful data structure found in a number of systems is the **chart**. Its value is that it allows alternative solutions to be stored simultaneously in a convenient and accessible manner. It is therefore a standard way of implementing a breadth-first parsing strategy (see 3.8.2 above).

Roughly speaking, a chart is a set of points or **nodes** with **labelled arcs** (sometimes called 'edges') connecting them. The nodes are in sequence ('ordered'), and the arcs can go in one direction only ('forward'). Two of the nodes have special status, namely the first, or 'entry' node, which has no arcs leading into it, and the last, or 'exit' node, which has no arcs leading from it. When used in parsing, the chart is set up initially with one arc for each possible reading of each word of the sentence, as in (13) for the beginning of (6); notice that the potential category ambiguity of the word *saw* is represented by two arcs labelled with the alternate possibilities.

(13)

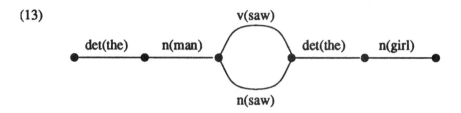

As each rule is applied, a new arc is added, connecting the outermost nodes of the constituent that is built, and labelled with the appropriate tree-structure. In (14) we can see the chart after NP rules have been applied. The labelling can consist of copies of the trees — usually given in the bracketed notation — as in (14a), or of 'pointers' to the arcs which have been subsumed, as in (14b).

(14a)

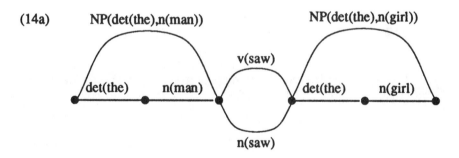

(14b)

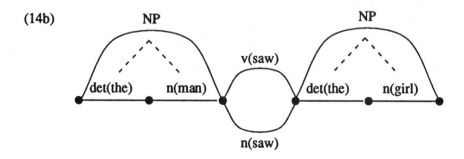

Continuing in this way, applying the other rules, a complete parse is represented by a single arc spanning the whole chart and labelled S, as in (15).

(15)

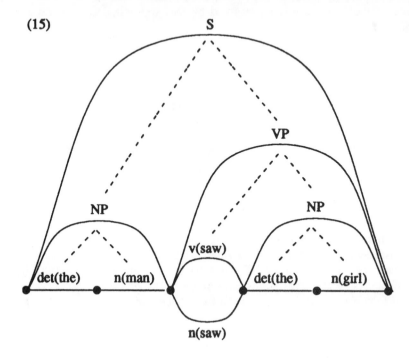

It should be noted that the arc labelled with the n reading for *saw* is present in each of the charts, even though it is not used in the construction of further arcs. In (16) (opposite) we give the (very complex) chart which would be built for the ambiguous sentence (5): there are two S arcs corresponding to the two readings, each with different substructures. (In fact, the chart has been simplified by leaving out some arcs which would be built but which would not be used, e.g. the arc for the n reading of *saw* and a false S arc spanning *the man saw the girl*.) A major advantage of the chart approach is that the parts of the two structures which are common to both readings are represented just once, and are 'shared'. These include all the lexical arcs on the 'bottom', and the arcs labelled in bold and drawn with solid lines. The two readings are otherwise distinguished by italic arc labels and dotted lines ('.. ..') for the reading 'girl with the telescope', and normal labels with broken lines ('- -') for the reading 'saw with the telescope'.

(16)

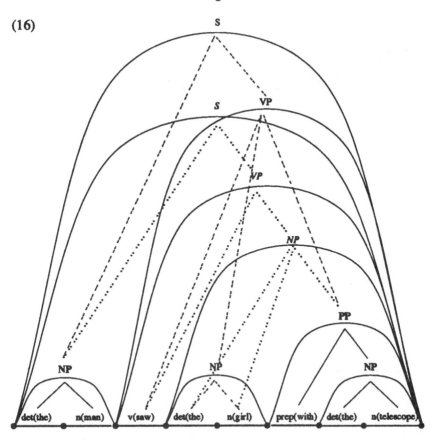

3.8.6 Production systems

Closely connected to the use of a chart as a data structure is the technique for implementing grammars called a **production system**. The idea is that the rules which say which sequences of arcs can lead to the construction of new arcs are all put together in a single database, in no particular order. This is the **rule set**, and the rules, or 'productions', can be thought of as 'condition-action' pairs, where the condition part is a 'pattern match' on the chart, and the action is the building of a new arc. By a **pattern match** is meant that the computer looks to see if the sequence of arcs specified by the rule can actually be located in the chart. It is up to the computer, and in particular the so-called interpreter part of the production system, to decide which rules can be applied and when. It should be noticed that the rules are **non-destructive** in the sense that, after a rule has been applied to a certain sequence of arcs, the old arcs are still there, and available to other rules. It means that care has to be taken that the interpreter does not apply the same rule more than once to the same sequence of arcs. Obviously, when many alternative rules might apply at the same time, the whole process can be very complex, especially when all combinations of rule sequences have to be tested. The crucial point is that the computational tasks of pattern matching and rule testing can be separated from the essentially linguistic tasks of stating which conditions can actually trigger which actions, i.e. separating the work of the computer and the work of the linguist, as described in section 3.2 above.

Finally, it should be noted that this architecture can be used not only for parsing but equally for other MT processes. The condition part of a production rule can be arbitrarily complex, it can specify the arcs to be looked for in as much detail as necessary. The only constraint is that the arcs must be contiguous. There is also no requirement that rules refer to sequences of more than one arc. Thus, for example, 'transformational' rules can be written which take a single arc with a specific labelling, and build a new arc with the same start and end points, but with different labelling. More detail about a particularly influential production system approach in MT is given in section 13.5 on the GETA-Ariane system.

3.9 Unification

In section 2.9.7 we described linguistic theories which make use of 'unification' of feature-based representations. This approach is closely connected with the emergence of unification as a computational technique, as found in programming languages such as Prolog, now much used in computational linguistics and MT. In fact, there are some important differences between unification as a computational device and unification as understood by linguists, which we will clarify below. However, the basic idea is similar in both cases.

Unification is essentially an operation carried out on data structures, and depends crucially on the idea of variables, described above. In the examples in (7), we saw variables used for feature values, but they could equally be used to represent words or whole structures. The idea of unification is that two structures can be unified if (and only if) they are identical, once values have been assigned to variables. So for example the structure with its accompanying conditions in (17a) — where variables are indicated in capital letters, preceded by '$' — can be unified with the structure in (17b), with the variables instantiated accordingly:

(17a) np(det($DET),n($N))
    if number($DET)=$NBR *and* number($N)=$NBR *and*
    gender($DET)=$GEN *and* gender($N)=$GEN
(17b) np(det(la),n(table))
    where $DET="la", $N="table", $NBR=sing, $GEN=fem

An entire programming style has been developed based on this idea, and is found in the much-used programming language Prolog. A parser written in Prolog consists of a set of descriptions of well-formed structures containing variables which are given values according to associated rules. In fact, the rule in (17a) is very similar to a Prolog 'clause'. If we put it together with some other rules written in the same formalism (which is not pure Prolog, but could easily be translated into it), you will see how a simple parser might be built (18).

(18a) s($A,$B)
    if $A=np(...) *and* $B=vp(...) *and* number($A)=number($B)
(18b) np($D,$N)
    if $D=det(...) and $N=n(...) *and* number($D)=$NBR *and*
    number($N)=$NBR *and* gender($D)=$GEN *and* gender($N)=$GEN

(18c) vp($X)
> *if* $X=v(...)$

(18d) vp($Y,$Z)
> *if* $Y=v(...)$ *and* transitive($Y) *and* $Z=np(...)$

In MT systems which use this idea, the structures which are unified in this way can be much more complex; in particular, the nodes of the trees represented in the rules can carry much more information, in the form of bundles of **features** (see section 2.8.3), which the very powerful but intuitively simple unification mechanism can operate on. In this way, complex data structures can be built up and manipulated by combinations of rules which individually express only simple relationships. Here the idea of the production system, described above, can be brought in: the 'rule set' is made up of independent rules about feature compatibility and tree structure, and there is an interpreter which figures out in which order the rules should be applied. The whole process continues until some specific configuration is arrived at, or no more rules apply.

3.10 Further reading

Within the space of one chapter we cannot cover, even superficially, all aspects of computer science, and not even all of computational linguistics. However, many of the available text books on computational linguistics assume a computational rather than a linguistic background in their readers, so the best sources for clarification and elaboration of the issues brought up here are general computer science textbooks, of which there are hundreds.

Here we give mainly further references for some of the more particular points made.

The question of character sets and processing languages which do not use the Roman alphabet is a major concern of researchers in the field of linguistic computing (as opposed to computational linguistics), and is addressed in journals such *Literary and Linguistic Computing, Computers & the Humanities,* and other journals. On the question of alphabetization, see for example Gavare (1988).

Computational lexicography is similarly a huge field. Two collections of papers, Goetschalckx and Rolling (1982) and Hartmann (1984), give a good view of current issues.

The procedure shown in Figure 3.1 is from Panov (1960).

For a discussion of parsing, see almost any computational linguistics textbook. De Roeck (1983) is a very simple introduction to some basic concepts, and Winograd (1983) is quite readable. For rather more advanced discussions, see King (1983), Sparck Jones and Wilks (1983), Thompson and Ritchie (1984), Dowty *et al.* (1985), Grosz *et al.* (1986) and Whitelock *et al.* (1987).

Charts and chart parsing in particular were first developed by Kaplan (1973) and Kay (1976). Winograd (1983) and Varile (1983) deal with the topic in a perspicuous manner.

Production systems were developed for use in cognitive modelling by Newell (1973). For a brief discussion see Davis and King (1977) or Rosner (1983);

for more detail see Waterman and Hayes-Roth (1978) or Stefik *et al.* (1982). The classic example of a production system for the purposes of MT is the system developed by Colmerauer (1970), the so-called 'Q-systems' formalism (see Chapter 12), which is in fact the forerunner of the programming language Prolog.

4

Basic strategies

This chapter is devoted to some fundamental questions on the basic strategies of MT systems. These concern decisions which designers of MT systems have to address before any construction can start, and they involve both design issues and theoretical issues. The first to be considered is whether a system is to be designed as a multilingual system or as a bilingual system. Next are decisions about whether the system is to adopt the direct method, the transfer method or the interlingua method. Then there is the computational environment as a whole, and distinctions between non-intervention (or 'batch') systems and interactive systems. Finally, there is the overall organization of lexical data in different system types.

In the previous two chapters we have already discussed issues which affect the basic design of an MT system. The choice of linguistic approach is crucial, determining both the basic theoretical framework and fundamental aspects of linguistic strategies and representations. On the computational side, the last chapter covered other crucial aspects, in particular the features of modularity and decoupling (or separation).

The basic design decisions to be outlined here are useful parameters for comparing and contrasting different systems.

4.1 Multilingual versus bilingual systems

Many decisions affecting MT system design hinge on the fundamental differences between multilingual and bilingual systems. **Bilingual** systems are those which translate between a single pair of languages; **multilingual** systems are designed to translate among more than two languages.

Bilingual systems may be uni-directional or bi-directional; that is to say, they may be designed to translate from one language to another in one direction only, or they may be capable of translating from both members of a language pair. As a further refinement we may distinguish between **reversible** bilingual systems and non-reversible systems. In a reversible bilingual system the process involved in the analysis of a language may be inverted without change for the generation of output in the same language. Thus, a system for English analysis might mirror directly a system for English generation in, say, an English–French bilingual system. The difficulties, both theoretical and practical, in designing truly reversible bilingual systems are so great that nearly all bilingual systems are in effect two perhaps quite similar uni-directional systems running on the same computer. Methods of analysis and generation for either of the languages are designed independently, without attempting structural reversibility. A bilingual system is therefore, typically, one designed to translate from one language into one other in a single direction.

A system involving more than two languages is a multilingual system. At one extreme a multilingual system might be designed for a large number of languages in every combination, as is the case of the European Commission's Eurotra project (Chapter 14), where the aim is to provide for translation from and to the nine languages of the European Communities in all directions (i.e. 72 language-pairs). A more modest multilingual system might translate from English into three other languages in one direction only (i.e. three language pairs). An intermediate type might cover, say, English, French, German, Spanish and Japanese but not all combinations of pairs and directions, for example Japanese into each of the European languages, all the European languages into Japanese, but would not be able to translate between any of the European languages. A potential user of such a system might be a Japanese company interested only in translation involving Japanese as a source or target language.

A 'truly' multilingual system is one in which analysis and generation components for a particular language remain constant whatever other languages are involved. For example, in a multilingual system involving English, French and German, the process of French analysis would be the same whether the translation were into English or German, and the generation process for German would be the same whether the source language had been English or French, and so forth. There have been, in fact, a number of 'multilingual' systems where analysis and generation components have differed according to the other language of the pair. An example is the early versions of Systran, e.g. the language pairs English–French, English–Italian, English–German. Originally, the English analysis modules were developed separately for each pair. Some resources and techniques were shared or copied, but basically the modules were independent: one could almost consider the modules as English-analysis-for-French-as-target, English-analysis-for-German-as-target, and so on. In this respect, Systran was not a 'true' multilingual system, but rather a collection of uni-directional bilingual systems. In particular, Systran's modules were in no sense reversible: the English–French and the French–English systems differed in almost every feature. It should be said that in recent years Systran's components and structure have become more uniform and compatible, so that today it is more like a genuine multilingual system (cf. Chapter 10).

In a 'true' multilingual system, uniformity would extend further: not only would analysis and generation components for particular languages remain constant whatever the other language(s) involved, but there would be a common linguistic approach applied to all the languages in the system, and there would be a common use of software as well. A good example is the GETA Ariane system (Chapter 13).

It should be now apparent that if it is intended to construct a multilingual system then it should be as truly multilingual as possible in all its aspects; all components which can in principle be shared between different languages should in fact be shared. In a system where, for example, the analysis of English for French as target language differs from the analysis of English for German as target language, it would be impossible to maintain the 'modularity' of the system (cf. Chapter 3). As we shall see, it would also be difficult to distinguish between those parts of analysis which are neutral with respect to the target language and those parts which are oriented towards the target language (cf. the discussion on transfer, section 4.2 below).

An obvious question at this point is whether a truly multilingual system is in practice — as opposed to theory — preferable to a bilingual system designed for a specific language pair. There are arguments on both sides; two of the most successful MT systems illustrate the pros and cons very well: GETA's multilingual Ariane system and TAUM's English–French Météo system (Chapters 13 and 12).

Among the most significant constraints imposed by the decision to adopt a multilingual approach rather than a bilingual one is that the isolation of analysis from generation means that no advantage can be taken of any accidental similarities between languages. By contrast, in a bilingual system similarities of vocabulary and syntax can be exploited. Take an example of potential lexical ambiguity (see section 6.1): when translating English *wall* into German it must be decided whether an external *Mauer* or an internal *Wand* is the correct translation, but such a decision is unnecessary when translating into French where the single word *mur* covers both senses. Likewise translation into French does not require distinguishing between two types of *corner* as does translation into Spanish: *esquina* ('outside corner') and *rincón* ('inside corner'). English analysis in a truly multilingual system would have to make these distinctions at some stage; but an English–French bilingual system would not — in fact it would be perverse not to take advantage of direct lexical correspondences. The Météo system is an example of a bilingual system which, although separating analysis and generation, exploits similarities and regular equivalences of English and French lexicon and syntax at every stage of the translation process.

4.2 Direct systems, transfer systems and interlinguas

There are broadly three basic MT strategies. The earliest historically is the 'direct approach', adopted by most MT systems of what has come to be known as the **first generation** of MT systems. In response to the apparent failure of this strategy, two types of 'indirect approach' were developed: the 'transfer method', and the use of an 'interlingua'. Systems of this nature are sometimes referred to as **second generation** systems.

The **direct approach** is an MT strategy which lacks any kinds of **intermediate stages** in translation processes: the processing of the source language input text leads 'directly' to the desired target language output text. In certain circumstances the approach is still valid today — traces of the direct approach are found even in indirect systems such as Météo — but the archetypal direct MT system has a more primitive software design.

In considering the operation of first generation MT systems, it should be borne in mind that computers available in the late 1950s and early 1960s were very primitive even in comparison with the humblest electronic calculators of today. There were no high-level programming languages, most programming was done in assembly code. In broad outline, first generation direct MT systems began with what we might call a morphological analysis phase, where there would be some identification of word endings and reduction of inflected forms to their uninflected basic forms, and the results would be input into a large bilingual dictionary look-up program. There would be no analysis of syntactic structure or of semantic relationships. In other words, lexical identification would depend on morphological analysis and would lead directly to bilingual dictionary look-up providing target language word equivalences. There would follow some local reordering rules to give more acceptable target language output, perhaps moving some adjectives or verb particles, and then the target language text would be produced.

The direct approach is summarized in Figure 4.1.

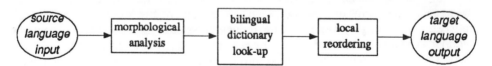

Figure 4.1 Direct MT system

The severe limitations of this approach should be obvious. It can be characterized as 'word-for-word' translation with some local word-order adjustment. It gave the kind of translation quality that might be expected from someone with a very cheap bilingual dictionary and only the most rudimentary knowledge of the grammar of the target language: frequent mistranslations at the lexical level and largely inappropriate syntax structures which mirrored too closely those of the source language. Here are some examples of the output of a Russian–English system of this kind (the correct translation is given second).

    (1) *My trebuem mira.*
        We require world
        'We want peace.'

    (2) *Nam nužno mnogo uglja, železa, elektroenergii.*
        To us much coal is necessary, gland, electric power.
        'We need a lot of coal, iron and electricity.'

(3) *On dopisal stranitsu i otložil ručku v storonu.*
It wrote a page and put off a knob to the side.
'He finished writing the page and laid his pen aside.'

(4) *Včera my tselyi čas katalis' na lodke.*
Yesterday we the entire hour rolled themselves on a boat.
'Yesterday we went out boating for a whole hour.'

(5) *Ona navarila ščei na neskol'ko dnei.*
It welded on cabbage soups on several days.
'She cooked enough cabbage soup for several days.'

The linguistic and computational naivety of this approach was quickly recognized. From a linguistic point of view what is missing is any analysis of the internal structure of the source text, particularly the grammatical relationships between the principal parts of the sentences. The lack of computational sophistication was largely a reflection of the primitive state of computer science at the time, but it was also determined by the unsophisticated approach to linguistics in MT projects of the late 1950s.

Before leaving the direct translation method, it should be noted that it continues to some extent in many uni-directional bilingual systems (cf. previous section): there may be less linguistic naivety than in the past, but the general idea of 'moulding' (restructuring) the source text into a target language output is retained: such systems take advantage of similarities of structure and vocabulary between source and target languages in order to translate as much as possible according to the 'direct' approach; the designers are then able to concentrate most effort on areas of grammar and syntax where the languages differ greatest.

The failure of the first generation systems (cf. section 1.3) led to the development of more sophisticated linguistic models for translation. In particular, there was increasing support for the analysis of source language texts into some kind of intermediate representation — a representation of its 'meaning' in some respect — which could form the basis of generation of the target text. This is in essence the **indirect** method, which has two principal variants.

The first is the **interlingua** method — also the first historically (cf. Chapter 1) — where the source text is analysed in a representation from which the target text is directly generated. The intermediate representation includes all information necessary for the generation of the target text without 'looking back' to the original text. The representation is thus a projection from the source text and at the same time acts as the basis for the generation of the target text; it is an abstract representation of the target text as well as a representation of the source text. The method is interlingual in the sense that the representation is neutral between two or more languages. In the past, the intention or hope was to develop an interlingual representation which was truly 'universal' and could thus be intermediary between any natural languages. At present, interlingual systems are less ambitious.

The interlingua approach is clearly most attractive for multilingual systems. Each analysis module can be independent, both of all other analysis modules and of all generation modules (Figure 4.2). Target languages have no effect on any processes of analysis; the aim of analysis is the derivation of an 'interlingual' representation.

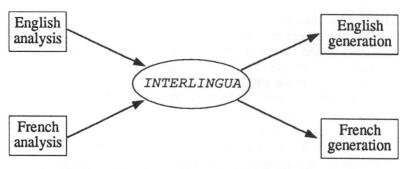

Figure 4.2 Interlingua model with two language pairs

The advantage is that the addition of a new language to the system entails the creation of just two new modules: an analysis grammar and a generation grammar. By adding one analysis module in Figure 4.2, e.g. a German analysis grammar, the number of translation directions is increased from two (English to French, and French to English) to four (by the addition of German to French and German to English). The inclusion of another generation module, a German generation grammar, brings a further two pairs (English to German and French to German). Compare Figure 4.3 with Figure 4.2 above.

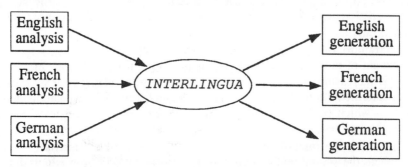

Figure 4.3 Interlingua model with six language pairs

The addition of two further modules for, say, Spanish, would increase the number of language pairs by another six (English, French and German into Spanish, and Spanish into English, French and German), and so on exponentially.

It may also be noted that such a configuration permits 'translation' from and into the same language, for example, the conversion of an English source text into the interlingual representation and then back into an English target text. This seemingly unnecessary 'back-translation' capability could in fact be extremely valuable during system development in order to test analysis and generation modules. Note that you might not necessarily expect the regenerated target text to be identical to the original source text, though you would expect them to be pragmatically equivalent (see Chapter 7 concerning choices in generation).

While the addition of new languages may appear easy in an interlingual system, there are major disadvantages: the difficulties of defining an interlingua, even for closely related languages (e.g. the Romance languages: French, Italian, Spanish, Portuguese). A truly 'universal' and language-independent interlingua has defied the best efforts of linguists and philosophers from the seventeenth century onwards (cf. Chapter 1). The particular problems involved will be considered in more detail in section 6.7.

The second variant of the indirect approach is called the **transfer** method. Strictly speaking all translation systems involve 'transfer' of some kind, the conversion of a source text or representation into a target text or representation. The term 'transfer method' has been applied to systems which interpose bilingual modules between intermediate representations. Unlike those in interlingual systems these representations are **language-dependent**: the result of analysis is an abstract representation of the source text, the input to generation is an abstract representation of the target text. The function of the bilingual transfer modules is to convert source language (intermediate) representations into target language (intermediate) representations, as show in Figure 4.4. Since these representations link separate modules (analysis, transfer, generation), they are also frequently referred to as **interface representations**.

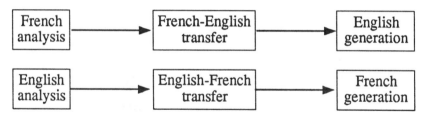

Figure 4.4 Transfer model with two language pairs

In the transfer approach there are therefore no language-independent representations: the source language intermediate representation is specific to a particular language, as is the target language intermediate representation. Indeed there is no necessary equivalence between the source and target intermediate (interface) representations for the same language. This distinction between language independence and language dependence will be examined in more detail in Chapter 6.

In comparison with the interlingua type of multilingual system there are clear disadvantages in the transfer approach. The addition of a new language involves not only the two modules for analysis and generation, but also the addition of new transfer modules, the number of which may vary according to the number of languages in the existing system: in the case of a two-language system, a third language would require four new transfer modules. Compare Figure 4.5 with Figure 4.4., and with the corresponding diagram for the interlingua system (Figure 4.3).

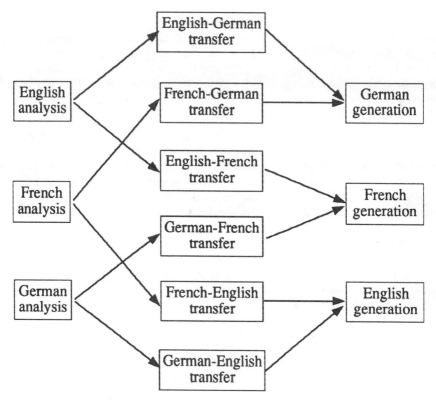

Figure 4.5 Transfer model with six language pairs

The addition of a fourth language would entail the development of six new transfer modules, and so on as illustrated in Table 4.1.

The number of transfer modules in a multilingual transfer system, for all combinations of n languages, is $n \times (n-1)$, i.e. not much less than n^2. Also needed are n analysis and n generation modules, which however would also be needed for an interlingua system.

Why then is the transfer approach so often preferred to the interlingua method? The first reason has already been mentioned: the difficulty of devising language-independent representations. The second is the complexity of analysis and generation grammars when the representations are inevitably far removed from the characteristic features of the source and target texts. By comparison, the relative complexity of the analysis and generation modules in a transfer system is much reduced, because the intermediate representations involved are still language-dependent abstractions (for more on this, see Chapter 6). At the same time, if the design is optimal, the work of transfer modules can be greatly simplified and the creation of new ones can be less onerous than might be imagined.

Number of languages	Analysis modules	Generation modules	Transfer modules	Total modules
2	2	2	2	6
3	3	3	6	12
4	4	4	12	20
5	5	5	20	30
...				
9	9	9	72	90
n	n	n	$n(n-1)$	$n(n+1)$

Table 4.1 Modules required in an all-pairs multilingual transfer system

4.3 Non-intervention vs. on-line interactive systems

The third major design feature to be introduced concerns the users of systems during the translation process, whether they play an active interventionist role, or whether they have no interaction with the system while it is processing the text.

The **non-interventionist** mode of operation has its roots in early computing practice where it was normal for computations to be performed in 'batch' mode: a 'job' was prepared, submitted to the computer and some time later the results would be printed out. The operators and programmers could not influence the operation of the computer once it had started a job. With later computational developments, particularly the advent of mini- and micro-computers, the 'conversational' style of running programs became more widespread, where users are able to intervene and interact directly with the computer. Many of the present-day MT systems were developed at a time when sophisticated human–machine interaction was not possible and only vaguely envisaged for the future. They were designed for 'batch' translation: a source text was input, the MT program was run and a target version output. Any revision could be undertaken only after the whole target text had been produced. More recently, many such MT systems have incorporated text-editing facilities enabling revision at terminals or on micro-computers. There are often also more sophisticated input facilities. However, the translation system itself is still 'non-interventionist': translation jobs are completed in 'batches' and there is no interaction during the translation processes with any human operators, users, translators or revisers.

By contrast the **interactive** mode of translation enables direct involvement on-line during the course of translation. Various types of interaction are possible: the computer may ask the user to supplement its linguistic information, requesting confirmation of its decisions, or selection from among alternatives. Most typical is the case where the source language sentence is ambiguous out of context, i.e. when translated as an independent sentence, which is the normal mode for MT systems (see Chapter 5 for problems involving lack of contextual information). In other instances, assistance may be sought with the selection of target language expressions when there are distinctions in the target language not made in the source. For example, the English verb *wear* has a number of possible Japanese translations depending on the object concerned (see section 6.1). This interaction could take place in two different ways as illustrated below: (a) assuming that the user knows Japanese, and (b) assuming that the user knows only the source language, English.

(a) To translate *wear*, please choose one of *haoru, haku, kaburu, hameru, shimeru, tsukeru, kakeru, hayasu, kiru*

(b) To translate *wear*, please indicate the type of the (understood) object from the following: coat or jacket, shoes or trousers, hat, ring or gloves, belt or tie or scarf, brooch or clip, glasses or necklace, moustache, general or unspecific

Other types of interaction will be described in more detail in section 8.3.3, where the distinctions made here are shown to be not quite as clear-cut as they seem initially.

4.4 Lexical data

The linguistic data required in MT systems can be broadly divided into lexical data and grammatical data. By 'grammatical data' is understood the information which is embodied in grammars used by analysis and generation routines. This information is stated in terms of acceptable combinations of categories and features (as described in section 3.8 above). By 'lexical data' is meant the specific information about each individual lexical item (word or phrase) in the vocabulary of the languages concerned. In nearly all systyems, grammars are kept separate from lexical information, though clearly the one depends on the other.

The lexical information required for MT differs in many respects from that found in conventional dictionaries. As already mentioned (sections 2.4 and 3.6) there is no need in MT for information about pronunciation or etymology, for lists of synonyms, for definitions, or for examples of usage. On the other hand, the information needed for syntactic and semantic processing has to be far more explicit than that found in dictionaries for human consultation: grammatical category, morphological type, subcategorization features, valency information, case frames, semantic features and selection restrictions. Because of these basic differences, the term **lexicon** is preferred to 'dictionary'.

Each of the design decisions mentioned above has implications for the organization of lexical data. In MT systems of the direct translation design there is basically one bilingual lexicon containing data about lexical items of the source language and their equivalents in the target language. It might typically be a list of source language items (either in full or root forms, cf. sections 2.4 and 5.1), where each entry combines grammatical data (sometimes including semantic features) for the source item, its target language equivalent(s), relevant grammatical data about each of the target items, and the information considered necessary to select between target language alternatives and in order to change syntactic structures into those appropriate for the target language (see particularly sections 6.4 and 7.1 below). The result can be a lexicon of considerable complexity.

In indirect systems, by contrast, analysis and generation modules are independent, and such systems have separate monolingual lexicons for source and target languages, and bilingual 'transfer' lexicons. The monolingual lexicon for the source language contains the information necessary for structural analysis and disambiguation (Chapter 5), i.e. morphological inflections, grammatical categories, semantic features, selection restrictions. Typically, for homographs and polysemes, each form has its own entry: for example, there will be two entries for *feed*, as a noun and a verb, and the noun *bank* will have two distinct entries for the two readings 'financial institution' and 'side of a river'. The bilingual lexicon for converting lexical items from source to target or to and from interlingual representations may be simpler, being restricted to lexical correspondences (e.g. that in French the first sense of *bank* is *banque* while the second is *rive*), and containing only the minimum of grammatical information for the two languages. The lexicon for generation is also often (though not always) less detailed than the one needed for analysis, since the information required for disambiguation is not necessary; however, as we shall see in Chapter 7, this view of the relative simplicity of generation may be a general weakness in MT system design. In addition, it should be noted that some indirect MT systems incorporate most of the information for the selection of target language forms in their bilingual transfer lexicons rather than in the monolingual generation lexicon (even if the choice of target item is properly a question of target language style or grammar), so that the generation lexicon is typically limited to morphological data.

In practice, the situation is sometimes further complicated in many systems by the division of lexicons into a number of special dictionaries, e.g. for 'high frequency' vocabulary, idiomatic expressions, irregular forms, etc., which are separated from the main or 'core' lexicons. This is because systems often have special routines devoted to handling less 'regular' items.

It is even more common to find separate lexicons for specific subject domains (e.g. biochemistry, metallurgy, economics), with the aim of reducing problems of homography (cf. section 5.2.2 below). For example, instead of a single lexicon containing a number of entries for the word *field*, each specifying different sets of semantic features and co-occurrence constraints, etc. and each relating perhaps to different target language equivalents, there might be a lexicon for physics texts with one entry and one target equivalent, another for agriculture texts, and so on. Such specialised subject lexicons are sometimes called **microglossaries**. We will return to the question of MT systems for specific subject fields or 'sublanguages' in Chapter 8.

The choice of an 'interactive' mode of operation can permit considerable simplification of lexical databases. If the system itself does not have to make decisions about the choice of target equivalents (whether *wall* is *Wand* or *Mauer*), or if it does not have to resolve ambiguities of grammatical category (e.g. whether *light* is a noun or adjective) or ambiguities of homonymy (e.g. whether *board* is a flat surface or a group of people), then the lexicon does not need to include complex grammatical, semantic and translational information, but may simply list alternatives for presentation to the human operator for selection.

From this brief outline it should be evident that the organization and content of MT lexicons are highly dependent on the methods used for analysis, transfer and generation and on the degree of human interaction envisaged in practical operation. These differences will emerge in the following chapters and are illustrated particularly in the descriptions of specific systems in Chapters 10 to 17.

4.5 Further reading

Most of the points covered in this chapter are covered in general articles about MT.

The contrast between bilingual and multilingual system design is rather briefly discussed in King (1982:140), and in Bennett *et al.* (1986:78f).

For a discussion of the differences between direct and indirect methods, see Johnson (1984), Tucker (1987), and Lehrberger and Bourbeau (1988:8–38). The Russian–English examples are taken from Knowles (1979). Descriptions of many direct systems are found in Hutchins (1986).

The choice of the interlingua and transfer methodologies is discussed in further detail in Chapter 6 of this book: see there for further references. Likewise, interactive and non-intervention systems are covered in Chapter 8, where further references are also given.

5
Analysis

This chapter is concerned with the specifically linguistic (rather than computational) problems which have to be faced in MT system design. It does not make reference to particular MT systems. Instead it discusses the issues in terms of an ideal model or a check-list to examine and evaluate particular systems.

The first general point to be made is that 'state-of-the-art' MT systems are not in general based on one single linguistic theory. As outlined in Chapter 2, a number of approaches to the linguistic description of natural languages have been influential in the design of MT systems. However, there have been very few systems based on a single linguistic model, and these have been predominantly experimental projects undertaking basic research using MT as a test-bed for computational linguistic theories. The great majority of MT systems are amalgams of different approaches and models, or even occasionally (particularly in the early years of MT research, cf. Chapter 1) with no discernible theoretical basis at all. Most commonly, systems are vaguely based on a general theory, such as transformational grammar or dependency theory, greatly modified by borrowings from other theories and by the demands of computational implementation.

MT research has often been criticised for ignoring developments in linguistic theory. There would appear to be a wide communication gap between theoretical linguistics and practical MT research. Some observers believe that there are good reasons for this situation: until recently, linguistic theories had not provided adequate accounts of all aspects of language use; a good linguistic theory may have given a convincing analysis of, say, quantifiers or coordination, but not explained all the peculiarities of actual usage in the coverage required for MT.

However, recent theories such as Lexical Functional Grammar or Generalized Phrase-Structure Grammar and their various derivatives have set out explicitly to cover as broad a range as possible, not only within one specific language, but also for different types of languages. In the past, and unfortunately it is still generally true today, much of linguistic theory was based on phenomena observed in English, the language of the majority of theoretical linguists. This neglect of other languages has been a further reason why linguistic theory has had less impact on MT than some observers might have expected. In other words, linguistic theories have rarely addressed questions of contrastive linguistics, i.e. the way in which different languages use different means to express similar meanings and intentions. Such questions are of course at the heart of MT.

Other reasons for the 'neglect' of linguistic theory by MT researchers are more practical: MT research is sometimes regarded as an 'engineering' task, a search for computational methods that work with the facts of language. The aims of many theoretical linguists are more abstract, concerned with investigations of human faculties in general, the nature of language itself, and the psychological foundations of language acquisition and use.

The result has been somewhat cynically described by Yorick Wilks (1989:59):

> "... the history of MT shows, to me at least, the truth of two (barely compatible) principles that could be put crudely as 'Virtually any theory, no matter how silly, can be the basis of some effective MT' and 'Successful MT systems rarely work with the theory they claim to.'"

The search for solutions that work, whatever their theoretical status and whether or not they fit the alleged principles of the project, has meant that MT systems inevitably present a confusing picture of disparate methodologies and that researchers have been obliged to take much more pragmatic attitudes to theoretical issues than their colleagues in computational linguistics and in linguistic theory.

5.1 Morphology problems

It is generally accepted in MT system design that the first and last tasks of analysis and generation respectively are the treatment of morphology. In the context of MT, morphological analysis (and generation) is frequently regarded not as problematic in itself but rather as a means of helping to simplify the more difficult problems of lexical, syntactic and semantic analysis and generation. For example, by including a model of morphological analysis, it is often possible to reduce the size of the dictionaries considerably, and thus the human effort in creating them, and the computer time in accessing them. Although English, for example, has a relatively impoverished inflectional morphology, the size of an MT lexicon can be almost halved by treating singular–plural alternations systematically and by limiting verb entries to 'root' forms (e.g. *like* as the origin of *likes*, *liking* and *liked*). With other languages, such as French and German, which have richer inflectional morphology, greater savings can be derived. Nevertheless, some older MT systems, and some small-scale experimental projects make use of **full-form dictionaries**, i.e. lexicons in which all inflected variants of the words appear. Two reasons are usually put forward for omitting morphological analysis: the perceived difficulties of dealing with irregular forms and the wide range of possible inflectional paradigms lead to complex and time-consuming components; and the ever-decreasing access times of modern computers outweigh the problems previously caused by very large dictionaries.

However, morphological analysis has other benefits, principally in the recognition of **unknown words**, i.e. word forms not present in the system's dictionary. From the identification of grammatical inflections, it is often possible to infer syntactic functions, even if the root word itself cannot be translated directly.

As mentioned in section 2.4, there are three main areas of morphology: inflection, derivation and compounding. In many respects the morphological systems of many languages are well understood and systematically documented, even for languages not as intensively studied as English and other 'major' languages of the world; nevertheless, the computational implementation of morphological analysis is not entirely straightforward. Even the relatively mundane task of recognising and stripping affixes requires an elegant solution. The potential complexities of morphological routines can be illustrated as follows: it would be easy to imagine a simple rule for English which recognised a word ending in *-ing* as the present participle of a verb. To get the root form of the verb, all that would be needed is a procedure to strip off the ending. It would work well for *foaming*, *trying* and *testing*, but not for *having*, *hopping* and *tying*, the root forms of which are not **hav*, **hopp* and **ty* but *have*, *hop* and *tie* respectively. These examples are well-known regular alternatives to the simple stripping rule, which must obviously be made more complex. And the rule must also ensure that *bring* and *fling* are not analysed as present participles of the 'verbs' **br* and **fl*! Although the solution is not computationally complex, this type of problem is quite common, and calls for some attention on the part of linguists.

Morphological analysis alone is sometimes sufficient to identify grammatical categories and structural functions, e.g. in English the suffix *-ize* usually indicates a verb, and German words ending in *-ung* are usually nouns. Frequently, however, morphological analysis cannot be divorced from syntactic analysis. Although German has a relatively rich inflectional morphology, providing indicators of subject–verb and adjective–noun agreement and marking case relations explicitly, it employs relatively few suffixes for these purposes, and many of the suffixes have multiple functions. A suffix such as *-en* can be highly ambiguous out of context, as Table 5.1 illustrates.

Most examples so far have been of inflectional morphology. Many languages have rich systems of **derivational** morphology and regularities in this area can also be exploited to reduce dictionary sizes. In English for example the recognition of negative prefixes such as *un-* and *non-*, the formation of adverbs from adjectives by the suffix *-ly* (though not all words with this ending are adverbs, e.g. *silly*); in French the suffix *-ment* is used to form adverbs (but again many words ending in *-ment* are nouns); and in German the suffix *-heit* can be used to form nouns from adjectives. However, derivational morphology has to be applied with care: for example, the English *-er* suffix frequently indicates a human agentive noun derived from a verb (a *dancer* is someone who dances, a *walker* someone who is walking), but there are often further meaning shifts involved: for example, a *computer* is a machine which computes, and a *revolver* is a weapon which has a mechanism which revolves.

noun plural
noun dative plural
weak noun singular non-nominative
strong declension* masculine singular accusative
strong declension* dative plural
adjective non-nominative masculine singular after definite article
adjective dative or genitive feminine or neuter singular after definite article
adjective accusative or genitive masculine singular without article
adjective genitive neuter singular without article
adjective dative plural without article
verb infinitive
verb 1st or 3rd person plural
verb past participle (strong verb)
a word which happens to end in *-en*

* articles, possessive and demonstrative adjective, etc.

Table 5.1 Possible interpretations of *-en* in German

The third aspect of morphological analysis involves the treatment of **compounds**. In English, terms are often coined by the simple juxtaposition of nouns (e.g. *steam engine*, *steam hammer*), and each component noun could appear in the dictionary; in the course of time, some juxtaposed nouns may be fused and become a single noun (e.g. *steamship*) and would be accommodated by inclusion of the full form in the dictionary. However, in languages such as German and Dutch, fusion is more common than juxtaposition (e.g. German *Dampfmaschine*, *Dampfhammer*, *Dampfschiff*), and novel original compounds are readily created (e.g. *Dampfschiffahrtsgesellschaft* 'steamship company'). A novel compound creates a problem for morphological analysis in an MT system: to treat it as an unknown word is unrealistic, since its meaning and correct translation can often be derived from its component parts; the difficulties lie in the multitude of feasible alternative segmentations, as exemplified in Table 5.2.

To illustrate the complexities that might arise with English examples, a morphological analysis routine might incorrectly segment *coincide* as *coin+cide*, *cooperate* as *cooper+ate*, *extradition* as *ex+tradition* or *extra+dition*, *mandate* as *man+date*.

Some of the possibilities ought to be excluded by the analysis program on semantic grounds if possible, but in other cases there may be a truly plausible ambiguity (e.g. *Wachtraum* as *Wacht+raum* or *Wach+traum*, *deferment* as *defer+ment* or *de+ferment*).

Alleinvernehmen	*Allein + Vernehmen*	'lone perception'
	All + Einvernehmen	'global agreement'
Beileid	*Bei + Leid*	'condolence'
	Beil + Eid	'hatchet oath'
Kulturgeschichte	*Kultur + Geschichte*	'history of culture'
	Kult + Urgeschichte	'pre-history of worship'
Uranbrenner	*Uran + Brenner*	'uranium pile'
	Ur + Anbrenner	'primitive kindler'
Wachtraum	*Wach + Traum*	'day-dream'
	Wacht + Raum	'guard-room'

Table 5.2 Examples of ambiguous compounds in German

5.2 Lexical ambiguity

Some of the morphological problems discussed above involve **ambiguity**, that is to say, there are potentially two or more ways in which a word can be analysed. More familiar, and more complex, are **lexical ambiguities**, where one word can be interpreted in more than one way. Lexical ambiguities are of three basic types: category ambiguities, homographs and polysemes, and transfer (or translational) ambiguities.

5.2.1 Category ambiguity

The most straightforward type of lexical ambiguity is that of **category ambiguity**: a given word may be assigned to more than one grammatical or syntactic category (e.g. noun, verb or adjective) according to the context. There are many examples of this in English: *light* can be a noun, verb or adjective; *control* can be a noun or verb. Especially common are noun–verb pairs, since almost any noun can function as a verb (examples in this sentence include *pair* and *function*); and almost any noun can function as an adjective (modifying another noun), hence the facility to produce new compound nouns in English, mentioned above. As an extreme but not rare example, *round* in the following sentences is a noun (1a), verb (1b), adjective (1c), preposition (1d), particle (1e) and adverb (1f).

    (1a) Liverpool were eliminated in the first round.

    (1b) The cowboy started to round up the cattle.

    (1c) I want to buy a round table.

    (1d) We are going on a cruise round the world.

    (1e) A bucket of cold water soon brought him round.

    (1f) The tree measured six feet round.

    Category ambiguities can often be resolved by morphological inflection: e.g. *rounding* must be a verb form, although *rounds* could be a plural noun or a third-person singular present tense verb. More frequently the ambiguity can be resolved by syntactic parsing. Thus in (1b) *round* could only be analysed as a verb because the syntactic context determines that, of the available options, only a verb would be appropriate here.

However, the problems increase when several categorially ambiguous words occur in the same sentence, each requiring to be resolved syntactically, as in (1c), where *want* could be a noun, *table* a verb. A good example is sentence (2).

(2) Gas pump prices rose last time oil stocks fell.

Each of the words in this sentence has at least a two-way category ambiguity: all can be nouns or verbs, and *last* can be noun, verb, adjective or adverb. (As a noun it is in addition semantically ambiguous: see 5.2.2. below.) Despite the individual ambiguities, there is in fact only one correct analysis of this sentence, although it requires more than simple knowledge of possible category combinations to arrive at it: for a simple parser (which looks only at categories, and has information about possible legal combinations of them), this sentence is massively ambiguous. Although this example has been deliberately concocted, numerous examples — perhaps less extreme — can be found in real life, especially in the headlines of English newspapers, which typically omit function words which would indicate categories. Two actual examples are shown in (3).

(3a) Foot heads arms body.

(3b) British left waffles on Falklands.

To understand (3a) demands the 'real-world knowledge' (see 5.3.2.3 below) that a British politician named Foot was made chairman of a committee investigating arms control. In the case of (3b), the sentence makes sense for British readers familiar with the use of *waffle* as a verb (where *left* is then interpreted as a noun indicating political tendency). The interpretation of *waffle* as a noun (with *left* as a verb) is dismissed on grounds of implausibility (see again 5.3.2.3 below); but for American readers who know *waffle* only as a noun (a kind of doughnut) the sentence is unambiguous, but surprising.

5.2.2 Homography and polysemy

The second type of lexical ambiguity occurs when a word can have two or more different meanings. Linguists distinguish between homographs, homophones and polysemes. **Homographs** are two (or more) 'words' with quite different meanings which have the same spelling: examples are *club* (weapon and social gathering), *bank* (riverside and financial institution), *light* (not dark and not heavy). Homophones are words which are pronounced the same but spelled differently (e.g. *hair* and *hare*), but since MT is concerned essentially with written texts, they need not concern us here. Polysemes are words which exhibit a range of meanings related in some way to each other, e.g. by metaphorical extension or transference (*mouth* of a river, *branch* of a bank, *flow* of ideas, *channel* of communication, *tide* of opinion, etc.). When the extension becomes too distant from the origin then the polysemes effectively become homographs: for example, a *crane* as a lifting device may have been a metaphorical transfer from the bird sense of the word, but the words are no longer thought of as polysemes. Conversely, the meaning of *ear* as in *ear of corn* might be thought to be a case of polysemy because of a physical similarity between the two concepts; but in fact the two words have different historical derivations (Latin *auris* and *acus*) and so technically are homographs. This demonstrates the fluidity of the difference, which in any case for MT (and computational linguistics) may be largely irrelevant.

Sometimes one use of a homograph set may be more prevalent than the others, as for example with *rail* which is the name of a genus of wading bird with a harsh cry, as well as something a train runs on. In this case, the homograph could be disambiguated according to text-type, so that the unusual usage is simply excluded from the dictionary unless it is appropriate to the subject field of the texts to be translated.

In MT analysis homography and polysemy can often be treated alike, since it is a question of identifying the sense in context of a particular written 'word'. Homographs of different grammatical categories can be resolved as described above, but for homographs of the same category syntactic analysis alone is insufficient: semantic information must be used. One common approach is to assign **semantic features** such as 'human', 'female', 'liquid', etc. and to specify which features are compatible in given syntactic constructions, via **selection restrictions**. For example it might be specified that the verb *drink* must have an 'animate' subject.

There are difficulties in devising a consistently applicable set of semantic features and in specifying the selection restrictions of nouns and verbs in terms of such features. Nevertheless they are widely used in MT systems, often in conjunction with case roles (see 5.3.2.1 below). But semantic features do not solve all problems, even in situations for which they have been devised. For example, consider the homograph *ball* with one meaning 'ball$_1$' the spherical object and another, 'ball$_2$' the dance party. The two could easily be distinguished in the following sentences by defining appropriate feature co-occurrence restrictions.

(4a) The ball rolled down the hill.

(4b) The ball lasted until midnight.

In (4a), *roll* would require a round object as its subject, i.e. 'ball$_1$'. In (4b), the verb *last* would expect a subject with temporal duration, which a 'ball$_2$' does have. However, in a sentence beginning as in (4c),

(4c) When you hold a ball, ...

the word *hold* is also ambiguous, requiring as its direct object in one case ('grasp') a physical object and in the other ('organize') an event. Since *ball* can be either a physical object ('ball$_1$') or an event ('ball$_2$'), there is no way out of the dilemma until, hopefully, the rest of the sentence provides further linguistic or contextual information.

5.2.3 Transfer ambiguity

Category ambiguities, homography and polysemy are all examples of lexical ambiguities which cause problems primarily in the analysis of the source language text. They are monolingual ambiguities. In MT there are also **transfer ambiguities** (or translational ambiguities) which arise when a single source language word can potentially be translated by a number of different target language words or expressions: several examples are given in the next chapter. The source language word itself is not ambiguous, or rather it is not perceived by native speakers of the language to be ambiguous; it is 'ambiguous' only from the perspective of another language. It is, therefore, a problem of translation — certainly a difficult one — but not a problem of linguistic analysis *per se*. Lexical transfer problems will be dealt with alongside other problems relating to transfer in the next chapter.

5.3 Structural ambiguity

5.3.1 Types of structural ambiguity

Whereas lexical ambiguities involve problems of analysing individual words and transferring their meanings, **structural ambiguity** involves problems with the syntactic structures and representations of sentences. Ambiguity arises when there is more than one way of analysing the underlying structure of a sentence according to the grammar used in the system. The two qualifications — "of a sentence" and "according to the grammar used in the system" — are important. The majority of MT systems are restricted to the sequential analysis of single sentences; they do not generally deal with larger units of translation such as paragraphs, and although some attempts are made to deal with features of the ways in which sentences are linked, e.g. pronouns, theme–rheme structure and so on, most such systems remain experimental. The second qualification is a reminder that no parser can go beyond the limitations of the grammar being implemented. If the grammar does not make distinctions which a human reader would make, then the parser will not be able to decide between alternative analyses. In the following sections there are a number of illustrations of this point: it is the grammar which determines whether a particular structure has more than one 'legal' interpretation and is therefore ambiguous. It is consequently valid to distinguish between 'real' ambiguities, for which a human might find several interpretations, and 'system' ambiguities which the human reader would not necessarily recognise.

5.3.1.1 Real structural ambiguity

Linguists in general are fond of writing about **real structural ambiguities**, in order to illuminate alternative syntactic interpretations revealed by formal analysis. Examples such as the following are well known (8)–(10):

> (8) Flying planes can be dangerous.
> (9) Time flies like an arrow.
> (10) The man saw the girl with the telescope.

For each of these sentences it is possible for human readers to find more than a single interpretation, as shown by the following paraphrases.

> (8a) It can be dangerous to fly planes.
> (8b) Planes which are flying can be dangerous.

(9a) The passage of time is as quick as an arrow.

(9b) A species of flies called 'time flies' enjoy an arrow.

(9c) Measure the speed of flies like you would an arrow.

(10a) The man saw the girl who possessed the telescope.

(10b) The man saw the girl with the aid of the telescope.

The recognition (by humans) of the ambiguities in these sentences may not always be easy (especially (9)); and **in context** — in a particular situation or in a specific text — the sentences may be quite unambiguous. For example, if (10) were to appear in a story, it would probably be obvious from the story-line who had the telescope, the man or the girl. However, since MT systems cannot make use of these contextual clues, except in a very limited way (see below), the sentences are effectively ambiguous. In these cases, the 'system' ambiguities coincide with 'real' ambiguities.

5.3.1.2 Accidental structural ambiguity

However, the generalization of such examples by the substitution of other verbs, nouns, prepositions, etc., leads to further structural ambiguities which would not be regarded as ambiguous by the human reader. Since the system lacks the information required to disambiguate, it treats real ambiguities and system ambiguities in the same way. We call such cases of ambiguity **accidental** (or 'system') **structural ambiguities**, and part of the interest in studying them is that in this way linguists can attempt to clarify what information should be added to the grammar so that the false reading is rejected.

Accidental structural ambiguities occur due to an accidental combination of words having category ambiguities, due to alternative grammatical uses for syntactic constituents, or due to different possible combinations of syntactic constituents. The types of structural ambiguities that occur differ from language to language, and, importantly, from grammar to grammar. However, it is useful to discuss here some of the types of ambiguity that a reasonably broad-coverage grammar of English might produce (or have to cope with), by way of exemplification.

Many ambiguities arise from the fact that a single word may serve in a different function within the same syntactic context. This is one possible consequence of the category ambiguities discussed in 5.2.1 above. Some examples of this have already been given: in (8), *flying* can either be a gerund governing a complement noun with the interpretation (8a), or an adjective modifying a noun (8b); in (9), *time* can be a subject noun, an imperative verb, or a modifying noun. These ambiguities are reflected in different structural interpretations of the same sentences; in terms of the Chomskyan model (see Chapter 2) they are **deep structure ambiguities**, because there are different 'deep structures' for the same 'surface structures'. As before, we can illustrate with real ambiguities: in (11a) the present participle *shaking* can function as an adjective (like *tiny* in (11b)) or as a gerundive verb (like *drinking* in (11c)).

(11a) He noticed her shaking hands.

(11b) He noticed her tiny feet.

(11c) He noticed her drinking beer.

The present participle can also be involved in an ambiguity between its use as a (verbal) noun and as a gerundive verb: compare the sentences in (12):

(12a) I like swimming.

(12b) I like tennis.

(12c) I like getting up late.

The word *that* in (13a) can be either a relative pronoun (equivalent to *whom* in (13b)) or a complementizer as in (13c):

(13a) They complained to the guide that they could not hear.

(13b) They complained to the guide whom they could not hear.

(13c) They complained to the guide that they could not hear him.

A final example of a deep structure ambiguity comes from the interpretation of a string of nouns either as a single constituent, i.e. as a compound noun, or with a constituent boundary in the middle. It is a particular problem in English which permits the omission of relative pronouns: consider the noun sequence *mathematics students* in (14a) and (14b):

(14a) The mathematics students sat their examinations.

(14b) The mathematics students study today is very complex.

In English the prevalence of noun compounds and the frequency of category ambiguities (particularly between nouns and verbs: see 5.2.1 above) means that this type of structural ambiguity is very common, and may accumulate to produce sentences like (2) above (reproduced here), which baffle most readers, until they have identified which words are functioning as verbs (*rose* and *fell*).

(2) Gas pump prices rose last time oil stocks fell.

Another type of structural ambiguity arises from lack of information about the attachment of (typically) prepositional phrases and relative clauses to preceding constituents of sentences. These are **surface structure ambiguities** in contrast to the deep structure ambiguities discussed above. We have already seen examples of this **attachment ambiguity** in (10) and (13a) above (reproduced here).

(10) The man saw the girl with the telescope.

(13a) They complained to the guide that they could not hear.

Sentence (10) is an example of **prepositional-phrase attachment ambiguity**. The prepositional-phrase *with the telescope* may modify either the preceding noun *the girl* or the main verb of the sentence *saw*. In (13a) the relative clause *that they could not hear* might refer to the guide or might be the content of the complaint. Further examples show other types of attachment ambiguity: in (15), the ambiguity lies in attachment of the *in*-phrase to either the first preceding noun *story* or the second *aircrash*; in (16a) the prepositional-phrase *to Susan* could attach either to the main verb *mentioned* as also in (16b) or to the embedded verb *sent* as in (16c); in (17a) the phrase *about the strike* could be attached either to the modifying adjective *concerned* as in (17b) or to the main verb *told* as in (17c).

(15a) Have you seen the story about the aircrash in the paper?

(15b) Have you seen the story about the aircrash in the jungle?

(16a) John mentioned the book I sent to Susan.

(16b) John mentioned the book I sent him to Susan.

(16c) John mentioned the book I sent to Susan to his brother.

(17a) I told everyone concerned about the strike.

(17b) I told everyone concerned about the strike not to worry.

(17c) I told everyone about the strike.

5.3.2 Resolution of structural ambiguity

When syntactic analysis produces more than one possible interpretation for a sentence, it is necessary to find a way of choosing the correct one. The reason for this is that often (though not always) the translation into the target language will be different depending on the interpretation chosen. For example, the Japanese translation of (10) has to be unambiguous: either (18a) or (18b); in German, the translation of *that* in (13a) differs from one interpretation to the other (19).

(18a) *Otoko wa BÔENKYÔ WO MOTTE IRU onnanoko wo mita.*

MAN subj TELESCOPE obj HOLDING GIRL obj SAW

'The man saw the girl who was holding the telescope'.

(18b) *Otoko wa BÔENKYÔ DE onnanoko wo mita.*

MAN subj TELESCOPE inst GIRL obj SAW

'The man, using the telescope, saw the girl.'

(19a) *Sie beklagten sich bei dem Reiseführer, DEN sie nicht hören konnten.*

(19b) *Sie beklagten sich bei dem Reiseführer, DAß sie nicht hören konnten.*

There are a number of options available for ambiguity resolution: the use of semantic or other linguistic information, the use of contextual clues, the use of non-linguistic 'real world knowledge', and interactive consultation. Other options include ignoring the ambiguity, using a 'best guess' default strategy or hoping for a 'free ride'.

5.3.2.1 Use of linguistic knowledge

Often, potentially ambiguous sentences can be disambiguated by reference to what might be called **linguistic knowledge**. There are various types of linguistic knowledge, but they all have in common that they make use of information about words and the way they combine, rather than the events in real life that sentences describe.

One such method is to provide parsers with information about co-occurrence restrictions, that is indications of how the presence of certain elements in a structure influences the likely presence of other elements. The clearest example is the use of **subcategorization frames** for verbs (cf. section 2.9.1). These indicate what types of complements are 'expected' by a particular verb. A verb such as *give* for example, expects to have a noun referring to a 'giver' as its subject, a noun referring to the thing 'given' as its direct object, and a noun referring to a 'recipient' as indirect object. Furthermore, we can specify to a certain extent what types of nouns fill these syntactic roles, by assigning semantic features to them, for example the 'giver' should be animate and so on. In this way, given a potentially ambiguous pair of sentences like those in (20) the parser may produce correct interpretations if it knows that *read* may be modified by a prepositional phrase introduced by *in* when the noun concerned belongs to the set of nouns marked as 'readable' (e.g. *book, magazine, newspaper*, etc.)

(20a) I read about the aircrash in France.

(20b) I read about the aircrash in the paper.

In a similar way, the sentences in (15) can be analysed correctly if similar information for *story* and the *in*-phrase is coded.

This kind of information can be handled also at a more general level, in terms of Valency and Case grammar (cf. sections 2.9.5 and 2.9.6). In Valency, verbs are characterised by the number and type of complements which either must or might be associated with them. In Case grammar, the roles of dependent complements are identified, such as Agent, Patient (or Object), Instrument, Manner, Accompanier, Location, etc. A typical generalization is that the subjects of transitive verbs are Agents, which are typically 'animate', 'potent', etc. For *give*, the expected case roles may be Agent, Recipient and Patient. The example sentences in (21) will be correctly analysed if the parser has access to the information that *write* takes an Instrument *with*-phrase and that the Instrument should be a physical object (21a); that an Accompanier of *visit* and similar verbs should be animate (21b); and that *tell* takes a Manner *with*-phrase, with a restricted range of possible fillers (*stutter, accent*, etc.).

(21a) He wrote the letter with a fountain-pen.

cf. He wrote the letter with the parcel.

(21b) He visited the museum with his brother.

cf. He visited the museum with the Elgin marbles.

(21c) He told the story with a funny accent.

cf. He told the story with a funny ending.

5.3.2.2 Contextual knowledge

In practice, very few sentences are truly ambiguous: if nothing else serves to disambiguate, then usually the context in which the sentence occurs will suggest that one or other reading is to be preferred. In discussing example (10) above it was suggested that the story-line might indicate which of the two characters had the telescope. It might have been mentioned in the previous sentence, or a previous paragraph, or perhaps even some chapters earlier. But it was also stated that very few MT systems are able to make use of such **contextual knowledge** for precisely the reason that there is no hard and fast rule about where to look for the piece of 'knowledge' which will help disambiguate in a particular case. From the other side, even assuming an efficient way of storing text-derived knowledge such as 'the man has a telescope', it would be difficult to know which pieces of knowledge were likely to be useful later, or how long they should be stored on the off-chance that they would be needed: for it would be clearly impracticable to extract and store every fact that could be inferred from every sentence of a given text, just in case it was needed to disambiguate something.

5.3.2.3 Real world knowledge

The third approach to ambiguity resolution when syntactic analysis is insufficient is to have recourse to what is generally called **real world knowledge.** An example of a structural ambiguity that is resolved by applying real world knowledge is sentence (22).

(22) The man saw the horse with the telescope.

In the similar earlier example (10) there was an ambiguity about the attachment of *with the telescope*. The same structural ambiguity is present in (22) too. But we know that *with the telescope* must modify *saw* because our knowledge of the world, and in particular of horses, makes the alternative improbable.

It should be noted that the line between real world knowledge and the linguistic knowledge discussed above is by no means clear cut. For example, in sentences like those in (23)

(23a) We will meet the man you told us about yesterday.

(23b) We will meet the man you told us about tomorrow.

there is no doubt that the adverbial *yesterday* attaches to the verb *told* in (23a) and that *tomorrow* attaches to *will meet* in (23b), rather than vice versa. It is a linguistic observation that the future tense of *tomorrow* is in agreement with the future tense of *will meet* and that the past tense of *yesterday* is in agreement with the past tense of *told*. But it is also a fact of reality that you cannot now make plans to do something in the past, and that you cannot already have spoken about something in the future. In other words, linguistic knowledge often correlates (not surprisingly) with real world knowledge.

Another example is a sentence like (24).

(24) The man saw the girl with red hair.

There is no ambiguity here for human readers because they know that hair cannot be used to aid vision. In linguistic terms, *hair* is not a permissible Instrument for the verb *see*. The semantic feature coding of potential Instruments for the verb is in effect a way of defining the physical act of seeing. Again, linguistic knowledge and real world knowledge coincide to a large extent.

The problem for MT systems is that it is at present impossible in practice to code and incorporate all the potential (real world) knowledge that might be required to resolve all possible ambiguities in a particular system, even in systems restricted to relatively narrow ranges of contexts and applications. Despite advances in Artificial Intelligence and in computing technology, the situation is unlikely to improve in the near future: the sheer complexity and intractability of real world knowledge are the principal impediments to quick solutions.

5.3.2.4 Other strategies

There are always going to be a residue of unresolved ambiguities (whether 'real' or 'system' ambiguities). In such situations the MT system could adopt strategies like those a human translator might apply in the same circumstances. The first might be to select the analysis which seems most 'natural' or most plausible. There has been ample psycholinguistic research into the question of which of competing structures are more easily understood, and this may be applied to build parsers which behave like humans when faced with these ambiguities.

The second strategy might be to ask the author if possible. Some interactive MT systems take this approach: they ask human operators to select the analysis which conforms with their knowledge of the subject and their understanding of the intention of the author. Consider an example like (25):

(25) investigation of techniques of stress analysis by thermal emission

The interpretation of this example would demand specialised scientific knowledge in order to determine whether it is *analysis by thermal emission,* or *investigation by thermal emission,* and whether it should be *techniques for analysis of stress* or *analysis of techniques of stress.* Interaction with a human operator is discussed in more detail in section 8.3.3.

The third strategy would be to make a **best guess,** based on the relative likelihood of one analysis over another, based only on which structures are more or less common, regardless of the words involved. For example, in complex noun-phrases like (25) a 'best guess' might be to assume that each prepositional phrase modifies the noun preceding it; or that adverbial phrases always modify the most recent verb. Obviously, this 'blind' approach will sometimes lead to wrong analyses, but if the 'guesses' are well motivated, the correct analysis may be made more often than not, and at very little cost.

Finally, it may be hoped that the ambiguity does not even have to be resolved because it can be retained in the target language. This option, sometimes called a **free ride,** is available usually only for languages of similar structure and vocabulary. Taking the familiar example (10) again, the ambiguity of the prepositional-phrase attachment can be retained in French and German (26) though not in Japanese (see (18) above).

(26a) *L'homme a vu la jeune fille avec le téléscope.*

(26b) *Der Mann sah das Mädchen mit dem Teleskop.*

One important point must be stressed. The distinctions that have been made among different types of ambiguities are irrelevant from the perspective of the system itself. What matters is not whether an ambiguity requires linguistic, contextual or real world knowledge but whether the relevant data are available which permit disambiguation. If the system can recognise that an ambiguity exists and it has the means to resolve it, then the system will obviously proceed to resolve it.

5.4 Anaphora resolution

Besides ambiguity resolution, which is often seen as the most important linguistic problem for MT, another major difficulty is the resolution of pronoun references or **anaphora resolution**. 'Anaphora' is the term linguists use to refer to an oblique reference being made to an entity mentioned explicitly elsewhere in a text. The most frequent linguistic device for this is the use of pronouns like *it*, *he*, *they*, etc., demonstratives like *this*, and phrases like *the latter*. The pronoun *she* for example may refer to a female already described as *woman*, and the pronoun *it* to a previously mentioned object, *a hat*, as in (27).

(27) The woman bought a hat and she paid for it by cheque.

The identification of pronouns involves, therefore, the identification of the earlier noun to which they refer, called the pronoun's **antecedent**. In (27) there is no problem since both *she* and *woman* are female, and are presumably assigned semantic features to reflect the fact. Likewise *hat* has no sex, and so *it* is the appropriate pronoun.

The establishment of the antecedents of anaphora is very often of crucial importance for correct translation. When translating into languages which mark the gender of pronouns for example, it is essential to resolve the anaphoric relations. Consider a set of sentences like those in (28).

(28a) The monkey ate the banana because it was hungry.

(28b) The monkey ate the banana because it was ripe.

(28c) The monkey ate the banana because it was tea-time.

In each case, the pronoun *it* refers to something different: in (28a) the monkey, in (28b) the banana, and in (28c) it refers to the abstract notion of the time of the action. For translation into German, where pronouns take the same grammatical gender as their antecedents, the appropriate connections must be made, as illustrated in (29). Since *Affe* ('monkey') is masculine, the corresponding pronoun is *er*; *Banane* ('banana') is feminine, and so requires the pronoun *sie*; and the appropriate pronoun for (28c) is *es*.

(29a) *Der Affe hat die Banane gefressen, da er Hunger hatte.*

(29b) *Der Affe hat die Banane gefressen, da sie reif war.*

(29c) *Der Affe hat die Banane gefressen, da es die Teestunde war.*

Making the correct anaphora resolution involves much the same types of knowledge — linguistic or otherwise — as for ambiguity resolution. In fact anaphora can be thought of as a sort of ambiguity, in that the antecedent of a given pronoun might be uncertain. In (28), where there is a choice between *monkey* and *banana* as antecedents, it is possible to invoke linguistic knowledge of co-occurrence restrictions to indicate that the former is more plausible in (28a), because *be hungry* requires an animate subject, and the latter is more plausible in (28b) because a fruit is more likely to be ripe than an animal is. In (28c) neither antecedent is appropriate, but a 'time-of-day' phrase is acceptable as the complement of *it was*.

However, as in ambiguity resolution, linguistic knowledge is sometimes not sufficient for the correct analysis. When translating sentences like those in (30) into French,

(30a) The soldiers shot at the women and some of them fell.

(30b) The soldiers shot at the women and some of them missed.

it is necessary to know whether *some of them* refers to *the soldiers* (masculine) or *the women* (feminine), not only for the pronoun gender (*quelques-uns* vs. *quelques-unes*) but also for agreement of the past participle in the case of *tombé(e)s* ('fell'). Here, to get the correct translations (31) it is the application of contextual or real world knowledge which gives an 'understanding' of the sequence of events being described.

(31a) *Les soldats ont tiré sur les femmes et quelques-unes sont tombées.*

(31b) *Les soldats ont tiré sur les femmes et quelques-uns ont raté.*

5.5 Quantifier scope ambiguity

A final problem to be discussed is that of **quantifier scope ambiguity.** This problem has been well studied in the field of natural language question-answering systems, where it is perhaps more crucial than in MT. This type of ambiguity occurs when the scope or range of a quantifier like *some, all, none* is unclear (cf. section 2.8.4). English in particular freely allows a syntactic phenomenon called 'quantifier raising', so that a sentence like (32a) has the true meaning expressed in (32b).

(32a) I don't think he'll come.

(32b) I think he won't come.

Sometimes quantifier raising can introduce an ambiguity as in (33a) and (34a), which can each be interpreted in two different ways (33b,c) and (34b,c).

(33a) All women don't like fur coats.

(33b) Not all women like fur coats, only some do.

(33c) There are no women who like fur coats.

(34a) All wires are attached to a pin.

(34b) There is one (large) pin to which all wires are attached.

(34c) Each wire is attached to its own pin.

Consider finally this notice, which was spotted in Japan. If you know that in Japan non-smokers are still somewhat in the minority, you will not so quickly assume that reading (35b) is the correct one.

(35a) No smoking seats are available on domestic flights.

(35b) There are no seats where you may smoke on domestic flights.

(35c) There are "no smoking" sections on domestic flights.

Many languages of course have similar (though not necessarily identical) quantifier scope ambiguities: with luck the same ambiguity may be present in both languages, in which case it may be possible to retain it (i.e. as a 'free ride'). But if not, the ambiguity must somehow be resolved. Since this often involves contextual or real-world knowledge, it may well be very difficult.

There are a large range of other linguistic problems that have to be solved, and in the next chapter we will be discussing several of those that concern contrastive aspects, that is problems that arise from specific differences between the language pairs involved. These are problems such as differing tense systems, modality, determination in noun phrases, thematisation, levels of politeness and formality, and so on.

5.6 Further reading

Discussion in the literature on the relationship between MT and theoretical linguistics has been quite heated and quite a few MT practitioners have taken the view that MT is an 'engineering' rather than theoretical problem.

In general, relatively little is written about morphological analysis in MT. Nevertheless, certain existing MT systems have significant morphological modules, notably the WOBUSU module in SUSY (Maas, 1980 and 1987:212–217; see also Chapter 11), in the work of the TAUM group (Lehrberger and Bourbeau, 1988:80–89; see Chapter 12), and GETA's Ariane system (Guilbaud, 1987:280–294; see Chapter 13).

For a discussion of compounding, see Selkirk (1982) and Lieber (1983).

Lexical ambiguity is discussed at length in Hirst (1987). Example (3b) was given to us by Scott Bennett. The discussion of homography and polysemy is based on Leech (1974:228ff).

Johnson (1983) has a brief discussion of parsing from the point of view of MT. Nirenburg (1987b) includes an interesting discussion of the question of linguistic vs. contextual or real-world knowledge.

Beyond the realm of MT, and particularly in the context of computational models of human parsing, syntactic ambiguity is even more widely studied. A good starting point might be Kurtzman (1984), Frazier (1985) and Pulman (1987). Disambiguation of attachment ambiguities is particularly spotlighted in Wilks *et al.* (1985) and Hirst (1987).

Anaphora resolution is discussed in Reinhart (1983), though not specifically from the point of view of Computational Linguistics or MT. For a discussion from the CL point of view, see Barwise and Cooper (1981), Hobbs (1983) or Hobbs and Shieber (1987).

6
Problems of transfer and interlingua

The last chapter was concerned primarily with problems of analysis, and the main focus was monolingual difficulties arising from the source language text. The next chapter will be concerned with the target language text generation. The present chapter concentrates on the interface between these two monolingual components.

Before discussing the different approaches according to the basic strategies described in Chapter 4 (direct, transfer, interlingua), we shall illustrate a few of the lexical and structural differences between languages.

6.1 Lexical differences

In the last chapter we discussed monolingual ambiguities which cause problems during analysis. **Transfer ambiguities** (or translational ambiguities) arise when a single source language word can potentially be translated by a number of different target language words or expressions, not because the source language word itself is ambiguous but because it is 'ambiguous' from the perspective of another language. Most differences in the lexical systems of languages arise from conceptual differences, but there are also those arising from stylistic or grammatical differences.

Stylistic translational ambiguities occur when the choice of target language lexical equivalent depends on differences of register or text-type. An example is the

French word *domicile* which could appear in English as either *home* or *domicile* according to the type of document being translated. This kind of difference is more common between languages which, unlike English and French, do not share similar cultural backgrounds. Japanese, for instance, has different words for kinship relations depending on whether it is the speaker's or hearer's kin being referred to, e.g. *kanai* '(my) wife' but *okusan* '(your) wife'.

Grammatical translational ambiguities are rather less common. These occur when there is a lexical choice in the target language which is conditioned by grammatical context. A familiar example is the translation of English *know* into French or German, where the choice between *connaître* or *savoir* and between *kennen* or *wissen* depends (roughly) on whether the direct object is a noun-phrase (1) or a subordinate clause or an infinitive (2).

(1a) I know the right answer.
Je connais la bonne réponse.
Ich kenne die richtige Antwort.

(1b) I know the author of that book.
Je connais l'auteur de ce livre.
Ich kenne den Verfasser dieses Buchs.

(2a) I know what the right answer is.
Je sais quelle est la bonne réponse.
Ich weiß, was die richtige Antwort ist.

(2b) I know who the author of that book is
Je sais qui est l'auteur de ce livre.
Ich weiß, wer der Verfasser dieses Buchs ist.

In some cases the choice may be open because both types of structure are possible in the target text (3).

(3) I know the quickest way to get from Norwich to Manchester.
Je connais la route la plus rapide de Norwich à Manchester.
Je sais comment aller le plus vite possible de Norwich à Manchester.
Ich kenne den schnellsten Weg von Norwich nach Manchester.
Ich weiß, wie man am schnellsten von Norwich nach Manchester kommt.

It may be argued that the difference between *connaître/kennen* and *savoir/wissen* corresponds to a conceptual difference between types of knowledge — knowing a fact and knowing how to do something — which is not reflected in English by a lexical choice. This would make the difference 'conceptual' rather than grammatical, though it would still be true that in translating from English into French and German the lexical choice can be made largely on the basis of grammatical facts alone.

A special type of grammatical ambiguity is that concerning anaphora. If the antecedent of a pronoun such as *it* in the sentences (28) of Chapter 5 has not been identified, then it may well have to be done during transfer, unless there is the relatively rare possibility of a straight lexical substitution. The latter is more likely with plural pronouns since a number of 'major' languages make no distinctions of gender (English *they*, German *sie*, Russian *oni*).

Conceptual translational ambiguities are the cause of the greatest problems in translation, and are the principal focus of debates about MT methodologies and system designs. They arise when a single 'concept' represented by one word in one language corresponds to a number of concepts, and hence words, in another language. This is by no means a rare phenomenon, even between closely related languages, and examples are plentiful, as illustrated in (4).

(4a)	English *wall*	German	*Wand* (inside a building)
			Mauer (outside)
(4b)	English *river*	French	*rivière* (general term)
			fleuve (major river, flowing into sea)
(4c)	English *leg*	Spanish	*pierna* (human)
			pata (animal, table)
			pie (chair)
			etapa (of a journey)
		French	*jambe* (human)
			patte (animal, insect)
			pied (table, chair)
			étape (journey)
(4d)	English *blue*	Russian	*goluboi* (pale blue)
			sinii (dark blue)
(4e)	French *louer*	English	*hire* or *rent*
(4f)	French *colombe* German *Taube*	English	*pigeon* or *dove*
(4g)	German *leihen*	English	*borrow* or *lend*
(4h)	English *rice*	Malay	*padi* (unharvested grain)
			beras (uncooked)
			nasi (cooked)
			emping (mashed)
			pulut (glutinous)
			bubor (cooked as a gruel)
(4i)	English *wear*	Japanese	*kiru* (generic)
			haoru (coat or jacket)
			haku (shoes or trousers)
			kaburu (hat)
			hameru (ring or gloves)
			shimeru (belt or tie or scarf)
			tsukeru (brooch or clip)
			kakeru (glasses or necklace)

It should be noted that even these correspondences are simplifications. In (4c), for example, French *pied* corresponds also to English *foot* (human, mountain), and *patte* to *paw* (animal) or *foot* (bird); in (4g) English *borrow* can also be German *borgen*, and *lend* can also be *leisten* ('lend help'). The example in (4i) is complicated by the fact that the Japanese translations of *wear* also translate the English *put on*: whereas English distinguishes the process from the resulting state without regard to the type of clothing, in Japanese it is the other way round. So *kaburu* is used not only for wearing a hat but also for putting it on.

There are many other examples of conceptual differences which could have been given: reflections of environmental or cultural differences, weather terms around the world, names of flora and fauna, culinary terms and so on. One example of this phenomenon which is often cited is the supposed abundance in Eskimo of words for 'snow'. In fact this is one of the great myths of linguistics. Eskimo actually has only two words for 'snow' (*qanik* for 'snow in the air', and *aput* for 'snow on the ground'), which is rather fewer than English, for example, (*snow, sleet, slush, hail, freezing rain, blizzard*).

For translation, there are particular problems caused by what are often referred to as **lexical gaps**, the absence in a language of one single word corresponding to a lexical item in the other language. These are not words specific to a particular culture, such as *mansion, cottage, marmelade, dacha, whiskey, vodka* (in these cases the lexical items are often borrowed untranslated), nor words which in one language carry a range of meanings covered by a variety of words in another as illustrated in (4), but 'universal' concepts which happen not to correspond to a single lexical item in a particular language. For example, English has nothing corresponding to French *gratiner* ('to cook with a cheese coating'), Russian *protalina* ('a place where the snow has melted'), Japanese *ōtosanrin* ('a three-wheeled pickup truck or motor van'). Likewise, English has lexical items which must be translated periphrastically: *snub* in French as something like *infliger un affront*, and in German as perhaps *verächtlich behandeln* or *derb zurückweisen*. In some cases the gaps are specific to grammatical categories; for example, German has adjectival forms for a number of adverbial and genitival expressions (e.g. *hiesig* corresponding to *hier* 'here', *derzeitig* corresponding to *der Zeit* 'of the time'), which are quite absent in English: there is no adjective for *here*, and a phrase such as *die derzeitigen Verhältnisse* has to be translated as *the circumstances at that time*. Some lexical gaps are the result of productive derivational morphology in one language which is not parallelled in another. A good example is the Dutch phrase *het Turks kennen* 'to know Turkish', from which the corresponding nominal *kenner van het Turks* can be formed. But in English the equivalent nominalization **knower of Turkish* is not possible, so the Dutch phrase must be translated as *someone who knows Turkish*. The transfer problems caused by such lexical gaps relate not so much to translation from the single lexical item to a periphrastic expression, but translation in the other direction. In the former, it may well be possible to decide on a particular 'standard' rendition; but in the latter, the variety of locutions may be so resistant to precise specification that the single lexical form is not selected when it would be appropriate.

6.2 Structural differences

Many relatively trivial syntactic differences between languages are well known, e.g. in French most adjectives follow nouns but in English adjectives normally precede the nouns they qualify. Other familiar differences are those between languages such as Japanese and Latin where the main (finite) verb of a sentence comes last and languages such as English and German where the finite verb comes after the first noun (phrase). However, there are many instances where it is less easy to equate a structure in one language with a structure in another in quite such a simple way.

A good example is the passive. In English, this is defined as any construction formed with the auxiliary verb *be* and the past participle. Even when translating into a language which has a similar construction, it is not always appropriate — or even possible — to use that construction. In (5a) the corresponding construction is acceptable; but in (5b,c), alternative constructions are preferable.

> (5a) *Le bâtiment fut construit en 1923.*
> 'The building was constructed in 1923.'

> (5b) *Ces livres se lisent facilement.*
> Lit. These books read themselves easily
> 'These books are easily read'

> (5c) *Ici on parle anglais.*
> Lit. One speaks English here
> 'English is spoken here.'

Because all these constructions can (sometimes) be used to translate an English passive, it is sometimes said — misleadingly — that there are three forms of the passive in French. However, the reflexive and impersonal constructions also correspond to other constructions in English. Further complications are introduced by the fact that in English it is possible to passivize indirect objects and prepositional objects, which is impossible in French (6).

> (6a) Mary was given a book.
> *Mary fut donné un livre.*

> (6b) This bed has been slept in.
> *Ce lit a été dormi dans.*

Some languages, such as German and Japanese, allow the passivization of intransitive verbs (7), which is not possible in English. It should also be noted that the interpretation of this construction is different in the two languages.

> (7a) *Es wurde getanzt.*
> Lit. It was danced.
> 'There was dancing.'

> (7b) *Toshio-ga tsuma-ni nigerareta.*
> Lit. Toshio was run away by his wife.
> 'Toshio's wife ran away on him.'

Another distinction is found in German, which has two forms of the passive expressing either a process or a completed state, using the auxiliaries *werden* or *sein*, respectively (8).

(8a) *Das Fenster wurde gebrochen.*
'The window was (i.e. got) broken.'

(8b) *Das Fenster war gebrochen.*
'The window was (i.e. had been) broken.'

These examples illustrate the diversity of both forms and functions of the 'passive'. Formal differences include verb morphology, different word orders, use of auxiliaries, alternative case markings on nouns, or combinations of all of these. The functional differences include thematization, depersonalization, and so on. Translation of such constructions is not a simple matter of deciding on structural equivalences.

Other examples are linked closely to particular lexical items or semantic fields. Consider the English and German translationally equivalent sentences in (9):

(9a) I like swimming.

(9b) *Ich schwimme gern.*

The main verb in English, *like*, expresses the 'pleasure' concept, with the activity itself, *swimming* as a dependent participial complement. In German, the main verb expresses the activity *schwimmen* ('swim'), with the notion of pleasure conveyed by the dependent adverb *gern* ('gladly'). Translation from English into German or German into English involves therefore a change of structure, either direct or indirect (i.e. via an interlingual representation, see below). A similar phenomenon is found in Spanish where the verb *soler* which takes an infinitival complement corresponds to the English adverb *usually* (10). A comparable translation problem can be found for almost any language pair.

(10a) *Juan suele ir al cine los sábados.*

(10b) Juan usually goes to the cinema on Saturdays.

Differences of structure within the same semantic field may be illustrated by the English and French equivalents for certain expressions of movement (11)–(13).

(11a) He walked across the road.

(11b) *Il traversa la rue à pied.*

(12a) She drove into town.

(12b) *Elle entra dans la ville en voiture.*

(13a) They flew from Gatwick.

(13b) *Ils partirent par avion de Gatwick.*

In each of the English sentences it is the mode of transport that is expressed by the verb (*walk*, *drive*, *fly*) and the direction is expressed by prepositions (*across*, *into*, *from*). In the French, it is the direction which is expressed by the verb (*traverser* 'cross', *entrer* 'enter', *partir* 'leave'), and the mode of transport is expressed by adverbial adjuncts (*à pied* 'on foot', *en voiture* 'by car', *par avion* 'by plane').

Another more complex illustration is found in sentences expressing 'naming' (14).

(14a) His name is Julian.

(14b) *Er heißt Julian.*

The English sentence uses the equative (copula) *is* with two arguments: the word *name* modified by the possessive adjective *his*, and the name itself *Julian*. In German the predicate *heißt* ('is named') has two arguments, the person named *er* ('he') and the name itself *Julian*. Further variations are found in other languages: for example in Russian a three-argument construction is used (14c) and in French there is a reflexive construction (14d).

(14c) *Jego zovut Julian.*
Lit. 'They call him Julian'

(14d) *Il s'appelle Julian.*
Lit. 'He calls himself Julian'

These are just a few of many grammatical phenomena we could have chosen to illustrate problems even — apart from (7b) — within a single language family group. Others include the interpretation of verb tenses (where different languages have differing ways of expressing temporal location, including systems of morphological tenses, uses of temporal adverbials, various auxiliaries); modality (expressing necessity, obligation, ability, intention, desire, and so on); quantifier scope (already alluded to in section 5.5); determiner systems (*the, this, that, a, some* etc.); and even systems of singular and plural.

One area of particular interest in MT is the translation of **idioms**. The term 'idiom' is rather over-used, and tends to cover everything from fixed phrases like *raining cats and dogs* or *kick the bucket* to slightly metaphorical uses of words such as *pay attention*. It should be said that texts which are rich in colourful idioms and flowery language are probably not ideal material for translation by machine. However, many MT researchers have made considerable efforts to tackle the problem. From the point of view of translation, 'idiom' can be defined functionally. A phrase that can be translated **compositionally**, even if clearly idiomatic in meaning, need not be treated as such (e.g. *to ask for the moon*, French *demander la lune*). On the other hand, any phrase for which the translation is not an obvious combination of the translation of its components must be treated in a special manner (as an 'idiom'). So phrases like *commit suicide* require special attention. Both the verb *commit* and the noun *suicide* have their equivalents in French (*commettre, suicide*), and indeed the direct object of *commit* is usually translated as the direct object of *commettre* as in *commit a crime* → *commettre un crime*. But if the direct object happens to be *suicide*, then the whole phrase must be translated differently, by the reflexive verb *se suicider*.

Idioms often occur in constructions which change their structure. Two examples will illustrate this. In French, a phrase like *donner un coup de poing* (literally 'give a blow with the fist') can be treated as an idiom since it translates into English as *punch*. However, in French the construction is a quite regular one — verb plus direct object — which can be augmented by insertion of an indirect object or an adverbial (15a), by modification of the direct object (15b) or by coordination with another similar construction (15c). All these are special problems for an MT system.

(15a) *Elle donna de temps en temps à son frère un coup de poing.*
Lit. She gave from time to time to her brother a blow with the fist.
'She punched her brother from time to time'

(15b) *Elle lui donna quelques coups de poing violents.*
Lit. She gave him several violent blows with the fist.
'She punched him violently a few times'

(15c) *Elle lui donna des coups de poing et de pied.*
Lit. She gave him blows with the fist and foot.
'She punched and kicked him'

The second example comes from Japanese, where the English verb *rain* corresponds to an expression meaning 'rain falls'. If the words occur in a straightforward finite clause, then translation by the English verb is usually correct (16a). But as a regular subject-plus-verb construction in Japanese, it can also be nominalized (16b) or made into a relative clause (16c). In these cases the translation requires special treatment.

(16a) *Kinō ame ga futa.*
Lit. Yesterday rain fell
'It was raining yesterday'

(16b) *Ame no furi kata wa odorokashita.*
Lit. The rain's way of falling surprised us
*'Its way of raining surprised us'
'It surprised us how (hard) it was raining'

(16c) *Kinō furi hajimeta ame ga mada futte iru.*
Lit. The rain which started to fall yesterday is still falling.
*'It which rained yesterday is still raining'
'The rain which started yesterday is continuing'

6.3 Levels of transfer representation

In describing the strategies for MT systems (Chapter 4), it was noted that the basic differences lie in the relative sizes of the three components: analysis, transfer and generation. The direct method stands at one extreme, the interlingua method at the other, with transfer-based systems between them. The well-known 'pyramid' diagram in Figure 6.1. is often used to illustrate this point.

The diagram shows source language analysis up the left-hand side, and target-language generation down the right. The apex of the pyramid represents the theoretical interlingual representation achieved by monolingual analysis and suitable for direct use by generation. However, the path to that interlingua is long, and, as the diagram is supposed to show, by cutting off the monolingual analysis at some point and entering into a bilingual transfer phase, one can avoid the difficulties of a full analysis (as described in Chapter 5). The diagram is also intended to suggest that the more the text is analysed, the simpler transfer will be (as depicted by the length of the line cutting across the pyramid). The extreme case is at the very bottom, where there is minimal monolingual analysis, and nearly all the work is done in transfer, as was the case with the early direct method systems.

To illustrate the various levels of transfer in these different types of systems, we describe the kinds of analysis that could be required, working 'upwards' from the base of the pyramid to the apex. In most cases, representations will be tree

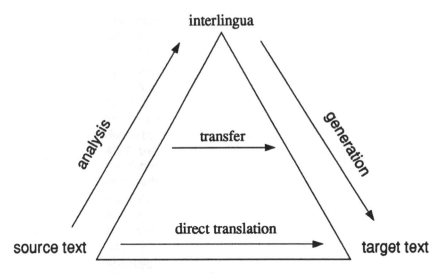

Figure 6.1 Transfer and interlingua 'pyramid' diagram

structures, and typically carry rather more information than is often shown when linguists discuss parse-trees or deep-structure representations (cf. Chapter 2). Our illustrative sentence will be sentence (17) and the target language French.

(17) Any government is dependent on its supporters.

In what follows, we take a deliberately eclectic and varied approach to the linguistic analysis. The reader should not be too concerned about the details of the representations, except to see what new information is introduced at each 'deeper' stage. It should be stressed that no specific method of analysis or representation is being especially promoted by us in this exercise.

6.4 Morphological transfer

The shallowest of analyses might be a word-by-word morphological analysis, resulting in a structure like (18).

(18)	any	government	be	dependent	on	it	supporter
	cat=det	cat=n	cat=v	cat=adj	cat=prep	cat=pospron	cat=n
		num=sg	num=sg			num=sg	num=pl
			pers=3			pers=3	
			tns=pres			sex=neut	

The analysis identifies grammatical categories, the syntactic number (singular or plural) of nouns, and the tense of verbs, but there is no identification of relations between words (e.g. determiners and nouns) or of groupings (noun phrases). In a crude word-for-word system transfer would consist simply in the substitution of source language words (with category features) by target words (with corresponding features), as in (19a), with perhaps the resulting target text (19b).

(19a)	quelconque	gouvernement	être	dépendant	sur	son	défenseur
	cat=det	cat=n	cat=v	cat=adj	cat=prep	cat=pospron	cat=n
		num=sg	num=sg			num=sg	num=pl
			pers=3			pers=3	
			tns=pres			sex=neut	

(19b) **Quelconque gouvernement est dépendant sur son défenseurs.*

The resulting translation would be clearly inadequate, even for a sentence such as this where little reordering is needed. It is relatively easy to think of English sentences — (20a) for example — for which this level of analysis results in almost incomprehensible and seriously ungrammatical output (20b).

(20a) Any responsible and well administered organisation must look
 after its female employees.

(20b) **Quelconque responsable et bien administré organisation doit
 regarder après son féminin employés.*

In practice, most of the direct translation systems do include minimal identification of local context so that the English sequence adj+noun would be inverted for French. However, because some French adjectives precede nouns (e.g. *bon, jeune*), exceptions would have to be indicated in the dictionary entries for these items.

These kinds of minimal structural changes are sometimes incorporated in a separate phase of direct systems which may operate after lexical substitution (cf. Figure 4.1): the arrangement is found particularly in direct systems with some modularity (e.g. Systran, Chapter 10). For this reason, 'local reordering' is often regarded as the beginning of 'generation' in these systems (see section 7.1 below.)

Example (20) illustrates another problem for word-for-word translation. The phrasal verb *look after* should be treated as a unit. Clearly it could be entered as a compound in the dictionary (with the French equivalent *soigner*). However, other phrasal verbs can be split (21).

(21a) He looked up the number in the directory.

(21b) He looked the number up in the directory.

With no identification of verb phrase structure, such compounds cause difficulties. How can *up* be related to *look*? And in (22), how can it be decided when *in* is part of the phrasal verb *fill in* and when not?

(22a) He filled it in.

(22b) He filled it in haste.

(22c) He filled it in yesterday.

(22d) He filled it in the morning.

The direct approach has particular problems with homographs; the usual method of resolving homograph ambiguities is to look at adjacent words for clues. For example, in the case of *empty*, which may be an adjective or a verb, it is the grammatical categories of adjacent words which are looked at: if *empty* comes between a determiner and a noun then it is presumed to be an adjective. But it may also come between another adjective and a noun, or at the end of a sentence. Listing all the possible category adjacencies for every adjective/noun and noun/verb homograph is clearly unsatisfactory, but this in essence is what direct systems have to do.

In the case of a word such as *enter* which may have a number of different translations (*entrer, s'enrôler, inscrire*) the program has to search for specific words (e.g. *room, service, ledger*). But there are obvious limits (computational, for example) on how much context can be examined, even if all the relevant words can be listed. Furthermore, there can no assurance against misleading contexts (23)

(23) The cleaner entered the service room.

However, even this approach — cumbersome as it is — is useless in cases such as the choice between *savoir* and *connaître* to translate *know*; only by examining the structural environment can a decision be reached (section 6.1 above). But without a structural analysis nothing can be done. The only solution, as many earlier direct systems found, is to give alternative translations and leave the choice to post-editors (section 8.3.2).

Obviously, direct systems hope that few structural and lexical choices have to be made. The more 'free rides' (section 5.3.2.4) that can be found, the simpler the dictionary entries can be. It is a reasonable assumption that fewer structural changes are required between cognate languages, such as French and Italian, than between unrelated languages, such as English and Japanese. Nevertheless, the paucity of structural analysis can be overcome only by the *ad hoc* inclusion of multiple-word entries, resulting in a huge bilingual dictionary containing structural transfer rules hidden in lexical transfer rules.

One answer to the problem of excessive lexical and structural detail in the dictionary is to conduct statistical analyses of texts and thus to derive probability measures for converting source language words or expressions into target words or expressions. No grammatical, semantic or lexical information need be involved, only information on the probabilities of source words corresponding to target words. The statistical approach was favoured by a number of the earliest MT systems (cf. section 1.3), and has now been revived by a group at the IBM Laboratories at Yorktown Heights, NY. Their tests of the approach on a large bilingual corpus of Canadian parliamentary proceedings have demonstrated that the use of probabilistic correspondences can produce context-sensitive translations with some success, with little or no use of grammatical information; the results have naturally aroused considerable interest (section 18.3).

6.5 Transfer-based systems

The next level of analysis after (18) is given by a syntactic parse resulting in a surface-structure representation. For sentence (17) this might result in a parse tree like (24) (next page).

Although there is now some structural information, we still do not have any information about functional relationships between elements. Using this structure as a basis for transfer into French, we might get internally coherent constituents, but we would not know what kind of structure the sentence as a whole should have, since there is no analysis of the syntactic or semantic functions of the elements.

(24)

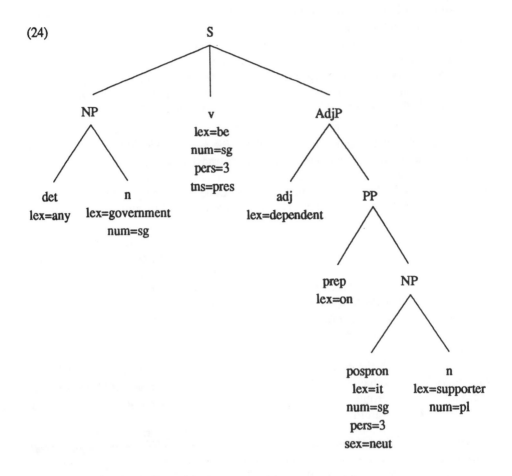

Nevertheless, some early transfer-based systems assumed that successful structural transformations between languages could be achieved at this 'depth' of analysis. For our example sentence (17) and for translation into French it might be sufficient. But in a relatively simple three-argument sentence such as (25a) it is essential to distinguish direct object and indirect object. This is even more obvious in a case like (25b) since structural changes are necessary.

(25a) The professor gave the student an assignment.

(25b) The student gave the teacher no offence.
L'étudiant n'a pas offensé le professeur.

It is now generally accepted that transfer must be based on a 'deeper' analysis, one which includes at least some indication of functional relations. For (17) the result might be as in (26), in which the syntactic functions of the constituents have been recognised, especially that the finite verb *be* is an auxiliary here, and the main predicate is the adjective. Other functions include subj[ect], compl[ement], qtf

(26)

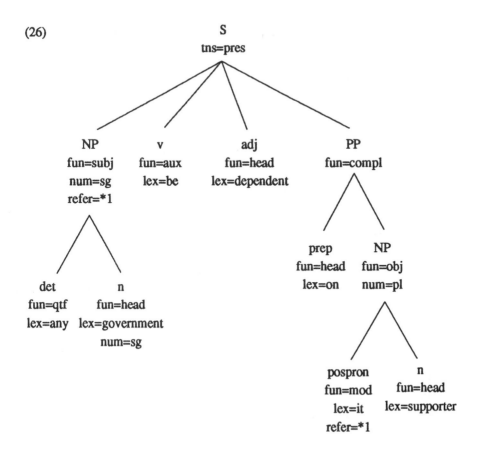

(quantifier), mod[ifier], and, for each constituent, head. Grammatical information such as tense and number has also been passed up to the highest appropriate nodes.

Notice that by matching up values for 'sex' and 'num', it is possible to recognise the anaphoric relation between the subject NP and the possessive pronoun, and to assign to both the refer(ence) index '*1'.

What is now involved in the transfer of this structure into French? There are two basic aspects: lexical transfer and structural transfer. Both these processes can cause problems (sections 6.5.1 and 6.5.2 below), but here for simplicity we may assume that lexical transfer consists of word-for-word replacement. The translation of the quantifier *any* might well be difficult — it has to be *tout* ('all') (see section 7.2.2). We know that the referent of the possessive pronoun (*its*) is the subject NP (*government*). For French the important question is whether it is singular or plural, since French possessive pronouns do not reflect the sex of the antecedent (i.e. 'his' and 'her' are the same), though they do agree in gender with the noun they modify. In this case, then, it so happens that it would not matter if the analysis of the anaphora was incorrect or incomplete: for translation into French, this is a 'free ride' (see 5.3.2.4 above). To transfer the preposition, we have to check which constituent the PP is attached to. Because the PP is a complement, its translation is determined by the head of the constituent (cf. *depend on, look for, finish with* etc.); by contrast, the translation of an adverbial PP often depends more on the object of the preposition itself (cf. *on the hill, in the city, at the bank* if the PP is a locative adverbial). The main structural change involves the auxiliary-plus-adjective, which is to be a straightforward verbal structure in French, i.e. *be dependent* is translated as *dépendre*. The result of these transfer operations is an input representation for French generation such as (27).

(27)

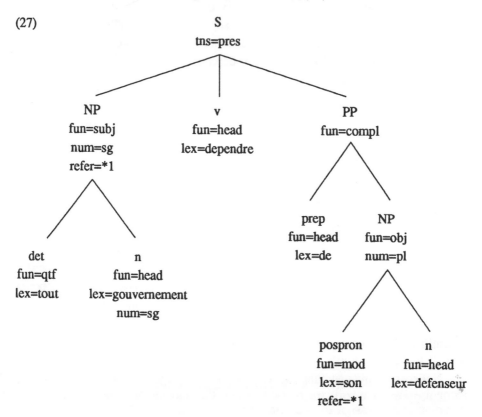

This particular illustration of transfer is relatively straightforward, but one could well imagine having to change the PP complement into a direct object, or having to make other basic structural changes (cf. some of the examples given in 6.2 above). This suggests perhaps that this level of representation is still a little too close to the English surface structure, and transfer might be somewhat easier if we could make our representation a little deeper, as we shall illustrate below.

Most transfer-based systems perform transfer on intermediate (or 'interface') representations at a level something like that illustrated in (26) and (27), as we shall see in later chapters dealing with actual systems. The main point to notice is that the representations remain language-specific: they typically have source and target language words in them, and they reflect the structure, whether superficially or in more depth, of the respective source and target languages. By contrast, interlingua-based systems attempt to provide representations which are language-independent both in lexicon and in structure.

Before discussing interlinguas, we must look more closely at problems of lexical and structural transfer in transfer-based systems.

6.5.1 Lexical transfer

Lexical transfer consists of the replacement of a source lexical item by a target lexical item. Obviously if there is only one target language equivalent (*north*, French *nord*, German *Nord*; *library*, French *bibliothèque*), then there is no problem, except where there are attendant differences of syntactic structure (see below). But only in the area of technical translation may such one-to-one lexical correspondences (of terms) be expected to be common: *screen – écran*; *hæmoglobin – hémoglobine*; *data processing – Datenverarbeitung*). Equally unproblematic for lexical transfer are many-to-one translations, e.g. German *Mauer* and *Wand*, both translate as English *wall*. The problems arise with the numerous one-to-many translations of lexical items (cf. the examples in section 6.1 above). In some circumstances it may be possible for an MT system to ignore certain translations, because they are rarely used or outdated (e.g. *computer* could be *Rechner* in German, but currently the more usual term is *Computer*), or because one of the possibilities occurs only in a particular sublanguage (section 8.4).

Where choices have to be made it is normal for lexical transfer to require inspection of surrounding context. This is the case with translating *know* (section 6.1) where translation into French or German can be determined from the identification of the complement as a clause or a noun phrase. Another example involves translating *eat* into German: *essen* is chosen if the subject is human, but *fressen* otherwise; in other words, the 'subject' or Agent must be identified and its semantic features checked for compatibility with the selection restrictions of the German verbs. More difficult are translations where the context is less easily defined in terms of adjacent vocabulary: a *library* is in German *Bibliothek* if it is part of an academic or research institution, but *Bücherei* if it is open to the general public. Many examples were given above of cases where for lexical transfer it is necessary to make a distinction that may be obvious to a human but which is difficult to express in terms of local contextually available information.

6.5.2 Structural transfer

Structural transfer is necessary when the structure inherited from the source language is inappropriate for the target language. In theory, the deeper the analysis goes, the less likely this problem is to occur, since the deepening analysis aims at neutralising the distinctions between languages.

Some problems of structural transfer are easier to solve than others. Consider a sentence like (28a) and its translation into French or German.

(28a) Jones likes the film.

(28b) *Le film plaît à Jones.*

(28c) *Der Film gefällt dem Jones.*

While *like* can be said to translate as *plaire* or *gefallen*, the corresponding structures do not match, since the subject of *like* has to be mapped onto the indirect object of *plaire* or the dative object of *gefallen*, while the object of *like* becomes the subject in both cases. This can be treated as a structural 'transfer rule' formulated in a quite straightforward way, perhaps something like (29) for English to French (with other transfer rules implied by the correspondence of similarly labelled elements, e.g. NP2 → NP2′).

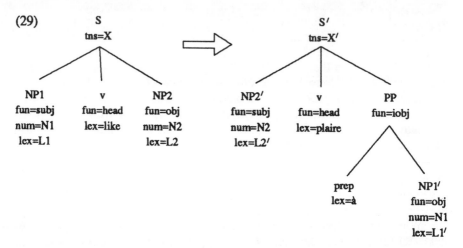

Rather more complex would be the 'transfer rules' for the examples above involving *like* and *gern* (9), verbs of motion in English and French (11-13), and naming verbs (14). All involve substantial structural changes. The partial example rule (30) gives a flavour of this complex structural transfer for *like* and *gern*.

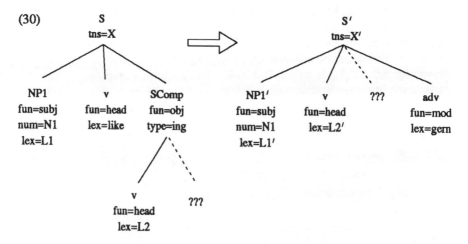

Notice that all the arguments of the embedded verb (indicated by the dotted line and '???') — which may also include further adverbials as in (31a) — have to be somehow transferred up into the top level structure.

(31a) John likes swimming with his friends in the summer.
John schwimmt im Sommer mit seinen Freunden gern.

It should also be noticed that rule (30) has to specify that the SComp contains a present participle (type=ing), since in other constructions *like* can take an infinitival SComp (as in 31b,c) where the transfer rule would again be different.

(31b) John likes his father to play cricket with him.

(31c) John likes to play cricket with his father.

Another example of the necessity for structural transfer comes from Japanese. The translation of sentences like those in (32) into Japanese involves a rule known as the 'animate subject constraint'.

(32a) The wind opened the door.

(32b) The earthquake destroyed the buildings.

(32c) A short walk will bring you to the station.

(32d) Our limited budget will not allow us to start a new project.

This constraint requires the subject of a verb which expresses an action in Japanese to be animate. This does not mean that all action verbs must have an animate subject, since in Japanese it is possible to omit the subject altogether, but formulations like those in (32) are not possible, because in each case the subject is not animate. Instead, the structure of the sentence must be transformed so that the implied subject is expressed, or omitted altogether, and the element which was the subject in the English must be expressed as an adverbial of the appropriate type. So the Japanese translations of the sentences in (32) would be structurally more like the English equivalents in (33).

(33a) By means of the wind the door became open.

(33b) The buildings were destroyed because of the earthquake.

(33c) By walking a short way, you will arrive at the station.

(33d) Owing to our limited budget, we cannot start a new project.

As a final example of structural transfer, we look at nominalizations in English, where it is generally possible, and even stylistically preferred, to construct sentences consisting of complex nominalizations connected by relatively vague verbs like *be, do, have*, rather than use relative clauses involving verbs. This is particularly the case in scientific writing: consider the examples in (34).

(34a) The possibility of rectification of the fault by the insertion of a wedge is discussed.

(34b) There has not been a substantial change in Tokyo residents' consumption of reservoir water despite the announcement by the Government of a period of rationing.

(34c) The extraction of moisture from the air by the dehumidifier made the room more comfortable.

In some languages, however, such constructions, even if they are grammatically possible, are considered very clumsy, difficult to understand, or anglicizations. Japanese and Czech are two such languages, and structure-preserving translations of the above sentences (i.e. translations which reflect the preference for nominalizations), while grammatically correct, would be regarded as stylistically inferior. Structural transfer is required to 'denominalize' the constructions, that is to say locate the underlying verb, identify the functional relationships of the components, and generate from there. The preferred structures would be more like the English equivalents in (35).

> (35a) We discuss whether it is possible to rectify the fault by inserting a wedge
>
> (35b) The amount of reservoir water that Tokyo residents consume has not substantially changed, even though the Government has announced a period during which it will be rationed.
>
> (35c) When they used the dehumidifier to extract the moisture from the air, it became more comfortable in the room.

6.6 Transfer with a structural interlingua

The problems of structural transfer underline the problems with representations which do not neutralize sufficiently the idiosyncracies of even the deep structures of the respective languages. As mentioned in section 2.9.2, it was once thought that the 'deep' structures of transformational-generative grammar might serve as interlingual representations, since they were held to be language-independent bases for semantic interpretations. A more common basis for an interlingual representation is the use of some of the ideas found in Case grammar.

Case roles (also known as 'deep cases', 'semantic roles', 'thematic roles' or 'theta roles') are semantic relations such as Agent, Patient, Experiencer, Instrument, etc., as discussed in section 2.9.6. Some of the less complex problems of structural transfer disappear when this sort of representation is adopted. Examples like (28) above no longer involve complex transfer, since the Case-based representation for both languages can be identical, except for the lexical items (36). Note the usual preference with a Case grammar analysis for a dependency representation rather than a phrase structure tree.

(36)

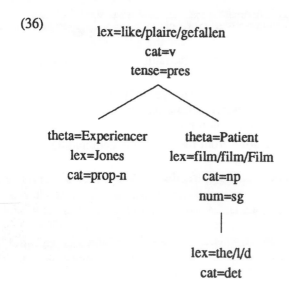

As an interlingual representation, this would be suitable as input to French or German generation, which will derive the appropriate surface structure from the representation, i.e. selecting the Patient as the surface subject, and the Experiencer as the indirect object (and making the necessary selections for tense and gender agreement).

Case structure representations are frequently supposed to reflect universals of syntax which could be regarded as interlingual. Use of Case roles is widespread in bilingual transfer-based MT systems, particularly when one of the languages is Japanese since Case grammar seems to be more appropriate as an analysis model for this language than the kind of phrase structure model often applied to European languages (cf. the examples in (32) where a Case-based analysis would identify the underlying roles of the surface subjects in the English sentences). Unfortunately, despite intensive study by linguists, there is no widely agreed set of Case relations, so researchers in MT systems adopting this approach are generally obliged to devise their own set of Case roles.

Returning to our example sentence (17), it will be recalled that the deepest level of representation so far proposed (26) still left us with some structural transfer regarding the change from the auxiliary-plus-adjective structure to the verb-plus-prepositional object structure of the French. This structural transfer could be avoided by the use of a Case-based representation as in (37). It is convenient here to adopt a feature-structure representation as seen in section 2.8.3.

(37)

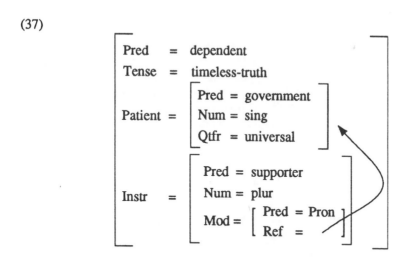

Some of the relationships represented in (37) have already been recognised in (26) and (27), e.g. the co-reference of the possessive pronoun (the Mod of *supporter*) and the Patient of the main predicate — we show here an alternative way of representing co-reference (an explicit 'pointer' instead of the co-indexing 'refer=*1' in (26) and (27)) — either method can be used in these representations. In other aspects the analysis is deeper, reflecting the recognition of *be dependent* as a single predicate, the description of *any* as a 'universal' quantifier, the suppression or replacement of syntax-oriented information such as category, lexical content of minor categories (determiner, possessive pronoun), and grammatical tense, all of which can all be recovered from the other more semantic information contained in the representation. Transfer to the equivalent French (38) is now little more than lexical replacement of *dependent* by *dépendre*, *government* by *gouvernement*, and *supporter* by *défenseur*. All other lexical items in the target text would be derived during generation (see next chapter).

(38)

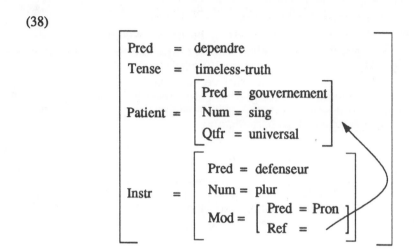

With structures such as (37)–(38) we are close to an interlingua-based representation, but only in respect to structural features; lexical transfer must still be done bilingually. As it happens, the conversion of (37) to (38) does not involve any 'translational ambiguity', but if instead of *government* we had *party* then a choice between *parti* (political party), *groupe* (party of travellers etc.), *partie* (legal term, as in *third party*) and *fête* ('celebration') would have to be made.

6.7 Interlingua-based systems

In interlingua MT systems, the result of source language analysis is a language-independent representation of the text which is the basis for the generation of the target language text. The advantages for multilingual systems have been mentioned already (section 4.2). The disadvantages arise from the fact that analysis and generation have to be strictly separated; it is not desirable to orient analysis towards a particular target language and it is not possible during generation to look back at the original source language text. The interlingua representation has to include all the information that might conceivably be required during the generation of any target language text (or rather more precisely: any target language included in the system now or intended to be added in the future). In effect this high degree of language-independence and neutrality means that interlinguas must strive towards universality in lexicon and structure: one might almost say, towards representing the 'meaning' of the text.

6.7.1 Structural representation in interlingua systems

One candidate for interlingua representation is the use of the formulae of propositional logic, and there has been some experimentation in this area. Taking once again our example sentence (17), a representation based on logical formulae might be something like (39).

> (39) all(X), government(X), indefinite(Y), plural(Y), support(Y,X,T), depend-on(X,Y,T), timeless(T)

Research has shown that it is generally not too difficult to arrive at this sort of representation given an input sentence such as (17). More difficult however is the generation of text from such a representation. For example, the sentences in (40) are only a selection of the possible texts that could be generated (in English) from (39), and it seems that the total absence of information relating to syntactic structure (e.g. indication of topic and comment, or choice of main predicate) makes such a representation inappropriate for translation (though well suited to multilingual **paraphrasing**, if that is an acceptable alternative to translation). In fact, (some of) the paraphrases in (40) could be said to distort the original message. Furthermore, no account has been taken of alternative surface forms for predicates such as 'depend-on(X,Y,T)' or 'support(Y,X,T)'. (It must be stressed that the use of something that resembles an English lexical item as the name of a logical relation should not be taken as an indication of a one-to-one relationship between the relation and the corresponding word.)

(40a) Every government has supporters which it depends on.

(40b) People who support all governments are depended on by them.

(40c) All governments depend on people who support them.

Most interlingua-based systems use representations which are essentially structured like those seen in the previous section for transfer-based systems: the difference is in the abstractness of the representation of structure, and in the treatment of lexical items.

There is general agreement among proponents of the interlingua approach that representations should be hierarchies of substructures showing clear inter-relationships. As already mentioned, in the earlier days of MT research on interlinguas, the Chomskyan theory of deep structures was thought to be attractive, but it is now agreed they are not sufficiently abstract, being too oriented towards the surface features of individual languages. Case grammar was also considered, but as already remarked, there is no agreement yet on a 'universal' set of case roles.

The implications of neutral structural representations can be illustrated by considering differences of word order between languages, and their significance. In English, word order is the primary means of distinguishing grammatical functions like subject and object. In (41), word order alone determines which noun phrase is the 'chaser' (the subject), and which is the 'chased' (the object).

(41a) The man chased the shark.

(41b) The shark chased the man.

Languages such as German and Japanese indicate grammatical functions with overt case-marking, so that word-order differences have other functions: in (42a) and (42b) the man is the topic of discourse (cf. section 2.7), while in (42c) it is the shark. But the underlying event described in (42b) and (42c) remains the same.

(42a) *Der Mann jagte den Haifisch.*

THE-nom MAN CHASED THE-acc SHARK

'The man chased the shark'

(42b) *Den Mann jagte der Haifisch.*

THE-acc MAN CHASED THE-nom SHARK

'It was the man that the shark chased'

(42c) *Der Haifisch jagte den Mann.*

THE-nom SHARK CHASED THE-acc MAN

'The shark chased the man'

Similarly in Japanese (43):

(43a) *Same ga hito wo oikaketa.*

SHARK-nom MAN-acc CHASED

'The shark chased the man'

(43b) *Hito wo same ga oikaketa.*

MAN-acc SHARK-nom CHASED

'It was the man that the shark chased'

In Russian, another highly inflected case-marking language, word order often indicates differences between definiteness and indefiniteness, i.e. between what is 'given' or 'presupposed' and what is mentioned for the first time (cf. section 2.7), as in (44).

(44a) *Ženščina vyšla iz domu.*

WOMAN-nom CAME OUT HOUSE-gen

'The woman came out of the house'

(44b) *Iz domu vyšla ženščina.*

'A woman came out of the house'

The implication for an interlingua is that it is not enough to indicate word order on its own: the interlingua must represent the significance in terms of syntactic relations (grammatical function), topic-focus relations (text function), determination, case role or whatever else the interpretation of the word-order dictates.

Passive, as we saw (in 6.2 above), is not a structure which can be equated across languages. In an interlingual representation it is not sufficient to characterise some structure simply as 'passive': rather the representation has to reflect the interpretation of those aspects of the meaning of the sentence as a whole which are indicated by the use of the passive.

Structural differences such as the *like/gern* examples in (9) can be treated in a (relatively) straightforward manner in transfer-based systems by structural transfer rules (section 6.5.2 above). But in interlingua-based systems the representation must be language-neutral. It could be one with an item corresponding to *like* as the head, or it could be one with an item corresponding to *swim*. The first would be a representation more like that of English, the second would be more like German. Either choice would be arbitrary, but neither would be neutral.

Another example was the expression of movement in examples (11)–(13). As we saw in section 6.2 above, in French the verb expresses direction and an adverbial phrase expresses the mode of transport, while in English the verb expresses the 'motion' and the prepositional phrase expresses the direction. One possible approach for a neutral interlingua representation might be to separate the two elements of 'motion' and 'direction' as in the partial representations shown in (45), where interlingual lexical units are conventionally indicated by angle brackets (for convenience English labels are used):

(45a) He walked across the road

Il traversa la rue à pied

$$
\begin{bmatrix}
\text{Pred} = \text{<MOTION>} \\
\text{Tense} = \text{past} \\
\text{Agent} = \begin{bmatrix} \text{Pred} = \text{Pron} \\ \text{Num} = \text{sing} \\ \text{Pers} = 3 \\ \text{Sex} = \text{male} \end{bmatrix} \\
\text{Instr} = \quad [\ \text{Pred} = \text{<FOOT>}\ ] \\
\text{Loc} = \quad \begin{bmatrix} \text{Pred} = \text{<CROSS>} \\ \text{Obj} = [\ \text{Pred} = \text{<ROAD>}\ ] \end{bmatrix}
\end{bmatrix}
$$

(45b) She drove into town.

Elle entra dans la ville en voiture.

$$
\begin{bmatrix}
\text{Pred} = \text{<MOTION>} \\
\text{Tense} = \text{past} \\
\text{Agent} = \begin{bmatrix} \text{Pred} = \text{Pron} \\ \text{Num} = \text{sing} \\ \text{Pers} = 3 \\ \text{Sex} = \text{female} \end{bmatrix} \\
\text{Instr} = \quad [\ \text{Pred} = \text{<CAR>}\ ] \\
\text{Loc} = \quad \begin{bmatrix} \text{Pred} = \text{<ENTER>} \\ \text{Obj} = [\ \text{Pred} = \text{<TOWN>}\ ] \end{bmatrix}
\end{bmatrix}
$$

A frequent option is to adopt the representation which is common to the majority of the languages of the system. For the 'naming' expressions above (14) (repeated here as (46a–d) for convenience) it is not obvious what could be an interlingual structure. However, the preponderance of constructions using a predicate corresponding to 'name' might suggest that underlying structure might

(45c) They flew from Gatwick.

Ils partirent par avion de Gatwick.

$$
\begin{bmatrix}
\text{Pred} = <\text{MOTION}> \\
\text{Tense} = \text{past} \\
\text{Agent} = \begin{bmatrix} \text{Pred} = \text{Pron} \\ \text{Num} = \text{plur} \\ \text{Pers} = 3 \end{bmatrix} \\
\text{Instr} = \quad [\ \text{Pred} = <\text{PLANE}> \ ] \\
\text{Loc} = \begin{bmatrix} \text{Pred} = <\text{LEAVE}> \\ \text{Obj} = [\ \text{Pred} = \text{"Gatwick"} \ ] \end{bmatrix}
\end{bmatrix}
$$

be something like (46e), which happens to correspond most closely in this case to the German (46b).

(46a) His name is Julian.

(46b) *Er heißt Julian.*

(46c) *Jego zovut Julian.*

(46d) *Il s'appelle Julian.*

(46e)
$$
\begin{bmatrix}
\text{Pred} = <\text{HAS-NAME}> \\
\text{Tense} = \text{present} \\
\text{Agent} = \begin{bmatrix} \text{Pred} = \text{Pron} \\ \text{Num} = \text{sing} \\ \text{Pers} = 3 \\ \text{Sex} = \text{male} \end{bmatrix} \\
\text{Compl} = [\ \text{Pred} = \text{"Julian"} \ ]
\end{bmatrix}
$$

6.7.2 Lexical representation in interlingua systems

The difficulties of devising neutral representations for syntactic structures are matched, perhaps exceeded, by those of establishing neutral representations for lexical units. As with structural differences, the problem for the interlingua approach is again two-fold: deciding on the most appropriate neutral representation, and discovering the procedures for extracting the necessary information from texts. As we have seen, in transfer-based systems there are no problems if for a particular language pair there are one-to-one equivalents; the problems come when there is more than one target word for a single source word. But for an interlingua in a multilingual system there are problems even if only one of the languages involved has two or more potential forms for a single given word in one of the other languages. If an interlingua is to be completely language-neutral, it must represent not the words of one or other of the languages, but language-independent lexical units, effectively **concepts** (see also 6.8 below). Any distinction which is (or can be) expressed lexically in the languages of the system must be represented explicitly in the interlingual representation. These distinctions can reflect grammatical, stylistic and most commonly conceptual differences (section 6.1 above).

It is a massive undertaking, even for closely related languages. For example, if Spanish is one of the languages included, the distinctions between the legs of humans, animals, chairs and tables (example (4c) above) has to be made in the interlingua even if when translating between English and German this distinction is irrelevant (*leg*: *Bein*). If the system were to include Japanese the interlingua ought, in theory, to distinguish eight different <WEAR> concepts, which would have to be identified each time the English word *wear* occurred (see examples (4i) above) — even if the target language were German, and the translation in every case would be *tragen*. The alternative would be to have a single <WEAR> concept in the interlingua, and the selection of the appropriate Japanese form would occur during the generation of the Japanese text. However such a unified concept would be unnatural for the Japanese: as unnatural, in fact, as a single concept for both *dove* and *pigeon* (cf. French *colombe*, German *Taube*) would be for English speakers. The situation is further complicated, as already described (in 6.1) by the fact that English and German, but not Japanese, distinguish between the process of 'putting on' and the state of 'wearing' clothes. A true interlingua would have to distinguish sixteen different concepts in this semantic field: <WEAR-HAT>, <PUT-ON-HAT>, <WEAR-COAT>, <PUT-ON-COAT>, <WEAR-GLOVES>, <PUT-ON-GLOVES>, etc.

In practice, nearly all interlingua systems do not do this; instead they rely on contextual information or real world knowledge when it comes to choosing between translation alternatives (see also section 6.8 below). In other words, they revert to a 'lexical transfer' approach with (more or less) interlingual structural representations, as described in 6.6 above.

The exception is to be found in those systems with an interlingua based on an existing language. To be a candidate, such a language has to be unambiguous, consistent and regular in its lexicon, i.e. have no homographs and polysemes, to be regular and unambiguous in syntactic structures, and to be expressive enough to embrace most (ideally all) conceptual differences of languages. No 'natural' languages meet the specification, but artificial languages devised for international communication and actually used like other spoken and written languages are sometimes thought to be possible candidates. One MT project (DLT at Utrecht) has in fact investigated the use as an 'interlingua' of a modified version of Esperanto, which is relatively free of homography and unambiguous in morphology. However, it is doubtful whether a system using a 'natural language' interlingua should strictly be called an interlingua-based system. This is because translation into this type of interlingua from, say, English is itself an MT system; likewise translation from the interlingua into French or another language. These sub-systems themselves can only be 'direct' or transfer-based, even if analysis and generation processes are simpler than when either source or target languages are true natural languages (for more on the DLT interlingua system see Chapter 17).

6.7.3 'Restricted' interlinguas

While a universal interlingua may not be feasible, in particular as far as the lexicon is concerned, we could nevertheless have a representation which is interlingual for exactly the languages we are dealing with. Such an interlingua would neutralise the differences between the languages in the system but take advantage of their accidental similarities. A system could be imagined for a set of Romance languages, for example, covering only French, Spanish, Italian and Portuguese. The interlingua approach might be feasible because these languages have much in common, both lexical correspondences and similarities in grammatical structures. The Eurotra project (Chapter 14) found that it was possible to establish 'euroversals' in certain semantic fields, i.e. interlingual lexical items having common ranges of meaning and reference for the European Community languages concerned.

An interlingua designed in this way for only a small set of European languages becomes even more feasible if we also impose restrictions on the breadth of coverage of such a system, so as to reduce the number of lexical items in the system and the problem of polysemy, or to control the number of syntactic constructions we expect to be able to treat. This 'restricted syntax controlled vocabulary' approach to MT system design is discussed further in Chapter 8.

At this point it is perhaps appropriate to comment on the use of the term 'interlingua' in the MT community. In this discussion, we have taken the term to mean a 'language-neutral intermediate representation'. By 'language-neutral', we have not of course meant that the representation has no linguistic content but only that it is not committed to or does not reflect the surface characteristics of a particular language. As this last section has shown, in practice an 'interlingua' is a representation FOR A GIVEN SET OF LANGUAGES which neutralizes their individual differences. This is of course a theoretically less committed viewpoint than the idea of a 'universal' interlingua, though in practical terms it is probably more tractable; indeed, there is a tendency in the most recent discussions of MT system design towards this conception. Finally, it should be pointed out that the perhaps natural gloss of 'interlingua' as 'intermediate language' can often be misleading. In most cases, an interlingua is a REPRESENTATION, i.e. a data structure in the computational sense of the word, and not a LANGUAGE in the usual sense at all. The exceptions are only the rare use of natural or auxiliary languages (e.g. Esperanto) as interlingual representations. It is therefore misleading for the term 'intermediate language' to be used when referring to the types of interface representations found in transfer-based or indeed in most interlingua-based systems.

6.8 Knowledge-based methods

The discussion so far has concentrated almost exclusively on linguistic approaches to problems of transfer and interlinguas. However, lexical translational differences are also, and inevitably, reflections of differences in cultural backgrounds and differences in conceptual divisions of the same 'reality'. The *rice* example (4h) is a good example of a cultural difference in the culinary sphere; the *wear* example (4i) illustrates a difference in the conceptual partitioning of a universal activity.

It has therefore been argued that translation should be based on non-linguistic **conceptual** representations, or — in alternative formulations — on representations of **meanings** derived from the processes of **understanding** of texts. Understanding a text involves relating what is said in a text (its linguistic content) to phenomena (entities, actions, events) outside the text (the non-linguistic 'reality'). Readers interpret texts with reference to what they know about the 'real world' or what worlds they can imagine. On the assumption that meanings and understanding are common and universal to all speakers of human languages, it follows that these 'conceptual' representations are interlingual, that they can serve as intermediate representations in MT systems, and that with the help of suitable 'knowledge bases' texts can be analysed into and generated from such interlingual representations.

We have seen already how reference to **real world knowledge** can assist in the analysis of texts (section 5.3.2.3). Its use in interlingua-based systems goes somewhat further. In this case the intention is not just to resolve ambiguities in the source text but to derive language-independent representations. Returning to the *wear* example (section 6.1 above), the knowledge base of a true interlingua ought to be capable of distinguishing the sixteen (or more) different aspects of wearing and putting on clothes. It would do so, presumably, on the basis of knowledge about different types of apparel (hats, coats, socks, etc.), about social, cultural, ethnic differences (ceremonial dress, working clothes, children's wear, tropical clothing, Arctic clothing, rainwear, etc.), and about the activities involved with them (making, buying, wearing, removing, washing, repairing, etc.)

The practical complexity of the task inevitably restricts the approach to highly restricted domains with relatively narrow contexts and applications. It is also true to say that knowledge-based MT systems have so far concentrated on the disambiguation of source texts and have not tackled the derivation of universal language-independent representations capable of providing information for generation in any other language. One MT project which is exploring the possibilities is described in section 18.1 below (the KBMT project at Carnegie Mellon University).

6.9 Example-based methods

Developments in computer technology, which are providing faster access to larger memories and data stores, are encouraging the investigation of methods based on access to huge corpora of texts in source and target languages. The basic argument is that translation is often a matter of finding or recalling analogous examples, discovering or remembering how a particular source language expression or something similar to it has been translated before.

Proposals for **example-based** methods are put forward generally as alternatives to knowledge-based approaches and as supplementary aids to the traditional rule-based methods of analysis, transfer and generation. The linguistic databank of 'examples' would be derived from a structural analysis of a large corpus of source texts and their translations in a target language produced by human translators. The result is bilingual sets of phrases; for example, English phrases containing *field* and their French equivalents in the database (Table 6.1).

the main fields	*les principaux domaines*
the following fields	*les domaines suivants*
these two fields	*ces deux domaines*
the specialized fields	*les domaines spécialisés*
the para-medical fields	*activités paramédicales*
the magnetic fields	*les champs magnétiques*
the coal fields	*les bassins-houiliers*
the coal fields	*les bassins*
the corn fields	*les champs de blé*

Table 6.1 Database of aligned examples

Whether *field* is to be translated as *domaine*, *champ* or *bassin* is determined by the frequency of phrases most similar in context to the given example. Exact matches will obviously cause few problems, but they will be rare; for instance, in the list above there is no match for *gold field*. The identification of 'similarity' depends on some measure of distance of meaning; in current proposals this is based on the classification of lexical items in semantic hierarchies, e.g. *field* might be listed under the heading 'range' along with *scope*, *sphere* and *arena*; and under 'enclosure' with *compound*, *yard* and *paddock*; and so forth. In the case of *gold field*, the hierarchy would indicate a smaller distance from *gold* to *coal* than from *gold* to *corn* and hence a higher probability for the translation of *field* as *bassin* than as *champ*.

The example-based approach is particularly attractive for the translation of complex noun phrases. Generally, Japanese noun phrases of the form 'N_1 *no* N_2' correspond to English noun phrases of the form 'N_2 *of* N_1'; but there are many exceptions: it is more idiomatic to say *application fee for the conference* than *application fee of the conference*, *conference in Tokyo* rather than *conference of Tokyo*, and literal translations from Japanese such as **holiday of a week*, **reservation of hotel* or *hotels of three are not permitted in place of *week's holiday*, *hotel reservation* and *three hotels*. There are similar difficult areas with other language pairs: consider the multiplicity of translations into English of the French *de*. The availability of analogous examples and probabilistic measures of distance could enable such problematic areas of lexical transfer to be handled more satisfactorily than attempts to devise rules based on grammatical categories and structures and the presence or absence of case roles, semantic features and the like. (We describe a proposed example-based MT system in more detail in section 18.2.)

Example-based techniques can also be used for translating sentences which are structurally similar to previously translated sentences. Again a similarity measure is required, though in this case it will be based on distribution of key elements such as grammatical words, or it may measure the similarity of certain sequences of grammatical categories, or a combination of these. For instance, the sample sentence in (47a) might be matched against any text consisting of a sequence such as that in (47b), where X may be any noun or adjective-plus-noun, and Y may be any noun phrase, and its translation a copy of the translation of (47a), with the non-matching parts translated separately.

(47a) Remove the bulb and replace it with a new one.

(47b) Remove the X and replace it with Y.

This approach could be likened to the use by a (linguistically sophisticated) tourist of a phrasebook, where new utterances can be built up by combining the appropriate elements of the phrases given. (For an experimental system based on this idea, see section 18.5.)

The example-based method should be distinguished from **corpus-based** approaches to MT. In the latter, systems (of whatever type) are developed for translating a subset of texts in a particular corpus and then applied to the translation of other texts in the same corpus. Example-based methods are not necessarily restricted either to particular corpora or to particular sublanguages (section 8.4). Initially, given the effort involved in building the databases, the method will almost certainly be applied within specific domains. However, as far as general vocabulary is concerned, examples taken from one corpus may be just as effective for translating texts in another subject area.

Although it is a natural assumption that example-based methods work best with structured sets of bilingual texts, the experiments at IBM mentioned earlier (section 6.3) show that correspondences of units in source and target texts can also be established by statistical means alone. However, to what extent this extreme position proves valid has yet to be demonstrated. (For more on this system see section 18.3.)

Finally, it should be evident that the example-based approach can be integrated in any of the basic models: direct, transfer, and interlingua. Unlike the knowledge-based method, which is dependent on semantic analysis to a high degree of abstraction, it can operate with relatively shallow analyses of surface structures and relatively simple lexical transfer procedures, i.e. it can be applied to any level of transfer: from morphological to interlingual.

6.10 Summary: comparison of transfer-based and interlingua-based systems

This chapter has illustrated the principal problems of converting lexical and structural information from one language into another for each of the three basic MT designs: direct, transfer-based and interlingua-based. At one extreme, the 'shallow' analyses of direct systems impose heavy burdens on bilingual lexicons and inevitably result in *ad hoc* treatments of structural changes. At the other extreme, the 'conceptual meaning' representations required for interlingua-based systems demand a complexity of semantic analysis beyond the limitations of current linguistic theory. It is generally agreed that transfer-based approaches are at present the best foundations for advances in MT. As we have seen, there are a number of options available: different levels of lexical and structural representation, and different potentials for interlingual elements.

In practical terms, the flexibility of the transfer-based approach overcomes one apparent drawback in comparison with interlingua systems, namely the cost of adding a new language to the system (section 4.2). Although in a multilingual system the transfer methodology requires the construction of a large number of transfer modules, the analysis modules are normally (as we have seen) simpler than interlingual representations, and they can be varied in depth and abstractness according to the languages concerned.

In certain respects, the differences between transfer and interlingua systems are relative. In practice, many systems which are described as 'interlingual' deal only with a single pair of languages, so they differ little in 'depth' of abstractness and universality from many transfer-based systems. But the main point which needs to be stressed is that whatever the framework the same problems of lexical and structural transfer are present: whether in an interlingua or a transfer-based system, the problems of knowing how to translate a certain construction (passive, say) or how to deal with a transfer ambiguity (*wall* into German) remain the same.

Within the transfer-based framework there are also many possible variants. The diagrammatic presentation in Figure 6.1 above is evidently a simplification. Transfer does not necessarily cut across the pyramid horizontally, i.e. between representations of equivalent abstraction. It can be imagined in some cases as cutting across diagonally, representing the respective amount of work done in analysis, transfer and generation, as shown in Figure 6.2. Also, where we have transfer between closely related language pairs having fairly similar structures, a relatively simple transfer can be achieved with a shallower degree of analysis taking advantage of the similarities, i.e. the base of the pyramid would be narrower to start with.

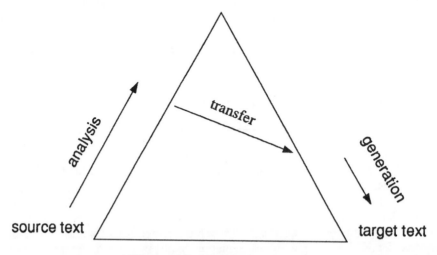

Figure 6.2 Modified pyramid

From a theoretical point of view there is one major advantage in the transfer-based approach. Although translation must involve monolingual linguistic analysis, it is concerned primarily with questions of **contrastive linguistic analysis**, namely the comparison of the devices that two (or more) languages employ to convey similar meanings. In the interlingua approach, all the contrastive linguistics is hidden in the monolingual analysis and generation, so there can be no separation of the linguistic theories driving the source language analysis, the bilingual transfer linguistics, and the target language generation. Any element of contrastive linguistics is implicit in the structure of the interlingua. With an interlingua system it is difficult to focus specifically on the contrastive aspects of translation, because the interlingua forces the linguist to abstract away from that aspect of translation. In a transfer system however, it is precisely in the transfer module that those purely contrastive differences are captured and dealt with, by whichever method or technique that is most appropriate: lexical substitution, structural change, universal items or features, reference to a knowledge base, statistical probabilities — in fact any of the options described in this chapter.

6.11 Further reading

General discussions of the transfer vs. interlingua problem are to be found in Krauwer and des Tombe (1984), Tucker (1987:22–26), Somers (1987b), Tsujii (1986, 1988) and Boitet (1988).

Examples of lexical translation difficulties are taken from many sources: indeed some of the examples are so widely cited as to have become clichés. The issue of the Eskimo word for 'snow' is discussed by Martin (1986) and Pullum (1989).

Similarly, structural translation difficulties are widely discussed, with the '*like/gern*' problem taken as the standard example.

The 'pyramid' diagram in Figure 6.1 is now a universal symbol, but was first used by the Grenoble team, and probably first appeared (in a slightly different form) in Vauquois (1968).

The 'animate subject constraint' is discussed in Nishida *et al.* (1980). Nominalizations are the subject of a paper by Somers *et al.* (1988).

Systems which use unification-based linguistic techniques and functional representations typify the 'structural interlingua with lexical transfer' approach and include the MiMo2 system (van Noord *et al.* 1990) and basic research work by Rohrer (1986), Kaplan *et al.* (1989), Zajac (1989, 1990) and Sadler *et al.* (1990). The issue is also discussed in Luckhardt (1987).

There have been several notable attempts at interlingua-based MT (see Hutchins 1986:Ch.10). Besides those mentioned in the text, contemporary approaches include those of the Japanese commercial systems of Fujitsu (Uchida 1988, 1989) and NEC (Harada 1986).

Using formulae of propositional logic is an approach currently being investigated by Hobbs and Kameyama (1990). References for the DLT system, which uses Esperanto as an interlingua, are given in Chapter 17. Carnegie Mellon's Knowledge-Based MT is discussed in section 18.1.

Experiments in Example-Based MT are described by Sato and Nagao (1990) (who call it 'Memory-based MT') and Sumita *et al.* (1990). The EBMT system proposed by the DLT group is described in more detail in section 18.2. The statistics-based approach of the IBM researchers is described in section 18.3.

7
Generation

In this chapter we shall discuss the **generation** of target language texts. We should immediately distinguish this use of the term 'generation' from its use in phrases like 'first generation' and 'second generation' which refer to historical stages in the development of MT systems (Chapters 1 and 4). An alternative term for the computation of target texts from intermediate representations is **synthesis.** Some authors have tried to make a distinction between 'generation' and 'synthesis', depending on the degree of specification of the input to this phase: 'synthesis' would involve more interpretation of the input structure than more straightforward 'generation'. In this and following chapters, however, we shall continue to treat the two terms as synonymous, and, generally, prefer the more common term 'generation'.

7.1 Generation in direct systems

We begin by looking at the notion of target language generation in direct systems of the 'first generation'. From an examination of the basic architecture of direct systems (see Figure 4.1, reproduced here as Figure 7.1) and from the description of transfer processes in these systems in the last chapter (section 6.4), it should already be clear that in a sense there is no interesting target-language generation at all, as such. In comparison with the 'indirect' interlingual and transfer-based systems (Figures 4.2 and 4.4) it is hard to say where analysis of the source language stops and generation of the target language starts: there is processing oriented towards the target language at an early stage (lexical substitution during

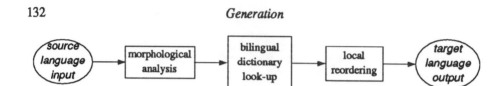

Figure 7.1 Direct MT system

dictionary look-up) and there is processing influenced by the source language at late stages (local reordering of structures).

The 'local reordering' phase can be seen as a mixture of transfer and generation. Input to the module is target language lexical items in source language word order. It is a 'transfer' process in so far as source text structures are transformed into target text structures (cf. Chapter 6), and it represents a 'generation' process in so far as the output consists of target language lexical items in target language sequences. An example of 'local reordering' was given in section 6.4 involving the reversal of the adjective–noun sequence in translating from English into French. The final phase ('text synthesis') is concerned, therefore, almost exclusively with procedures to ensure correct word endings (e.g. *try* plus *-ed* as *tried*) and morphological agreement (e.g. adjectives and nouns in French). It is the only stage which can be rightly called one of 'generation' in that it involves only target language information and operates independently of the source text. Nevertheless, it is rudimentary, consisting only of morphological processing.

In direct systems, therefore, generation is based as much as possible on source language structures: nothing is changed more than strictly necessary for the production of an 'acceptable' target language word order. As we saw in section 6.4, most of these changes are determined by specific information attached to source language lexical items; very little is controlled by general operations. The inextricable mixture of transfer and generation is now seen as a major disadvantage of direct systems (particularly those of the 'first generation'). The lack of modularity means that improvements are almost impossible once the systems are in operation. Later direct systems have increased modularity, and some separation of 'transfer' and 'generation' procedures is found, although the basic orientation of the processing to specific source and target languages remains. Examples of systems which exhibit these features are given in the descriptions of Systran (Chapter 10) and of Météo (Chapter 12).

7.2 Generation in indirect systems

In general, indirect systems reflect a more sophisticated attitude to the linguistic and computational aspects of MT system design. Nevertheless, when it comes to target language generation, several systems still go about it in a rather crude manner. First, it is not infrequent to find a mixture of transfer and generation: they may well have a distinct and independent analysis phase (i.e. one that takes no account of target language structures), but they do not necessarily make a clear separation of transfer and generation procedures (for example, METAL, described in Chapter 15). Second, the basic approach in most cases can be characterized as 'pre-determined' in that only the first and most straightforward possibility is considered at each point in the generation process. The disadvantages of this approach is discussed later (section 7.3) after describing typical generation procedures.

7.2.1 Generation in transfer-based systems

In a transfer system, the generation phase is generally split into two modules, 'syntactic generation' and 'morphological generation'. In **syntactic generation** the intermediate representation which is output from analysis and transfer resembles a deep-structure tree of the older type of transformational-generative grammar (cf. example (27) in section 6.5). It is converted by 'transformational rules' into an ordered surface-structure tree, with appropriate labelling of the leaves with target language grammatical functions and features. The basic task of syntactic generation is to order constituents in the correct sequence for the target language.

For example, if a sentence is labelled 'passive' in the deep structure, syntactic generation will create a node for the auxiliary verb, labelled with the appropriate tense information, and will assign the 'past-participle' label to the main verb. Similarly, if a noun phrase has a clausal modifier and this has to appear as a relative clause in the target, syntactic generation involves the selection of an appropriate relative pronoun and an appropriately tensed verb form. Sometimes, an argument of a verb which was, for example, the direct object in the source language has to be a prepositional object in the target language (cf. French *chercher* and *regarder* with direct objects, and English *look for* and *look at*). Assuming that transfer retains the simpler direct object construction in the intermediate representation, it will be in the syntactic generation module that the prepositional phrase structure is created.

The resulting 'surface' structure is then input to **morphological generation**, which interprets strings of labelled lexical items for output as target sentences. It is generally relatively straightforward: the labelled string '*dog*+plural' to give *dogs* in output, German '*machen*+past+plural' to give *machten*, etc. In some cases morphological rules are a little more complex (e.g. French '*remplir*+imperfect+3rd-person+plural' → *remplissaient*), and of course there must be special rules to handle irregular forms ('*go*+past' → *went*). In general, morphological generation can usually be handled by a combination of general and special-case procedures, on a word-by-word basis.

It is appropriate at this point to look at a simple example based on Ariane (a system described in detail in Chapter 13). This example is derived from the German-to-French version, with some details altered for the sake of clarity. The representation for the input sentence (1) after lexical and structural transfer is given in (2).

(1) *Das Energieproblem ist zu einer grossen Herausforderung geworden.*
'The energy problem has become a major challenge'

It should be noticed that the basic structure of (2) is somewhat like that of the German sentence: the main verb is still at the end, and some of the values of label features also derive directly from the German analysis. For example, the analysis of *Herausforderung* ('challenge') as a derived verbal noun in German has been retained in the features for the French equivalent, given here by the underlying verb *défier*. Other features have been inserted during lexical and structural transfer, particularly the values for the lexical units themselves.

(2)

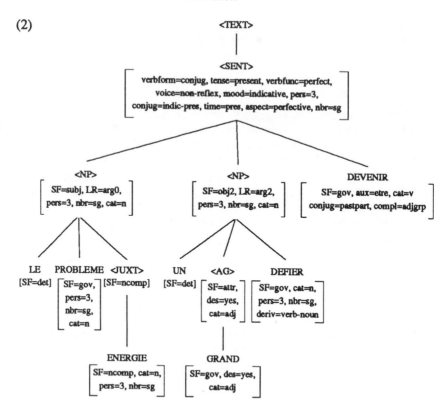

The task of syntactic generation is to convert this representation into a surface structure for the corresponding French sentence. It involves for example looking at the labelling on the top node <SENT> in order to select an appropriate verb form. In this case the labels 'perfective' and 'present' indicate the introduction of an auxiliary, and the 'aux=etre' label on the DEVENIR node specifies which auxiliary it should be. In a similar way, the labelling of <JUXT> as 'ncomp' indicates that the noun complement *énergie* must be transformed into a prepositional phrase introduced by *de*. A further task of syntactic generation is the distribution of number and gender information to relevant terminal nodes. For example, determiners and adjectives should agree in number and gender with the governing noun in a noun phrase; the auxiliary verb, which is to show the tense (from features on <SENT>), should agree in number with the subject noun (phrase); and the past participle should also agree in number and gender with the subject. The resulting surface structure tree (3) may still show constituents from the intermediate representation, but they are ignored in final output.

This structure is now subjected to a simple **morphological generation** routine. This works through the tree top-down and left-to-right. Each time it comes to a terminal node, the set of labellings are interpreted according to morphological rules. For example the node labelled LE [nbr=sg, gend=f, vwl=yes] corresponds to the string *l'*; ETRE [tense=pres, pers=3, nbr=sg] to *est*; GRAND [des=yes, nbr=sg, gend=m] to *grand*; and so on. The result is the surface string (4).

(3)

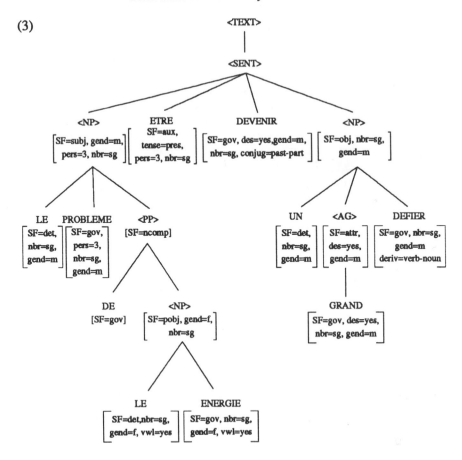

(4) *Le problème de l'énergie est devenu un grand défi.*

Morphological generation is generally no more complex than this: the problem of generating *l'* rather than *la* in (4) can be handled by a kind of agreement feature ('vwl=yes'), though it should be noted that such essentially phonetic rules are sensitive to word order rather than grammatical constituency. For example, the choice between *a* and *an* in English is determined by the next word in the sentence, not by the head noun. Other problems for morphological generation include the choice of different stems for different endings, e.g. *good+er* → *better*, French *aller*+2nd person+sing+present → *vais*. There are however a number of rather more subtle problems. Sometimes a morphologically derived form is available as an alternative to a full form: for example, *painter* and *artist* (which differ little semantically). And, just as in morphological analysis, compounding can be a major headache, when some means has to be found for deciding whether or not elements should be recombined as compounds, e.g. *drainage filtering system* vs. *system for filtering during drainage*, or German *System für Übersetzung* vs. *Übersetzungssystem* ('translation system').

7.2.2 Generation in interlingua systems

In essence, the procedures for generating texts in interlingua-based systems parallel those described for transfer-based systems. Generation includes stages of syntactic and morphological generation. The main difference is that the starting point, the input, is not a 'deep-structure' syntactic representation, such as (2), but an interlingua representation based probably on predicate–argument structures. Examples of such structures were given in section 6.7. The 'deep' syntactic structure must first be generated from the interlingual representation by a stage often known as **semantic generation.**

The process may be described using example (5), which has been adapted from (37) in section 6.7. As before, interlingual lexical items in the representation are indicated by angled brackets, with English labels for convenience.

(5)

$$
\begin{bmatrix}
\text{Pred} & = & \text{<DEPEND>} \\
\text{Tense} & = & \text{timeless-truth} \\
\text{Patient} & = & \begin{bmatrix} \text{Pred} = \text{<GOVERNMENT>} \\ \text{Num} = \text{sing} \\ \text{Qtf} = \text{universal} \end{bmatrix} \\
\text{Inst} & = & \begin{bmatrix} \text{Pred} = \text{<SUPPORTER>} \\ \text{Num} = \text{plur} \\ \text{Mod} = \begin{bmatrix} \text{Pred} = \text{Pron} \\ \text{Ref} = \end{bmatrix} \end{bmatrix}
\end{bmatrix}
$$

The 'deep' structure to be generated is (6) (also given as (27) in section 6.5).

Starting with the topmost Pred <DEPEND>, the 'semantic generation' module must select a verb in the target language (in our case, French) as head of the sentence. The choice of *dépendre* entails the formation of a complement structure ('fun=compl') corresponding to the Inst in (5). This consists of an appropriate prepositional 'case' marker and a dependent noun phrase, corresponding to the structure of the Inst, with as its head the target language equivalent of <SUPPORTER>, i.e. *défenseur*, and the feature 'num=pl' derived in an obvious way from the 'Num=plur' feature in (5). At the same time, the feature 'timeless-truth' is attached to the top node (S) as the target language feature 'tns=pres'. The Patient feature structure in (5) is converted into an NP with the feature 'fun=subj', with the noun *gouvernement* (the target equivalent of <GOVERNMENT>) as its head, and its quantifier (Qtf=universal) giving the determiner *tout* and the singular number for the whole NP. Finally, the generation module produces a representation of the reference link (Ref) from the Mod of <SUPPORTER> to the subject NP. It is achieved by creating a possessive pronoun (posptron) with a referential co-index to the subject NP (i.e. attaching the feature 'refer=*1' to both nodes): for French (unlike English with *his*, *her*, *its* and *their*), only the number of the antecedent

(6)

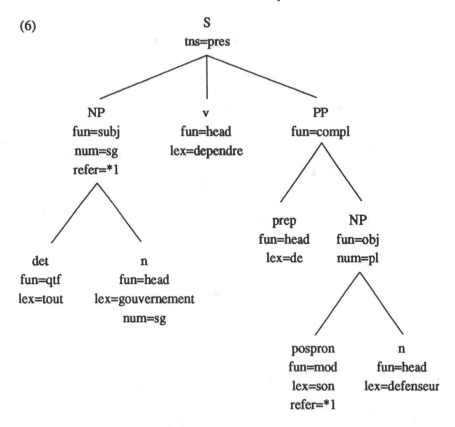

is important for choosing the appropriate possessive pronoun (*son* or *leur*, though number and gender agreement with the noun it modifies may result in a different surface form, e.g. *sa*, *leurs* etc.). The number information from the antecedent is added to the representation.

Subsequent stages of syntactic and morphological generation would then proceed as outlined above for a transfer-based system. The result would be (7a), the translation of (7b) (example (17) in section 6.3).

(7a) *Tout gouvernement dépend de ses défenseurs.*

(7b) Any government is dependent on its supporters.

7.3 Pre-determined choices and structure preservation

In certain respects the approaches to generation in indirect systems are merely more sophisticated versions of the approach in the earliest direct systems. There are two major problems with this model: the assumed 'pre-determination' of target language generation, and the implication of 'structure preservation' as a methodology in translation.

In the context of generation **pre-determination** means that for any given deep representation that is derived from an interlingua or from transfer, there should be one (and only one) corresponding surface structure. The opposite approach would be where choices have to be made between the possible surface structures which may be generated from the same representation.

The reasons for adopting pre-determination as a strategy in generation seem to be computational: a generation module in which the correspondence between one representation and another (deep and surface syntax, or intermediate representation and text in the extreme case) is easier to implement and maintain. It means that once transfer is complete, the remainder of the translation process is a straightforward process. It may involve a lot of computation, but it should not be complicated. The alternative entails the development of algorithms for choosing appropriate structures; it introduces added complexity.

The assumption of pre-determination goes against what is known both by linguists and by translators: that there is no one-to-one correspondence between meaning and form. From the linguist's point of view, this is expressed by observing that, just as one surface string may have several different possible deep structures (structural ambiguity, section 5.3 above), so a given deep structure can be mapped onto different surface structures. In Chomskyan linguistics this fact was captured by the postulation of optional transformations which preserved meaning (section 2.9.2) A translator knows very well that there are hundreds of ways that a given text can be expressed in the target language: in fact, most translators would regard the task of expressing the meaning of a source text, rather than initial understanding of the text, as the aspect of translation which requires most skill.

Although MT is not, of course, the same as human translation, the somewhat naïve assumption that generation should be pre-determined in this sense has the result that systems tend to produce rather stilted translations with very little variety in style. In itself, this may be seen as an advantage, especially when MT is used for technical translations, where the main requirement is accuracy and fidelity to the original (see Chapter 9); but on the whole the principle results in MT output of a lower quality than it might be.

The basic problems are too close adherence to the structures of source texts and the treatment of sentences independently. To avoid making choices during generation, it is seen as preferable to retain the structure of original sentences in texts: structure preservation is adopted as the option of first choice. If at all feasible, the structure of the source language is preserved in the generation of the target language; and, as a result, translations are as literal as possible. Rearrangement of structures takes place only under certain predefined conditions. In this respect, MT is in direct contrast with human translation, where preservation of sentence structure is normally the LAST choice; even the sequence of sentences is often changed. Only when the exact meaning of the source text is perhaps unclear (and the original author is unavailable for clarification), do translators generally resort to translating more or less phrase by phrase.

Text generation is a major concern of many researchers outside MT in the field of natural language communication, in particular those interested in database interrogation. In this context the aim is to respond in natural language to users' requests for information. The factual content of the texts to be generated is derived from the internal representation of the information in the database. Initially, the most popular technique for generating responses was that of **direct replacement,** in which representations were merely transformed into natural language sentences more or less in the pre-determined manner described above. The inflexibility of the approach became soon obvious. It was clear that the most appropriate and natural reply to a query ought to take into account the context in which it was made; it should not make unnecessary and unnatural repetitions, and it should relate to what has gone before, i.e. the generation of texts has to make full use of ellipsis, pronominalization, and topic-comment structuring, any of which might differ from one language to another (consider how in examples (5) and (6) above it was assumed that the possessive pronoun in the source text should appear as a possessive pronoun in the target.) Text generation is now seen as a series of decision points involving choices conditioned by a vast range of information including, but by no means restricted to, the propositional content of the texts to be generated.

This approach to text generation would take into account information about the pragmatic situation, whether 'new' or 'old' information is being communicated, what links are being made to previous sentences, etc. (section 2.7) For example, consider again the sentences in (8) (which we saw in the last chapter).

(8a) *Der Mann jagte den Haifisch.*
THE MAN-subj CHASED THE SHARK-obj

(8b) *Den Mann jagte der Haifisch.*
THE MAN-obj CHASED THE SHARK-subj

If the input representation to the generation module were to retain the 'subject' specification of the original, i.e. *Mann* in (8a) and *Haifisch* in (8b); and if the rules for generating English state that the 'grammatical subject' should appear first in the sentence (which is the norm in English), then the resulting translation would be as in (9).

(9a) The man chased the shark.

(9b) The shark chased the man.

But this would be wrong for (9b). While (8a) and (9a) have both the same topic (*Mann* and *man*), (8b) and (9b) do not (*Mann* and *shark*). In fact, (9b) corresponds to (10a). What should happen is that the marked thematization of (8b) should be preserved (cf. section 2.7). In order to retain the same topic-comment structure, *man* should be the first noun in the English. This means either a 'focus' construction (10b) or a passive structure (10c).

(10a) *Der Haifisch jagte den Mann.*
THE SHARK-subj CHASED THE MAN-obj

(10b) It was the man that the shark chased.

(10c) The man was chased by the shark.

Other factors which should influence text generation come broadly under the heading of 'style'; for example, the choice between an adjectival phrase and a relative clause (11), between different types of passive (12), and between alternative expressions for generic nouns (13).

(11a) the late trains

(11b) the trains which are late

(12a) The cake is eaten.

(12b) The cake gets eaten.

(12c) Someone eats the cake.

(13a) The lion is dangerous.

(13b) A lion is dangerous.

(13b) Lions are dangerous.

In the context of translation two further points should be made. First, the kinds of choices just exemplified are often conditioned by quite different criteria in different languages: for example, heavy pre-nominal modification is quite permissible in German but only rarely in English, cf. (14) and (15).

(14) *die in den letzten zehn Jahren entwickelnden Industrien*
   THE IN THE LAST TEN YEARS DEVELOPING INDUSTRIES
   'the industries (which have been) developing in the last ten years'

(15) the above mentioned problem

Second, the syntactic devices used to express various choices are not always equivalent between languages: German expresses thematization by word order (16a) while this is not always possible in English (16b) or French (16c). English has available a variety of alternative devices (16d,e). In these examples the issue of quantifier scope is also involved, a problem in generation just as in analysis (cf. section 5.5).

(16a) *Nur Kuchen hat das Kind gegessen.*

(16b) * Only cakes has eaten the child.

(16c) * *Seulement des gâteaux a mangé l'enfant.*

(16d) The child has eaten nothing but cakes.

(16e) It is only cakes that the child has eaten.

7.4 Stylistic improvements in generation

The structure-preserving approach continues to be popular for good practical reasons. On the one hand, problems of analysis and transfer are complex and difficult to resolve. If a simple version of generation produces reasonable results — ones which, though not perfect, can be post-edited relatively easily or serve the purpose of conveying more or less accurately the meaning of the original text to the reader — then it makes sense to adopt it. On the other hand, until fairly recently most MT systems have translated between Indo-European languages with broadly similar basic structures. As a general rule, for these languages a verb in the source language corresponds to a verb in the target language, an adjective corresponds to an adjective, a subject–predicate structure remains more or less constant, and so on. Exceptions can be treated by special procedures in 'structural transfer' (section 6.5.2). But the basic assumption can be maintained that it is in fact possible to retain source language sentence structures.

The inadequacy of this approach became obvious when more MT research tackled translation between languages of greater typological diversity (notably English and Japanese). One example was illustrated in the previous chapter: the so-called 'animate subject constraint' in Japanese. An even greater difference between the two languages is the 'action-orientation' of English and the 'process-orientation' of Japanese. In English it is more natural to express events in terms of someone doing something, while in Japanese it is the tendency to focus on the object undergoing the action. For example, a natural translation of (17a) would be (17b) rather than (17c). Although grammatical and meaningful, sentence (17c) refers to the physical capacity of sight and might imply that the speaker has been cured of blindness.

(17a) I can see Mount Fuji.

(17b) *Fuji-san ga mieru.*
'Mt. Fuji can be seen'

(17c) *(Watashi wa) Fuji-san wo miru koto ga dekiru.*
'It is possible (for me) to see Mt. Fuji'

In confronting these problems, a clear division between the respective roles of analysis, transfer and generation needs to be maintained. The analysis module should be expected to deal with source language ambiguities, the transfer module with questions of contrastive lexical and structural differences, and the generation module should be expected to handle any problems which are matters of choice in the target language. In all the examples so far the criteria for choosing among different expressions of a given 'meaning' can be stated without reference to the source language: the differences between the alternatives in examples (11)–(13) are features of English, and are quite independent of the way the same ideas might have been expressed in a source language, be it French, Russian or Japanese.

The first requirement, therefore, is some means in the generation module for determining the criteria to be applied in particular instances. Sometimes this is easier than others: a structure-preserving translation into English of (14) would not actually be completely ungrammatical, but in order to block its generation there would need to be a 'preference rule' stating that noun modifiers consisting of anything much more than an adverb and an adjective are not to be produced. Similarly it should be possible to formulate a rule which would allow (18a) but prevent a large noun phrase appearing as an indirect object before a short direct object as in (18b).

(18a) John gave the man a book.

(18b) * John gave the man he met yesterday in the park after he'd been for a hamburger a book.

On the other hand, without considerable contextual and pragmatic information it might be impossible to choose between the two variants in (19).

(19a) The boy gave his sister a book.

(19b) The boy gave a book to his sister.

More complex and problematic would be the coding for choosing from amongst the permutations of translations for the German sentence (20a), where for each component part in the English representation — very roughly as in (20b) — there are various possibilities (20c).

(20a) *Technologische Fortschritte sind ein entscheidender Bestandteil der Entwicklung, insbesonders für Länder, die für ihr Energiebedarf vom Import abhängen.*
TECHNOLOGICAL ADVANCES ARE A(N) ESSENTIAL INGREDIENT OF-THE DEVELOPMENT ESPECIALLY FOR COUNTRIES WHICH FOR THEIR ENERGY-NEED FROM-THE IMPORT DEPEND

(20b)

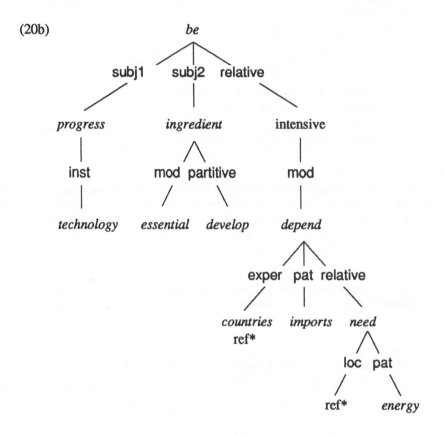

(20c) Technological progress/advance(s)...
    Progress/Advance(s) in technology...
    ... is/are an essential ingredient of development...
    ... is/are an ingredient which is essential for/in development...
    An essential ingredient of development is technological progress/advance(s)...
    ... especially/particularly for (those) countries...
    ... (which are) dependent on imports for their energy needs...
    ... which depend on imports for their energy needs...
    ... whose energy needs are dependent on imports...
    ... whose energy needs depend on imports

It should be noticed in particular that whatever the criteria for making the choices are, the corresponding choices in the German source text are more or less irrelevant.

An important point to note about this view of generation is that it requires a high degree of language independence, i.e. that intermediate representations should go further towards neutralizing the accidental syntactic characteristics of source languages. It is a problem for both transfer-based and interlingua systems, but in this case the motivation is clear: the interface structure should contain just the information that is necessary to permit appropriate decisions to be made by the generation module.

In this section, we have suggested that there are problems of generation which are just as complex as, though subtly different from, those of analysis, and that in most MT systems they have not been properly addressed. Generation should not only handle the mundane questions of morphological agreement and basic word order, but should also tackle what for a human translator might in the end be classified as matters of style. Some help in the selection of appropriate output may well come from access to databases of 'example' translations (as described in section 6.9), but more research is needed on computational stylistics, and particularly computational implementations of the findings of comparative stylistics. The need is for methods of ensuring the generation of structures which are idiomatic for the target language, e.g. the 'process orientation' of Japanese, the 'action orientation' of English in (17) above, and the preference in French for more 'dynamic' expressions (21a) than in English (21b).

(21a) *Les gens ont applaudi sur le passage des troupes.*

(21b) People cheered as the troops marched by.

The task is far from easy, but it must be tackled if significant improvements in MT output are to be achieved.

7.5 Generation as the 'reverse' of analysis

It is a common assumption by newcomers to computational linguistics in general and to MT in particular that generation ought to be the mirror image of analysis, and the assumption is probably reinforced by diagrams of indirect MT systems, by diagrams such as Figure 6.1 (Chapter 6) and by some of the general descriptions of systems. Our discussion so far, in this and previous chapters, especially on analysis procedures, should have dispelled this misconception.

Nevertheless, there has recently emerged a style of programming based on logic, using the Prolog programming language, in which this literal interpretation of generation as the reverse of analysis can actually be realised. Prolog is claimed to be a non-procedural programming language, which means that programs written in it do not specify how something is to be computed but describe what has to be computed. Prolog programs describe sets of data and logical rules. The sequence in which the former interact by the application of the latter is determined by an 'interpreter', which decides which rules are appropriate, and when to apply them. Only when there are several candidate rules that could be applied does the order in which the programmer happened to write them down have any significance.

In this respect Prolog is said to embody the 'separation of algorithms and data' discussed in Chapter 3 (the data are the programs; the algorithms are more or less hidden from the programmer), and this is hardly surprising since, in fact, the development of Prolog grew out of work on Q-systems in what later became the Météo project (see Chapter 12).

One consequence of this program design is that Prolog programs — at least simple ones — are, under normal circumstances, reversible. A Prolog program defines a set of relationships between sets of data: in the case of a parser, the program will define a relationship between a set of possible texts (strings of words) and the corresponding representations. Because of the way Prolog works, we can in principle use EXACTLY THE SAME PROGRAM either to compute a representation given a string of words or to compute the string of words given the representation. In this sense, a Prolog program written as a parser can also be used as a generator: we can use it to ask either "What is the structure corresponding to this sentence?" or to ask "What is the sentence corresponding to this structure?"

A number of researchers have adopted this basic idea in experimental MT systems and are investigating the limits of its applicability. Using Prolog they are attempting to build reversible (typically bilingual) MT systems where the grammars used for analysis are also used for generation just by running them backwards. Unfortunately it is often the case that in striving to maintain reversibility the grammars remain too simplistic, and the system ends up as a low-level interlingual one where the intermediate representation is little more than a surface phrase-structure tree: only sentences where there are no gross structural differences (e.g. of the *like/gern* type) can be translated. When structural changes involve deleting parts of the structure, reversibility becomes much more problematic: a reversed deletion is an insertion, and it is often difficult to control the arbitrary insertion of underspecified parts of a structure.

An alternative to this 'reversible procedural' approach involves the use of feature unification (see section 2.9.7) and the definition not of reversible analysis grammars as such, but of collections of well-formedness conditions or **constraints** on feature bundles, which, when applied to one structure (which might be a simple string of words) combine and unify to give a new structure. The approach can be used both for analysis, where a string is given as input and a representation 'emerges', or for generation, where the representation is given as input. In order to translate, the constraints must also specify mappings between representations, so that input can be the source string and output the target string. The Eurotra 'E-framework' (Chapter 14) is in part an implementation of this idea, though for practical reasons there are aspects of the formalism which make it not fully reversible.

It is frequently assumed that reversible grammars are most appropriate for interlingua systems, where the 'analysis' and 'generation' modules share a common interface; but there is nothing against a transfer-based reversible system, as long as the transfer rules themselves are also reversible.

In both types of 'reversible' system, an additional issue is the general underlying principle that translation itself is in some sense reversible, i.e. that because a sentence S can be translated as S', then S' must be translated as S in the opposite direction. Unfortunately, this is far from the case in reality. Nevertheless, several basic research MT systems have taken the challenge of reversibility seriously, since there is a clear reduction in development costs to be had if large amounts of linguistic data can be used for both analysis and generation.

The best known example of an MT project explicitly investigating reversible grammars is Rosetta (described in Chapter 16). This interlingua model makes the further theoretical claim that grammars should not only be reversible, but that they should be 'isomorphic', i.e. that for every rule needed for one language there should be a corresponding rule in the other language. Other reversible MT systems written in Prolog make less strong theoretical claims. They include ULTRA, a multilingual system with all combinations of English, German, Spanish, Japanese and Chinese, under development at New Mexico State University, Las Cruces; a related project XTRA, investigated at various centres as its developer changed laboratories; SWETRA at the University of Lund, developed chiefly for English–Swedish, but with parallel experiments for French, Polish, Russian, Georgian and Irish translation; and CRITTER, a sublanguage system developed in Canada to translate agricultural market reports between English and French (see section 18.7) In each case, analysis and generation are both handled by **definite clause grammars** (DCGs), a formalism for augmenting essentially phrase structure rules, developed specially for Prolog programming.

7.6 Further reading

General discussions of the problem of generation are very scarce in the MT literature. For example, the section of Nagao's (1989) book on 'sentence generation' is actually about differences in English and Japanese sentence structure, and so is really about transfer, while McDonald's (1987) article is a view of MT generation from an 'outsider' working on information retrieval systems. We must consult descriptions of the target-language generation modules of individual systems; the example of Ariane generation in section 7.2.1. comes from Guilbaud's (1987) description of the German–French version.

One notable research project which was chiefly interested in generation was the SEMSYN project (Laubsch *et al.* 1984, Emele *et al.* 1986, Rösner 1986a,b) in which a German generation module was devised for producing output from the intermediate representations of a Japanese–English MT system.

The issue of pre-determined choice in target-language generation is hinted at in various descriptions of the Ariane system (for references see Chapter 13), and the fact that the correspondence between a text and its possible translations is one-to-many rather than one-to-one is implicit in several early discussions of transfer in Eurotra and the notion of 'isoduidy', an invented term indicating the relationship between two translation equivalents (or more generally, linguistic representations which are equivalent alternatives at a given level of abstraction) (see Johnson *et al.* 1985, Arnold 1986).

The problem of structure preservation as a first choice is discussed in Somers (1987b, 1990) and in Somers *et al.* (1988).

An important contribution to the discussion of 'stylistic' improvement of MT has been made by DiMarco and Hirst (1988, 1990).

The example with *Technologische Fortschritte* (in section 7.4) and a discussion of the requirements for intermediate representations come from Somers (1987b).

For more information on ULTRA, see Farwell and Wilks (1991). The XTRA system is reported in Huang (1988). See Sigurd (1988) for a discussion of SWETRA. References on Rosetta and CRITTER are given in Chapters 16 and 18 respectively. For information on the use of Prolog for natural language processing, and on DCGs, textbooks such as Pereira and Shieber (1987), Gazdar and Mellish (1989) or Gal *et al.* (1991) are recommended.

8
The practical use of MT systems

In this chapter we turn to examining the 'modes of use' of MT, the ways in which computers can be used for translation and the practical environments in which MT systems are and can be used. We include discussion of different types of systems, the kinds of users envisaged, what kinds of hardware facilities are required and provided, and how these factors affect the designs of systems.

There is a common view, represented diagrammatically in Figure 8.1, which places human translation and MT at two ends of a spectrum of translation methods with various kinds of human–machine cooperation between them. At one extreme are wholly computerised systems with no human involved producing translations of a high quality: fully automatic high quality translation (FAHQT). At the other extreme is human translation involving no mechanical aids whatever as it has been practised for centuries. Beween them come **Human-Aided Machine Translation** **(HAMT)** and **Machine-Aided Human Translation (MAHT)**. Both encompass a range of system types and methods: not only are the acronyms and names confusing but it is sometimes difficult to categorise systems as one or the other, hence the term **Computer-Aided Translation** (or 'Computer-Assisted Translation') is often used to cover all types. Essentially, however, MAHT includes the use of (generally) computer-based tools as aids for professional translators, whereas HAMT covers the use of MT systems to produce translations with the assistance of human operators before, during or after the computerised processes.

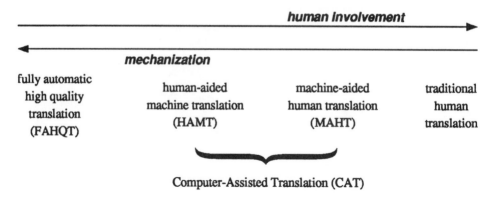

Figure 8.1 Human and machine translation

8.1 Fully automatic high quality translation (FAHQT)

The notion of **fully automatic high quality translation** (commonly known by its acronym FAHQT) came into currency in the first period of MT development (section 1.3). The term originated with Yehoshua Bar-Hillel, who consistently argued from 1951 that fully automatic translation of a quality comparable to that of human translators was not merely an unrealistic aim for research but also impossible in principle. His criticisms of contemporary research, particularly in a 1958 report (more widely available in 1960), were interpreted as condemnations of MT activity as a whole, and undoubtedly influenced the later ALPAC report of 1966 (cf. section 1.3). However, Bar-Hillel's main objective was to direct MT efforts to the more realistic aims of 'Human-Aided Machine Translation'.

His arguments against FAHQT were that translation involved certain human abilities which no computer could ever replicate. In particular, he focused on the problem that we now know as 'real world knowledge' (see section 5.2.1), and his example was the now famous lexical ambiguity problem with *pen*: sentence (1) can be understood only if we assume *pen* here to mean 'a child's playpen' rather than 'a writing utensil'.

(1) The box was in the pen.

Even given an appropriate context, it is the knowledge that we have about the relative sizes of typical pens and boxes which allows us to make the correct disambiguation, and hence the correct translation. Bar-Hillel argued that we cannot envisage incorporating this kind of knowledge into an MT system, and that since this kind of knowledge is essential for FAHQT, the aim of FAHQT is itself impossible.

It should be said that more recently both these assertions have come to be questioned. There are claims that real-world knowledge can be incorporated into MT systems and there are certain projects which are attempting to do this, looking for help and support from research in Artificial Intelligence (cf. Chapter 18). On the other hand, there is a school of thought which disputes the claim that 'understanding' of this nature is *a priori* required for translation, whether by humans or by computers. Nevertheless, there seems to be general agreement about the present impossibility of developing fully automatic systems capable of translating to a high standard without either human assistance at some stage or controls or restrictions on the language of texts. We can have either fully automatic translation or high quality (computer-based) translation, but we cannot have both. As far as Figure 8.1 is concerned, FAHQT at one end is unachievable and human translation at the other end is not a topic of this book; what we discuss in this chapter is the area in between.

8.2 Machine-Aided Human Translation (MAHT)

Machine aids have been available to translators for a long time. There can be few translators still using only pen and paper (certainly not most technical translators); typewriters and dictaphones are familiar pieces of equipment. It is computational aids which are changing the ways translators work, threatening (in the opinion of some) the image of translation as more an art, craft or skill than as a technique or job. There is, of course, no reason for fearing that the availability of computer-based aids should make translation any less intellectually and artistically demanding, any more than the availability of dictionaries and typewriters does. The fear stems from a belief (usually held by translators of literary works) that computerisation necessarily implies a loss of humanity.

At the most basic level, the word processor (or word processing program for a microcomputer) may be regarded as a 'machine aid'. But its use can scarcely be called MAHT. At the very least, MAHT must involve a computer-based linguistic aid, such as a program for checking spellings, grammar or style of the translation. The availability of **spelling checkers** depends on the target language; for English, there are very good and efficient spelling checkers available, for other languages the picture varies according to the commercial attractiveness of the particular language. Most spelling checkers are based on very large dictionaries with very fast look-up, but have no linguistic 'intelligence' (e.g. to spot *there* as a misspelling of *their*), though some have quite ingenious algorithms for trying to guess the correct form of a misspelling. **Grammar checkers** and **style checkers** are slightly more sophisticated tools, working typically by pattern matching, although some use parsers of the computational linguistic kind. Grammar checkers look for errors such as the non-agreement of subjects and verbs, word repetition (e.g. *the the*), sentences lacking finite verbs, and so on. Style checkers look for features considered to be stylistically awkward, such as clichés, sentences beginning with conjunctions or ending with prepositions, sentences which are too long or too short, and so forth. Of course, not all translators would find a need for such aids.

Of more direct value is the increasing availability of **on-line reference works** such as dictionaries, thesauri, encyclopaedias and other general sources of information which translators may consult. Laser disks and CD ROMs, holding large amounts of information in convenient form, can now be integrated in word-processing environments and accessible on-line. Particularly attractive are the **on-line bilingual dictionaries** now available commercially.

The integration of the various resources has led to the development of what is generally known as the **translator's workbench** (or translator's workstation). Typically, systems are based on microcomputers (even small personal computers) with split-screen or multi-window facilities: one part of the screen is the work area for the target text, function keys open windows or subdivide the screen for perusal of on-line dictionaries, consultation of other on-line information sources, and perhaps searches of a store of previous translations on similar topics or for the same customers; full integration means that information can easily be transferred from one window to another. Source texts can be input directly at the keyboard or in machine-readable form, received on a diskette, or transmitted via a telecommunications link, or converted from a print copy by an optical character reader (OCR). Facilities are frequently provided for the creation of **text-oriented glossaries**, lists of the words occurring in a particular text (excluding common vocabulary and perhaps other non-technical words on a 'stop list') with suggested equivalents in a target language: the lists may be in alphabetical order or in the order of occurrence in the original, and the equivalents may come from translators' own glossaries or from other (on-line) sources. There is often an alternative option in the form of **automatic term look-up**, the consultation of in-house and external terminological databases for technical and specialised words in a particular text. These workbench facilities can save much effort by translators; it has been estimated that technical translators spend as much as 60% of their time consulting dictionaries and reference works in terminology research.

Usually, translators will use these aids and facilities much as they do printed dictionaries and reference works and enter translations manually, but there are programs being developed which allow lexical substitution semi-automatically and provide a kind of draft translation. Programs for **machine pre-translation** replace source words and phrases which have unique target language equivalents (e.g. terminology which has to be translated consistently) while leaving in the original those words which have many possibilities in the target or which cause particular problems; the latter would include words such as English *use* when translating into French (*usage*, *emploi*, *utilité*, etc.), and all function words (prepositions, conjunctions, pronouns, etc.) and common adjectives and verbs such as *several*, *any*, *make*, *occur*. This sort of pre-translation is in some sense a mechanization of the activity, familiar to translators, of checking through a text for unfamiliar or technical vocabulary for the translation of which some research may have to be done.

8.3 Human-Aided Machine Translation (HAMT)

Whereas in MAHT the human translator is in charge, using machine aids or not as required or desired, in HAMT it is the system itself which takes the main responsibility for translation, with human assistance to help in the process when needed. Human involvement may be either during the process, in an 'interactive' mode, or outside the process, in 'pre-editing' or 'post-editing' stages.

The use of the term 'interactive' may be confusing and requires clarification; it refers strictly to human involvement during the actual processes of translation (analysis, transfer, and generation) when the computer seeks assistance in the interpretation of structures, the resolution of ambiguities and the selection of lexical items. It does not refer to any interaction between users and systems before or after translation processes. In many systems pre-editing and post-editing is done interactively: in the case of pre-editing, the system foresees what problems it is going to have and interacts with the user, for example, by flagging unknown words and asking the user to provide target language equivalents before it starts translating; in the case of post-editing, the system alerts users to places in the text where alternatives have been offered and asks for choices to be made. These may be called examples of **interactive pre-editing** and **interactive post-editing**. Of course, in actual systems there may be borderline cases where it is unclear whether something is 'pre-editing' or 'participating in the translation process', but here we attempt to maintain the distinction for the sake of clearer exposition of the basic concepts.

8.3.1 Pre-editing

Typically pre-editing involves checking source texts for forseeable problems for the system and trying to eradicate them. It can include the identification of names (proper nouns), the marking of grammatical categories of homographs, indication of embedded clauses, bracketing of coordinate structures, flagging or substitution of unknown words, etc. In its extreme form, it involves the reformulation of the text using a 'controlled language'.

An example of pre-editing, without restrictions on vocabulary and syntax, is found in the SUSY system (described in Chapter 11). This system has the option of marking source texts with special symbols, e.g. proper names are indicated by an '=' sign (e.g. *Tom=*); paragraph and section headings can be distinguished (by the prefix *$U*), so that the system does not try to analyse them as sentences; a clause without a finite verb can have the prefix *$S*; a sentence with an embedding can be flagged *$SA*, and the beginning and end of embeddings indicated by *$EA* and *$EE*; the disambiguation of homographs can be helped, for example, by marking a following word as a finite verb (*$FIV*); the non-idiomatic use of an apparent idiom can be flagged; and so on. Pre-editing is optional, which means that the system will look out for these 'flags', but will still attempt to produce a translation even if they are not there: pre-editing can improve the overall standard of the translation, but it is not indispensable.

Closely related to pre-editing is the use of **controlled language** in source texts. The approach has been successfully applied with Systran and other systems. It recognises that major obstacles to quality MT output stem from the inability of systems to interpret certain constructions correctly and from the problems caused by homographs and ambiguities. The use of controlled language is aimed at adapting source texts to constructions and vocabulary which the system can deal with. The writers of texts for translation are thus restricted to particular types of constructions and to the use of terminology and even words of common vocabulary in predefined meanings. For example, *replace* can mean two different actions in (2).

(2a) Remove part A and replace it with part B.

(2b) Remove part A, adjust part B and then replace part A.

In (2a) it means 'exchange' and in (2b) 'put back'; a controlled vocabulary would restrict usage to only one of these. Similarly, *switch* can be either a noun or a verb; writers are asked to use it only as a noun and to use for the verb *diverge*, *transpose*, *substitute* as appropriate. Simple and clear unambiguous sentences are the goal. So, for example (3a) might be replaced by (3b).

> (3a) Loosen main motor and drive shaft and slide back until touching back plate.

> (3b) Loosen the main motor. Loosen the drive shaft. Slide both parts until they touch the back plate.

There is evidence that in technical writing such restrictions actually produces better source (English) texts. Xerox has been using this approach with Systran for over 15 years and has found that the texts that their writers produce are clearer and more understandable. The main advantage, however, is that the output from the MT system needs little or no post-editing. The extra expense involved in producing source texts is easily justifiable when, as in the case of Xerox, translations of technical manuals are needed in a number of different target languages.

The use of controlled language with MT systems must be distinguished from the 'sublanguage' approach to MT (section 8.4 below). In the latter case, the system itself is designed to deal with the vocabulary and typical constructions of a specific subject area and/or document type; but there need not be any restrictions on writers or on the texts input to the system. Controlled language is not limited to a sublanguage, it may range over all the subject areas covered by a particular user; and the MT system itself is not designed to deal only with texts in the controlled forms, it can deal with uncontrolled input (even if less successfully). However, it is certainly possible for the two approaches to be combined; indeed there could be obvious advantages in a system dealing with a controlled sublanguage, and an example is given below.

8.3.2 Post-editing

The task of the post-editor is to correct output from the MT system to an agreed standard: minimally in the case of texts wanted only for information purposes, by someone familiar with the subject matter, and thoroughly in the case of texts for widespread publication and distribution (see section 9.7).

In early systems, post-editing was typically done by hand, even with paper and pencil in some cases, but more recently on a word processor. Every error has to be spotted by the editor: there is no help from the system itself. Every lexical and structural change has to be done by retyping. A basic requirement is that the source text is available with the MT output on the same screen, and that one word may be easily substituted by another throughout a text.

With a more sophisticated program it is possible to incorporate function-key facilities for transposing words and phrases. In translating the Spanish (4a), an MT system might generate (4b).

> (4a) *En este studio se buscará contestar dos preguntas fundamentales.*

> (4b) In this study it will be sought to answer two fundamental questions.

Within the text, the best rendition might be (4c), which retains the same topic-comment structure as the original, but is more natural.

(4c) This study will seek to answer two fundamental questions.

If changes of this kind are common, then it ought to be possible to produce active verb forms from passive forms (and vice versa), and to change a 'prep + X, *it*...' construction to a construction with X as the subject.

Interactive post-editing represents a further advance. The system alerts the editor to sentences or phrases which may be wrongly translated (e.g. contain an ambiguity it could not resolve, or a construction it could not analyse). It provides the option of correcting similar errors automatically throughout the text once the editor has replaced a mistranslation by a corrected form. More sophisticated still are **linguistically intelligent word processors**; these could spot certain structural ambiguities and enable alternative structures to be generated; or automatically change gender agreements in a whole phrase, e.g. if a masculine noun has been changed by the editor into a feminine one, then all the dependent adjectives and determiners would also be changed; or insert appropriate prepositions automatically, e.g. if *discuss* is changed to *talk*, then *about* is inserted before the direct object. However, such systems are still some way in the future at the moment.

8.3.3 Interactive MT

The third mode of human assistance occurs in **interactive** systems. The idea of an MT system which halts during translation processes and asks users for help to solve problems of ambiguity and translational equivalents has been current for many years. However, there are still few truly interactive systems available.

A good example is the TransActive™ mode of operation with the ALPSystem (now marketed by the ALPNET company). This is the MT component of a package for translators providing multilingual word processing, access to on-line glossaries, etc., and can operate either interactively or non-interactively. When in interactive mode, as it progresses through the analysis of each sentence in the source text, it asks various types of questions. These questions may have to do with lexical problems, such as disambiguating a homograph, or choosing from a choice of target translations; they may have to do with syntactic ambiguities and ask the user to choose among paraphrases of the alternative readings; and some of the questions may be of a more stylistic nature. (Notice the mixture of questions to do with analysing the source text and with decisions about the target text.) To some extent, the questions that are asked are more or less under the control of users since they build the dictionaries which drive the interactions. If a user puts eight different translations of some word in the dictionary, the system will require a choice from those eight every time that word appears. However, users typically build a series of domain-specific dictionaries and indicate for any particular text which is to be the preferred source of equivalents. In many cases there will therefore be only one equivalent within each specific domain.

The difficulty with this kind of interactive system is that there are often so many interactions for a single sentence that it might have been quicker for the user to translate from scratch. Furthermore, it is frustrating and irritating to have constant repetitions of the same interactions with the same lexical items. The system has, of course, no memory of similar problems and the earlier responses, nor could it be expected to 'know' (even if it could 'remember') whether a given query would elicit the same response in a different situation. Some probabilistic 'learning' from previous interactions has been claimed for some recent systems (e.g. Tovna), where preference is given to changes which have been made frequently.

8.3.4 Interactive systems for monolingual users

It may be noted that the assumption so far is that interaction involves knowledge of both source and target languages, i.e. the user is expected to be a translator. An alternative scenario can be envisaged where the user is monolingual: either knowing only the target language or knowing only the source language. In the former case it is clear that input and analysis must be fully automatic: a user ignorant of Arabic, Chinese or Japanese scripts, for example, cannot be expected to do any pre-editing of texts or provide any help in disambiguation. All that is possible is for assistance in the generation of fluent output, which could be done interactively.

Greater involvement is possible when monolingual users know only the source language and the system takes responsibility for producing the target text. There are two possible scenarios here: either the text has already been written, or it is composed at the time of translation. In the first case the system interacts with some user (who may be the original author) in order to ask questions when it encounters unknown words, ambiguities or structures which it cannot interpret, whether the problems are those of analysis or transfer or generation. For example, if translating from English into German, it may ask whether a particular occurrence of *wall* is referring to an interior or external structure (note that the system must solicit the information without referring to German words or linguistic facts, which will be meaningless to the user).

In the second case, the system interacts with the user in the composition of a source text which it can be sure of translating accurately into the target language. A typical situation is one in which someone wants to communicate a message, write a business letter, or participate in some kind of on-line dialogue. At its simplest (as in a project under development, see section 18.5), a system designed for a specific domain has a set of pre-translated set phrases (like a phrase-book) or of partial sentences with slots into which the user can insert phrases and which the system can translate in the usual way. There are two possible modes in which the system can operate. In a **menu-driven** mode, the system builds texts from series of questions. In the case of a business letter the user could be asked what type of letter it is to be: a complaint, an enquiry, a response to an enquiry, an order, and so on. This choice determines a rough template, the details of which must be filled in: the addressee's name, dates, the items being ordered, etc. for each of which further standard options are available. An alternative **dialogue** mode is where it is the user rather than the system who initiates the procedure, by proposing a draft source text. The system accepts the user's input in the normal way, and then tries to find the best pre-translated set phrase (or phrase template) that matches the input, and asks questions to ensure the phrase selected corresponds to the user's intentions, or makes suggested changes to the input to make it more like one of its set phrases. This mode is being used in a system which aims to act as an intermediary in an on-line dialogue with another user (perhaps also monolingual), so there are both user–system dialogues when the content of the text is being negotiated, and user–user dialogues, which are the object of the translation.

The quality of the output is assured because the set phrases and partial sentences have been carefully selected, and because there will be no problems with ambiguity as users will know what they want to say. The situation is quite different from the standard MT environment. With no pre-existing source text, the emphasis is on text generation rather than analysis and transfer. Instead of trying to extract meaning from a text, here the system tries to extract meaning from a user. What is important is not the way something is expressed but what 'message' is intended. This system of **interactive composition** in an unknown language or 'MT without a source text' is clearly quite different from conventional MT where everything that needs to be discovered about the meaning has to be found in the words of the text.

8.4 Sublanguage systems

Human intervention or assistance is the most normal response to the difficulties of achieving MT output of good quality. The other is to minimise problems by imposing restrictions on the types of texts. One option, already mentioned (section 8.2), is to control the language of source texts. Another is to design systems for a specific well-defined range of texts. At its extreme, systems can be designed to translate just one particular corpus of texts, e.g. aircraft manuals from English into French (as in the TAUM-Aviation project at Montreal University from 1976 to 1981) or abstracts of articles on the textile industry (as in TITUS, see below), or even just one text. More common are systems intended for one particular subject domain where the texts are written in a particular **sublanguage**.

The 'sublanguage' approach to MT originated from work at Montreal on a system designed specifically to translate weather forecasts from English into French (Météo described in Chapter 12). It was recognised that the range of vocabulary and syntactic structures can differ quite significantly from those of the 'standard' language. An example of the 'sublanguage' of meteorological reports is (5a). Other sublanguages are those for stock market reports (5b), and for the law (5c).

(5a) Tomorrow cloudy with periods of light rain becoming heavy towards dawn.

(5b) On Monday the indicator plunged 13·76 points in a sell-off touched off by the news of a sharp boost in oil prices. Mines plunged sharply.

(5c) I the undersigned ... do hereby certify and attest that the document hereunto annexed is a true and faithful account.... In witness whereof I have hereunto set my hand...

In fact, nearly all specialisms have their own jargon, whether it be the language of natural science (*electron, catalyst, ion, protein*), of linguistics (*phoneme, parse, pragmatics*), of wine tasting (*smooth, fruity, bouquet*), or of military affairs (*missile, ballistic, magazine*). In many specialisms the terminology has been standardised, including words of the common vocabulary used in special meanings (*field* and *mass* in physics, *tree* and *generate* in formal linguistics, *tank* and *force* in military language). This fact has been recognised since the earliest MT systems by the provision of specialised dictionaries, which users can activiate as needed for translating texts in particular subject domains.

Characteristic grammatical features are rarely specific to one sublanguage, but certain styles are more typical than others. Some have been illustrated already: the omission of definite articles is typical of operating manuals in English (as in (3a) above), whereas in French manuals a typical usage is the infinitive verb form in imperatives (6); the nominal style with passives is typical of much report literature in English but it is not so acceptable in Japanese; and complex noun compounds are common in technical manuals. Other examples are the custom in English for minutes of meetings to be written in the past tense (7a) but in French in the present tense (7b); and for legal documents to contain multiple embeddings, with no punctuation (8).

(6) *Ouvrir le régulateur.*

(7a) The working group's attention was also drawn to the fact that ...

(7b) *L'attention du groupe de travail est également attirée sur le fait que* ...

(8) The requirement that affidavits in opposition to summary judgment motions must recite that the material facts relied upon are true is no mere formality.

Another feature of sublanguages is that some grammatical properties of individual words differ from standard language. For example, the verb *present* in medical language does not require a direct object, so that (9) is acceptable in a doctor's report, but ungrammatical in standard English; and in the language used by airline pilots, *overhead* can function as a preposition (10), which is not normal in everyday English.

(9) The patient presented with a cold.

(10) Our routing tonight takes us overhead Paris.

MT systems can be designed to deal strictly with one particular sublanguage. The advantages are, generally, the availability of clearly defined terminology, the reduction of homography since other subjects are not involved, the concentration on grammatical problems which are frequent and typical in texts of the domain, and the creation of a system for a specific task with identifiable measures of success and acceptability. However, while this may be true in some cases (meteorology and the stock market, described in Chapters 12 and 18 respectively), in some sublanguages the pecularities heighten the difficulties and complexities of analysis rather than reduce them, as in the case of legal language.

There are further difficulties. It is relatively rare to find texts restricted to a specific subject; a medical text may well include chemical and physical terminology and may refer to administrative and economic aspects of medical treatment, etc.; a chemistry text may include mathematical terms and refer to biological systems; and so forth. In addition, systems designed specifically for one particular sublanguage may not be easily extendible to another.

Although restriction to a sublanguage does not necessarily imply the 'control' of the language of input texts (section 8.3.1 above), the two features are often found together. One reason has already been given, namely that actual documents are rarely limited to one sublanguage. Another is that even restriction to a sublanguage does not ensure that all ambiguity has been tackled, hence we find **controlled sublanguage** systems.

An example is the TITUS system designed by the Institut Textile de France (described in more detail in section 18.4) for translating abstracts connected with the textile industry. Abstracts in one of four languages (English, French, German and Spanish) are entered interactively, with the computer asking for help with homographs (e.g. *control* meaning 'command' or 'test') and with ambiguous or 'unacceptable' constructions. Automatic translation into the other languages enables abstractors to check whether the correct analysis has been made.

8.5 Use of low quality MT

We have discussed revision of the output (post-editing), preparing the input (pre-editing and controlled language), interacting with users, translators and writers, and limiting the range of systems to sublanguages. There is one further option for the practical utilization of MT systems, namely the use of unrevised output from systems with no constrained or controlled input. Obviously, from what has been said in previous chapters, this 'raw' output is often of a relatively low quality. Nevertheless, there are many circumstances in which this is acceptable.

Experts in scientific fields need access to current documentation in languages they cannot read, e.g. reports on space technology in Russian. The output from an MT system is unlikely to be very good, but for technical readers who know enough about the field, who know what is going on generally in this science, and who can maybe even guess roughly what the article is about, it may well provide sufficient material to get at least some idea of the content of the text. In particular, they should have enough information to say whether they do or do not want this or that paragraph translated 'properly'. It is an economically sound use of low quality MT output, and indeed, for many people with financial and time constraints it is better to have a crude translation than no translation at all. It may not be what the designers of the MT system had in mind, but it is clearly a valued and practical use. Indeed, it has been reported that users of raw MT in the late 1960s came to learn 'Anglo-Russian' and claimed to prefer the raw output because it was more 'accurate' than the results of post-editing.

Such raw MT output may be even more useful to someone knowing the grammatical rudiments of the source language but not enough vocabulary to read texts fluently. For example, someone with expertise in road building and with an elementary knowledge of German could 'understand' a primitive 'translation' such as (11), where most of the terminology has been translated but the rest of the text has been left in the original.

(11) PROBLEM DES WATER-RUN-OFF VON ROAD SURFACE, WIE WIND DIRECTION,
UNEVEN UND RUT, CAMBER DER ROAD UND LENGTH DES RUN-OFF PATH,
WERDEN DISCUSS. SIEBEN DIFFERENT TYPE VON ROAD SURFACE MIT DIFFERENT

METHOD ZUR MEASUREMENT IHRER SKIDDING RESISTANCE UND ROUGHNESS
WERDEN DESCRIBE.

An expert reader should be able to judge from this version of an abstract
whether the original full text is likely to be of interest. Such output could also
be of value as a 'pre-translation' for a translator, just as a pre-translation (section
8.2. above) could also be used as a very 'raw' translation for an expert with some
knowledge of the source language.

Another context in which low quality MT would seem to be useful has been
investigated in Japan. A fully automatic bi-directional MT system connected
English and Japanese monolingual users in an on-line 'conversation' via a
telecommunications satellite linked to computers in Europe and Japan. Although
there were many mistranslations, especially due to the colloquial or conversational
style of the input, it was nevertheless possible for bilingual conversations to take
place, with both partners typing in messages and reading responses in their own
languages. There is an obvious saving in time in comparison with writing a letter,
having it translated (particularly expensive in the case of English from and into
Japanese), and sending it by airmail, etc.

We may conclude with the words of J.C. Sager who remarked in connection
with Systran that MT can offer 'a choice to the customer, varying from the
cheap and nasty of the dime store to the Tiffany or Cartier of translation' (Sager
1986:166). There is no single mode of use for MT, but a whole gamut of variations,
with different qualities, different user profiles, different best-use scenarios, different
hardware requirements, and consequently of course, different costs. In this chapter
we have seen examples of this variety. In the next chapter we look at how the
acceptability, suitability and usability of MT may be evaluated.

8.6 Further reading

In general, MT from the users' perspective is well documented in many of the
proceedings of the Aslib series of conferences (Snell 1979, Lawson 1982, 1985,
Picken 1986, 1988, 1990), and Vasconcellos (1988) consists of numerous articles
on various aspects of MT, HAMT and MAHT, mostly from the viewpoint of
translators.

Bar-Hillel's report on MT, in which he made the point about 'real world
knowledge', was written in 1958, but is most widely available as Bar-Hillel
(1960). For a discussion, see Hutchins (1986:153–7).

For a discussion of the necessity for understanding in translation, see Johnson's
(1983:35f) brief remarks on the subject with reference to MT, and Tsujii (1986)
for a more general discussion.

For a general discussion of machine aids for translators, see Somers and
McNaught (1980), Lawson (1985), Magnusson Murray (1988) and Stoll (1988). A
survey of commercially available tools suitable for multilingual word-processing
(including translation) appeared in *LT/Electric Word* 13 (May/June 1989); see also
Becker (1984) and Section I of Vasconcellos (1988). For information on spelling
checkers, see (almost) any personal computing magazine. A good example of

a grammar or style checker is IBM's CRITIQUE system (Richardson and Braden-Harder, 1988). Lexical and terminological aids are discussed in Section II of Vasconcellos (1988). Term-banks in particular are discussed in Snell (1983); see also Chapter 3 of Bennett *et al.* (1986).

Proposals for machine pre-translation have been put forward by Bédard (1990).

The idea of the 'translator's work-bench' originated with Erhard Lippmann (1971) and Martin Kay (1980); it has been championed especially by Alan Melby (1982, 1983, 1987) with his 'multi-level translator workstation', and was incorporated in the commercial HAMT system developed by ALPSystems (Tenney, 1985). The idea has also been taken up by researchers in Malaysia (Tong, 1987).

Pre-editing is not widely covered in the literature. The idea of restricted syntax and controlled vocabulary is discussed briefly in Somers (1983:150f), and experiments by Xerox with Systran are reported by Elliston (1979) and Ruffino (1982).

Post-editing is discussed in five articles in Lawson (1982:97–136), in Wagner (1985), Vasconcellos (1987) and by McElhaney and Vasconcellos (1988), these last two articles concerning experiments at the Pan-American Health Organization in Washington DC with PAHO's SPANAM Spanish–English system.

Research on linguistically intelligent word processors has been a focus of interest in recent work by the Grenoble MT research group (Boitet and Gerber 1986, Boitet 1987, Zajac 1988).

The philosophy behind interactive systems is discussed by Johnson and Whitelock (1987). Interactive translation in ALPSystem is described in Bateman (1985) and in Weaver (1988). Another truly interactive system is the METAL system (see Chapter 15).

The scenario involving a monolingual user was first proposed by Kay (1973), and is the basis of the Ntran system (Whitelock *et al.* 1986, Wood and Chandler 1988) and the DLT system (see Chapter 17). Dialogue-based MT is discussed in Boitet (1989b) and Somers *et al.* (1990).

The sublanguage approach was pioneered by Raskin (1974) and is typified by research in Canada (Kittredge 1987, Lehrberger and Bourbeau 1988, Isabelle *et al.* 1988). For a general discussion of sublanguage, see Kittredge and Lehrberger (1982).

The use of 'raw' MT output, or MT output of a lower quality is discussed in Somers and McNaught (1980); the acceptability of raw Systran output for example is confirmed by van Slype (1979) and more recently by Bostad (1986) and Habermann (1986). The example of partial German–English translation is from Canisius (1977:267f). The preference of raw output for its 'accuracy' is reported by Martin Kay (personal communication). The comments of Sager are from Sager (1986:166).

TransActive is a trademark of ALPNET.

9
Evaluation of MT systems

The different modes of use of MT which were discussed in the last chapter are motivated to a considerable extent by the inadequacies of the translations produced by systems. Fully automatic high quality translation is not at present possible; in general, the 'raw' translations produced by MT systems must be revised or post-edited. Alternatively, the input to MT systems must be pre-edited or adapted to the limitations of systems. A major question to be asked about any MT system is, therefore, how good are its raw translations, what is the potential for improvement, and how may it be best and most cost-effectively used in practice?

What may be surprising is that despite some 40 years of research on MT there is still no generally accepted methodology for the evaluation of systems. Although the ALPAC report did include some evaluations of then existing systems it is only since the initial assessments of the Systran system for the European Communities in the late 1970s that the topic has received much attention. Most evaluations take place under contract and often under confidentiality agreements. Consequently there is little constructive criticism of methodology. A major deficiency is that many evaluations are undertaken by people with little or no expertise in MT techniques, unable to judge what is possible and what is unrealistic, unable to estimate the potential rather than current performance. On the other hand, 'evaluations' made by MT researchers are often minimal and misleading: the demonstration of a system with a carefully selected set of sentences or sentence types is not the basis for claims about a large-scale system. In view of the misconceptions and misunderstandings concerning nearly all aspects of MT, one role of evaluation must be to introduce realism in public discussions of what MT systems can and cannot do and what they may be able to do in the future.

With no generally accepted methodology all that can be done here is to indicate the principal areas in which evaluation can take place, what aspects should be taken into consideration, and some of the methods which may be employed.

9.1 Types and stages of evaluation

At the outset we need to distinguish various stages in the development, installation and operation of MT systems. At each stage systems can be evaluated for performance and efficiency. The first stage is the development of a prototype system, the design of the basic system, writing programs, compiling dictionaries, etc. Evaluation will be restricted to the testing of processes alone, without consideration of potential operational environments. It will be the concern primarily of the system developer, who wants to know whether the programs written for the system are in fact performing in the ways intended and who wants to discover whether the output is acceptable as a 'translation'. Such evaluations can be, in fact normally will be, continuous during the development stages of a system, i.e. the programmer or the linguist will want to know the effects of any changes of coding or of a grammar rule. However, from time to time during development the designers of the system will undertake more extensive tests, e.g. running texts of some size against the system and testing the adequacy of the dictionary information and the grammar. These tests may be called **prototype evaluations**.

The second stage is the development of a system which can operate in the intended environment, the design and provision of facilities for inputting text, for compiling and updating dictionaries, for revising (post-editing) output, for interacting with the computer, etc. This stage will include also improvements in the robustness and computational efficiency of programs, the integration of the system in a particular computer environment, e.g. adaptation to particular operating systems or particular computer hardware. These **development evaluations** are concerned not only with the linguistic capabilities of the system but also with operational capabilities. Before offering systems to potential users, the developers will want to be assured that the system does what it is claimed to do, whatever type of system it may be, and that modifications and improvements can be made without radical changes to programs and facilities. In the case of systems to be marketed, they will also, of course, want to evaluate the economic viability of the system as a commercial product, potential sales and leasing agreements, servicing costs, etc.

The third stage is the evaluation of a system by its potential purchasers. They will want to know not only whether the system performs as the designers or vendors claim but also whether it can be used cost-effectively in their particular circumstances. These **operational evaluations** will include assessments of how much and what kind of human input is required to produce acceptable translations, what working conditions are required and what qualifications are needed by operators, what technical facilities are required, how compatible the system is with existing equipment, how improvements can be introduced, etc.

Closely related to these concerns are those of the actual users of the system, particularly professional translators. They will want to know how much work will be involved in pre-editing, post-editing or interactive operation, whether productivity will be increased, how much time and effort is saved, and the impact on working practices. Typically, these **translator evaluations** are included within operational evaluations, but they do represent a distinct area of concern, since the individual attitudes of translators can have major impact on the success or otherwise of MT systems in organisations.

The final stage of evaluation is that of the recipients of translations. They will be concerned primarily with quality, cost and speed. Inevitably these **recipient evaluations** will be comparative: whether the introduction of the MT system produces translations faster and/or more cheaply than human translation while maintaining quality. What they want is good, fast and inexpensive translation.

9.2 Linguistic evaluation of 'raw' output

Common to all stages is the testing of the linguistic quality of the output, the quality of 'raw' translations. This is an evaluation of the basic computer processes. Here there are important differences between **glass-box** evaluations and **black-box** evaluations, between assessment by those who have access to all the workings of the system and assessment by those who can work only with inputs and outputs. The former is available generally only to the researchers and developers of prototype systems, while potential purchasers and users are restricted to black-box evaluations. In examinations of systems we may further distinguish between overall assessments of 'quality' and more detailed identifications of 'errors'. The former tend to produce more subjective evaluations, while the latter provide more objective practical data.

9.2.1 Quality assessment

The most obvious tests of the quality of a translation are: (a) its fidelity or accuracy, the extent to which the translated text contains the 'same' information as the original; (b) its intelligibility or clarity, the ease with which a reader can understand the translation; and (c) its style, the extent to which the translation uses the language appropriate to its content and intention. Each factor can be independent: a translation which is faithful to the original may be difficult to understand; a translation easy to read may have distorted the original message; and an intelligible rendition may be in a quite inappropriate style.

Various tests have been proposed and implemented to provide measurements of fidelity. As part of the ALPAC investigation (Chapter 1), people were asked to read the output of an MT system and then judge how much more 'informative' the original was. This procedure can obviously be criticised as being excessively subjective. Rather more objective tests of fidelity have been proposed in more recent years. In the case of instruction manuals, a practical **performance evaluation** is feasible: can someone using the translation carry out the instructions as well as someone using the original? Another proposal involves **back-translation**: the MT output is translated back into the original language and the result compared with the original text, though of course there is a risk that any shortcomings are magnified by the double process.

For **intelligibility** (or clarity) a number of evaluations have asked readers to rank output from, e.g. 'perfectly intelligible' to 'hopelessly unintelligible'. Generally, only individual sentences are evaluated. But, by isolating sentences from their contexts, such tests are made even more subjective and uncertain than they might be. More objective tests have employed readability scales, such as the well-known Flesch scales, use of the Cloze technique, and comprehension tests. The Flesch scales are based on average sentence lengths, use of complex nominalizations, etc. The Cloze technique involves the masking of words in sentences and texts and asking readers to suggest words to fill the blanks: the correlation between suggested and original words is an index of 'readability'. Comprehension tests (well developed for educational purposes) can be employed to evaluate the intelligibility of the translated text as a whole, by testing readers' understanding of its content.

Measurements of **style** are as subjective as the global rankings of intelligibility. Nevertheless, the appropriateness of a particular style is an important factor. Determiners and copulas may be legitimately omitted in some contexts e.g. newspaper headlines and chapter headings. The translation of an English imperative (1a) by a French imperative would not be appropriate in an instruction manual, where the acceptable style is the infinitive (1b).

(1a) Open the control valve.

(1b) *Ouvrir le régulateur.*

9.2.2 Error analysis

While performance tests, comprehension tests, Flesch readability scales, etc. are certainly valuable and reasonably reliable global evaluations of translations, in most instances the most useful practical information is obtained from **error counting**. It is an index of the amount of work required to correct 'raw' MT output to a standard considered acceptable as a translation. In a typical case, the reviser (post-editor) counts each addition or deletion of a word, each substitution of one word by another, each instance of the transposition of words in phrases, and calculates the percentage of corrected words (errors) in the whole text. The method cannot be completely 'objective' for a number of reasons. Firstly, revisers differ in what they consider to be errors; some will ignore stylistic infelicities if they do not affect intelligibility and accuracy. Secondly, there are different levels of acceptability which are dependent on the particular circumstances in which the revision is taking place. But since operational evaluations (see below) are made for specific situations the estimation of error correction has a practical value.

For many purposes, however, the simple counting of errors is insufficient. What is needed is a **classification of errors** by types of linguistic phenomenon and by relative difficulty of correction. Some lexical errors are easily resolved by simple changes to dictionaries, while others may have implications for grammatical rules and for a whole range of vocabulary items. Some grammatical mistakes may be corrected by simple adjustments to a few lexical entries, others might involve alterations to the basic design of whole translation modules. This kind of detailed evaluation of errors is clearly essential for developers of systems, but it is also of value to potential purchasers who want to know how and whether quality can be improved.

All the above tests can be and have been used to compare different MT systems. An additional method, particularly for research systems, would be the application of **bench-mark** tests. The performance of systems would be compared in the translation of a corpus of texts covering the whole range of linguistic phenomena which an MT system should be expected to deal with. Performance could be evaluated in terms of quality (overall fidelity and intelligibility), error rates and production speed, thus also providing potential purchasers with an indication of basic achievement. However, as yet, no bench-mark tests for MT systems exist and there will be obvious difficulties in reaching agreement about the selection of texts, what should be tested and how performance should be measured. The difficulty of defining a suitable bench-mark is exacerbated by the fact that MT systems differ widely in languages treated, types of texts, involvement of users in pre-editing, or interaction, and many other factors.

9.3 Evaluation by researchers

The continuous monitoring of performance is obviously crucial in the development of prototype systems. The principal tool is the **diagnostic trace**, a record of the stages through which a program goes to produce output. Typically, a text fragment (often a single sentence) is submitted to the system for processing and the results of each stage are displayed (on screen or in print) to enable researchers to examine the actual operations taking place. On this basis they can discover whether the program is doing what is intended, and, if it is not, where the mistakes are occurring. In many cases researchers will be testing a single part of the system, e.g. an analysis module or just the transformation of structures in a transfer module. In other cases they may want to test the whole system.

The errors identified combine problems of computational treatment and linguistic analysis. In theory, programming errors are relatively easily rectified, since it should already be known exactly what results are intended. Linguistic errors involve closer examination, distinguishing between omissions, incompleteness and mistakes in lexical data or grammatical rules and unsatisfactory application of data and rules in procedures of analysis, transfer and generation. In the identification and analysis of errors the researchers are guided by most of the approaches outlined above, from subjective evaluations of fidelity and intelligibility to classifications of error types. In effect, they see translation errors in the same way that post-editors do: what needs to be changed in order to produce 'acceptable' output. However, researchers are usually concerned with particular types of errors connected with the specific problematic linguistic phenomenon which they are dealing with at the time.

At various times during development, MT systems are evaluated as whole systems. This is when researchers test programs against larger fragments of texts in prototype evaluations. At this stage they look for more than erroneous treatments of specific constructions and vocabulary items. Evaluation of errors should be more exhaustive, with the aim of determining which errors can be corrected only by revision of basic procedures and which errors are simply a matter of correcting dictionary data and can therefore be left for later development stages. Typically a system will pass through a series of such prototype evaluations.

9.4 Evaluation by developers

At some point, an MT system passes from a research project to a development project: changes in the basic design are no longer undertaken and the emphasis is on the creation of a practical system. The provision of facilities for users to input text, to compile and update dictionaries and to edit output texts entails the introduction of further types of evaluation. The linguistic evaluation of translations continues, but now the main concern is to identify errors which can be corrected within the capabilities of the system. Features which cannot be corrected will have to be dealt with by the provision of other software facilities.

During the development phase, it will be decided precisely what the limitations of the system are, what types of texts it can deal with satisfactorily, what subject domains should be covered in the dictionaries and the grammar rules, and what facilities must be provided to users, if these aspects were not already part of the original systems. The objective of development evaluations is to ensure that before being offered to potential users the system performs as intended and produces translations which are believed to be acceptable in known circumstances. The developers should discover precisely what improvements are feasible within the basic design, and how and at what cost they may be achieved.

Evaluations during development involve typically translations of substantial text corpora (covering the intended subject domain of the system) and the identification and classification of errors. The perspective will approximate that of potential users. Normally, the most frequent or least complex errors will be tackled first. After the dictionaries have been updated and some rules changed as appropriate, the corpora are tested again. The cycle is repeated until the results are 'acceptable', or it is considered that further investment of development time cannot be justified.

9.5 Evaluation by potential users

In many cases, system developers and potential users work together closely. Often, systems are in fact designed for specific users, who may participate in the development, may select corpora to be tested, and may be involved in evaluation. Such users will often know as much about the internal workings of the system, its limitations and potential, as the developers themselves.

More typical, however, is the potential user or purchaser who can evaluate a system only by its performance, as a 'black box' to be assessed by its results. Whereas the principal focus of evaluation by researchers and developers is the linguistic quality of the translation, the potential purchasers are concerned primarily with the capabilities, acceptability and cost-effectiveness of the system in their particular environments. From this perspective (Figure 9.1), the MT system is just one component in a broader configuration of systems.

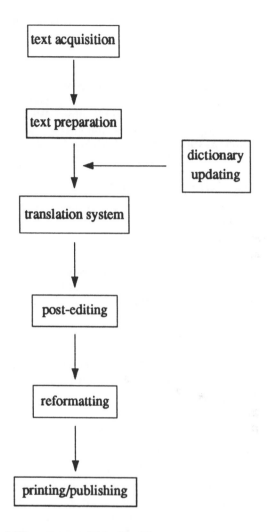

Figure 9.1 MT system within broader context

Text acquisition includes the production or receipt of a machine-readable text: word-processing, text transmission, optical character recognition (OCR) of printed or typed texts. Text preparation involves at least the separation of graphs and figures from the alphabetic text. In the case of 'restricted language' systems (section 8.3.1), preparation obviously embraces all the operations involved in checking and controlling the vocabulary and grammar of input texts. An important stage is often a preliminary examination of the text for unknown words and the consequent updating of dictionaries. After translation comes the revision of texts (post-editing), the reformatting of the text by insertion of graphs and figures, and finally stages in the preparation of translated text for printing and, possibly, publishing. In this context, translation is by no means the most expensive part of the operation: text input and preparation and text post-editing and printing may be more significant in total costs.

The capabilities of a system are to be assessed in the light of the user's particular needs. These should be precisely established. What types of texts does the user intend to translate (e.g. patents, abstracts, manuals, reports)? What subject areas do they cover? Are they intended for specialists or for the general public, for information purposes only or for publication? What volume of texts (of each type and/or in each subject domain) are anticipated? And are they all to be dealt with by the system? Are there any time constraints on the production of translations?

9.5.1 Linguistic assessment

When evaluating the linguistic capabilities of the system, the user should also examine the linguistic characteristics of the texts to be translated. Particularly important are vocabulary considerations. If texts cover a wide range of subjects there may be problems of homography which the system cannot deal with satisfactorily. If the vocabulary of texts is well covered by existing terminology standards the problems of dictionary compilation may be lessened; otherwise the user may have to undertake terminological research. A high proportion of compounds and nominalizations may also have an impact. Other linguistic factors to be considered include the occurrence of structures or features which the system may not cover (e.g. interrogatives, imperatives, subjunctives, particular tenses). Certain styles may cause problems, e.g. the system may not be able to parse 'telegraphic' constructions (2a) for (2b), long noun strings (3) or sentences containing parentheses (4).

(2a) Arrive London Tuesday.

(2b) I will arrive in London on Tuesday.

(3) mains cable socket switch indicator

(4) The new system will (if installed correctly) increase production.

The submission of representative texts for translation should allow users to assess the limitations of the system and its potential for improvement and extension. Users do not, however, have access to information about grammars and programs, do not know the linguistic model on which it is based (if any), and may not be able to judge these aspects in any case. They are limited to examining output and analysing errors in order to determine how much human revision is required if translations are to be brought to an acceptable standard. Their difficulty is in identifying those errors which can be easily rectified (e.g. by changes to dictionary entries) and in recognising those errors which reveal major deficiencies of the basic design. Furthermore, some errors (e.g. pronouns) which look important may in fact be easy to correct in post-editing while they are very difficult to correct in the program. Users need to be aware that certain linguistic phenomena cause problems for all MT systems, e.g. complex sentences, coordination, ellipsis, fragmentary sentences, telegraphic phrasing, complex noun phrases.

In many cases, only discussion with developers can establish which errors can be rectified easily and which cannot. Nevertheless, a proper evaluation should involve careful selection of texts, the making and testing of hypotheses about the way the system operates, by choosing suitable examples and counter-examples, and the detailed analysis of results. From such evaluations potential users should have an inventory of linguistic phenomena that are satisfactorily processed, and of those phenomena not processed at all; they should have available an explanation for good translations as well as poor translations, for good grammatical analyses as well as poor ones; they should know, in brief, why some kinds of texts are suitable for the system and why others are not. Ideally, they should also understand the basic nature and content of the linguistic components of the system, e.g. whether it analyses deep structure as well as surface structure, whether it uses an intermediate representation, what kind of information is taken from the dictionary, and when and how it is used, etc. Potential users should aim to be capable of making informed judgments of the true possibilities of improving the quality of output and extending the system to other domains and languages.

9.5.2 Evaluation of limitations, improvability, and extendibility

No MT system can ever be regarded by its designers as complete, least of all 'perfect', in its performance. Both developers and potential purchasers need to know what the limitations of the system are, and how it may be improved. Some limitations are obviously inherent in the basic design: most systems are limited to sentence analysis, thus no treatment of cross-sentence anaphora (section 5.4) can ever be possible. Many systems provide little or no semantic feature analysis of nouns, and thus the treatment of multiple noun–noun compounds such as (5) is severely restricted. However, many limitations are less obvious and can only be established with effort.

(5) fan nozzle discharge static pressure water manometer

To a great extent, assessment of the potential improvability of a system depends on detailed knowledge of the basic design and internal workings of all components of the system. Some failings of a system may be easier to overcome than others, and these phenomena may differ from system to system: what one system can achieve easily may be difficult in another. Changes in dictionary information may result in improvements but may also have an impact on other components; changes of grammar rules or of other procedures relating to linguistic structures carry the risk of a 'ripple effect', where the desired output is achieved but the change causes a new error elsewhere. While many commercial systems permit users to make changes to dictionaries of technical vocabulary, they prohibit alterations to basic vocabulary (i.e. common verbs and nouns) and forbid any changes of basic grammar and structural analysis. Improvements of basic design can be undertaken only by linguists and programmers employed by the vendor.

It is particularly difficult to assess a system's ultimate potential improvability. Many researchers have argued that MT systems based on the direct translation approach have much lower improvability potential than transfer systems. Their argument appears to be borne out by experience with the early Georgetown system, whose computational complexity (Chapter 1) precluded any changes after installation, and with the Systran Russian–English system at the US Air Force, where for over twenty years expansions and changes to dictionaries improved output quality, but are now found to be more likely to degrade it, due to the ripple effect mentioned above. However, nobody is able to assess these limits in advance, least of all for systems based on the transfer or interlingua approaches where operational experience is very much more recent.

Equally important is the potential extendibility of systems to other subject domains and other languages. Systems designed for one particular subject area are inherently more difficult to extend to other areas, not only because of differences in vocabulary but also because differences of grammar and style constitute different sublanguages (section 8.4). It should be noted that many systems which claim to be applicable to all subject domains have in fact been based on a particular subject area; at present many Japanese microcomputer systems are intended for translation of texts in computer science or electrical engineering. Extendibility to related subject areas could well be simply a matter of extending the dictionaries, although the dangers of homography should not be underestimated. Extendibility to less similar domains not only entails the creation of necessary dictionaries, but it may also require more fundamental changes to grammar rules and basic features of components. It is therefore important to establish the modularity of a system and the support given by developers and vendors for extending and improving systems for their users.

The extendibility of a system is highly dependent on the modularity of its analysis, transfer and generation components. A basic question is whether components developed for one language pair can be applied or easily adapted for another language pair. In theory, transfer and interlingua systems should be more easily extendible than direct systems. However, the claim has yet to be substantiated. A number of basically direct systems have added new pairs of languages without great difficulty (e.g. Systran and Weidner); as yet it is not known whether indirect systems have found it any easier.

9.5.3 Technical assessment

The computational features of the system may be easier to determine than the linguistic ones, and may often have more influence when evaluating MT systems. The particular hardware and software requirements of a system may inhibit some potential purchasers (although the usual advice is that it ought not to). What ought to be more important are the computational limitations of the system itself. There may, for example, be limits on the size of dictionary entries, on the character set, on the number of lexical items in dictionaries, on the length of sentences that can be analysed, on the size of texts that can be processed at any one time. There may be software or hardware features which determine the average processing times, which restrict access to dictionaries, and which reduce compatibility with other computer equipment such as OCRs, word processors or printers. Questions of software reliability and robustness are more difficult to answer, but at least purchasers should be able to reach agreement with developers or vendors about future maintenance of software and hardware.

9.5.4 Assessment of personnel requirements and ease of use

MT systems are usually installed in organisations employing professional translators. Their attitudes to computers, to MT and to changes in work practices are crucial to any successful introduction of an MT system. An important part of any evaluation must therefore be an assessment of how the system will be integrated with other components of the translation process (Figure 9.1 above).

Ideally, the operation should involve persons with computer expertise in natural language processing, linguists with knowledge of computational linguistics, translators with knowledge of MT, and terminologists familiar with computational tools. In practice, systems are run by translators who have to learn its capabilities and limitations by trial and error. Adaptability and a positive attitude are essential. But so too is adequate training. If translators are to become post-editors they have to learn new skills; the revision of MT output differs from the revision of human translation.

How much revision is required is therefore an important consideration; the linguistic evaluation of a system should provide some estimate of the types and frequencies of errors which need correction for the texts to be translated. An excessive amount of post-editing (or interactive correction) lowers morale and increases any antagonism towards MT. The low quality of some systems is known to have been a considerable irritant. If some texts are to be only lightly revised (e.g. if they are needed for information only) then the reluctance of professional translators to put out low-quality work has to be overcome. Whatever procedures are adopted, revisers should be positively involved in improvements to the system, by expanding and updating dictionaries, by proposing changes in grammar rules, etc. Above all, they need good facilities, e.g. split-screen editing, 'user-friendly' tools for correcting and replacing words, for transposing and transforming phrases and sentences, and for checking spelling

The adequacy of the basic 'core' dictionary supplied with the system is a major factor. Translators are likely to be antagonistic if they have to supply dictionary information for large quantities of common vocabulary. Special dictionaries are another matter; but the facilities for entering and updating data must not be complex: in particular, users should not be expected to know linguistic terminology, and differences between, e.g. 'transitive' and 'intransitive', should be illustrated by clear examples. Particularly desirable features are mnemonic codes, automatic generation of verb and noun paradigms, and checks for consistency.

Other facilities which enhance the practical acceptability of systems include the statistical monitoring of usage (sizes of texts, amounts of correction, frequency counts of vocabulary, etc.), and the comprehensiveness and readability of the documentation for the system.

9.5.5 Evaluation of costs and benefits

No MT system will be used, however good its quality, if it cannot compete in terms of cost with human translation. Inevitably, a major feature of any evaluation by potential users and purchasers has to be an assessment of the costs of installing and running a system and of the expected savings to be obtained in comparison with existing operations. A major overhead with many commercial systems is the need to build up collections of data such as customised dictionaries, but also, for example in one case, corpora of previously translated texts for use as examples: in any case, the efficiency of the system increases with use, so initial cost estimates may be considerably misleading, and a true estimate of MT costs may be impossible to achieve until the decision to invest time and money has already been taken. Costings are, of course, based not on the translation system itself in isolation but on the total operational environment (Figure 9.1).

Typically, the potential purchaser will submit texts for translation, and monitor and measure all production costs up to the final versions of translated texts, identifying all direct and indirect costs. These should include all costs of transcription and transmission (e.g. OCR, word processing), of preparing texts for input (checking, correcting, reformatting, perhaps controlling vocabulary and style), of updating dictionaries, of human interaction (if relevant), of recovering and post-editing texts, and of production and printing. A comparison will be made with the costs of producing the same quality of output by human translators, including all costs of acquisition, preparation, transcription, preliminary reading, dictionary consultation, typing, retyping, revision, proof-reading and printing. It should also be remembered that human translators need breaks, and cannot work intensively for long periods. Ideally the comparisons should involve the same texts with both human translation and human revision, and MT and human revision.

Against the costs should be set the relative benefits, which vary from system to system. Major benefits could include: faster production of translations, higher rates of productivity (which are particularly marked if large volumes of text in one specific subject domain are being translated), greater degrees of consistency in terminology (the importance of this factor may outweigh many perceived drawbacks), simultaneous output in many languages (which may well compensate for high costs of text preparation, e.g. in a 'restricted language' system, section 8.3.1). To these should be added expected benefits from future improvements in the translation system and in other facilities, particularly those for pre-editing, post-editing and formatting. Furthermore, the costs of maintaining dictionaries may well diminish: initially users have to enter large numbers of lexical entries; after some time the number of new items declines (unless, of course, new subject domains are undertaken).

The final stage of operational evaluation should always be a trial of the system in the actual working environment for a reasonable period of time (e.g. six months). Only then should the final decision be made.

9.6 Evaluation by translators

Professional translators are almost invariably the direct users of MT systems; few have yet been developed for non-translators, although more can be expected in the future. It has been made clear already that translators are likely to be closely involved in evaluations of systems for purchase and installation, even if in large organisations they may not make the final decision, which may be taken primarily on grounds of costs and benefits.

Translators' concerns are predominantly with the amount of work involved in pre- and post-editing, and the facilities available for substituting words, transposing phrases and changing texts. The quality of the MT system's output is obviously important; if translators consider that too often there will be more work in revising than in translating from scratch, then they are going to reject the system and oppose its introduction. Gains in productivity have to be substantial, and the revision work must not be tedious. Judgement is however often clouded by translators' attitudes; they have been trained to produce high quality work, sometimes even to improve the clarity and style of original texts. Translators are naturally reluctant to be responsible for what they consider an inferior product. Their instinct is to revise MT output to a quality expected from human translators, and they are as concerned with 'stylistic' quality as with accuracy and intelligibility.

In assessing MT they need to adopt a different attitude, to acknowledge that perfectionism is neither always desirable nor always appreciated, particularly if it results in higher charges. An MT system gives them the option of adjusting 'stylistic' quality to users' needs without sacrificing accuracy and consistency. In evaluating MT, therefore, translators should be less concerned with the fluency of the output than with the amount of revision required to produce documents at agreed levels of quality.

Some translators will undoubtedly decide that the changes in working practices which MT systems bring are not tolerable and they will continue with non-automated methods: the demand for good quality translation means they will not lack employment. Those translators who are prepared to be adaptable and to learn new skills and techniques will constitute a new 'breed' of translators. Nevertheless, adaptability should not be all in one direction: the attitudes and evaluations of translators ought to have much greater impact on the design of MT systems than has often been the case in the past. Too frequently, systems have been developed with little or no consultation with translators, who as principal users could make significant practical contributions.

9.7 Evaluation by recipients

Recipients of translations are interested in how much they have to pay for them, how quickly they have been done, and how acceptable they are in terms of quality and readability. Judgements by recipients ought to be included in evaluations by users and purchasers since, after all, those receiving translations have to see benefits as well.

Cost and speed are the only criteria in the case of MT output which has been revised to the standard of human translation. In theory, an MT system should permit both lower costs and faster production. It is, however, possible that the quality may not be as high as that produced wholly by human translation. The operators of the MT system may decide that the costs of high quality revision cannot be justified. Perhaps the recipient wanted the translation quickly and sufficient time could not be devoted to revision. It is for the recipient to decide whether the advantages of speed outweigh the disadvantages of lower quality.

What levels of quality are acceptable depend on the readership and use of the translation. Accuracy, style and readability may be crucial for instruction manuals and for text intended for general publication; and these will be assessed on the lines indicated earlier (section 9.2.1 above). However, if the recipient is an expert in the subject and only wants to scan the text for basic information a low level may be perfectly adequate, e.g. 'raw' output or lightly edited texts. Omission of articles, wrong prepositions, stylistic awkwardness, and many other types of 'errors' may all be accepted as long as the text is comprehensible and the information being sought can be extracted.

9.8 Further reading

Lehrberger and Bourbeau (1988) provide a thorough discussion of the linguistic evaluation by users, with a check-list of other factors. Dyson and Hannah (1987) give a useful summary of what potential users should look for when evaluating systems. The collection edited by Vasconcellos (1988) includes a number of general discussions of methods for evaluating systems, and the economic aspects are well covered by van Slype (1982).

For the evaluation of particular systems a good source is the proceedings of Aslib conferences, e.g. Lawson (1982), Picken (1985, 1986, 1987, 1988, 1990), Mayorcas (1990). Important evaluations are those of Systran by van Slype (1979) and of Logos by Sinaiko and Klare (1972, 1973). Contributions towards a methodology for MT evaluation have also been made by Melby (1988) and King and Falkedal (1990). Karlgren (1987) discusses the value of raw MT output for various purposes.

10
Systran

As a system with over 20 years of operational service, a period far longer than any other MT system, Systran cannot be ignored by any book devoted to MT. It is also a good example of the 'direct' approach to MT design, even if in certain respects a number of modifications make it less typical of this approach than older projects (see Chapter 1) and than a number of current low-priced personal computer systems.

10.1 Historical background

The genesis of the Systran system can be traced back to the earliest efforts in MT during the late 1950s. Its designer, Peter Toma, was the principal programmer of the SERNA implementation of the Georgetown University GAT system for Russian–English translation, demonstrated in 1960. (The subsequent Georgetown systems installed in 1963 and 1964 at Euratom in Ispra (Italy) and at the Oak Ridge National Laboratory of the US Atomic Energy Commission were later computational implementations of the GAT programs.) Toma had in fact begun MT research in 1957 at the California Institute of Technology before joining the Georgetown University project, the largest in the United States during the first decades of MT research (section 1.3). He left Georgetown in 1962 to set up his own company and to continue work on Russian–English MT, producing two systems AUTOTRAN and TECHNOTRAN for the fields of atomic energy and medicine. In 1964 Toma moved to Germany, where with the support of the Deutsche Forschungsgemeinschaft he began development of the Systran Russian–English system. At this stage, the prototype, showing clear signs of its GAT-SERNA ancestry, was evaluated at the University of the Saarland with a view to adaptation as a system for Russian–German translation; however, eventually the Saarbrücken group decided to develop their own system SUSY (Chapter 11).

In 1968 Toma founded Latsec Inc. in La Jolla, California, to develop the Russian–English system for the United States Air Force (USAF). Systran (an acronym for '*System translation*') was tested in early 1969 at the Wright-Patterson Air Force Base (Dayton, Ohio) and since July 1970 has continued to provide translations for the USAF's Foreign Technology Division to this day. Subsequently, Systran was used by NASA during the joint US–USSR Apollo–Soyuz space project (1974–75), and in 1976 it replaced the Georgetown system at Euratom.

The most significant development, however, was the demonstration in June 1975 of a prototype English–French version of Systran to representatives of the Commission of the European Communities (CEC), as a result of which a contract was concluded to develop versions for translation between languages of the European Communities. The contract with Toma's new company, the World Translation Center (WTC), included an agreement for substantial development of the systems by staff of the CEC's translation department. Work began in February 1976 on the English–French version, followed by the development of systems for French–English and English–Italian. By March 1981 it was considered that each system was producing reasonable enough output to set up a pilot production service in Luxembourg. Since this date, the CEC has developed Systran systems for a number of other language pairs which are in operational use.

As well as in the United States, numerous companies were set up to promote and develop Systran, e.g. the Systran Institut in Germany, the World Translation Corporation in Canada, and the Systran Corporation of Japan. The latter developed systems for Japanese–English and English–Japanese translation during the 1980s. In addition agreements were made with various other organizations, particularly with users for the joint development of lexical databases. The complex situation was simplified, after a series of negotiations spread over a number of years, when the Gachot company in France acquired all the US and European companies involved. Since 1986 the only company with Systran rights which remains outside is the IONA company which owns the Systran Corporation of Japan and the rights to the Japanese programs.

There are now many large users of Systran (section 10.5 below) and the number of language pairs grows year by year. Table 10.1 shows the language combinations available and in development at the time of writing. In addition, from its central computer at Soisy-sous-Montmorency (near Paris), the Gachot company offers a translation service for many of these pairs and some are available on the Minitel network in France: the first MT system for use by the general public.

A sign of the maturity of Systran was the World Systran Conference in February 1986 organized by the Commission of the European Communities and held in Luxembourg. This conference — the only one so far dedicated to a single MT system — brought together all the main Systran users to exchange experience and to discuss future developments.

Available	Under development
English ⇔ French	English ⇔ Chinese
English ⇔ German	English ⇔ Korean
English ⇔ Japanese	English → Arabic
English ⇔ Russian	English → Danish
English ⇔ Spanish	English → Dutch
English → Italian	English → Finnish
English → Portuguese	English → Norwegian
German → French	English → Swedish
German → Italian	French → Dutch
German → Spanish	French → German
	French → Italian
	Italian → English
	Portuguese → English

Table 10.1 Systran language pairs

10.2 The basic system

The ability of Systran developers to produce a wide range of language pairs points to a relatively high degree of modularity in the system design. It is reflected in the following features. There are two main types of programs: (a) system programs, written in assembler code, which are independent of particular languages; these are control and utility programs, such as those responsible for dictionary look-up routines; and (b) translation programs which are broken down into a number of stages, each with separate program modules. Translation programs for analysis and generation are claimed to be independent of particular language pairs, the analysis module for a particular language is constant whatever the target language concerned and the generation modules are likewise constant whatever the source. Furthermore, a common Romance language analysis 'trunk' has been developed which can be implemented whenever a Romance language (French, Italian, Spanish, Portuguese) is the source in a system. This modularity has been largely achieved since Gachot acquired Systran, and it also enables the relatively straightforward introduction of new techniques wherever they seem appropriate.

Nevertheless, in certain respects, the basic procedures of Systran remain much as first conceived for the USAF Russian–English system. The main component remains the large bilingual dictionaries containing not only lexical equivalences but also grammatical and semantic information used during analysis and generation. Much of this information is in the form of algorithms to be invoked during various stages of the translation processing. While programs of structural analysis and generation are largely independent, the main translation processes are driven by bilingual dictionaries of considerable complexity. Nevertheless, the compilation of bilingual dictionaries for new versions of Systran does not always have to start from scratch, as in many cases there need be only minor differences in the coding of source lexical items when coupled with new target languages. This fact has recently encouraged the compilation of dictionaries containing equivalents for a number of different target languages ('multi-target').

10.2.1 Dictionaries

The lexical databases for Systran are divided into the Main Stem dictionary, a bilingual dictionary of single-word entries, and various multi-word 'contextual' dictionaries. In the Main Stem dictionary every source language word (in its root form, except for English where full forms are given) is given a complete morphological, syntactic and semantic description: grammatical category, government, valency, agreement, transitivity, noun type ('animate', 'countable', 'abstract', etc.), semantic markers ('physical property', 'container', 'device', 'food product', etc.); and also a translation of the base form into an equivalent target word, accompanied by the grammatical information needed for its generation. A distinction is made between homographs with different grammatical categories, which have individual entries, and homographs of the same category, which are handled like polysemes by the 'contextual dictionaries' to be described below. This distinction is a reflection of Systran's predominantly syntax-based approach to translation, i.e. first, syntactic problems are dealt with, and then semantic information is invoked to resolve residual problems. It should be noted that for each source entry only a single target equivalent is given: this is in effect the 'default' translation which remains if it has not been changed by other dictionaries; for example, the English *station* has the default French translation *poste*.

The Systran 'contextual' dictionaries are derived automatically from a single source dictionary which can be regularly updated. They provide the data to enable analyses or translations to be modified according to context, and form a battery of dictionaries which apply at various stages of analysis and translation.

(a) The 'Idiom' dictionary is designed to deal with invariant (fixed) expressions (e.g. *on the one hand*, *in order to*), which may in some cases correspond to a single target form.

(b) The 'Limited Semantics' dictionary defines the scope of syntactic relations within noun phrases, e.g. by identifying *hydraulic brake* as a lexical unit and thus preventing an analysis of *hydraulic brake fluid* in which *hydraulic* modifies *fluid*. Other compounds may be identified as lexical units to ensure uniform translation (e.g. *machine translation* as *traduction automatique* and not *traduction de machine*). It also includes therefore entries for noun phrases which form a single semantic unit, e.g. French *pomme de terre* (corresponding to the single English word *potato*.) In some versions of Systran these two functions are divided between different dictionaries. The 'limited semantics' dictionary is also used to ensure the interpretations of otherwise ambiguous strings as noun phrases, e.g. *equipment cooling* as 'cooling of equipment', rather than as a noun with following modifier: 'equipment which is cooling ...'.

(c) The 'Homograph' dictionary lists the syntactic contextual information required for the resolution of certain homographs. For example in French, between a transitive verb (e.g. *prendre*) and its direct noun object (e.g. *chapeau*) there is normally a determiner (e.g. article *un* or possessive pronoun *son*), but there are exceptions (e.g. *prendre note* 'make a note of') and these are indicated in the homograph dictionary.

(d) The 'Analytic' dictionaries contain the exceptions to general syntactic rules which apply to particular words. For example, English *nor* breaks the 'normal' rule for conjunctions in that it can be followed by an inverted subject noun and verb, as in ... *nor could he see the difficulties*. These dictionaries may operate at various stages of analysis.

(e) The Conditional Semantics dictionary intervenes at the stage of transfer to make the final target language lexical selection. It incorporates both syntactic and semantic information to distinguish between potential target equivalents. For example, the default translation of English *grow* in French is *grandir*, but with an 'animate' complement it is to be *élever* and with a 'plant' as object it is *cultiver*. In some cases the number of contextual specifications is large: 400 entries distinguish the translations *huile* and *pétrole* for English *oil*.

10.2.2 Computational aspects

As stated earlier, there are basically two types of programs in Systran. The 'systems programs' written in assembler code are independent of the languages involved and include the general programs for input, dictionary look-up procedures and control of the translation processes. The 'translation programs' differ according to the specific languages being treated. As we shall see, these are divided into programs for the analysis of a source language, for transfer and for generation. These programs are written in a higher-level 'macro-language'.

Systran uses a linear data structure, comprising a sequence of records ('byte areas'), one for each word in a sentence. Each byte area consists of the word itself and the grammatical information and translation equivalents associated with the word in dictionary entries. By convention each byte stores a particular type of information. For example, byte 1 indicates the primary category (verb, noun, adverb) of the word, byte 2 the person and number of verbs, byte 3 the surface case (nominative, accusative, etc.) of nouns or the tense, mood and voice of verbs, byte 4 the gender and number of nouns, and so forth. The attributes of specific bytes vary relative to the values of other bytes (e.g. byte 3 according to whether byte 1 is 'noun' or 'verb'), but the essential feature to note is that Systran routines point to information stored in fixed byte locations. A rule to deal with a 'limited semantics' expression, for example *current practice*, might be coded in the 'macro-language' as in (1).

(1) CURRENT $C-B26 PRACTICE (PW)

Byte 26 specifies the adjectival modifier. In this case the rule applies if byte 26 of the principal word (PW) *practice* points to *current*. Likewise, the rule in (2) succeeds if the word which is pointed at by byte 102 has the 'semantic feature' ATTACH, i.e. *remove* must have a direct object such as *clamp*, *bolt*, etc.

(2) REMOVE $C-B102 ATTACH

Other bytes may trigger the initiation of subroutines, e.g. a positive value in a 'homograph notification byte' would start a homograph resolution routine (see 10.2.3 below).

During syntactic analysis, pointers are set up between specific bytes of different words, e.g. the link between an adjective and its governing noun is recorded by a pointer from byte 16 of the adjective to the address of the noun and by a pointer from byte 26 of the noun to the address of the modifying adjective. Similarly, after a subject noun has been identified, pointers are set up between it and the first word of the predicate, using specific bytes in the words concerned.

As this brief outline indicates, the data structure and low-level programming of Systran continue to reflect the computational practices of the 1960s and 1970s and are typical of many 'first generation' MT systems. Nevertheless, they have not prevented modifications and developments in a number of respects, as we shall see.

10.2.3 Translation processes

The basic stages of translation are: Preprocessing, Analysis, Transfer and Synthesis (Figure 10.1). It will become evident that the uses of the terms 'analysis', 'transfer' and 'synthesis' differ in certain respects from those found in other systems and from the usages adopted in this book.

The first stages involve dictionary look-up and morphological analysis and apply to the whole text.

1. Input: a program loads the text and identifies formatting information, e.g. titles, paragraphs, indentation.

2. Idiom dictionary look-up: invariant forms (fixed expressions) are identified, and single grammatical categories assigned (e.g. *in order to* as a preposition)

3. Main dictionary look-up: the remaining words of the text are searched for in the main stem dictionary and the information is copied into the byte areas of the data structure.

4. Morphological analysis is activated during dictionary look-up when applicable. If English is the source language, there is no morphological analysis as the dictionaries contain full forms; but in the case of languages like Russian or French stems and endings are entered in the dictionary separately. Morphological analysis entails the identification of potential combinations of stems and endings. It may also be applied to any words not found in the main dictionary in order to infer grammatical and category information.

5. Compound nouns are identified, by access to information from the 'Limited Semantics' dictionary; note that items which occur in the Limited Semantics dictionary are always treated as compounds. This causes problems when two words which otherwise form a compound happen to occur in sequence, for example the compound *femme de ménage* ('charlady') might occur in (3a) where the intended meaning is (3b).

(3a) *Il parla à la femme de ménage.*

(3b) He spoke to the woman about housekeeping.

The next stages of Analysis are applied to each sentence in turn:

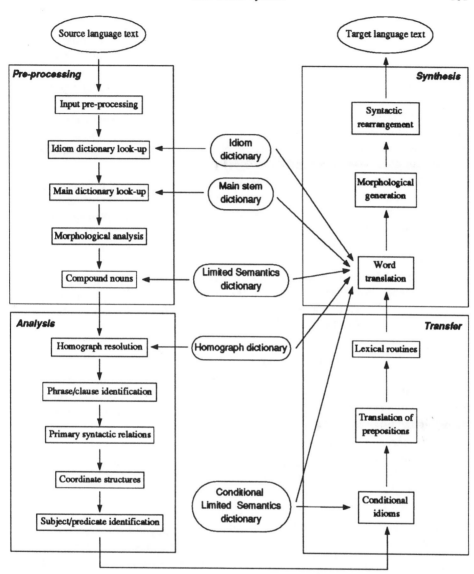

Figure 10.1 Systran translation process

6. Resolution of homographs is achieved by examining the grammatical categories of adjacent words in a single pass of each sentence. This is particularly complex in the case of English, since each word with potentially more than one grammatical category (i.e. most English words) has to be checked for its grammatical context in the string; e.g. *states* could be a verb in third person singular or a plural noun, but in the context of a preceding adjective *many* it can only be the latter. More general rules such as the following for French are also invoked: in most cases, a French verb cannot be followed immediately by a noun; there must be an intervening article or possessive pronoun. Any exceptions (e.g.

prendre note) are, as we have seen, noted in the Homograph dictionary. In the case of any unresolved homographs, the most frequent grammatical category is assumed. Note that this 'disambiguation by near context' is quite different from the parsing typically found in more recent MT and natural language processing systems.

7. Sentences are segmented into main and subordinate clauses by searching for punctuation marks, conjunctions (e.g. *because*), relative pronouns (*that*), etc. Markers for beginnings and endings of clauses are inserted. Eleven types of subordinate clause are recognised in English.

8. The 'primary syntactic relations' are determined, such as relations between nouns and modifiers (articles and adjectives, possessive nouns), between adjectives and adverbial modifiers, between verbs and objects, between prepositions and their 'object' noun (phrases), the relations of infinitives and gerunds to other words, etc. This pass also identifies the main finite verb, tense information, negation, comparatives and superlatives.

9. Words related by 'enumerations' are identified, such as coordinate structures within phrases. For example, in (4a), the coordination of *smog* and the phrase *pollution control* must be identified; in (4b) the coordination to be identified is that of *smog* and *pollution* as modifiers of *control*.

   (4a) Smog and pollution control are important factors.

   (4b) Smog and pollution control is under consideration.

In this case, syntactic information is available (*are* and *is*), but in other cases semantic information is necessary: for example, in (5a) the coordination of *zinc* and *aluminium* (as types of *components*) is licensed by the sharing of the semantic marker 'chemical element'.

   (5) zinc and aluminium components

A supplementary routine finalises syntactic relations, e.g. in (6) the syntactic status as 'object' of *demand* already established for *speed* in the previous stage is assigned also to *accuracy*.

   (6) The task demands speed and accuracy.

10. Subject and predicate are identified, going beyond the 'surface' phrase structures to 'deeper' analyses. It is a relatively simple process: already identified finite verbs are potential predicates and nouns (or pronouns) not already identified as 'objects' are potential subjects. In this way, sentences are marked as declarative, interrogative, or imperative.

11. Deep (case) relations are identified, i.e. relations between predicates and arguments, and including therefore the identification of grammatical subjects in passive sentences as the 'logical' objects of the verb. In most versions of Systran, this stage subsumes (or is preceded by) routines for establishing relations between prepositions and their governors (e.g. noun or verb).

Both stages 10 and 11 may involve consultation of the Analytic dictionaries to deal with infrequent and exceptional structures.

The Transfer program has three parts:

12. Lexical transfer of 'conditional idioms'. Standard idioms and fixed phrases have already been dealt with during analysis via the idiom dictionary

and Limited Semantics dictionary (stages 2 and 5). At this stage, other words receive 'idiomatic' translations under certain conditions which are defined in the Conditional Semantics dictionary. These conditions presuppose structural analyses of earlier stages. For example, if *agree* is in the passive, it is translated as French *convenir*, otherwise it appears as *être d'accord*; other examples involving *grow* and *oil* have already been mentioned (section 10.2.1). The homograph *lead* is to be translated as *plomb* when identified as a 'chemical element', which may have been achieved during the recognition of coordinated structures (e.g. *steel and lead*). The contexts consulted are generally the fairly simple relations of subject to verb, adjective to noun, adverb to verb, etc.

13. Translation of prepositions not already dealt with in the preceding stage. Selection is determined by dictionary information attached to verb forms or by codes attached to governing or dependent words.

14. Structural transfer using 'lexical routines', i.e. tests specified in the dictionaries for particular words or for particular syntactic or semantic categories of words. For example, the selection of appropriate translations of *as* in French (*comme, pendent que, à mesure que, puisque*) triggers alternative selections of constructions and verb tenses. As another example, routines assigned to *expect* ensure the correct constructions in French with reflexive and subjunctive, e.g. (7).

(7a) He expects to come.

(7b) *Il s'attend à ce qu'il vienne.*

The last stage, Synthesis, has also three basic parts:

15. Assignment of the default translation (in the Main Stem dictionary) for any word not already translated during transfer; for example, English *station* may have the default French translation *poste*, which would be selected if alternatives such as *gare* have not been already selected from contextual information.

16. Morphological generation, on the basis of structural information about case, gender, number, time, etc. from earlier stages and on the basis of information (in the Main Stem dictionary) about inflections and dependency restrictions, e.g. that French verbs of motion (*partir*) are conjugated with the auxiliary *être* in the past tense instead of *avoir*, and that a dependent infinitive follows directly after some verbs (*aimer aller*) rather than the normal *de* (*proposer de sortir*).

17. Generation of target word order, e.g. rearranging the word order from an English adjective–noun sequence to a French noun–adjective sequence. In French generation, this stage also deals with elision, e.g. *le homme* → *l'homme*, and with the translation of *it* by reference to the grammatical gender (male, female) of an antecedent noun in the previous sentence (usually the last) and, in this way, selecting *il* or *elle*.

10.3 Characteristics of the system

The Systran MT design is generally characterised as based on the direct approach. It is evident, however, from the description of the stages of translation that it could almost be classified as a transfer system. It would appear to have clearly separated phases of analysis, transfer and synthesis; it would seem at first sight that the analysis stages take no specific account of target language data and that at least part of generation is independent of the source language. It is these features which lead to the claims by the developers already described above.

It must be conceded that the basic design of Systran has changed considerably over the years since the first Russian–English system was introduced in the early 1970s. At this time, its ancestry in the Georgetown systems of the 1960s was still apparent. The analysis of Russian was influenced profoundly by the needs to generate English; sequences which could be adopted unchanged in English were not analysed in depth, and structures which are peculiar to Russian were given English-like analyses. The generation of English output was likewise dependent on information about the original Russian text. Some of this mixture can be found in the present USAF version, although efforts have been made to increase its modularity and to isolate independent modules of Russian analysis and English generation.

With the English–French system for the CEC, the Systran developers moved towards much greater degrees of modularity in order that programs designed for one language as source or target could be transferred to another version with a different target or source. As a result the programs for the analysis of English are now common to all Systran systems with this language as source.

Nevertheless, Systran cannot truly be characterised as a transfer system for a number of reasons.

First, there is no separation of linguistic data into monolingual databases for analysis and synthesis, with the bilingual databases confined to straight lexical and structural transfer. Instead, Systran retains the typically 'direct' feature of large bilingual dictionaries accessed at various stages of analysis and generation. It is, however, true that different parts of the bilingual databases are accessed and applied at each stage: during analysis only the source language information is used for morphological processing, homograph resolution and the identification of structural relations. It is also true that some essentially monolingual databases are available: the Homograph dictionary appears to contain only source language information about collocations of certain lexical items, and the Analytic dictionaries seem to be restricted to structural idiosyncrasies of source languages. In these particular respects, monolingual analysis is not oriented to specific target languages.

Second, despite the labels there is no clear separation of transfer and generation. In 'Synthesis', for example, are found the main processes of lexical transfer (stage 15) and structural transfer (stage 17). 'Transfer' is confined to routines specific to particular source or target lexical items: 'transfer ambiguities' (stage 12), problems of prepositions (stage 13), and lexically conditioned structural transformations (stage 14). The only monolingual process is that of morphological generation (stage 16), which is a feature typical of earlier direct systems (section 6.3)

Third, there is no complete analysis of sentences. Various relationships are identified: nouns are linked to modifiers (adjectives and articles), adverbs to verbs, subordinate clauses are marked, coordination is specified, subjects of verbs are identified, and so forth. Structural analysis is partial and selective; no non-terminal categories are recognised (e.g. noun phrases, verb phrases) and there is no attempt to build a full dependency or constituency representation. There is, in brief, no linguistic model or framework which is guiding analysis. The sole acknowledgement to linguistic theory is the distinction between surface relations (identified in stages 7 to 9) and deep structure relations (in stages 10 and 11).

The relative paucity of structural analysis means that much more 'grammatical' information has to be attached to individual lexical items in the dictionary than in the case of other systems, as pointed out earlier (section 6.3). In particular, as there are no representations on which general structural transfer rules can be based, the data for structural transfer have to be contained in the coding of specific lexical items.

Fourth, it appears that analysis is blocked in some cases. Once a string has been identified as an 'idiom' or 'compound' (stages 2 and 5) it is marked as a 'translated' unit. In subsequent stages there is no further analysis of the string. For example, the recognition that *hydraulic brake* is a compound means that further constituency analysis (as adjective and noun) does not take place. It should be noted, however, that this practice is by no means confined to direct systems.

Fifth, there is clear evidence of a residual preference for 'lexicographic' solutions (typical of direct systems of the first generation). It is seen not only in the precedence of lexically-driven structural transfer (stage 14) to general structure transfer rules (stage 17), but also in the prominence given to dictionary translation (idioms and compounds). One consequence is that syntactic information is not available when it could be used. Homograph resolution (stage 6) is based entirely on the examination of preceding or following words, within specified ranges. It can take no account of clause boundaries because these are not established until later (stages 7 and 8). This strategy of translating by default (which requires only shallow analysis) followed by 'repair' where possible, is typical of the first generation approach.

Finally, there is evidence of inconsistency in the application of semantic features, again, perhaps, because of the lack of a general model or framework. In origin, the semantic markers were indicators of subject domains. They now include generalised markers (PRPHY [physical property], MATER[ial], CONTNR [container], PROF[ession]), semi-specific markers (CHCOM [chemical compound], FPROD [food product], FINAN[ce]) and specific markers (MONTH, CITY, COUNTR[y]). Their primary function is to assist in the disambiguation of 'enumerations' (stage 9) and in the selection of target items (in stages 12 and 15), e.g. PROF ensures the selection of *employer* rather than *utiliser* when translating *employ*. But semantic markers are not used for semantic analysis as such. This may explain why they are not ordered in hierarchies. The marker PROF is not subordinated to HUM[an] and to AN[imate], for example, and so each would have to be assigned to the lexical items *teacher* or *lawyer*, if it is considered necessary for transfer. As the last comment implies, there appears to be no general guidance on the assignment of semantic markers; they are applied empirically to solve particular problems, with the obvious dangers of inconsistency and arbitrariness. The *ad hoc* nature of semantic markers is particularly evident in the Russian–English system. For example, the preposition *do* is translated as *up to* if the preceding verb or noun is '+increase' and as *down to* if it is '+decrease', and the preposition *po* is translated as *along* if the following noun is '+linear', as *over* if '+nonlinear' and as *using* if '+metal tool'. Some success in regularising and simplifying the application of semantic markers was achieved with the development of the English–French system for the CEC and this has continued with later systems developed there and by the Gachot company.

From the computational point of view, Systran is also typical of first generation systems in its choice of programming environment and its general computational approach. The data structure used is primitive, while the translation process is controlled directly by a sequence of procedures written in a relatively low level programming language. Even the (relatively recent) provision of a 'rule writing macro language' does not compensate, since the formalism does not encourage the declarative style of linguistic programming seen in later systems.

The general conclusion is that although successful efforts have been made to introduce greater degrees of homogeneity and conformity (in particular, the development of a common 'trunk' for the Romance languages), Systran still reflects the eclectic character of first generation direct MT systems. It still lacks a coherent linguistic theory at its base; many routines are designed empirically for specific problematic constructions associated with particular words in particular languages; there is little generality in lexical and structural transfer; the main burden of the translation process is carried by information contained within the large bilingual dictionaries. As a consequence, methods are inconsistent, coverage and quality are uneven, and modifications of lexical information can often have unexpected consequences.

10.4 Improvability

Since much of the success of the Systran translation programs depends on the quality of their bilingual dictionaries, it has been the enhancement of dictionary entries which has received most attention by those involved with the development of systems. For example in the CEC's English–French system, to block the erroneous translation of (8a) as (8b), semantic codes were incorporated which linked the adjective *faulty* and nouns categorised as 'devices'.

> (8a) The committee discussed faulty equipment and office management.
>
> (8b) *Le comité a étudié l'équipement et l'administration de bureau défectueux.*

As another example, to ensure the correct translation of phrases including *éviter* a routine was inserted to generate a present participle, so that (9a) is translated as (9b) and not as (9c).

> (9a) *éviter que l'argent soit dépensé*
>
> (9b) prevent the money being spent
>
> (9c) prevent that the money be spent.

However, such is the complexity of Systran's dictionaries that special care has to be taken to ensure that an 'improvement' introduced to deal with one particular problem does not degrade performance in another part of the system: this is the 'ripple effect', see section 9.5.2. (Some of these dictionaries are now very large: the Russian–English ones contain some 350,000 entries, the English–French and German–English nearly 150,000, and the English–German nearly 100,000 lexical items.) Experience with the USAF Russian–English system has shown that improvements from the addition of dictionary entries, homograph routines, etc. are often accompanied by degradations of output quality in other parts of the process: errors were appearing where none had occurred before. On aggregate there was progress, but it was not uniform and there were substantial losses. This is the penalty for Systran's lack of an overall linguistic theory which would give clearer guidance to researchers charged with such improvements. One answer was to take greater care; proposed changes are checked against a benchmark corpus of Russian texts (ca. 50 million words), and accepted only if there is no degradation. Improvement of the system is now a matter of 'fine tuning' and not of making large-scale modifications.

Later systems, it may be hoped, may avoid (or at least delay for a longer period) the quality degradation experienced in the USAF model. There will always be this danger if changes are introduced piecemeal with no clear guiding framework, but there is little alternative with Systran: lexical data are typically irregular, and changes have to be introduced by trial and error. Amendments to the CEC's systems are consequently done on test versions and introduced into production versions only after extensive trials.

Most improvements to Systran systems, other than expansions of lexical data, have therefore been relatively peripheral, which does not mean that they are unimportant for users, particularly post-editors. In French and Italian the minutes of meetings are conventionally recorded in the present tense, but in English the custom is to use the past. At the CEC a routine was inserted to convert tenses (present to past, perfect to pluperfect, future to conditional, etc.) and to change words such as *demain* into *the day after*, rather than the normal *tomorrow*. Another improvement was the introduction of routines to deal with some types of words not found in the dictionaries. In the earlier versions, such as the USAF Russian–English system, such words were left untranslated. At the CEC, routines were written to deal at least with those which have regular endings: some routines assigned a probable semantic marker (e.g. a French word ending in *-meter* would be coded as a device, one ending in *-ologie* or *-isme* as a branch of science), others offered provisional target language endings, so that *-ogue* (as in French *radiologue*) would be rendered *-ogist* (giving *radiologist*).

10.5 Evaluations, users, and performance

The two longest-standing users of Systran systems, the USAF and the CEC, have both undertaken thorough evaluations of quality and performance on a number of occasions. The USAF Russian–English system has been in use since 1970, producing nearly 100,000 pages of texts per year mainly for information gathering purposes. It has been estimated that less than 5% of output contains errors; the system itself flags texts for not-found words, acronyms, potentially suspect adjective–noun and noun–noun compounds, uncertainty in disambiguation, known problem words, and places where some revision of word order may be necessary. In fact only 20% of texts is flagged. Such is the overall quality of raw translations that users are now offered direct access to the system, submitting texts from personal computer terminals, usually short extracts. The USAF has recently extended its Systran services to translation from French and German and has plans for developing a Chinese–English system as well.

The English–French system at the CEC was extensively evaluated in October 1976 and in June 1978. In both evaluations comparisons were made between CEC documents in the form of human translation after revision, 'raw' unedited MT, and revised MT, each in terms of their intelligibility, their fidelity to the original, and types of errors. The raw MT output was found to have improved between the two dates in most respects, e.g. the scores of intelligibility (clarity and comprehensibility) rose from 47% to 78%, correction rates decreased from 40% to 36%. In subsequent years further expansion and improvements to dictionaries (the main source of errors) have lowered the error rate for this version to 11% in 1987. For other systems at the CEC, the rates are higher but still encouraging: French–English 14%, German–English 21%, English–Italian 29%, English–German 30%; but others are not yet satisfactory, e.g. German–French 67%.

Use of Systran at the CEC continues to grow — although more slowly than once anticipated — not only with more translators using raw MT output as 'pre-translation' drafts and with more fully post-edited translations being produced, but also with more requests for rapid minimal post-editing for texts where lower quality is acceptable, e.g. documents read for information gathering only. It is claimed that texts can be produced for this service at a rate of up to 5 pages an hour.

The use of Systran raw output for information purposes is found at many of the large companies and organisations which have installed Systran systems or which have contracts with agencies using Systran. In fact, the Systran vendors now concentrate their promotions of systems on this use rather than on the production of texts for post-editing. Major users are General Motors of Canada, where an English–French system produces literature for the Canadian market, the NATO headquarters in Brussels, the Dornier company in Germany, the German national railways (Bundesbahn), the Nuclear Research Center (Kernforschungszentrum) in Karlsruhe, the International Atomic Energy Authority, the French company Aérospatiale, and the Xerox company. The latter, in fact, is one of the biggest users, translating English technical manuals into five languages (French, German, Italian, Spanish, Portuguese) at a rate of some 60,000 pages a year. The noteworthy feature of this application is that texts are written in a controlled language, restricted in syntax and standardised in terminology and vocabulary usage, in order to reduce problems of ambiguity and homography for the MT systems and thereby to minimise and sometimes eliminate the need for post-editing. In the Xerox multilingual environment (one source and many targets) the costs of preparing texts before input are fully justified by the much lower revision costs. As a by-product, it is claimed that the use of 'Multinational Customized English' results in better-written original documents, to the benefit of English users. In coming years, Xerox intends to develop Systran systems for translating from English into Scandinavian languages (Danish, Norwegian, Swedish and Finnish).

Finally, the Gachot company has begun to make its systems available to smaller, casual users: in France, as already mentioned, to all Minitel subscribers; and in the United States, to anyone with a terminal linked to the mainframes at the Systran organisation at La Jolla, California. Systran has come a long way from the days when all input was on punched cards and output on computer printout had to be manually revised and then retyped. Its durability and wide usage demonstrate, above all, that MT is serving practical translation needs with success.

10.6 Sources and further reading

The literature on Systran and its users is now very large. For basic initial orientation and references see van Slype and Pigott (1979), Hutchins (1986), Wheeler (1987), and Whitelock and Kilby (1983), which is particularly valuable for its detailed treatment of the linguistic and computational processes. The most accessible descriptions by the inventor himself are Toma (1976, 1977).

For more recent information see the papers given at the World Systran Conference (1986), and by Gachot (1989) and Trabulsi (1989). The Xerox implementation is described by Elliston (1979) and by Scott (1990). For recent descriptions of the USAF setup see Bostad (1988), and for the CEC see Pigott (1989). The earlier evaluations of the CEC systems are summarised by van Slype (1979).

11
SUSY

11.1 Background

Research on MT at the Universität des Saarlandes in Saarbrücken, Germany began in the mid 1960s with the development of a parser for German. A more substantial project began in 1967, just at the time when elsewhere MT research was coming to a stop as a result of the ALPAC report (section 1.3). This explored the possibility of adapting the Systran system for Russian–German translation, but the attempt failed and the group started work on its own prototype. In 1972 the project combined with other activities on data processing and mathematical linguistics to form the Sonderforschungsbereich 100 Elektronische Sprachforschung (SFB-100) ('Special Research Group 100: Electronic Language Research'), funded primarily by the Deutsche Forschungsgesellschaft ('German Research Association', a government body). The Russian–German prototype was the starting point for research on the multilingual system known as SUSY (Saarbrücker Übersetzungssystem 'Saarbrücken Translation System'). The languages involved have been German, Russian, English, and French (also briefly, Esperanto); the emphasis throughout has been the analysis and generation of German.

Over a period of 20 years, SUSY underwent many changes in response to developments in the field. There are consequently problems of presenting the system. This chapter describes basically the mature version of the SUSY-I system of the mid 1980s, programmed in Fortran, and implemented until 1981 on a Telefunken TR440, and thereafter on a Siemens computer. The later SUSY-II demonstrated further developments, incorporating insights from the earlier version and showing substantial influences from the Eurotra project (Chapter 14) with which many researchers at Saarbrücken were heavily involved. Indeed, work on Susy came to an end in 1986, because in effect the research had merged with the work on Eurotra.

11.2 Basic system design

Susy is basically a **transfer** system with monolingual analysis and synthesis (generation) phases and a bilingual phase in which lexical and structural transfer takes place. The structures that are computed are essentially dependency tree structures, a reflection of the predominance of the Valency grammar approach among German linguists (section 2.9.5). The input can be optionally pre-edited. There is no interactive post-editing. Due to the incorporation of 'fail-soft' modules, Susy always produces some sort of output.

The system is highly **modular** in one major respect: the translation process is broken down into separate sub-processes. The modules are applied in strict sequence. In general, analysis and synthesis modules are language-specific, while transfer modules are designed for specific language pairs. However there are also, in the version we describe, some modules which are not independent of particular pairs, especially in analysis. In this respect, Susy is not quite a pure multilingual transfer system, where, it will be recalled (Chapter 4), the analysis module for a source language should combine with any target languages in the system. Close inspection of some Susy analysis modules reveals that they do take account of target languages. This explains why the different versions of Susy reported in the literature often diverge slightly in their details. While the principle of multilinguality may be undermined as a result, the modularity of Susy must be seen as a positive feature. It permits revisions and changes in some parts of the analysis and synthesis processes while retaining other parts from previous versions, both in order to incorporate new linguistic ideas and approaches, and to adapt the analysis modules of one language pair for use with a different language pair.

In another respect, Susy does not score highly. There is generally no clear separation of linguistic and algorithmic aspects, although again there have been differences between versions. The early Susy system had effectively no such separation in the sense that, although highly modularised, the various modules were directly programmed in Fortran. The major innovation of the later Susy-II version was the use of a rule-writing formalism.

The basic stages of processing in Susy are as in Figure 11.1.

The substages (or 'operators' in the Susy terminology), with their titles, are as follows. Text input (LESEN) may be preceded by an optional stage of pre-editing. Dictionary look-up (WOBUSU) and its associated morphological analysis is followed by homograph resolution (DIHOM) and then by various levels of syntactic parsing: SEGMENT identifies clauses and phrases and a tentative dependency structure, NOMA identifies nominal groups and VERBA verbal groups. The whole sentence receives a complete parse by KOMA (complement analysis), and problems of lexical and structural ambiguity are dealt with by the semantic disambiguation module SEDAM. The single stage of transfer (TRANSFER) involves both lexical and structural transfer.

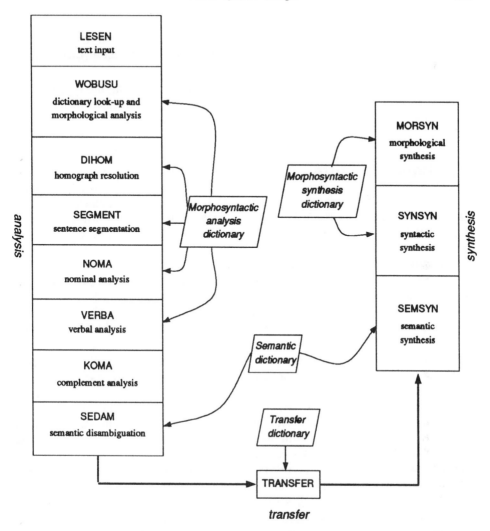

Figure 11.1 Translation process in Susy

The target language is generated by passing through the stages of semantic synthesis (SEMSYN), syntactic synthesis (SYNSYN) and morphological synthesis (MORSYN).

There are separate monolingual dictionaries for source and target languages, containing essentially morphological and syntactic data for lexical items. Each language has separate dictionaries for analysis and synthesis; the largest are the German analysis dictionary with 140,000 entries, and the German synthesis dictionary with 14,000 entries; others are much smaller. Semantic processes involve 'semantic dictionaries' for source and target languages; in this case the same monolingual dictionary is used for both analysis and synthesis, the largest being again for German (75,000 entries), with others much smaller. Semantic dictionaries include semantic features and syntactic and semantic conditions for polysemes, in particular for prepositions. The bilingual transfer dictionaries comprise basically lexical equivalences with some information on structural contexts. Their relatively small sizes (only English–German more than 10,000 entries) reflect the experimental nature of the SUSY project.

We describe the operation of the modules after first outlining the type of data structure found in SUSY, the pre-editing options and the mechanism for ensuring some output if any component fails (the RESCUE operator).

11.3 Data structure

As in any modular system, the data structure is very important, since it ensures communication between modules. We can consider it from two points of view, the computational and the linguistic. From the computational point of view, the data structure of SUSY is similar to that found in Systran; it is motivated by programming convenience, in the SUSY case the programming language being Fortran. SUSY uses a data structure where there is one data record per word, and these are stored in a sequential file. The 'word record' is divided into 'cells', each of one or more bytes, corresponding to specific information about the word. The translation process consists of successively rewriting the file, changing the values in appropriate cells.

From a linguistic point of view, the data structure is a dependency tree structure, in which the governor–dependent relationships for each word are identified. In a noun phrase such as *the very big system*, the noun *system* is the governor with immediate dependents *the* and *big*, and the adjective *big* having *very* as its dependent. At the sentence level, the main verb is taken to be the overall governor, with its complements (subject, object, etc.) and modifiers (circumstantial adverbials) as dependents. The dependency information is augmented by indications of the types of dependents, e.g. subject or object, modifier or determiner, and so on.

Although both Systran and SUSY use rather crude low-level data structures, the linguistic interpretation is more sophisticated in SUSY. Specifically, some of the cells are used as 'pointers', permitting the sequential file structure to be used for representing tree structures, in the following way. Each word record is numbered consecutively, according to the position in the sentence of the word it represents. Each byte in the word record is capable of storing a single character: a letter or integer. The first cell might consist of 20 bytes, say, and is used to store the string itself. The next five cells might be one byte each, and contain grammatical information from the dictionary (e.g. category N=noun, V=verb, etc., and if a noun whether S[ingular] or P[lural], or if a verb its person, number and tense, etc.). The next cell might be 30 bytes containing the stem (root) form and morphological information, e.g. that the stem allows only certain endings, and so on. (The sizes and nature of the cells suggested here are for illustrative purposes, and do not necessarily reflect accurately the exact structure of SUSY word records.)

We assume, again for the purpose of illustration, that bytes numbered 75 and 76 are used to store pointer information: in byte 75 will appear the record number of the governor of the current record, and in byte 76 a code indicating what sort of dependent it is (e.g. S[ubject], O[bject], M[odifier] and so on). In this way we might have the data structure shown in Figure 11.2 for the sentence (1):

(1) The file contains secret information about every employee.

Record no.	1 2 3 4 5 6 7 8 9101112131415161718192021222324252627282930313233435			70717273747576777879 80
1	THE	D	THE	2D
2	FILE	NS	FILE	3S
3	CONTAINS	V3SP	CONTAIN	0
4	SECRET	A	SECRET	5M
5	INFORMATION	NS	INFORM	30
6	ABOUT	P	ABOUT	5M
7	EVERY	Q	EVERY	8Q
8	EMPLOYEE	NS	EMPLOY	60

Figure 11.2 Data structure (simulated)

The information in bytes 75 and 76 effectively represents the following dependency tree (2):

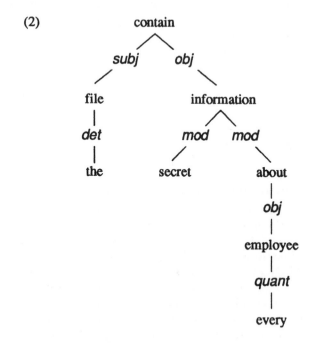

Although the data structure may be rather crude computationally, it can be seen that by using this pointer mechanism it can be used in a linguistically quite sophisticated way. There are, however, problems when alternative analyses are possible (e.g. caused by category ambiguities, as we shall illustrate). The creation of alternative tree structures means that there have to be copies of word record files differing perhaps only in the details of one or two codes.

11.4 Pre-editing and the fail-soft RESCUE operator

SUSY provides the option of pre-editing source texts by inserting special codes to aid analysis. Pre-editing permits the enhancement of the system's performance, but is not an essential feature of it. The analysis processes look out for these codes but are also able to operate without them. Examples of some of the SUSY codes have been given in section 8.3.1. When we look in more detail at the SUSY analysis stages, we will see the effect of codes in different modules.

A characteristic and innovative feature of SUSY is the explicit incorporation of the **fail-soft** operator RESCUE, which comes into operation whenever something has gone wrong with any of the modules. Each module includes consistency checks to see that the input and output conform to what is expected. In other words, there are minimum entry requirements for each module. Within each module there is the expectation that certain computations will have been successful and a new result produced. If the expectation is not fulfilled (because the rules are too strict, or the input is very unusual) then the appropriate RESCUE operator is triggered: a mechanism which attempts to complete the work of a module by relaxing or ignoring the constraints which prevented the production of some output.

In this respect, SUSY is a 'try anything' system. Whatever the input it will be able to produce some sort of translation, even if no more than a partial word-for-word version. Moreover, the triggering of this special procedure means that the system itself is 'aware' that the result may be of a low quality and can indicate the fact this when producing output.

11.5 Analysis

11.5.1 Text input and dictionary look-up

The first module, called LESEN ('read'), is a stage of non-linguistic preprocessing. LESEN reads the text into the initial data structure, divides the text into sentences, and assigns each word an identifying number. It also normalises the text, which means taking account of typographical information (notably, for German, whether the word begins with a capital letter). For each word, a 'word record' is created, as described above (section 11.3) and including any pre-editing information.

The output of LESEN is passed to the next module, called WOBUSU (*Wörterbuchsuche* 'dictionary look-up'). Only words marked during pre-editing as proper names, e.g. *Tom=* are ignored. There are three monolingual dictionaries in SUSY: a high-frequency dictionary of grammatical words, a stem dictionary which includes all irregular forms and all irregular stems, and an idiom dictionary. The dictionary entry gives the stem or the full form, a lemma (or lexical item) and the corresponding morphological and syntactic information. It also gives, depending on the category, certain paradigmatic information. For example, for a noun the information concerns its gender, plural form, prepositional valency (e.g. *Lust AUF Kuchen* 'desire for cakes', *Vertrag MIT Guinea* 'treaty with Guinea'), and so on. For a verb, the dictionary indicates whether it includes a separable prefix, what inflectional paradigms it belongs to, which verb type it belongs to (e.g. full, auxiliary, modal), whether it combines with *zu*, which form of passive is available (none, personal, impersonal, or both), whether the past participle can be used as an adjective, what case its reflexive pronoun takes, if appropriate, which auxiliary verb (*haben* or *sein*) is found in compound tenses, and what its valency frame is (including up to three prepositional objects).

11.5.2 Morphological analysis

The WOBUSU module also incorporates morphological analysis, which is broken down into two sub-modules, INFLECTION and COMPOUND.

The first module, INFLECTION, deals with single words and attempts to give an analysis in terms of stem + affix. It examines all possible segmentations of words and filters out those which are not plausible combinations of stems and affixes, i.e. where the proposed stem or affix form does not exist. For example, the word *Speichern* would be segmented as follows:

(3) SPEICHERN+0 SPEICHER+N SPEICHE+RN
    SPEICH+ERN SPEIC+HERN SPEI+CHERN
    SPE+ICHERN SP+EICHERN S+PEICHERN

When the stems (the parts before +) are looked up in the dictionary, only four are found to be plausible: namely *SPEICHERN* (the infinitive of the verb *speichern* 'to store', *SPEICHER* (the stem form of the noun *Speicher* 'store', or the stem form of the verb *speichern*), and *SPEICHE* (the stem of the noun *Speiche* 'spoke' of a wheel). Of these four possibilities, it can immediately rule out *SPEICHE+RN* since *+RN* is not a possible ending. Each of the remaining solutions is for the moment equally plausible, and the alternatives are stored in the word record, namely

(4) SPEICHERN+0 infinitive of *speichern*
    SPEICHER+N dative plural of noun *Speicher*
    SPEICHER+N inflected form of verb *speichern*

The resolution of this ambiguity is left to a later module. In this example there are only three alternatives, but multiple output from INFLECTION is quite frequent in German, which as we have seen (section 5.1) has a number of highly ambiguous endings out of context.

If INFLECTION fails to provide at least one solution, then the COMPOUND module is activated. This deals with compound words and derivations, which are a major problem for a language like German which permits very free and productive derivation and compounding. Whereas in English, compounding is an essentially syntactic phenomenon in that it concerns identifiable words used in sequence, in German it is a morphological problem. Individual elements of compounds are joined together to make single 'words', which are rarely listed as such in dictionaries.

The COMPOUND module works in a similar manner to INFLECTION, but segmentation is more complex: not simply identifying stem + affix, but recognising patterns of multiple affixes and roots:

$$(P (Z)) R (S)$$
$$(P) (G) R (S)$$
$$(P) R ((F) R)^n (S) \quad n{\geq}1$$

where brackets indicate optionality, the index *n* repetition, and

P = prefix
S = suffix
R = root
F = compounding unit *e*, *es*, *s*, *n*
G = pre-morpheme *ge*
Z = morpheme *zu*

For example (5).

(5) *herauszubringen* ('to bring out') = HERAUS+ZU+BRINGEN (P Z R)
ausgebildete ('educated'+inflection) = AUS+GE+BILDET+E (P G R S)
Geburtstagsgeschenke ('birthday presents') =
GEBURT+S+TAG+S+GESCHENK+E (R F R F R S)

If both INFLECTION and COMPOUND fail to suggest an analysis, the word is treated as 'unknown'. However, because German is highly inflected, it is often possible to guess the syntactic category of unknown words from their endings. In this way, the results of either module which provide plausible combinations of endings and unverified stems can be passed on to further stages. For example, the ending *-te* usually indicates a finite verb, as in *pflegte* ('cared for'), though it might not (e.g. *Kette* 'chain').

The results of INFLECTION and COMPOUND are passed to a final sub-module of WOBUSU, which deals with the identification of fixed phrases. The operation of morphological analysis before the recognition of fixed phrases allows SUSY to treat semi-fixed idioms which are nevertheless susceptible to grammatical inflection, e.g. noun phrases which take case endings, idiomatic verbs which are inflected for tense and agreement, and so on.

11.5.3 Homograph disambiguation

In the data structure resulting from WOBUSU is a sequence of words which have been looked up in the dictionary, many of which are ambiguous in category. The next phase DIHOM (*Di*sambiguierung von *Hom*ographen 'homograph disambiguation') attempts to resolve these ambiguities. The technique used is based on compatibility and distributional information, and is therefore more like 'stochastic parsing' models than the more traditional grammar-based approaches.

DIHOM consists of three sub-processes. Two general routines dealing with impossible sequences and with the ranking of possible ones are preceded by routines for the treatment of 'special cases'. These are specific items or classes of items which require a particular strategy for disambiguation. One special case is the German word *bis*, which can be a subordinating conjunction, a coordinating conjunction, an adverb or a preposition. It can be treated as a special case because this particular combination of category ambiguities is unique to this word. Other examples are non-contiguous conjunctions such as *weder ... noch* ('neither ... nor'), *um ... willen* ('for ... sake'), *not only ... but also*, and so on.

The second sub-process is called INHIBIT, which in some accounts precedes the routines for special cases. This looks for and eliminates impossible sequences of categories. In German the sequence determiner + finite verb is impossible; therefore, if a determiner is followed by a word which could in isolation be interpreted as a finite verb (e.g. *das Verlangen* 'the demand'), this reading would be eliminated. A further example from German is that a finite verb form may not follow immediately after a preposition (**mit machte*); thus *vererbten* in *aus vererbten Grundstücken* cannot be a finite verb ('[they] inherited') but must be an adjective (derived form the verb), thus meaning 'from hereditary lands'.

The third and chief process in DIHOM is the calculation of 'weightings' for the remaining ambiguities based on tables of probabilities and compatibilities. 'Probabilities' measure the likelihood of two categories occurring in sequence: it is a purely statistical measure which results in not a single solution but a ranked list of solutions. For example, if a noun–adjective ambiguity follows a determiner then it is more likely to be a noun, but the adjective possibility is still accepted, with a lower score. 'Compatibility' is a similar measure which takes account of mutual probabilities, i.e. when there are two ambiguous words occurring together the probability of the solution for one depends on its compatibility with the solution for the other. Compatibility testing also looks for relationships between words over longer distances: for example, if there is a relative pronoun then there should be a finite verb somewhere to its right. The final step is to combine weightings for individual words in the calculation of a ranked order of probabilities for the word sequences.

It is easy to see how the fail-soft mechanism (section 11.4) can take advantage of this approach: if in later modules it is found that the preferred homograph disambiguation was wrong (because it does not permit the analysis to proceed) then it is a relatively simple matter to backtrack and try the next ranked solution.

The probability and compatibility scores were initially estimated by linguists and then adjusted over a long period in response to incorrect translations. The alternative of basing these measures on large-scale corpus analysis (cf. section 18.2) does not seem to have been used.

11.5.4 Phrasal analysis

The next module is called SEGMENT, and its purpose is to identify clause boundaries within the sentence, i.e. segment the sentence into main clause, subordinate clauses, parenthetical clauses, and so on. Clause boundaries are identified by looking for punctuation marks (for which conventions are stricter and hence more reliable in German), for subordinating conjunctions and for relative pronouns. A major difficulty is the recognition of the scope of conjunctions, e.g. whether *und* ('and') coordinates two nouns, or two noun phrases, or two verb phrases, or whatever. This module also includes a kind of validity checking, which looks for obligatory elements within clauses. For example, the main clause in a sentence should have a finite verb, an infinitival clause should contain an infinitive verb form, and so on.

A different segmentation routine was written for English (PHRASEG) and French based more closely on the analysis of surface structure, particularly the positions of nouns and finite verbs. It was introduced because the punctuation conventions of English and French differ so markedly from those for German (see section 2.3).

The output of SEGMENT (or PHRASEG) is passed to two stages of phrasal analysis dealing with noun groups and verb groups. The two modules are NOMA (*Nominalanalyse*) and VERBA (*Verbalanalyse*) respectively, though some descriptions of SUSY have different names for these modules.

NOMA operates on the segments identified by the previous module, and consists of twenty or more sub-processes dealing with the internal structure of noun phrases. These sub-processes are each devoted to specific analysis tasks such as apposition, numerals, adjectival groups, embedded structures and so on. Some are based on the identification of 'markers' (such as punctuation or specific words, e.g. *for instance*, as signs of apposition); others are based on semantic features to establish valency relations. The main sub-process, however, is the one which deals with the recognition of simple groups such as preposition + determiner + noun, determiner + adjectival group + noun, etc. The procedure is based on lists of permissible sequences (rather as in COMPOUND above), with plausibilities based on congruences of case, gender and number as appropriate. The 'longest match' principle is applied, i.e. the longer sequences of categories are tested first.

NOMA is followed by a similar process of verb group analysis, VERBA. Just as NOMA treats different types of noun structure, VERBA deals with compound verb groups, modal auxiliaries and so on. This is a major task for German which has relatively few inflected tenses (e.g. in comparison with French), but allows many combinations of auxiliaries and modal verbs, e.g. (6); as the translation indicates, there are similar problems in English.

> (6) *Die Aufgabe hätte getan werden sollen.*
> 'The task ought to have been done'

11.5.5 Structural analysis

The output from NOMA and VERBA provides the building blocks for the next stage of the analysis, namely the structural or complement analysis carried out by the KOMA module ('*Komplementanalyse*'). The purpose of KOMA is to determine the valency structure for each clause. For example, KOMA determines which of the noun groups identified by NOMA should fill the argument (or 'complement') slots for the verb identified by VERBA in a verbal clause. In the case of complex noun groups, its task is to establish the internal valency and argument relations. Verb arguments include nominal groups, prepositional phrases, infinitival and subordinate clauses. Arguments of nouns are adjectival groups, plus prepositional phrases and certain types of subordinate clause, e.g. *daß*-clauses as in (7a) or infinitivals as in (7b).

> (7a) *die Idee, daß er kommen soll* 'the idea that he should come'
> (7b) *sein Versprechen, pünktlich zu kommen* 'his promise to come on time'

KOMA works by first attempting to fill up the valency slots appropriate for the main word in the clause, e.g. subject and object for a finite verb. This is achieved by checking for compatibility in terms of syntactic case and number, and, to a certain extent, by checking for simple semantic feature co-occurrence restrictions. Remaining elements are analysed as adverbials or appositionals, though again there is some checking for semantic compatibility (e.g. adverb of direction with a verb of movement).

The module also attempts to reconstruct elliptical structures, e.g. from (8a) to (8b).

(8a) *Der Bauer lacht und singt.*

(8b) *Der Bauer lacht und der Bauer singt.*
'The farmer laughs and [the farmer] sings'

Similarly, for English, KOMA tries to find the 'deep' subjects in sentences like (8c) and (8d).

(8c) John persuaded him to go home.

(8d) John promised him to go home.

As a consequence of the analysis in terms of valencies, passive constructions are represented in active forms, as this example (9) of the output from KOMA illustrates.

(9a) *Die durchgeführten Versuche werden von dem Chemiker als Erfolg bezeichnet.*
'The experiments carried out are declared a success by the chemist'

(9b)

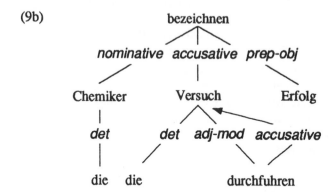

11.5.6 Semantic disambiguation

The final module in the analysis phase is called SEDAM (*Semantische Disambiguierung*). Its procedures are based primarily on semantic features assigned to nouns and some pronouns in the 'semantic dictionaries' and on various types of semantic rules attached to entries. Semantic features are of two kinds: those taken from a restricted set of presumed universals (human, abstract, animate, etc.) and those from a language-specific set of features developed initially for noun groups (geographical location, vehicle, profession, animal, plant, etc.). The first set is hierarchically structured, so that superordinate features are not entered in dictionaries but are created automatically as appropriate. The rule sets attached to entries are invoked for changes, deletions and insertions in structures, and are controlled by syntactic or semantic specifications of contexts.

The purpose of SEDAM is to allocate an interpretation to syntactic structures which are semantically ambiguous or vague. For example, a noun referring to a process may be modified in a number of ways which are not made explicit: a modifying noun might refer to the agent of the process (e.g. *human understanding*), or to the object (*satellite launching*), or to the method (*computer simulation*), or to the location (*inner-city deprivation*), and so on. Such ambiguities are resolved by the application of rules expressing semantic preferences.

Another type of semantic disambiguation which SEDAM attempts is the distinction of homographs of the same category, i.e. words which up to this point can be correctly assigned to a single syntactic category, but for which there are two (or more) distinct meanings and uses. For example, *trade* can refer to an occupation or profession, or to commerce in general. The first sense may be isolated by the presence of a possessive pronoun (*his trade*) or preceding preposition (*by trade*); the second may be excluded if the noun is plural. Most distinctions are, however, based on co-occurrence restrictions applied to semantic features, e.g. in recognising the various uses of *raise* ('cultivate', 'express', 'produce', 'bring up', etc.). Evidently, these distinctions are in part motivated by the need to provide the information necessary for lexical transfer into particular languages; it is not clear to what extent the SUSY researchers regard them as applicable more widely.

Included in SEDAM, also with a view to transfer problems, are routines for identifying 'semi-fixed' expressions, e.g. the phrase *take into consideration*, in structures where other components may interrupt (10).

(10) The Commission took the plan into consideration.

The basic task is to interpret the verb + prepositional phrase as a single unit with *Commission* and *plan* as its subject and object arguments respectively.

Prepositions are dealt with by a special routine which examines valency relations and the semantic features of arguments and which creates 'artificial words', in effect interlingual elements, which are left unchanged during the subsequent transfer processes.

11.6 Transfer and synthesis

TRANSFER is a sequence of processes, using the bilingual dictionary to replace source language lexical forms by their target language equivalents. Normally, the corresponding dependency structure is preserved, though exceptionally this can be altered by TRANSFER. This module also includes a sub-process which attempts to translate words which WOBUSU identified as unknown. The main part of TRANSFER is the simple translation of lexical units which is made on a word-by-word basis, without looking at the surrounding context. There are some special purpose sub-modules within TRANSFER that deal with particular cases such as the translation of negation, the treatment of surface case relations within noun groups, and so on. For certain language pairs, additional TRANSFER modules are needed, for example to deal with the lack of determiners when translating from Russian as the source language.

The task of SYNTHESE is to construct target language sentences on the basis of the output from TRANSFER. It consists of three sub-processes dealing with semantic, syntactic and morphological generation.

SEMSYN (*Semantische Synthese*) has the task of generating idioms or 'semi-fixed' constructions where appropriate, or of producing the correct prepositions for verbs and nouns (e.g. translating *to* with geographical names: *in die Schweiz, zu Berlin, nach Europa*), and of translating 'artificial words' into target lexical items. Artificial words are lexical units formed during analysis and include disambiguated homographs (e.g. *Schloß₁* 'lock', *Schloß₂* 'castle') and discontinuous multi-word lexical items (e.g. *Landwirtschaft betreiben* as the translation of *to farm*, compound prepositions such as *away from*, English phrasal verbs such as *take down*, and so on).

SYNSYN (*Syntaktische Synthese*) takes the output of SEMSYN and produces a sequence of lexical items (i.e. word stems) with the associated morphological information necessary for morphological synthesis. Part of the task of this module is to determine the correct surface word order, as well as the surface case endings of nouns and various agreement phenomena, depending on the target language concerned (e.g. dative plural ending in German, subject–verb agreements in many languages, and number–gender agreement in French noun groups).

There are a number of interesting sub-processes within SYNSYN. One called SGKOMP deals with compounds and derivations. For example, when translating the French phrase *système de traduction* ('translation system') into German it creates a compound noun *Übersetzungssystem* rather than the noun phrase *System von* [or *für*] *Übersetzung*. Another module SNOADJ determines which of various possible realizations for certain modifier–noun combinations should be chosen, e.g. whether *Israeli lemons* or *lemons from Israel* should be output.

One of the more complex sub-processes of SYNSYN is SPORE, which deals with the synthesis of pronouns and possessive adjectives. In German, for example, pronouns must agree in grammatical gender with their antecedent nouns. In (11), *it* refers to *file* (which is feminine in German *Datei*) and not *system* (which is neuter), and so should be translated as *sie* and not *es*.

(11) If the system deletes a file, the user can recover it by ...

There is a similar problem with German possessive adjectives, which must likewise show grammatical gender concord with antecedents, often conflicting with natural gender (12).

(12) *Die Gemeinschaft und ihre Mitglieder*
'The community and its members'
Lit.: The community and her members

Some attempt is also made to deal with anaphora across sentence boundaries using a system for weighting potential antecedents according to their positions and roles in preceding sentences.

The process of translation is completed with the MORSYN (*Mor*phologische *Syn*these) module, the aim of which is to convert the stem + morphological feature units into target text strings. This is sometimes relatively straightforward, though with some languages (especially German) morphological forms are highly dependent on surrounding context; for example, German adjective endings depend not only on the case and gender of the noun which the adjective modifies, but also on what sort of determiner the noun group has: *ein guter Mann, der gute Mann*. Similarly, both English and French have cases of morphological alternation which is contextual rather than grammatical (French *du* replacing *de le*, elisions before vowels *l', d'*, choice of English *a* or *an*). Finally, MORSYN also deals with capitalization and punctuation, both particularly important for German output.

11.7 Conclusion

In most essentials, Susy is an example of a transfer-based system, but in some respects it is a hybrid. From the computational point of view it exhibits a basically first generation type of architecture similar to that found in Systran (Chapter 10). Linguistic routines are written not in some higher-level rule-writing formalism but directly in the low-level programming language Fortran. Weak points of Susy are consequently the programming environment and the attendant primitive data structure and simplistic mode of processing, in particular the single non-branching sequence of modules.

Nevertheless, the linguists working on Susy have shown that it is still possible to maintain a consistent linguistic approach, though of course the details of their implementations are only accessible to readers familiar with low-level programming practices. It must also be said that the abundant use of acronyms — only partially revealed in this discussion — can be distracting or even confusing if in English-language descriptions they differ from those in German accounts.

One characteristic of Susy's hybrid 'direct' ancestry is the emphasis in the first stages of analysis on non-linguistic methods. It is not until the SEGMENT procedures that there is anything which would be called 'parsing' in the traditional (computational linguistics) sense. Many problems are resolved on the basis of *ad hoc* rules which search for particular categories or even particular words in as yet unstructured strings, or which weigh the probabilities and compatibilities of sequences of categories irrespective of structural relations.

It may be noted also that analysis procedures are not entirely monolingual. Target language oriented analysis is found particularly in SEMSYN. It is doubtful, for example, that a strictly monolingual analysis of English would identify so many different meanings of *raise* if it were not to be translated into German where choices have to be made between *vorbringen, züchten, anbauen, aufwerfen, erzeugen, aufbringen, anheben*, etc. In a 'true' transfer-based system these selection problems would be handled by bilingual lexical transfer routines.

In general, the translation quality of Susy is comparable to that of other contemporary systems, and indeed Susy has been used in several practical experiments. In a collaborative project Susy was linked with Kyoto University's TITRAN system to translate titles of documents between German and Japanese, using English as a 'switching language'. A less successful experiment was the use of Susy by the translation service of the German Bundessprachenamt ('Federal

Language Office'), which faltered due to an unwillingness to accept lower quality translations. By contrast, a successful automatic indexing experiment made use of the German analysis modules to derive standardised (root) forms of words in abstracts and full texts together with some indicators of structural relationships.

Despite these partial successes, the developers of SUSY recognised that the original system had its limitations, and started working on an essentially new project SUSY-II. The intention was to develop a linguistic rule-writing formalism, a simplification of the analysis stages (reduction to three basic processes), a more satisfactory treatment of structural ambiguity, and the introduction of preferential rule application. Some of these new approaches were explored by other researchers at Saarbrücken engaged on a parallel MT project for French–German translation (ASCOF). However, these plans for SUSY-II were in turn overtaken by events, and in 1986 work on MT in SFB-100 was terminated, with efforts at Saarbrücken concentrating on the German contribution to Eurotra.

11.8 Sources and further reading

The information for this chapter is derived from numerous sources in English and German. In particular, there is a large set of reports and working papers published by SFB-100 itself, under the general title *Linguistische Arbeiten*, in two series (the second starting in 1982). For those able to read German, and interested in very precise details of the implementation of SUSY, some of these may be worth seeking out.

The most thorough English-language description of SUSY is Maas (1987), though also worth consultation are Maas (1977), Luckhardt (1982), and Hutchins (1986:233–9), the latter an outsider's viewpoint. Useful references in German include Maas (1978) and Blatt *et al.* (1985), and from the *Linguistische Arbeiten* reports, Luckhardt (1976) and Luckhardt and Maas (1983).

The German–Japanese collaboration is described by von Ammon and Wessoly (1984/5); the Bundessprachenamt experiment is described at its outset in Wilms (1981); the automatic indexing project is described in Kroupa and Zimmermann (1987); a comparison of SUSY and SUSY-II can be found in Maas (1981) and in Luckhardt (1985), while Maas (1984) describes SUSY-II in detail. The ASCOF project is described in Biewer *et al.* (1985).

12
Météo

In this chapter we describe the Météo system developed by the TAUM group in Montreal for translating weather bulletins from English into French. The system was installed in 1976 and has been in daily operation from the following year to the present time. Its success is based primarily on the completeness and accuracy which could be achieved by the restriction to the sublanguage of meteorological forecasts.

12.1 Historical background

Research on natural language processing began at the University of Montreal in 1965 with the creation of CETADOL (Centre d'Études pour le Traitement Automatique des Données Linguistiques 'Centre for Automatic Linguistic Data Processing Studies') under the direction of Guy Rondeau. At this time, the Canadian government introduced its bilingual policy, which required all official documentation to be available in both French and English. The demands on translation services grew considerably and the Canadian National Research Council began sponsorship of MT research. Between 1968 and 1971 the main focus of the centre became machine translation and the group was renamed TAUM (Traduction Automatique de l'Université de Montréal). The group developed a prototype English to French system, adopting the transfer-based approach and written in the 'Q-systems' software developed by Alain Colmerauer. Already, TAUM had realised the advantages of a sublanguage approach for solving many semantic difficulties of translation (cf. section 8.4) and in 1975 it received a contract to develop a system for translating public weather forecasts.

The task was in many respects ideal for MT treatment. The translation of weather reports is both very boring and highly repetitive. Job satisfaction was already low and there was a high turnover of translation staff when the Canadian government decided to make bilingual weather forecasts available throughout the country. TAUM was asked to develop a system for the Translation Bureau of the Canadian Secretary of State. A prototype was demonstrated in 1976, and Météo began full-time operation in May 1977. Since that date, weather forecasts translated by Météo have been transmitted daily from the Canadian Meteorological Center in Dorval (a suburb of Montreal) for use by the press and television networks. In October 1984 a new version Météo-2 was installed for operation on microcomputers. Météo-2 is written in the programming language GramR developed by John Chandioux Consultants Inc. (Chandioux was the principal designer of the original system). The old mainframe version in the Q-systems program is no longer used: Météo-2 has proved to be faster, more reliable and more cost-effective. A further development in 1989 was the installation by the same company of a Météo system for French–English translation of bulletins issued by the Quebec Weather Office.

In this chapter we describe the original Q-systems implementation of the English–French system.

12.2 The translation environment: input, pre-processing and post-editing

The Météo translation program at the Canadian Meteorological Center is embedded in a larger system which receives the reports from the communication network, pre-processes the data for the Météo system, sends any material which Météo cannot translate to human editors, reformats the Météo output and transmits the final version across the network. At present, the system is translating some 37,000 words every day of the year (over 8 million words p.a.) at an accuracy of over 90%.

Weather reports are received in standard formats, as exemplified in Figure 12.1: a coded heading, a statement of the origin of the bulletin, a list of the regions to which the bulletin applies, the forecast itself, and at the end a terminator. This format is rigidly adhered to. The vocabulary of the bulletins is likewise fixed and predictable, being restricted to the set phrases of the headers, place names, and descriptions of meteorological conditions. This means that it is relatively easy to scan the input text for 'unknown words' which are almost invariably caused by transmission errors. These are virtually the only errors which result in reports being sent for revision by human translators.

The first operation involves the identification of translation units and transforms them into a Q-system format, with individual words and punctuation separated by '+' and the beginnings and ends of phrases by '-01-' and '-02-'. In addition, it marks each unit by an identifier so that, if necessary, revisers can quickly locate the original phrase. These identifiers consist of the source, e.g. Toronto, and a running number. For the bulletin in Figure 12.1 the output would be as in Figure 12.2.

FPCN11 CYYZ 311630

FORECASTS FOR ONTARIO ISSUED BY ENVIRONMENT CANADA AT 11.30 AM EST WEDNESDAY
MARCH 31ST 1976 FOR TODAY AND THURSDAY .

METRO TORONTO

WINDSOR.

CLOUDY WITH A CHANCE OF SHOWERS TODAY AND THURSDAY.

LOW TONIGHT 4. H1GH THURSDAY 10.

OUTLOOK FOR FRIDAY... SUNNY

END

Figure 12.1 Weather report as received

-01- $(TORONTO,2) + FORECASTS + FOR + ONTARIO + ISSUED + BY + ENVIRONMENT + CANADA
+ AT + 11 + H + 30 + AM + EST + WEDNESDAY + MARCH + 31ST + 1976 + FOR + TODAY + AND
+ THURSDAY + . -02-/

-01- $(TORONTO,3) + METRO + TORONTO + , + WINDSOR + . -02-/

-01- $(TORONTO,4) + CLOUDY + WITH + A + CHANCE + OF + SHOWERS + TODAY + AND +
THURSDAY + . -02-/

-01- $(TORONTO,5) + LOW + TONIGHT + 4 + . -02-/

-01- $(TORONTO,6) + H1GH + THURSDAY + 10 + . -02-/

-01- $(TORONTO,7) + OUTLOOK + FOR + FRIDAY + = + SUNNY + . -02-/

Figure 12.2 Formatted weather report

As this example shows, pre-processing includes some regularisation, the original *11.30* becomes *11 + H + 30*; it also includes the expansion of abbreviations, for example *kmh → kilometres per hour, Jan → January, BC → British Columbia* etc.

It is in this form that the report is sent to the Météo program. The completed translation is formatted as precisely as the original. For the example above, the output is given in Figure 12.3.

In this particular example, it will be seen that Météo failed to translate *high Thursday 10* because of an input error: the numeral *1* instead of the capital letter *I* in *H1GH*. The failure is identified automatically by the system and marked for the attention of the post-editors. Human intervention is therefore involved only when the system fails to translate a phrase, and this is generally because of corrupt input. Post-editing is done at terminals using a minimum of simple commands.

12.3 The translation processes

The linguistic data of Météo consist of three bilingual dictionaries for 'idioms', place names and general (meteorological) vocabulary, and three processing modules for the syntactic analysis of English, the syntactic generation of French, and the morphological generation of French.

Although the TAUM group adopted the transfer-based approach for its major MT research, an essentially 'direct' design was developed for the Météo

U

FPCN1 CYYZ 311630

2

PREVISIONS POUR L ONTARIO EMISES PAR ENVIRONNEMENT CANADA A 11 H 30 HNE MERCREDI
LE 31 MARS 1976 POUR AUJOURD HUI ET JEUDI.

1

TORONTO ET BANLIEUE

WINDSOR.

0

NUAGEUX AVEC POSSIBILITE D AVERSES AUJOURD HUI ET JEUDI

0

MINIMUM CE SOIR 4.

-0

HIGH THURSDAY 10.

2

APERCU POUR VENDREDI... ENSOLEILLE.

Figure 12.3 Météo ouput

sublanguage system. There was no need for a transfer module, partly because
the 'telegraphic' style of English reports is almost the same structurally as that
of French reports. Also absent is a module for the morphological analysis of
English; not only is the range of vocabulary limited but morphological variation
is restricted, e.g. verbs appear only as present or past participles. Consequently,
all lexical variants are entered in the dictionary.

Linguistic analysis is somewhat simplified by the restricted syntactic range of
meteorological reports: no pronominal reference, no relative clauses, no passives;
above all, the phrases are short. On the other hand, the omission of prepositions and
articles caused problems, and led the developers to incorporate analysis procedures
based on semantic features.

12.3.1 Dictionary look-up

Translation begins with the extraction of lexical data. The Idioms dictionary
indicates that, for example, an English phrase such as *blowing snow* is to be
translated as *poudrerie*. For Météo, an 'idiom' is any sequence of more than one
word which has to be treated as if it were only one word; 'idioms' are thus defined
in a purely practical way, and, more significantly, in bilingual contrastive terms.

The Place-names dictionary contains only those names which differ in English
and French (*Newfoundland → Terre Neuve*), which are phrasal (*Greater Vancouver
→ Vancouver et banlieue*, *Metro Toronto → Toronto et banlieue*), or which must
include some linguistic information to ensure correct output (e.g. names which
are plural, contain a definite article, or are feminine). All other place names can
be omitted, as the program treats any 'unknown' item as if it is a proper name
and does not attempt translation.

The main dictionary is the General dictionary containing, as already noted, all morphological forms. Every entry for an English word indicates a French equivalent, a grammatical category, semantic features, and target morphological information. For example (1),

(1) AMOUNT = N((F,MSR),QUANTITE)

where N indicates a noun, F feminine gender and MSR a measure noun. The grammatical categories are the traditional ones (adjective, adverb, conjunction, determiner, etc.).

For nouns, the morphological information is restricted to indications of gender (F or not) and of plurality. No indication of plural endings for French nouns is necessary, since, with all English forms being entered, they are given directly (e.g. *area → région, areas → régions*). Any differences of number between the languages are treated likewise (*skies → ciel*). For adjectives, the syntactic information concerns simply whether it should precede a noun in French or not; and the morphological information indicates the modifications needed to produce feminine and plural forms: F0 (no change), F1 (regular *-e* ending), F2 (*-eau →* *-elle*), P0 (no change), P1 (regular *-s* ending), P2 (*-al → -aux*).

The syntactic information for adverbs and verbs is minimal. Entries for adverbs indicate whether they may be attached to adjectives, verbs or prepositions; and verbs are marked simply as either transitive or intransitive, with no other subcategorisation.

Semantic features are attached to nouns, adjectives, adverbs and prepositions. Some examples are shown in Table 12.1.

Feature	Examples
time zone	*HAE (heures avancées de l'est)*
month	*juillet, novembre*
day	*lundi, vendredi*
measure	*degré, médiocre, supérieur, à peu près, environ*
place	*secteur, comté, avoisinant, partout, au dessus de*
direction	*est, du nord*
time point	*fin, matin, par la suite, avant*
time duration	*matinée, annuel, pour peu de temps, au cours de*
possibility	*risque, bon, faible, peut-être*
met. phenomenon stationary	*humidité, brume, nuages, chaud, dense*
met. phenomenon falling	*neige, pluie, grêle, abondant*
met. phenomenon blowing	*rafale, vent, venteux, fort*

Table 12.1 Examples of features

Since there is no transfer dictionary, all translational variants are listed in the dictionary, differentiated usually by appropriate semantic features (2).

```
(2) ABOUT = P((MESURE),ENVIRON)
    ABOUT = P((TEMPS),VERS)
    AREA = N((LIEU),REGION)
    AREA = N((CONDITION METEO),ZONE)
    CONSIDERABLE =
              ADJ((CONDITION METEO,TOMBANT),FORT)
    CONSIDERABLE =
              ADJ((CONDITION METEO,STATIONNAIRE),MARQUE)
```

Choice between variants takes place during the final stages of syntactic analysis, as we shall see.

12.3.2 Syntactic analysis

From an examination of weather reports, the TAUM researchers established a classification of all the phrases which occur. They found that just five types of tree structure were needed. The task of the analysis program is thus defined as the discovery of the particular tree for a given input phrase.

The first phrase type (labelled MET0) consists simply of a list of place names, for example (3).

(3) RED RIVER, INTERLAKE, BISSET, BERENS RIVER.

The next three types have a more complex structure captured by the rule formalisms in (4), where round brackets indicate tree structure, curly brackets alternatives, and square brackets optional elements.

(4a) MET1 $\left(C(\{\begin{smallmatrix} Adj \\ GN \end{smallmatrix}\}, [Cmod]), [T], [L]\right)$

(4b) MET2 $\left(GN(\{\begin{smallmatrix} highs \\ lows \\ etc. \end{smallmatrix}\}), [T], [L], GN(\{\begin{smallmatrix} Temp\ to\ Temp \\ Temp \end{smallmatrix}\}), [T], [L]\right)$

(4c) MET3 $\left(GN(outlook\ for\ T), C(\{\begin{smallmatrix} Adj \\ GN \end{smallmatrix}\}, [Cmod]), [T], [L]\right)$

MET1 (4a) expresses meteorological conditions, e.g. *mainly sunny today, sunny with moderate southwesterly, winds 25 kilometers per hour*. The construction consists of a 'condition' node (C) and an optional time (T) and/or location (L), where the condition is expressed by an adjectival (Adj) or nominal group (GN) followed by an optional complement (Cmod). An example is shown in (5).

The phrase type MET2 (4b) is for phrases which express maximum and minimum temperatures, e.g. *highs today 15 to 18, lows tonight near 3*. The structure represents an introductory GN such as *highs, lows, temperature range* and so on, followed by a temperature or pair of temperatures. Optional time and place adverbials can appear before or after the temperature(s), as in (6).

Phrase type MET3 (4c) applies to phrases giving the weather outlook, e.g. *outlook for tomorrow, continuing mainly sunny*. The structure is similar to that of MET1, with the addition of a nominal group (GN) before the meteorological condition (C), as exemplified in (7).

(5)

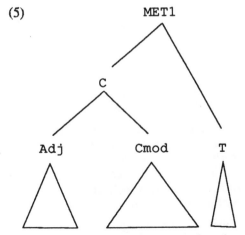

mainly sunny with moderate winds today

(6)

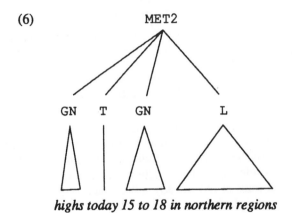

highs today 15 to 18 in northern regions

(7)

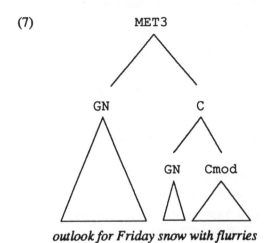

outlook for Friday snow with flurries

The final phrase type covers the bulletin header indicating its origin, for example as in (8).

(8) FORECAST FOR MANITOBA ISSUED BY ENVIRONMENT CANADA AT 6 AM CST
APRIL 8TH 1976 FOR TODAY AND FRIDAY.

These are invariant with only place names, dates, days and hours changing. The label for these stereotypical phrases is ORG.

Syntactic analysis is accomplished in three stages by use of a fairly traditional (from the linguistic point of view) bottom-up parsing technique, the computational features of which we shall look at in section 12.4. From the point of view of linguistic processing, it is sufficient to mention that the procedure creates at each stage all possible partial solutions, which are successively pruned as they are combined until, in the final stage, there is just one analysis.

The first stage involves the recognition of dates, hours and degrees of temperature. Strings such as *in the low 20s* are transformed into *21 à 23*, and the English time periods AM and PM are changed into the French 24-hour equivalents. Next comes the identification and translation of time expressions such as *afterwards, this evening, on Monday evening, early in the evening*, etc. Syntactically they are adverbs or noun phrases optionally preceded by prepositions; semantically they are recognised by semantic 'time' or 'place' features (as in (4) and (5) above). The analysis includes the treatment of conjoined expressions such as *in the afternoon or evening*. In this case an article must also be inserted: *dans l'après-midi ou la soirée*.

The next stage identifies the remaining noun phrases, i.e. those expressing meteorological conditions. The procedure involves both the syntactic categories of lexical items and also their semantic features. Matching these features helps both correct analysis and selection between alternative French translations (it should be recalled that lexical transfer has already taken place, and such cases are treated as ambiguities). For example *heavy* has three possibilities (9) depending on whether it modifies nouns such as *rain, wind* and *fog*.

(9) ADJ((TOMBANT),ABONDANT)
    ADJ((STATIONNAIRE),DENSE)
    ADJ((SOUFFLANT),FORT)

The matching of features ('TOMBANT', etc.) to those attached to the modified nouns ensures the correct renditions: *pluie abondante* 'heavy rain', *vents forts* 'heavy winds', *brouillard dense* 'heavy fog'.

Similar feature matching ensures the translation of *bank* as *rive* or *banc* (10a) and of *around* as *environ* or *vers* (10b), the latter using the definitions given in (2) above.

(10a) river banks → *rives du fleuve*
      cloud banks → *bancs de nuages*

(10b) around 10 degrees → *environ 10 degrés*
      around noon → *vers midi*

The features also help to resolve ambiguous structures such as coordination: compare *gusting winds and snow*, where the adjective modifies only the first noun (because snow does not gust), and *persistent rain and sleet*, where both nouns are included in the scope of the adjective.

Finally, analysis recognises that meteorological conditions (C) can be complements (Cmod) of other conditions (C), thus forming more complex sub-trees (11).

(11)

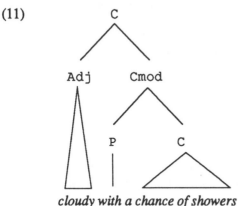

cloudy with a chance of showers

Furthermore, phrase types (MET1, MET2, etc.) can themselves be conjoined as larger units, 'sentences' (S). The result of syntactic analysis is thus a single tree, dominated by the S node, with English words as terminal nodes and the standardised types of phrase structures specifying the non-terminal nodes.

12.3.3 Syntactic and morphological generation

The task of syntactic generation is to derive the French word order from the structural representation and the information attached to lexical items. Expressions of time and location are placed after expressions of meteorological conditions; adjectives are placed after the nouns they modify (except when indicated otherwise, e.g. *gros*); and articles are inserted. It involves also the selection of the correct prepositions as translations of English *in* with places: *in Montreal, in Nova Scotia, in Ontario, in Manitoba.* It is *à* if the noun never has an article (*à Montréal*), *en* if the noun is feminine (*en Nouvelle-Écosse*), *en* if the noun is masculine and begins with a vowel (*en Ontario*), and *au* if the noun is masculine, begins with a consonant and can have an article (*au Manitoba*).

The final stage of morphological generation is concerned primarily with ensuring the correct endings of adjectives (feminine, plural, etc.) and with contextual adjustments: *le été → l'été, ce été → cet été, un beau été → un bel été, à le → au, de le → du,* etc.

12.4 The computational processes

From a computational point of view, Météo is constructed as a single unified system in the fashion of a **production system** (see section 3.8.6). There is a single

data structure and rule-writing formalism for all modules. The data structure is in
the form of a **chart** (see section 3.8.5), the arcs of which are labelled with feature
bundles. There is no overt control structure to determine the order of application
of grammar rules. These are interpreted, in the manner typical of a classical
production system, as pairs of pattern matches on the chart and actions which
build a new arc on the chart. This production system architecture corresponds to
a bottom-up breadth-first parser. The software was written by Alain Colmerauer,
and called **Q-systems** ('Q' for 'Quebec', allegedly). Q-systems are regarded as
the prototype of the (now well-known) programming language Prolog, which has
a similar computational architecture.

12.4.1 The data structure

As just stated, the data structure in Météo is a chart, the arcs of which are
labelled with feature bundles. The initial process of dictionary look-up (section
12.3.1) builds the initial configuration of the chart by constructing one arc for
each reading of each lexical item. Thus, multi-word items like *Thunder Bay* or
blowing snow have a single arc (12a), while an 'ambiguous' word like *heavy* (cf.
(9) above) has parallel arcs in the chart (i.e. arcs connecting the same pair of
nodes), as in (12b).

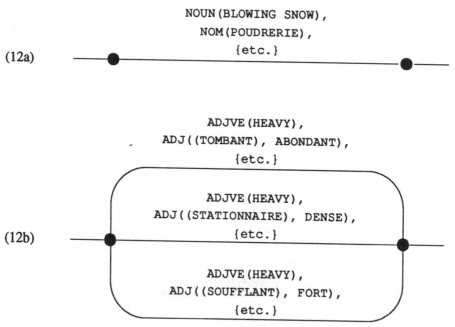

As each rule is applied, the pattern matcher looks for a sequence of arcs as
defined by the rule's 'pattern-match' part, and then builds a new arc which spans
the whole sequence and which is labelled in accordance with the rule's 'action'
part. So, for example, a rule that builds a noun group from the sequence adjective

plus noun (e.g. *intermittent rain*) would take the part of the chart in (13a) and build a new arc as in (13b).

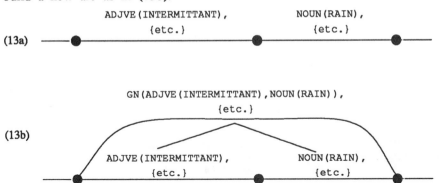

When building a new arc it is essential to indicate which arcs have been subsumed (actually 'used') in its construction: for example, if the adjective is *heavy*, the new arc must indicate which reading of *heavy* has been accepted. It should be noted that the arcs subsumed by rules are not 'thrown away': they are still part of the data structure, and can participate in other rules. In this way, competing alternative partial structures can be maintained until the final complete analysis has built a single arc for the whole structure. A legitimate interpretation is one which has been appropriately labelled by one of the five phrase types given above (MET0, MET1, etc.). And likewise, the whole bulletin should conform to the expected structure, i.e. a single header (ORG) followed by any combination of the other phrase types.

From a computational point of view, there is no distinction between the processes of analysis and generation. Like analysis, generation is activated by rules involving pattern matches on the chart and the construction of further arcs. The two processes are, however, kept separate. At the end of analysis, the chart is 'tidied up' and unneeded arcs are removed before the chart is passed to the generation module. But this is essentially a strategy to increase computational efficiency (it is easier to search a smaller database for possible pattern matches), rather than a strict modularisation of the translation procedure as a whole.

12.4.2 Rule formalism

The rules are rather similar to the GETA rules (Chapter 13) in that they define a tree and then describe features on each of the branches of the tree. The left hand side of a rule is a sequence of arcs on a chart and the right hand side specifies the new arc. For example (14) shows the morphological rule which interprets *worse* as the stem *bad* plus a suffix *-er*.

(14) WORSE == ADJ(BAD,/) + * (ER)

The rule defines on the left hand side a tree 'WORSE' (a single node) and builds on the right hand side a tree with two branches, one as ADJ with a subordinate element BAD and one as * with a subordinate ER.

Another, more general, rule (15) identifies this as a comparative construction.

(15) `ADJ(A*,/,U*) + *(ER) == ADJ(A*,/,U*,INV(MORE))`

Here `A*` and `U*` are variables: `A*` may apply to any lexical item, and `U*` to any list of features. In the case of the output from (14), `A*` corresponds to BAD, `U*` is null (an empty list), and `*(ER)` is an exact match. The result on the right hand side of (15) is a single-node tree which has copied `A*` and `U*` and incorporates the feature `INV(MORE)`.

12.4.3 Rule application

The Q-system procedure is a classical production system in the sense that the rule-set is an unordered set of these linguistic rules. The process is controlled purely by the state of the database (the chart). This determines which of the rules in the rule-set can be applied next. Often, more than one rule can be applied, in which case both possibilities must be tried, theoretically 'in parallel'. However, since this would involve potentially huge computational resources, maintaining perhaps dozens of only slightly different copies of the database, the system in fact applies alternative rules in sequence, and backtracks when appropriate if the first rule applied turns out to be the wrong one. This feature of the Q-systems architecture is now, of course, very familiar to Prolog programmers, but when first implemented in Météo it was an innovation.

There are major disadvantages with this 'unstructured' approach to linguistic processing which are largely avoided in Météo by virtue of its compactness: the rule set is relatively small, and this is because the text type is very restricted. While the production system architecture may be appropriate for Météo, it does not follow that it is generally applicable for translation systems, as indeed the TAUM researchers discovered when they attempted to use the approach in their second much larger MT system, Aviation (see below).

There are potential disadvantages also in the use of a single unified rule-writing formalism and associated computational mechanism for a number of disparate kinds of process. Dictionary look-up, parsing, and morphological generation are all performed by the same rewrite-rule production system strategy. The mechanism has to be powerful enough to accommodate the most complex of those tasks, namely parsing. But to use all the power of a general rewrite mechanism for the relatively trivial tasks of dictionary look-up (involving only adding information to single arcs) and morphological generation (involving only string handling) may be seen as excessive. It does not matter so much for Météo because of the smallness of its scale, but these aspects of Météo's design are not necessarily desirable in larger systems.

12.5 Summary and discussion

Although Météo is clearly a second generation MT system, it departs from the classical architecture in interesting respects. Its linguistic strategies are well-motivated and finely tuned to the task on hand and from the computational point of view it is sophisticated, and for its time innovative.

In basic design, Météo is a direct system of a distinctive character. The limitation to the idiosyncratic nature of meteorological bulletins and the limitation to English and French translation in one direction led to a unique approach, which may well not be applicable in other circumstances. As we have seen, analysis lacks a morphological component, it is preceded by dictionary look-up which deals with any problems of 'idiomatic' or compound expressions, it is based on a mixture of English syntactic information and French semantic features, and the results are representations unique to the sublanguage of weather reports. Whereas analysis is bilingual, oriented to a specific target language, generation is wholly monolingual; but it is restricted to relatively minor syntactic manipulations and to morphological formations. It might, theoretically, be argued that Météo is in some senses an 'interlingua' system, with the intermediate representations between analysis and synthesis serving as 'pivot' texts. From this perspective, they are abstract representations of the information structure of bulletins which happen to have French labels. But the lexical units are not 'interlingual' concepts in any sense (e.g. *poudrerie* cannot be regarded as a unified (universal) concept). It is doubtful that these representations could be used as the basis for generating texts in any other language.

There seems to be no doubt that Météo is a clear example of a direct translation system, one which 'translates as it goes along'. The most typical 'direct' feature is the placing of lexical transfer before any syntactic analysis. Here it is done for perfectly good practical reasons. First, the vocabulary is highly restricted, there are very few homographs, and these are treated as category ambiguities (e.g *heavy* in section above). Second, the system is aimed exclusively at English–French translation: nothing is gained by postponing lexical transfer, and furthermore the knowledge of possible transfer ambiguities can be helpful in syntactic analysis. Third, source language lexical items are not actually replaced during analysis: the possible translation is added as extra lexical information to terminal items.

Météo is untypical of second generation systems in its weak modularity. There is no separation of the operations of analysis, transfer and generation; but it is modular in that the algorithmic and linguistic parts are separated: linguistic knowledge is expressed declaratively in an unordered set of rules, and the algorithmic knowledge which defines the procedural interpretation of the rules is captured by the Q-systems architecture. This means that extension of the sublanguage (e.g. to include gale warnings or reports on road conditions) could be achieved by adding linguistic rules and updating the dictionaries, without any change to the software. This was confirmed in practice by the rewriting and re-implementation of the software (on microcomputers and using the more efficient GramR language) without having to revise the linguistic foundations of the system.

What distinguishes Météo above all is the orientation to a particular sublanguage; this explains the preference for semantic analysis of structural relations and the use of features which would be unusual in general parsers ('blowing', 'falling'). The limitations of the approach are seen in part by the absence of any equally successful sublanguage MT systems and in the difficulties encountered by the TAUM group when they researched an English–French system for translating maintenance manuals for the hydraulic systems of jet aircraft (the Aviation project). There was a clearly identifiable sublanguage, but one which was much more complicated; in particular there were severe problems of multiple lexical, syntactic and pragmatic ambiguity in compound noun phrases and imperatives (19).

(19a) vertical stabilizer lower spar bar attachment fittings

(19b) Insert selector lever actuating arm in slot of selector lever.

The Aviation project differed in a number of respects from Météo (it was a transfer-based system and with much greater modularity), but the Q-systems approach proved ultimately unsatisfactory for this particular more complex sublanguage and the project came to an end in 1981.

The success of Météo is the best 'advertisement' for MT; it is successful because it is an exactly appropriate application: it performs satisfactorily and economically a translation task that humans do not enjoy doing, and which might otherwise not get done. The future of Météo, which is no longer being developed in any substantial way, is presumably to do its job until it is superseded by some better idea, or until the need to translate weather bulletins disappears. In fact, in recent years, some of the previous members of the TAUM group have been researching a system (RAREAS) which would generate bulletins in both languages directly from the raw meteorological data.

12.6 Sources and further reading

Basic descriptions of Météo are given by Chandioux (1976), Chevalier *et al.* (1978), summarised by Whitelock and Kilby (1983) and by Hutchins (1986: 228–231). Information about recent developments is given by Chandioux (1989a,b). For some details of the Aviation project, with further references, see Lehrberger and Bourbeau (1988); and for RAREAS see Kittredge *et al.* (1986).

13
Ariane (GETA)

13.1 Historical background

Perhaps the most influential individual person in the history of post-ALPAC MT research was Bernard Vauquois, who led a team of researchers at the Universiy of Grenoble until his untimely death at the age of 56, in 1985. The Grenoble group started work on MT as early as 1960, and, even before the ALPAC report in 1966, was developing a system incorporating characteristics of what are now generally called 'second generation' systems. In particular, the Grenoble group, at first known as CETA (*Centre d'Etudes de la Traduction Automatique* 'Centre for the Study of Machine Translation'), concentrated on the development of formalisms for expressing linguistic information and the algorithms which implemented them, and on the idea of doing translation by computing a succession of 'linguistic representations'. The original CETA system, developed between 1960 and 1970, for three language pairs (into French from Russian, German and Japanese, though with most work being done on the Russian–French system) was an interlingua system. A change in computer facilities in 1971, among other reasons, led the Grenoble team (now renamed GETA: *Groupe d'Etudes pour la Traduction Automatique*) to rethink the design of their MT system and to design a 'transfer' system, officially known as Ariane, though often referred to simply as 'the GETA system'.

The principal research work continued to be done on Russian to French translation, although there was also substantial research on a German–French system which used the same generation programs as the Russian–French version. From time to time there were other languages investigated by researchers who came to Grenoble: Portuguese, Malay, Japanese, and Chinese. GETA has consistently encouraged the training and establishment of MT projects throughout the world, notably in Southeast Asia, Japan and China. The most important practical application of Ariane came through involvement in the French national project launched in 1983. The aim of the Calliope project, as it was called, was the development of a French–English system for aeronautics and an English–French system for computer science and data processing. However, after a bright start the project ended in early 1987.

The GETA system is important not only because it is a good example of a 'second generation' system, but also because the research at Grenoble was very influential. Many of the Japanese MT systems are quite similar in design to the GETA system, especially Kyoto University's Mu system, which itself influenced several of the Japanese commercial systems. Early work on Eurotra was much influenced by Grenoble (see Chapter 14), as was later work at Saarbrücken; the TAUM group at Montreal collaborated closely with GETA, and many researchers starting work in the field after 1975 have taken GETA's work as a reference point.

The system has gone through a number of improvements and modifications: Ariane-78, Ariane-85 and the most recent version Ariane-G5. The long-term goal has been to develop an MT 'engine' as the foundation for multilingual translation. This chapter describes basically Ariane-78.

13.2 General description

Ariane is a transfer system with analysis and generation both split into morphological and syntactic modules. Transfer also has two phases: lexical and structural transfer. Computationally, Ariane is interesting in its use of special-purpose rule-writing formalisms for each of the modules, and a (theoretically) strict separation of linguistic and algorithmic knowledge at each stage. The system is truly multilingual in the sense that the formalisms and the algorithms which implement them are quite independent of the languages to be treated; also from a linguistic point of view the analysis and generation programs for a given language-pair can be re-used for different target or source languages respectively. The representation levels used in Ariane are also of interest from a linguistic point of view, in that they are **multi-level** structures which combine dependency relations and constituent structures, and contain both deep and superficial linguistic information.

Figure 13.1 shows the general architecture of the system. The figure shows source language analysis up the left-hand side, transfer across the top, and target language generation down the right. The lozenges represent intermediate data structures, while the solid square boxes characterise the linguistic processes. The inner shaded box represents the software system itself, with the separate software tools implementing rule-writing formalisms shown in oval boxes.

The flow of the translation process follows a standard linguistic stratification: the source text string of characters undergoes morphological analysis resulting in a flat labelled tree. Multilevel analysis gives an intermediate source structure, which then undergoes a two-stage transfer: in lexical transfer the source-language lexical

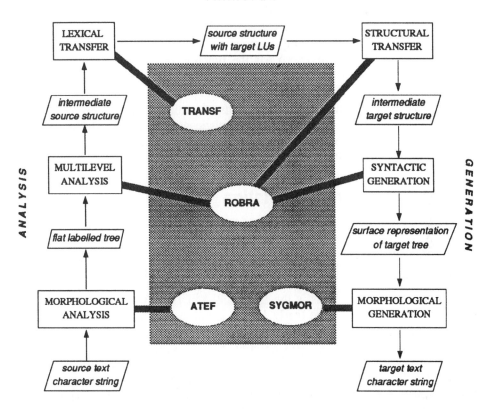

Figure 13.1 Configuration of the Ariane system

items, or 'lexical units' (LUs), are replaced with the corresponding target-language LUs giving a source-language structure with target-language LUs. Structural transfer produces an intermediate target structure which is input to syntactic generation and morphological generation.

Ariane has four rule-writing formalisms, effectively task-specific very-high-level programming languages, each with its associated implementation, the details of which are hidden from, and in theory of no interest to, the linguist writing the rules. The four software packages correspond to four different types of linguistic data-processing, in accordance with four different types of data structure and associated manipulation. This is an important feature of Ariane (distinguishing it, for example, from Météo) since each of the formalisms is specifically designed to facilitate a certain type of computation, with just enough (computational) power and flexibility for the allotted task.

ATEF is designed for morphological analysis, and maps strings of characters onto bundles of features arranged on a flat labelled tree. ROBRA (used for three of the six stages, in particular for the two most significant stages) is a very powerful software tool, which permits the description of **tree transductions**, i.e. it allows rules to take as input arbitrarily complex tree structures, to manipulate these structures, and to output new tree structures. TRANSF is a slightly less powerful formalism (used for lexical transfer), which takes trees as input but does not have the power to rearrange them, only altering the labels on the branches. SYGMOR (used in morphological generation) has the function of converting labelled trees into character strings; it realises a finite state deterministic automaton, reflecting the lesser complexity of this phase.

We shall describe the Ariane formalisms in some detail (section 13.5) First however, we look more closely at the linguistic aspects of the GETA system, and in particular, the linguistic theory embodied in the analysis (and generation) procedures, and in the intermediate representation(s) used.

13.3 Multi-level representation

One of the most positive characteristics of the GETA approach is its incorporation of linguistic theory in both procedures and representations. Within the overall modular system design, each of the modules is motivated linguistically. At the heart of the linguistic approach taken by the GETA group is the representation which is aimed at as the output of analysis and, after lexical and structural transfer, the input to generation. This is the **interface structure**, where the influence of linguistic theories of the time (early 1970s) is particularly evident.

The interface structure is the linguistic representation resulting from a stratified linguistic analysis which we will describe below (section 13.4). As might be expected from the modular approach, there are various 'levels' of analysis. These are reflected in the linguistic representation, which combines simultaneously information at different levels: morphological, syntactic, and 'logico-semantic'. It is this 'multi-level' representational structure which is particularly noteworthy and which has been highly influential.

At the morphological level, the representation captures the difference between textual strings such as *dogs* and their morpho-lexical interpretation, e.g. lexical unit *dog*, noun plural. The syntactic level is a representation in terms of phrase structure constituents, such as noun phrase and verb group, together with (surface) syntactic relations, such as subject and object, complement and modifier. The so-called logico-semantic level is a deep syntactic representation showing dependency relations (heads and modifiers) of a logical nature, e.g. predicates and arguments or circumstantial elements with their semantic roles (goal, cause, location, etc.).

The representation for the sentence (1a) is shown in (1b).

(1a) *La Commission prépare un rapport de synthèse pour le mois prochain d'après les avis des experts.*
'The Commission is preparing a synthesis report for next month according to expert opinion'

It should be noticed first that at each terminal node in the tree is shown the lexical value of the node in a canonical form (i.e. *le* for all articles, singular form for nouns, infinitive for verb and so on). At both terminal and non-terminal nodes there appears (in square brackets) a three-valued label. This label gives the values at the three principal levels of morpho-syntax, surface syntax, and deep

(1b)

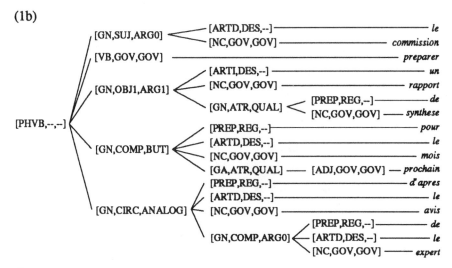

Key:

morphosyntactic labels: ADJ - adjective; ARTD - definite article; ARTI - indefinite article; GN -noun group;
    NC - common noun; PHVB - verbal sentence; PREP - preposition; VB - verb

syntactic labels: ATR - atribute; CIRC - circumstantial; COMP - complement; DES - designator; GOV -
    governor; OBJ1 - direct object; REG - 'regisseur' (head); SUJ - subject

logico-semantic labels: ANALOG - analogic; ARG0 - deep subject; ARG1 - deep object; BUT - goal; GOV -
    governor; QUAL - qualifier

syntax, i.e. the values of three principal features, MS (morpho-syntax), SF (syntactic function) and LS (logico-semantics). At each node there is also a large number of other feature–value pairs giving further pieces of information (not illustrated here), including lexically derived information such as grammatical gender, and morphologically derived information such as number, tense and so on.

The structure itself is rather flat from a typical phrase structure point of view, in that there are few intermediate constituents. For example, there are no separate prepositional phrases since prepositions are treated as parts of nominal groups. An essential feature to be noticed is that, looking from the top of the tree (the left-hand side in this diagram) each non-terminal node has exactly one daughter whose syntactic and deep syntactic label is GOV. In this way, the representation is not just a phrase structure tree but also, simultaneously, a dependency tree with 'lowered' governors. This can be demonstrated by reconstructing the tree, taking each governor as the root and its sisters as dependents, to give the dependency representation (2), with logico-semantic functions also shown where appropriate. Notice that the logical function of *experts* is ARG0, i.e. the 'deep subject' of *avis* ('opinion') treated as if it were a nominalized verb.

(2)

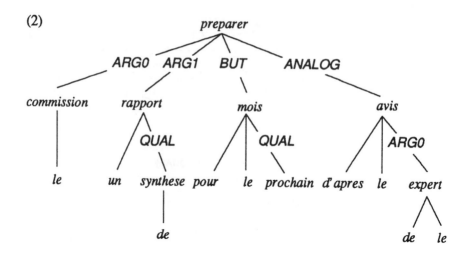

13.4 Linguistic processes

13.4.1 Morphological analysis

The linguistic processes involved in arriving at an interface representation such as (1b) are roughly as follows. First, the text is subjected to a morphological analysis phase, using rules written in the ATEF formalism (described below). This phase gives the labellings for each terminal node, based on the combination of dictionary look-up and string segmentation. Often, the results of morphological analysis are ambiguous. The labellings are attribute–value pairs, as in (3) for our example sentence (1a).

The output from morphological analysis is a (set of) flat labelled trees, where each minimal tree consists of a single dummy parent node dominating as many daughter nodes as there are words in the sentence, but where there are (as yet) no intermediate constituents. Each such flat tree will contain one reading of any ambiguous items, so there will be as many outputs as there are combinations of possible morphological analyses of the individual words.

13.4.2 Multi-level analysis

The next phase is the multi-level analysis, the most complex part of the system and employing the powerful ROBRA formalism (described in more detail in section 13.5.2 below). It involves a combination of 'parsing' to build an initial syntactic tree structure, and a kind of 'transformational' stage where surface syntactic tree structures are mapped onto deeper representations, where, for example, discontinuous lexical units are 'joined up' and surface syntactic functions like subject and object are replaced by logico-semantic relations.

The 'parsing' phase involves the application of rules which take sequences of LUs and build intermediate constituents. So, for example, a rule to build a GN

(3) la   LU="LE", CAT=ARTD, GNR=FEM, NBR=SG

la   LU="LUI", CAT=PRON, GNR=FEM, NBR=SG, CASE=OBJ

commission LU="COMMISSION", CAT=NC, GNR=FEM, NBR=SG, SEMFEAT=etc

prépare   LU="PREPARER", CAT=VB, NBR=SG, PERS=1/3, TNS=PRES

un   LU="UN", CAT=ARTI, GNR=MASC, NBR=SG

un   LU="UN", CAT=CARD

rapport   LU="RAPPORT", CAT=NC, GNR=MASC, NBR=SG, SEMFEAT=etc

de   LU="DE", CAT=PREP

synthèse   LU="SYNTHESE", CAT=NC, GNR=MASC, NBR=SG, SEMFEAT=etc

pour   LU="POUR", CAT=PREP

le   LU="LE", CAT=ARTD, GNR=MASC, NBR=SG

le   LU="LUI", CAT=PRON, GNR=MASC, NBR=SG, CASE=OBJ

mois   LU="MOIS", CAT=NC, GNR=MASC, NBR=SG, SEMFEAT=etc

prochain   LU="PROCHAIN", CAT=ADJ, GNR=MASC, NBR=SG

d'après   LU="D'APRES", CAT=PREP

les   LU="LE", CAT=ARTD, GNR=M/F, NBR=PL

les   LU="LUI", CAT=PRON, GNR=M/F, NBR=PL, CASE=OBJ

avis   LU="AVIS", CAT=NC, GNR=MASC, NBR=S/P, SEMFEAT=etc

des   LU="DE", CAT=PREP LU="LE", CAT=ARTD, GNR=M/F, NBR=PL

experts   LU="EXPERT", CAT=NC, GNR=MASC, NBR=PL, SEMFEAT=etc

Key: CASE case: OBJ - object

CAT category: ADJ - adjective; ARTD - definite article; ARTI - indefinite article; CARD - cardinal number; NC - common noun; PREP - preposition; PRON - pronoun; VB - verb

GNR gender: FEM - feminine; MASC - masculine; M/F - either masxuline or feminine

LU lexical unit

NBR number: PL - plural; SG - singular; S/P - either singular or plural

PERS person: 1/3 - either 1st or 3rd person

SEMFEAT semantic features

(noun group) node might look for a sequence of article, noun, adjective. Roughly speaking, such a rule might look for a tree structure as in (4a) and produce a structure as in (4b), having introduced an intermediate GN node and filled in some syntactic functions. The '?' sign indicates a value not yet specified.

(4a)

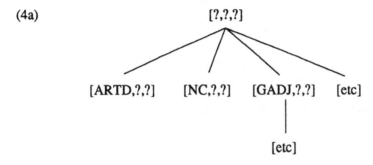

(4b)

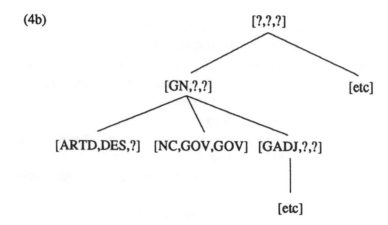

Because ROBRA is a tree transduction formalism, the rules do not have to be simple re-write rules as found in a standard phrase structure grammar: constraints such as number and gender agreement can be easily built into the rules. The rule sketched above, for example, would be conditioned by the compatibility of the values for features like NBR and GNR on the apprropriate nodes.

Alongside the analysis of phrase structure, rules which refer to the internal structures of already constructed constituents operate, reassigning the values of features or rearranging the shapes of tree structures. This activity is part of the analysis of syntactic and logico-semantic functions, and may, for example, depend on the application of subcategorization information relating to GOV nodes. Sometimes, nodes are deleted or inserted, as with the representation of a sentence like (5a), where a dummy deep subject is introduced into the structure for the embedded sentence (5b), or with sentence (6a) where the surface subject of the verb has no true logical role (6b).

(5a) *Charles espère venir.* 'Charles hopes to come'

(5b)

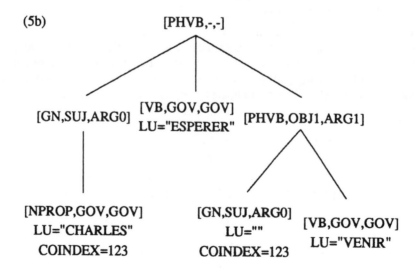

(6a) *Il semble nécessaire de restaurer le statue.*
'It seems necessary to repair the statue'

(6b)

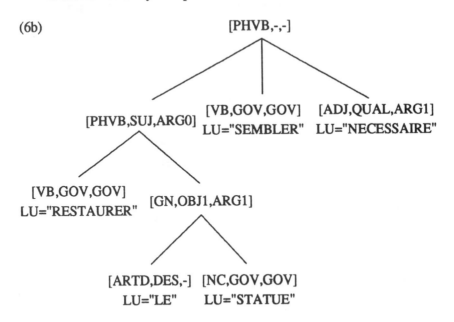

One of the major justifications for the multi-level type of representation is that it allows a 'safety net' approach to translation. If something goes wrong in the later stages of analysis, there will probably be a well-formed syntactic tree structure which can be passed to generation and from which some kind of translation can be produced, even if of a lesser quality than desirable.

13.4.3 Transfer and generation

The output of multi-level analysis is a tree structure showing dependency and phrase structure relations, and indicating logico-semantic as well as surface syntactic functions. The next stage of the translation process is lexical transfer, in which source language LUs are replaced by corresponding target language items. Often, the choice of target LU depends on the surrounding context. In the case of example (6), there could be a straightforward lexical transfer rule for *statue* to give the corresponding English word; on the other hand, there might be several different translations for *restaurer*, including *restore*, *repair* and *refresh*, depending on the nature of its object, so in this case the rule might stipulate the subtree showing the verb with its ARG1, and specify the semantic features attached to the GOV of the ARG1.

The structure is passed to structural transfer which makes the necessary structural alterations, including renumbering ARGs, introducing or deleting case-marking prepositions, and, quite often, restructuring the tree. Input is source-language structures (with target-language LUs already inserted), while the output should be the corresponding target-language (deep) structures. The tree transduction formalism ROBRA is again involved, for manipulations such as changes in argument notation (7) and (8), and the more complex tree structure changes in (9).

(7) A supplies B with C → *A fournit C à B*

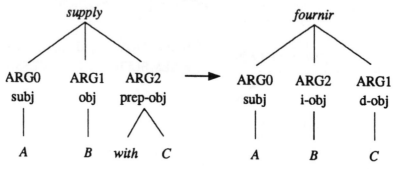

(8) A likes B → *B plaît à A*

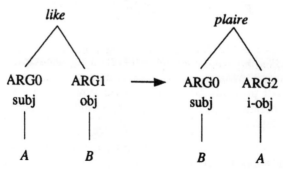

(9) *A schwimmt gern* → *A aime nager* ('A likes swimming')

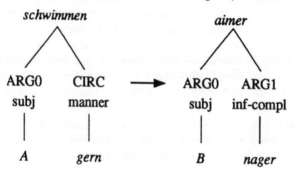

In generation, the next stage of 'syntactic generation' involves the assignment of surface structure labels, that is, the choice of surface subjects and objects, the selection of appropriate verbal auxiliaries and so on, the rearrangement of word order, and the setting of values for morphological variables (e.g. number and gender agreements). It involves again the restructuring of trees and hence the use of the ROBRA formalism.

Morphological generation is the final stage of the translation process. The associated rule-writing formalism, SYGMOR, has the function of converting the labelled trees output by the syntactic generation phase into character strings, including punctuation. First trees are transformed into strings of pairs of values and attributes, and then these are output as surface strings.

13.5 Rule-writing formalisms

As already mentioned, the four software packages of Ariane correspond to four different types of linguistic data-processing: strings to trees (ATEF), trees to trees (ROBRA and TRANSF), and trees to strings (SYGMOR).

The underlying computational structure of Ariane is a 'production system' (cf section 3.8.6). The declarative aspect is strictly separated from the procedural aspect, i.e. the linguistic knowledge to be expressed is separated from the knowledge of how that lingustic knowledge is to be applied. It will be recalled that a production system consists of a data structure, a rule set and an interpreter. In this case, the data structure is the linguistic representation, implemented as a chart with labelled arcs indicating tree structures. The rule set is, of course, the set of linguistic rules written in the formalisms. And the interpreter is the underlying computer program which implements the rule-writing formalism.

The system as a whole works like a production system in that (at least in theory) the linguist writes the rules as productions. The linguist does not describe explicitly the translation processes, but rather writes linguistic rules which describe the configurations to be searched for in the data structure (i.e. tree structures, or sequences of arcs) and what changes are to be made (i.e. what new structures are to be added to the chart) if the configurations are found. It is left to the software to determine which rules are applicable to the data structure at any time, to apply the rules, and to repeat the cycle. Likewise, the software will incorporate methods of resolving rule conflicts, of knowing when all the applicable rules have been applied and when the process has terminated. In theory, none of this needs to be stated explicitly by the linguist.

In order to improve the efficiency of the production system, the rules can be divided by linguists into smaller 'subgrammars', which are effectively self-contained production systems. To a certain extent, the linguist can indicate which subgrammars should come into play at which point in the processing, thus permitting some procedural control over the flow of processing. In this respect, the separation of algorithms and linguistic information is compromised, although, it should be stressed, within the subgrammars the pure production system architecture is respected.

However, MT processes are often too complicated for a pure production system architecture, and in practice linguists at GETA have been forced to find ways of introducing procedural controls into the declarative mechanism for the sake of efficiency and practicality. In addition, although the chart is an excellent data structure for representing ambiguity, rules can refer only to single arcs and not to bundles of arcs spanning the same set of nodes. This means that it is not possible to refer explicitly to ambiguous structures, and linguists must rely on the rule set and the way the interpreter implements the rules to disambiguate ambiguous sequences.

13.5.1 ATEF

ATEF stands for *Analyse de textes en état fini* ('finite state text analysis') and its task is the mapping of strings of characters onto bundles of features arranged on a flat labelled tree, as in (3) above. The rules written in the ATEF formalism operate roughly by stipulating string segmentations and corresponding feature assignments. The application of a rule is restricted by conditions relating to information found in the lexical entries for the substrings. The feature assignments are given either in absolute terms or with reference to the lexicon. For example, the rule applying to *condensed* and the lexical entry in (10) is approximately as in (11) (the exact formalism has been simplified for the purposes of illustration):

(10) LU=CONDENSE, CAT=V, CONJ=NO, TNS=PAST, VOX=PAS

(11) $X + "D" ==
        [LU=$X, CAT=V, CONJ=NO, TNS=PAST, VOX=PAS] /
        CAT($X)=V and end($X)="E"

where $X is a string variable ending in *e* and is in the lexicon with category (CAT) verb (V).

ATEF was innovative as a tool for computational morphology in many ways, especially in listing both stems and endings in the lexicon. So for example, a rule something like (12) might deal simultaneously with both present and past participles, assuming that the respective lexical entries for the strings *d* and *ing* as verbal suffixes would give the appropriate values for TNS and VOX.

(12) $X + $Y ==
        [LU=$X, CAT=V, CONJ=NO, TNS=TNS($Y), VOX=VOX($Y)]
        if CAT($X)=V and end($X)="E" and CAT($Y)=VBSUFX

Another feature is the possibility in ATEF of 'string transformations' as part of rules, allowing for substrings to be replaced by other substrings. This is important when morphological rules are applied sequentially, as in the treatment of English derivational morphology. An illustration is the word *unhappiness*. First the suffix *-ness* is identified as one for deriving nouns from adjectives; then the *-i* ending is changed to give *unhappy*, and lastly a rule deals with the prefix *un-*. By having a rule to change *i* to *y* (reflecting a regular English morphophonemic pattern), there is no need to include the stem *happi-* in the lexicon, which would duplicate information associated with *happy*.

13.5.2 ROBRA

The heart of the GETA system is the ROBRA rule-writing formalism. ROBRA is used for three of the six stages that make up the translation process, and in particular for the two most significant stages, namely multi-level analysis and structural transfer. As we have seen, these stages involve complex 'tree transductions'.

In this section we look in detail at an actual example of a rule written in the ROBRA formalism: a rule for compound nouns. In this way, it should be possible to get a clearer idea of the kinds of linguistic generalizations that the rule formalism allows or encourages, as well as some indication of the nature of the formalism. In discussing the example rule, we will also indicate some of the other features available in the formalism.

Figure 13.2 shows the rule (slightly simplified) as it would appear to the linguist. Line numbers have been added to facilitate discussion.

```
1      COMPN: 1(2(3,4))  /
2
3      CAT(3) -E- N -ET-
4      (CAT(4) -E- N -OU- SUBD(4) -E- CARD)
5      -OU-
6      CAT(3) -E- PREF -ET- CAT(4) -E- N
7
8      ==
9
10     1(3,4)  /*<--2/
11     4:4,
12     -SI- SUBD(4) -NE- CARD
13     -ALORS- SF(4) := GOV,
14     SF(3) := JUXT,
15     RS(3) := QUAL,
16     VAR(1) := VAR(4)
17     -SINON- SF(3) := GOV,
18     SF(4) := JUXT,
19     RS(4) := QUAL,
20     VAR(1) := VAR(3)
21     -FSI-
22     1:1, K:=NP, UL:='*NP', VLI:=N
```

Figure 13.2 Example ROBRA rule

The rule has a name, COMPN 'compound noun' (line 1), which is used mainly as a useful mnemonic for linguists when they are trying to debug the system: a trace of the rules which have been applied will refer to this rule by this name, though otherwise it has no significance. The body of the rule is a left-hand side (lines 1–6) and a right-hand side (lines 10–22). The left-hand side gives the pattern match to be sought in the data structure, while the right-hand side details the new data to be created. In this sense, the rule is like a production rule, or pattern–action pairing.

The pattern-match part of the rule consists of a tree structure, or 'schema' in GETA terminology, (line 1) and a set of 'conditions'. The bracket notation is a fairly standard way of representing the tree structure in (13):

(13)

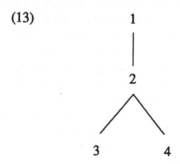

The conditions (lines 3–6) stipulate that either (i) the CAT[egory] at node 3 should be N[oun] and the category at node 4 should be N or the value of SUBD should be CARD[inal], or (ii) that the category at node 3 should be PREF[ix] and the category at node 4 should be N. The operator —E— means 'equal', —ET— means 'and', and —OU— means 'or', with bracketing giving the operator precedence. In other words, this rule will apply to any of the three trees shown in (14).

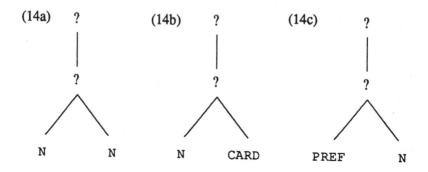

As it stands, the rule would match trees where node 2 has further unspecified daughters (or indeed sisters). Sometimes it is desirable to stipulate in the tree schema that the nodes identified should be contiguous, or that there should be no other sister nodes. This can be done using the 'anti-node' formalism, so that the tree with nodes 3 and 4 as contiguous sisters would be expressed as 1 (2 (3, *, 4)); the asterisk indicates that there must not be other nodes in this position. In the general case, however, the tree formalism (line 1) will in fact match a potentially infinite range of structures with arbitrary numbers of sister nodes at each level.

The condition part of the pattern-match can be quite complex. Often the same or similar conditions are repeated in many different rules. For this reason the ROBRA formalism allows the definition of macros or 'formats', defined separately which stipulate that two nodes must agree in number and gender, where the statement of 'agreement' may actually be quite complex. For example, a format for agreement might be defined as in (15), which says that CONCORD (A, B) is true if A and B have the same value for NBR and either they agree in GNR or the value for NBR is PL[ural]:

(15) CONCORD (A, B) ==

NBR (A) -E- NBR (B) -ET-

(GNR (A) -E- GNR (B) -OU- NBR (A) -E- PL)

This format would then be called in appropriate places, with actual node numbers in place of A and B, for example CONCORD (3, 4). Such a formalism has the advantage of enabling the linguist to state declaratively that there is a relationship CONCORD which may exist between two nodes, and to define this independently of any rules which use it. A second advantage is that, if the name chosen for the format is relatively transparent, complex conditions can be expressed in more meaningful ways and individual rules are easier to understand.

Returning to our example rule, we note that it covers three cases of noun compounds, namely noun+noun (*ville dortoir* 'dormitory town', *homme grenouille* 'frogman'), noun+cardinal number (e.g. *salle 15* 'room 15', *figure 6*), and prefix+noun (e.g. *contre-pas* 'half pace').

After the == sign (line 8) comes the right-hand side of the rule, which details the target tree structure to be built. Like the left-hand side, this has two parts, a structural part (line 10) and a set of assignments ('affectations' in GETA terminology) to the new structure, corresponding to the conditions on the left-hand side.

The 'target schema' details not only the new tree structure in (16), but also, by way of confirmation, an indication that the old node 2 has disappeared: /* ←2/ (the asterisk is again an anti-node or non-existent node). If a rule is to create a new node the confirmation would be, e.g. /6←*/, i.e. with the new node and anti-node in the reverse positions.

(16)

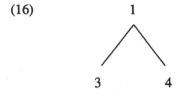

The affectation part of the right-hand side is a mixture of copying of information, adding new information, and performing complex operations. In line 11 we have a case of simple copying: the attribute–value assignments for the new node 4 are copied from the old node 4. In line 22, the old node 1 is copied onto a new node 1 and three new attributes are added: K, UL and VLI with values NP, *NP and N respectively. Lines 12–21 illustrate a series of complex assignments. Here we see affectations dependent on values of other attributes, expressed by logical operators: —SI— means 'if', —NE— 'not equal', —ALORS—

expressed by logical operators: −SI− means 'if', −NE− 'not equal', −ALORS− 'then', −SINON− 'else' and −FSI− 'end if'. The value assignments are to be as specified in lines 13–16 if SUBD (4) is not CARD, otherwise they are to be as specified in lines 17–20. The former would be the case for (14a) and (14c) above, and the latter would apply to (14b). It should be noticed that assignments can either be given in terms of literal values, as in SF (4) :=GOV (i.e. the syntactic function (SF) of node 4 must be GOV); or they can be given in terms of other variables, as in VAR (1) :=VAR (4). Furthermore, just as we saw in the case of the conditions, affectations can also be expressed in formats, whenever sets of affectations are used repeatedly in different rules. The mechanism and motivations for its use are the same as for condition formats.

The three tree structures in (17) show the end result of applying this rule.

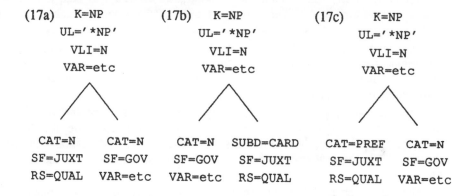

(17a)   K=NP   (17b)   K=NP   (17c)   K=NP
        UL='*NP'   UL='*NP'   UL='*NP'
        VLI=N   VLI=N   VLI=N
        VAR=etc   VAR=etc   VAR=etc

CAT=N	CAT=N	CAT=N	SUBD=CARD	CAT=PREF	CAT=N
SF=JUXT	SF=GOV	SF=GOV	SF=JUXT	SF=JUXT	SF=GOV
RS=QUAL	VAR=etc	VAR=etc	RS=QUAL	RS=QUAL	VAR=etc

The formalism can be criticised for being less declarative than intended; note the presence of the procedural 'if–then' in the affectation part. The possibility of including such procedures allows rules to be combined just because they have similar conditions and affectations, even though they may refer to essentially different constructions. In this example, the linguist has been encouraged to deal with three different types of compound noun on formal rather than linguistic grounds. The noun+number type (14b) differs clearly from the other two; it is the only one where the left daughter becomes GOV (17b) and it has one particular condition, tested in line 4 and repeated in the affectation at line 12.

13.5.3 TRANSF and SYGMOR

As we have already remarked, the TRANSF formalism used for lexical transfer is a slightly less powerful tree transducer. TRANSF takes trees as input but unlike ROBRA does not have the power to rearrange them; it is able only to alter the labelling on branches. Thus it has the pattern-matching capability of ROBRA, i.e. locating arbitrarily complex tree structures in the data structure, but it cannot create new tree structures. It is entirely appropriate for lexical transfer. Any structural changes required by the choice of target LUs are handled by the subsequent application of ROBRA (as described above.)

The rule-writing formalism SYGMOR was designed for morphological generation. Its function is to convert labelled trees into strings of characters (including punctuation marks.) There are two transducers; the first converts trees to strings of items, each of which is a bundle of attribute–value pairs; the second transducer maps these bundles onto actual strings. The whole process, though relatively simple, can be quite flexible and includes, for example, string transformation rules which allow regular morphological rules to be captured (e.g. the doubling of certain consonants in English *-ing* forms: *put* → *putting*).

13.6 Concluding remarks

The GETA system is rightly regarded as the archetypal 'second generation' MT system, i.e adopting a linguistics-oriented highly modular indirect translation approach, clearly separating algorithmic and linguistic processes, a stratified approach to analysis and generation, with little semantic processing and no AI-type 'understanding' and no interactive facilities. It represented a considerable advance on earlier direct 'first generation' systems of the pre-ALPAC era but it also exhibits some characteristic shortcomings of this design type.

The main problem lies in the use of the high-level rule-writing formalisms. In order to provide as general a set of formalisms as possible, the computer scientists at GETA had to design particularly powerful formalisms and software. In effect, they are like programming languages, albeit attuned to a special purpose. But this means that linguists have very few constraints, other than some undefinable notion of good programming practice, and the ideals of declarative programming can quickly become submerged. A good example is the use of 'flags' in rules: as a set of rules becomes more and more complex, it becomes increasingly difficult for the linguist to predict exactly what the effect will be of adding or changing a rule here or there. Since the underlying architecture is that of a production system, the linguist is not supposed to incorporate control information in rules, i.e. information which tells the interpreter which rule to apply next. However, for the sake of efficiency and avoidance of spurious computations, it is tempting to specify affectations in one rule which are to be tested in the condition part of another rule, i.e. 'flagging' that the first rule has applied so that the second rule can 'know' this. There is no problem if the 'flags' have an intrinsic linguistic validity, but if they do not, the declarative nature of the system is undermined. A criticism of the GETA approach is that this type of 'cheating' is in fact inevitable and necessary, and that when a system gets to a substantial size the idealised declarative model may be simply inappropriate. Whether later systems based on Prolog and other declarative languages are open to the same criticism remains to be seen.

A second, more local, problem concerns the linguistic representation used in GETA. The multi-level tree structure aims to capture simultaneously surface and deep structure, but in some cases there is a conflict between these two. For example, discontinous elements (e.g. in English phrasal verbs) must be represented as discontinuities at the surface level, but at the deeper level ought really to be merged as single nodes. This is done to a certain extent using the value of the LU (lexical unit) attribute, but the tree structures still include redundant or partially empty branches which represent surface elements with no deeper roles.

The strengths of the GETA system are its linguistic and computational techniques, particularly in the areas of morphological and syntactic analysis and transfer. Its weaknesses are the inadequate treatment of semantics and the poverty of its lexicographic databases. The only relatively large-scale test was that of the Russian–French version on abstracts in space science and metallurgy with a dictionary of some 7,000 Russian lexical units.

These deficiencies, however, are far outweighed by the substantial pioneering achievements of the GETA research group, which influenced profoundly the direction of MT research from the mid 1960s. The innovative theoretical work on Ariane reached a peak in the early 1980s. Since then the focus of attention in the GETA group has changed slightly. At the time of his death, Vauquois was working on a new, more declarative rule-writing formalism, called 'static grammars'. During the 1980s there has been much work at GETA on improving the environment for linguists working on MT, with better debugging tools and special rule-writing packages which allow linguists to write rules in a more familiar way and which automatically compile the actual formalism, and so on. The most recent new area of research at GETA, now under the direction of Christian Boitet, is the development of an interactive 'dialogue-based' MT system (cf. section 18.5). It is a sign that this long-standing research group remains at the forefront of MT research.

13.7 Sources and further reading

The GETA system is exceptionally well documented both in the public domain of collections on MT and Computational Linguistics, and in conference proceedings, as well as in the semi-private domain of GETA's own technical reports. The information in this chapter has been derived from all of these sources, too numerous to list.

The Grenoble group's early attempts at MT are documented in Vauquois' (1975) book. A representative collection of articles by Vauquois throughout his life has been published under the editorship of Christian Boitet (Vauquois, 1988). Other major general articles about the GETA system are Boitet and Nédobejkine (1981), Vauquois and Boitet (1985), Boitet (1987,1989a), Guilbaud (1987). Whitelock and Kilby (1983) and Hutchins (1986, 1988) give outsiders' views of the system and further references.

The project to commercialize the GETA system, called Calliope, is described in Brunner (1985); Joscelyne (1987) is a journalistic appraisal of its failure. Work on environments for rule writers is described in Boitet and Gerber (1986). Static grammars are described by Vauquois and Chappuy (1985).

14
Eurotra

This chapter describes what has probably been the biggest MT project yet, both in terms of number of personnel and amount of expenditure, and in the wide geographical distribution of the research groups involved. The Eurotra project has initiated and promoted basic research and development of the linguistic and computational requirements of complex multilingual MT system design, which will remain of lasting benefit to future developments.

14.1 Background

The increasing demands for translations in the European Community as a consequence of its multilingual policy had led the Commission to the introduction of Systran in 1976, initially for English–French translation and later for other pairs (Chapter 10). It was recognised, however, from the outset that inherent limitations in the Systran design reduced its potential as a multilingual system producing good quality output. In 1978 discussions began on a project for 'the creation of a machine translation system of advanced design (Eurotra) capable of dealing with all the official languages of the Community'. At that time these were Danish, Dutch, English, French, German, and Italian; Greek was added soon afterwards, and in 1986 Portuguese and Spanish were added. Eurotra is intended, therefore, to translate between nine languages, in all 72 language pairs.

The planning stage came to fruition with the formal approval of the Council of Ministers in November 1982 to set up a research and development programme in three phases. The first, 'preparatory', phase (1982–84) was to establish the organisational framework, with research groups funded in each member state, and to define the basic linguistic and software specifications. The second phase from 1984 to 1988 was to be devoted to the linguistic research necessary for a small prototype system (with about 2,500 lexical items per language), to be tested on a particular corpus; and the third phase (1988 to 1990) was intended to enlarge the system to deal with more complex texts, working with about 20,000 lexical items in each language, and progressively less restricted to a particular text corpus. The domain of the prototype was limited to technical texts in the field of information technology. The final result was not to be a fully operational system but a 'pre-industrial prototype' as the basis for possible industrial development after the end of the research programme. As such, the emphasis was on quality of output —reasonable to good, without significant human involvement — and on extendibility rather than on speed of performance.

The initial Council decision was amended in November 1986 to take account of the accession of Spain and Portugal. The inclusion of Spanish and Portuguese inevitably meant a protraction of the development of a prototype and consequently, at the same time, the Council agreed to an extension of the second phase.

Progress, however, was slower than anticipated. The European Parliament set up an independent evaluation committee which reported in late 1987. The Pannenborg report was critical of failures to resolve problems of management and lack of central resources. It considered that an exclusive emphasis on linguistic foundations had led to the neglect of computational possibilities (e.g. interactive operation) and insufficient attention to dictionary compilation. It confirmed that a prototype was unlikely by 1990 and that no commercial system would appear by 1993. Nevertheless, the project was held to have made fundamental progress in the specification of interfaces and had succeeded in promoting computational linguistics research in member countries (which had been specified as a secondary aim of the programme). Its positive recommendations included more realistic deadlines, the ending of the research phase in 1988 and the establishment of closer links with industry for the development of a practical system, all of which contributed to the Council's approval in July 1988 of the transition to the third phase. By December 1989 there were 18 institutions involved in the project, located in 12 member states and comprising over 150 scientists, postgraduates and engineers (mostly active part-time only), with a central Commission staff in Luxembourg and under the general direction of Sergei Perschke.

A subsequent assessment in March 1990 (the Danzin report) confirmed the importance of the project as a stimulus to basic research in language technology, but also the unlikelihood of an operational MT system. It anticipated that the result of Eurotra would be a 'scientific definition prototype' rather than a 'pre-industrial development prototype'. It would have a limited lexicon, because not enough work has been done on terminology to achieve the planned 20,000 word coverage. However, there were already sufficient potential applications (monolingual as well as multilingual) of the Eurotra research to justify work already done, and the report recommended the continuation and broadening of the computational linguistics research framework established by the Eurotra project beyond 1991 to stimulate inter-European projects in basic and applied research and development of computer-based language tools.

Having begun as an ambitious R&D project to develop a multilingual MT system based on the latest advances in computational linguistics, Eurotra has at the time of writing entered a second round of funding, known as the 'transition programme', during which the emphases will be on laying the foundations for development of an industrial prototype by improving the performance, both linguistic and computational, and on encouraging more basic research on the theoretical foundations of MT in a multilingual framework. What is described in this chapter is not a prototype system but the specifications for a potential system which have been only partially implemented. Early articles about Eurotra concentrate on the political and administrative problems (which are in fact highly relevant to the system design), and give very general information about the nature of the translation problem to be solved. More technical articles began to appear around 1986, referring to a computational approach called the '<C,A>,T framework', later superseded, but nevertheless containing the seeds of what was finally to be adopted. Furthermore, the status of the various reports differs: some have been agreed by all participants, many exist as proposals. The basic design framework only became settled towards the end of the project, and there remain differences between researchers working in different environments. It is often difficult to establish from the writings of Eurotra-supported researchers whether they are giving an 'officially' approved view or not. A recently published set of articles can be regarded as definitive, and have informed the present description.

14.2 Organisation and system design

The requirements of decentralisation and multilinguality determined the development and design criteria of the system. While general administration and coordination was located in Luxembourg, all research was carried out by teams for each language in each Community country. Two groups had special functions not focused on a single language (Table 14.1), and other groups were involved in the project from time to time, notably ISSCO (*Istituto per gli Studi Semantici e Cognitivi*) in Geneva, and GETA in Grenoble.

Decentralisation on this scale demanded from the beginning a clear framework for the research and development of separate modules. Eurotra is the first attempt to create a genuinely multilingual system. A crucial decision, taken in 1978, was that Eurotra would be a transfer-based system, although perhaps, with the benefit of hindsight, as some observers have suggested, with originally 30, then 42, and finally 72 language pairs, it would have made more sense to choose an interlingua approach. However, it should be remembered that at that time, this approach had been so firmly discredited that the option was barely discussed (cf. section 1.3). The basic specifications for interface structures, for core formalisms and for software were drawn up by teams with members from throughout the Community; individual research groups worked on the analysis and generation modules for their own languages, and worked in pair-wise collaborations on the 72 transfer modules.

Definition of the interface structure (IS) was obviously crucial. In theory, since this is a transfer-based system, the IS for any one particular language could differ from one language pair to another, e.g. there could be one French

Task	Group	Location
Administration	DG XIII-B, CEC	Luxembourg
Danish	Københavns Universitet	Copenhagen
Dutch	Rijksuniversiteit Utrecht	Utrecht
	Katholieke Universiteit Leuven	Leuven
English	UMIST (University of Manchester Institute of Science and Technology)	Manchester
	University of Essex	Colchester
French	Université de Nancy II	Nancy
	Université de Paris VII	Paris
	Université de Liège	Liège
German	IAI (Institut für Angewandte Informationswissenschaft)	Saarbrücken
	IKP (Institut für Kommunikationsforschung und Phonetik)	Bonn
Greek	Eurotra Greece	Athens
	Panepistemio tou Rethymnou	Crete
Italian	Gruppo Dima	Turin
	Università di Pisa	Pisa
Portuguese	Universidade de Lisboa	Lisbon
Spanish	Universidad de Barcelona	Barcelona
	Universidad Autónoma de Madrid	Madrid
Terminology	Dublin City University	Dublin
Documentation and software clearing-house	CRETA (Centre de Recherches et d'Etudes en Traduction Automatique)	Luxembourg

Table 14.1 Participants in Eurotra

IS when translating into German and another French IS when translating into Spanish. However, this would have been not only less practical, obviously, but it would also have undermined the aim of having monolingual analysis and generation components which are neutral with respect to target and source languages, respectively. For this reason, there was agreed a common set of principles defining in general what the ISs should look like, and what level of abstraction of linguistic information they should contain.

In Eurotra translation is regarded as a **mapping** from a source text to a target text, where the mapping is defined in steps corresponding to **modules** of the system. In the three basic stages, 'analysis' is the mapping from source text to a representation R_s reflecting the source text, 'transfer' is the mapping of R_s onto a representation R_t reflecting the target text, and 'generation' is the mapping of R_t onto a target text (Figure 14.1).

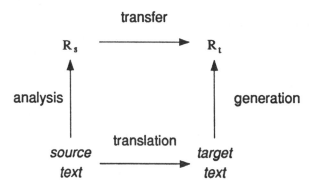

Figure 14.1 Notion of 'mapping'

With 72 language pairs there is an obvious requirement that transfer is kept as simple as possible; but as a consequence, the analysis and generation modules are correspondingly more complex than in other transfer-based systems. Because of this complexity, analysis and generation are also broken down into a series of mappings (Figure 14.2), giving the Eurotra framework its basically stratificational nature. The intermediate levels of representation are linguistically motivated, and up to five types of representation are envisaged (although some groups were able to define the sequence of mappings from text to IS in fewer stages).

The representations at the top of the figure, i.e. the final representation in analysis and the initial representation in generation, are the interface structures (ISs) mentioned above. It should be noticed that there is no stipulation that there must be the same number of levels of representation on both sides. The levels typically reflect the familiar distinctions of morphological, surface syntax (constituent), relational, and deep syntax descriptions of linguistic phenomena. They are characterised as follows:

- ETS (Eurotra Text Structure): the input text as received with formatting and publishing codes, including non-textual data and diagrams.
- ENT (Eurotra Normalised Text): the input text, stripped of all non-textual data and coding and roughly equivalent to an ASCII file.
- EMS (Eurotra Morphological Structure): a representation of words and morphemes in the form of a sequence of labelled word trees and punctuation marks.
- ECS (Eurotra Constituent Structure): a representation of surface syntactic constituency structure based on relations of syntactic categories.

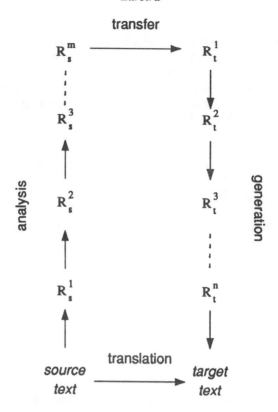

Figure 14.2 Complex mapping

- ERS (Eurotra Relational Structure): a representation of surface grammatical relations (subject, object, etc.) together with syntactic categories, broadly similar to LFG f-structures.
- IS (Interface Structure): a representation based on semantic dependency incorporating case frame structures and semantic features (animate, human, etc.) IS representations are the input to and output from transfer components.

14.3 Computational approach

In the terminology of the Eurotra project, the mapping between two levels of representation is called **translation**, an unfortunate choice of term, which should obviously not be confused with the ordinary sense of text-to-text translation (which for Eurotra is seen as a special case of 'translation' as defined here).

The Eurotra rule-writing formalism, called the **E-framework**, grew out of the earlier well-publicised '<C,A>,T' framework, and has much in common with it. The E-framework falls within the class of **unification-based** grammar formalisms (section 2.9.7), though, unlike many other such frameworks, it has not been designed with a view to dealing primarily with surface syntactic analysis. Rather, the E-framework is a more general mechanism for handling structured feature-based linguistic objects, and fits neatly the overall stratificational linguistic approach of Eurotra.

14.3.1 Objects and structures

At each level the representations consist of primitive objects and structures built from these primitive objects. The primitive objects are **feature bundles** (cf. section 2.8.3), where features are attribute–value pairs and where the possible values of features and the possible combinations of attributes are defined by a 'feature theory' for each level of representation. For example, the feature theory for a morpho-syntactic level of representation might stipulate that if there is an object with an attribute–value pair where the attribute is 'category' and the value is 'noun', then the same feature bundle should have also an attribute 'case' with a value such as 'nominative' or 'accusative', a 'gender' attribute with a value 'masculine' or 'feminine', and so on. For each level of representation there is a defined set of features.

The legal primitive objects or categories at each level of representation are also defined by the feature theory: in practice this means that each level of representation is described by a set of 'feature declarations' which say what the features are (the attributes and their possible values), and the 'co-occurrence restrictions' on the features, which state which feature values are mutually compatible.

Turning now to the definition of **structures**, these are defined by rules which express the two structural properties of **dominance** (i.e. mother–daughter relationships) and **precedence** (i.e. ordering among sisters), cf. section 2.8.2. For example, at the syntactic level there may be a rule stating that an object having the features in (1a) might also have a structure made up of two objects, one a feature bundle including the features in (1b), and the other with the features in (1c). This kind of information is captured by the familiar type of rewrite rule.

(1a) {category=np, gender=masculine, case=nominative, number=singular}

(1b) {category=determiner, gender=masculine, case=nominative, number=singular}

(1c) {category=noun, gender=masculine, case=nominative, number=singular}

The 'rules' defining legal structures are collected to form the grammar of each descriptive level, where 'grammar' is understood in the formal sense of a set of context free rewrite rules defining the possible structural relationships of feature bundles.

It is important to note the 'declarative' nature of the feature theory and structural definitions. What the system does with these definitions is quite separate, and will now be discussed.

14.3.2 Translators and generators

The objects that are of interest to the MT system (at a computational level) are called **consolidated** objects, by which is meant structures which are well-formed according to all these rules. There are also **unconsolidated** objects, the provenance of which will be revealed below, and which are structures which may or may not be well-formed: they are 'hypothetical structures', waiting to have their validity confirmed or denied. They may be structures which are only partially specified, or with inconsistent or incomplete feature specifications, or in need of restructuring.

The computational device which attempts to consolidate unconsolidated objects is called a 'generator'. This is again an unfortunate choice of terminology, since what a generator does here is not the 'generation' of target text. In fact, the term is used as the equivalent of a generative grammar in the mathematical sense (see section 2.9.1); hence it is declarative, and not a procedural device.

The unconsolidated objects are the results of 'translation', the process of mapping between levels of representation. Translation is done by 'translators', which take as input a single consolidated object (the output of the previous step) and process it top-down to produce as output a series of unconsolidated sub-objects which are passed to the next generator. In other words, translators take the output from a previous generator and change it in some way to provide input to the next generator; or more simply, they transform the structure and the features from one level to the next.

The **generator** performs the job of consolidation in a number of ways. In general terms, it can alter the dominance relations of a structure, primarily by inserting or removing nodes (though not by inverting them); and it can affect precedence either by imposing order on an unordered set of sisters or, again, by inserting or deleting sisters (but not by reversing their order).

There are three main types of rules found in a generator: structure-building rules, feature rules, and filter rules. Each of them has two variants.

Structure-building rules are either 'b-rules' or 'l-rules'. **B-rules** ('b' for 'building') are the most common type of rule, and most closely correspond to the conventional context free rewrite rule. A b-rule identifies a mother node and a list (possibly empty) of daughters, all specified as feature bundles. For example, (2) describes a simple noun phrase (perhaps for French) at the ECS level: np is the name of the rule (for debugging and control purposes); the '*' is a Kleene star and indicates iteration; the '^' indicates optionality. Informally, we can describe (2) as a rule defining a noun phrase with an optional determiner phrase, any number of adjective phrases (ap) where the adjective is prenominal (adj_type=ante), an obligatory noun, and any number of post-nominal adjectives; all the elements must agree in gender (G) and number (N), the capital letters indicating variables.

```
(2) np = {cat=np, gend=G, nb=N, def=DF}
         [^{cat=detp, gend=G, nb=N, def=DF},
          *{cat=ap, gend=G, nb=N, adj_type=ante},
          {cat=n, gend=G, nb=N},
          *{cat=ap, gend=G, nb=N, adj_type=post}]
```

A b-rule can be applied in four different modes, depending on the circumstances in which it comes into play. In one mode, corresponding to traditional bottom-up parsing, the daughters specified by the rule unify with a sequence of nodes, the mother node is built and the dominance relations are established. In a second mode, the rule provides confirmation of a structure; in this case both the mother and the daughters unify. In a third mode, where the mother unifies with a node which has no daughters, the rule serves to create a new structure. And in the fourth mode, if the set of daughters is partially matched, then the rule might serve to insert an additional sister node.

L-rules ('l' for 'leaf') are also structure-building rules, but are restricted to rules which describe single feature bundles. They typically describe the atomic dictionary entries for the level concerned.

Feature rules apply only to objects in which dominance relations have been consolidated. They serve to refine such objects: by adding information (in the form of new features), in the case of **i-rules** ('i' for 'insertion'); or by causing features to propagate through the structure, in the case of **f-rules** ('f' for 'feature'). For example, the f-rule in (3) shows values for tense and aspect being passed up from the main verb (role=gov, cat=v) in a sentence to the governing (cat=s) node.

(3) s_tense =
          {s_tense=T,s_aspect=A,cat=s}
          [{s_tense=T,s_aspect=A,role=gov,cat=v},
           *{}
          ]

The i-rule in (4) shows the insertion (identified by the '!') of a determiner in a (Dutch) noun phrase, with gender number and determiner type (msdefs) according to the marking on the mother node (np).

(4) np = {cat=np,msdefs=D,nb=N,nl_gender=G}
              [^{cat=quantp,pos=predet},
               !{cat=detp,msnb=N,nl_gender=G,msdefs=D},
               *{cat=ap},
               {cat=n},
               *{}]

Filter rules, like feature rules, apply to objects where dominance has been consolidated, and they serve, as their name implies, to disallow structures which do not conform to certain specifications. In this way, they act as a safety valve by enabling the explicit suppression of structures which result from 'over-generation', i.e. the unforeseen superfluous results of rules, and by describing explicitly the conditions under which a structure can be accepted. Filter rules are, thus, of two types: **s-rules** ('s' for 'strict') specify acceptability conditions for structures, and **k-rules** ('k' for 'killer') explicitly suppress illegal or unwanted structures.

Some additional comments on filter rules are appropriate here. First, notice that their presence undermines slightly the declarative nature of generators in general. This is particularly true for the k-rules. Second, since s-rules can be regarded as restatements of the admissibility conditions for objects, it is difficult to know exactly how the description of legal objects should be divided between b-rules, i-rules, f-rules and s-rules. On the other hand, it might be seen as a strength of the formalism in that it gives the linguist a choice and the linguistic description is not confined by the tools available. However since s-rules are in effect a device to allow the grammar writer a 'second chance' in ensuring processes work as intended, they are almost as non-declarative as the k-rules. Nevertheless, if filter rules are applied in a principled way (rather than as an *ad hoc* escape hatch), their availability should not undermine the general elegance of the E-framework.

Translators, as mentioned above, serve to map consolidated objects from one level onto sets of unconsolidated objects at the next level. Two basic principles have been developed to guide the definition of translators. The first, often referred to as the 'one-shot' principle, requires that between two representations the translator does not create any intermediate representations, i.e. elements(s) of one representation must be directly converted into element(s) of another. The second principle is that of 'compositionality', which states that interpretations of structures are functions of the interpretations of their components in a formally defined way, i.e. the translation of a complex expression should be a function of the translation of the basic expressions it contains together with their mode of combination — in this respect Eurotra shows the influence of the Rosetta project (Chapter 16) — though translators operate between representations and not (as in Rosetta) between derivation trees.

Each translator consists of a set of **t-rules** of two types. **Default t-rules**, as their name suggests, express automatic mappings from the feature theory at one level to that at the next. They are defined implicitly according the intersection of the feature theories of the two levels. **Explicit t-rules** define mappings which are not given by default, or contradict the default mappings. As such, they take priority over default t-rules when translators are activated.

Orthogonal to the explicit–default distinction is a distinction between **feature t-rules** (f-t-rules) and **structure-building t-rules** (b-t-rules), the former are used to map features, the latter to map structures. In general, f-t-rules are very simple mappings of one (or more) feature–value(s) at one level onto the next, as in (5), which maps a value for syntactic aspect onto semantic aspect (e.g. between the ECS level and the ERS level).

```
(5) t_simple = {syn_aspect=simple} =>
                {sem_aspect=perfective}
```

B-t-rules tend to be more complex. In example (6) a prepositional phrase (cat=pp) with the syntactic function of complement (sf=compl), formed with the preposition *of* at ECS, is mapped onto a simple noun phrase at ERS. The label OBJ is a variable name with no special significance; the '~' indicates explicitly that this node will be deleted; the '?' indicates that cat can have any value.

```
(6) tpp_compl =
          ~:{cat=pp,sf=compl}
            [ ~:{cat=p,gb_lu=of}, OBJ:{cat=?}]
      => OBJ:{sf=compl}.
```

As this description of the various rule types making up the E-framework demonstrates, the Eurotra linguists have available a rich computational formalism. But this richness means it is almost inevitable that different 'styles' of rule-writing emerge. For example, one group may write a large number of very simple and partly repetitive rules, while another group may try to capture similar linguistic facts with a small number of much more complex rules. Likewise, there are often alternative ways of doing the same thing, using different combinations of different rule types, and there is no firm guidance about which should be used.

14.3.3 Implementation

The importance of software tools adequate to the task of multilingual MT was recognised by the establishment of a strong team within Eurotra devoted to the development of efficient computational facilities. A major restriction was the need for software which could run on the fairly wide variety of machines favoured by the various research groups. In fact, the UNIX[TM] operating system was quickly agreed upon as a communal standard, and the E-framework software has been written in Prolog, in keeping with its generally declarative style and its unification basis. Needless to say, some implementations of the Eurotra software performed more efficiently than others. An example of the kind of problems encountered was the relative inefficiency of the Prolog compiler with such large programs. The Danzin report mentions an overall twenty-fold increase in performance between 1987 and 1990 thanks to an increase in computing power from 1Mips to 4Mips or 5Mips depending on the site, the introduction of the Yap[TM] compiler developed in Portugal to replace the standard Prolog interpreters (at least doubling and in some cases quadrupling efficiency), and a ten-fold improvement in the application software.

In the terminology of the Eurotra community itself, 'implementation' has come to mean not the installation of the basic software, but the development of the translation pairs themselves. At the time of writing, roughly the beginning of the 'transition programme' (see section 14.1), work on analysis and generation modules for all nine community languages is well under way, with transfer modules (of varying quality) for almost all 72 language pairs also under development. There is of course great variation also in the sizes of the linguistic modules amongst the different groups, not least because some began much later than others, and there is a similar variation in the sizes of the dictionaries, with lexical entries now numbering on average 4,000 in both monolingual and transfer dictionaries.

14.4 Linguistic aspects

Apart from an innovative computational approach to MT, the Eurotra project is remarkable for its significant contribution to the promotion of computational linguistics, and especially of contrastive linguistics, throughout the member states. At the beginning of the project, relatively little work had been done in a formal framework on any of the languages involved, with the obvious exceptions of English and to a lesser extent French and German. There are now large computational grammars of Greek, Danish, Dutch, Italian, Portuguese and Spanish. In the following section, we attempt to give some indication of the results of the important contrastive linguistic work undertaken in collaboration by the various Eurotra groups.

14.4.1 Research on linguistic topics

The breadth of coverage of linguistic phenomena in the project is indicated by the range of sentence types that most of the Eurotra implementations can handle: adverbial and subordinate clauses, verbless sentences, appositions, headlines and parenthetical expressions, infinitives and control verbs, participle constructions, basic coordination, all temporal as well as modal forms, morphological analysis (inflectional and derivational), etc., with research continuing on problems such as ellipsis, negation, quantifier scope, and pronoun anaphora resolution.

Among the topics in which the Eurotra linguists can claim to have made significant advances, we may mention particularly tense and modality. These are two areas where cross-linguistic differences are notoriously treacherous. Even within the relatively small set of closely related languages that Eurotra deals with, there are great differences in the number of morpho-syntactic verb tenses and their corresponding uses (cf. the example sentence (7) in the next section). For example, the English present perfect form (*have* plus past participle) may indicate either an activity which has recently been completed or one which was begun in the past and continues. The two uses may result in different tenses in any of the other languages in the system. With so many different tense systems a pair-wise case-by-case treatment was simply impossible, and recognition of the problems triggered research into the specification of a feature system for indicating the temporal reference of any given morpho-syntactic tense and which would be common to the European languages involved, i.e. a 'euroversal' feature system for tense.

Modality (expressed in English by modal auxiliaries such as *can, must, may, might*, etc.) is equally complex, and, unlike time and tense, had not previously been studied extensively from a contrastive point of view. In certain respects, the problems were greater since the languages in the system do not even share the same morpho-syntactic means for expressing modality: auxiliary verbs, verb inflections, adverbials, or combinations of these. Again, a 'euroversal' system of modality features had to be worked out.

A general lexicographic problem for Eurotra was the need to develop a common perception of canonical form (cf. section 2.8.4), particularly in order that IS representations could be as interlingual as possible and that transfer could be restricted largely to lexical items. The need was to define the underlying head–modifier structures for various types of construction. It involved issues such as the role of prepositions (whether functioning as case markers or having lexical content — contrast *on* in *depend on the weather* and *sit on the floor*), the 'featurization' of modifiers such as determiners and quantifiers, and the treatment of compounds not as unanalysed units but as lexical items with structure.

In the general design of Eurotra it was important that the different language groups were assured of relative independence in matters of linguistic principle. Although all groups were constrained to use the E-framework, to aim at a common IS representation in analysis and to start from a given IS representation in generation, they were free to develop their own approaches to analysis and generation of their own language. The British group, for example, chose to skip the ERS level of representation, deriving IS structures directly from ECS representations. Likewise, there has been no centrally imposed common treatment of coordination, agreement, anaphora and so on. For these reasons, it is not possible to present a single 'Eurotra linguistic approach', since, apart from IS, there is none. We can, however, give some impression of the general stance of Eurotra in the next section, by illustrating briefly the analysis process of a sample sentence.

14.4.2 An illustrative example

We select for exemplification the German sentence (7) used in the most recent description of Eurotra. In the article from which this illustration is taken, the example is worked through to transfer and generation of Danish.

(7) *Die Industrie kennt dieses Problem seit einiger Zeit.*
'Industry has known about this problem for some time'

The representation after morphological analysis is a shallow structure, as in (8a). In fact the representation (as at other levels) is much richer than in the simplified tree diagram. This is shown in (8b): the feature bundles for the daughters give the lexical and morphological feature information associated with each word, where angle brackets indicate lists of daughters (the dots indicate parts of the representation omitted here for brevity, and are not part of the formalism).

(8a)

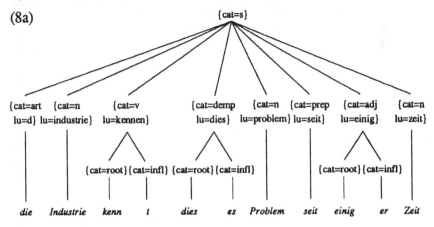

```
(8b) {cat=s}
      <{cat=art, lu=d, msdefs=msdef, gender=fem,
        nb=sing},
       {cat=n, lu=industrie, gender=fem, nb=sing},
       {cat=v, lu=kennen, mstense=pres, nb=sing,
        pers=3}
       <{cat=root, lu=kenn},
        {cat=infl, lu=t}>,
       {cat=art, lu=dies, msdefs=msdef, gender=neut,
        nb=sing},
       <{cat=root, lu=dies},
        {cat=infl, lu=es}>,
       {cat=n, lu=problem, gender=neut, nb=sing},
       {cat=prep, lu=seit, ....},
       {cat=adj, lu=einig, ....},
       <{cat=root, lu=einig},
        {cat=infl, lu=er}>,
       {cat=n, lu=zeit, gender=fem, nb=sing}>
```

At this stage no intermediate constituents have been recognised, of course, though the treatment of inflectional morphology as a substructure should be noted. Ambiguities, such as the grammatical case and gender of *einiger*, are recognised in morphological analysis and are to be resolved at some subsequent stage.

The next stage is the translation of the EMS structure to a (set of) unconsolidated ECS structure(s), which the ECS generator then consolidates. Inflectional information is converted into features, and the lower nodes such as root and infl are discarded. The b-rules at this level are principally those of the 'bottom-up parsing' type (see above), taking sequences of nodes and creating a more structured representation, perhaps as in (9) (we show only the most relevant feature values, and for increased legibility show the structure in a more traditional tree form). Some readers might be surprised at the constituency structure of this analysis: the German ECS module is much influenced by Government and Binding theory (see section 2.10.3), hence the structure with the verb under comp. It is a good example of the way that representations at intermediate levels (i.e. other than IS) are not centrally legislated, but can be decided by individual language groups.

(9)

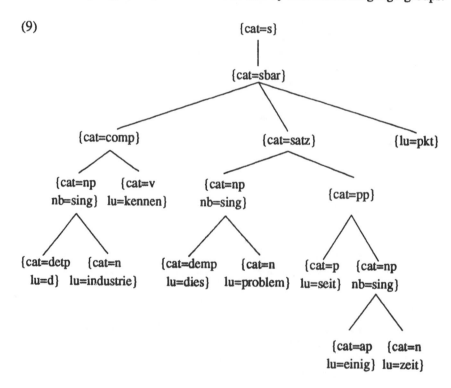

Consolidation at this level includes the 'percolation' of syntactic features from the leaves to the appropriate dominating nodes. For example, the case, gender and number of a noun phrase is given by unification of the possible values for these features on the daughters, typically by a b-rule such as (10).

(10) np = {cat=np, case=C, nb=N}
      [^{cat=detp, case=C, nb=N, gender=G},
       *{cat=ap, case=C, nb=N, gender=G},
       {cat=n, case=C, nb=N, gender=G}].

Recall that the '^' symbol indicates optionality, and the '*' repetition; capital letters indicate variables.

The representation at ERS level reflects dependency relations and syntactic functions such as governor, subject, modifier and so on; with these elements presented in a centrally legislated canonical order. The representation of our example sentence is roughly as in (11): again for clarity's sake, some feature values are not shown.

(11)

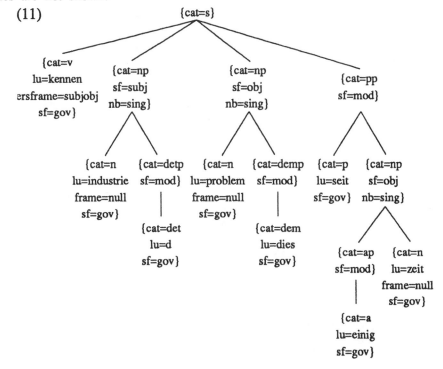

The IS structure is, in the case of this example sentence, very similar to the ERS structure, though the labellings reflect the deeper analysis (12). In fact, the full labelling of the IS tree is quite extensive: we show here, for example, that the cat=s node carries values for aspect, tense, sentence-type, and so on. Other labels are also present at all nodes (see below).

Transfer to an English IS consists just of replacing lexical items (13a). In our example sentence, the surface tense and aspect of the main verb will be changed from the German simple present to the present perfect in English. However, at the IS level, the time labelling for both languages is the same, the appropriate values having been calculated at a previous point in the German analysis (probably at ERS level) by a rule stipulating the values sTENSE=simul and

(12)

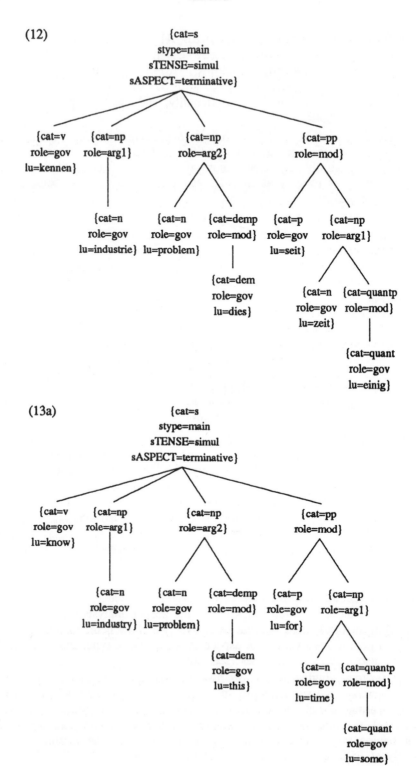

(13a)

'sASPECT=terminative' whenever the morpho-syntactic tense is present and there is a modifying prepositional phrase with *seit*.

In order to give a better indication of the complexity of the IS representation, we reproduce here more or less in full the English IS for this sentence (13b).

The reader's attention should be drawn to three interesting aspects of the IS representation. First is the inclusion in the feature bundles of traces of the rules which have been used to build the structures, seen as values of the feature $rule. Although clearly not part of the structure from a linguistic point of view, the inclusion of this information in the data structure is of obvious benefit to researchers working on the system. The second point concerns the features with unfilled values which show up in the IS as an underline character ('_') followed by a number. These are features which, perhaps by default, appear on each node at this level, but for which no value has been established, either by the translator, or by the unification process of the generator. From (13b) we can see that there must be a default rule that all nodes at IS level have the features sTENSE and sASPECT; but for all nodes except the mother node and its governor, the features are unvalued. The third point of interest is a related computational issue. It is the number of features with value no. These negative values are necessary because the Eurotra software is essentially unification-based: it was found that irrelevant features were being inserted into the structure by the unification process. It became necessary, therefore, at all levels (and most often at the 'lower' levels) to make explicit not only which feature–values apply, but also which ones do not. Researchers report this as a major disadvantage of the unification approach, perhaps unforeseen (or at least underestimated) by the developers of smaller experimental unification-based systems.

Obviously, the representation in (13b) is too unwieldy for the human linguist to manage comfortably, and in Eurotra, as in other systems such as Ariane and METAL (Chapters 13 and 15), some attention has been paid to making the huge data objects that the system manipulates more accessible for the researchers. For example, structures such as the ones shown in (13a) can easily be produced and investigated. What we have been able to show here is the size and complexity of the data structures created and handled by the Eurotra system, which in this respect can be said to be a typical large-scale second generation MT system.

14.5 Conclusions

Eurotra is undoubtedly the most ambitious MT project at the present time. As yet, the huge research effort has not resulted in even a 'scientific pre-development' system, but this must be seen in perspective. The basic linguistic knowledge required for a multilingual system did not exist when the project began. Linguistics research did not provide the necessary detail, and other MT systems did not organise data in ways which could be adopted for an advanced multilingual design. Now it can be said that a large part of this fundamental research has been accomplished. Much, of course, remains to be done. Eurotra has been above all a project for European linguists.

(13b)

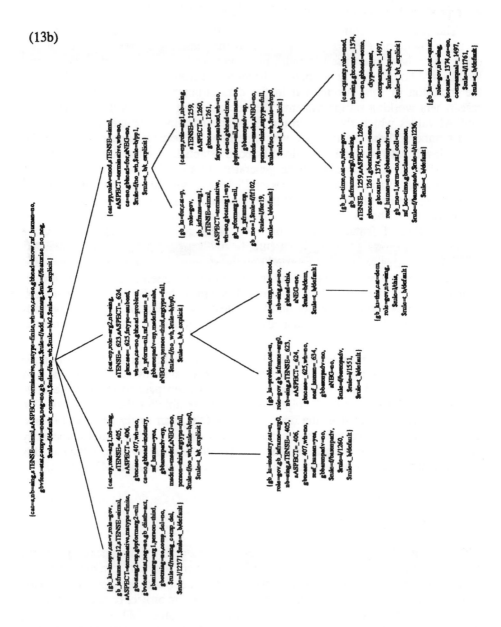

As well as the mainstream Eurotra research, there has been some significant related 'spin-off' research, including two experimental MT systems (CAT and MiMo) based on and derived from Eurotra at an earlier stage in its development, and the development of a logic grammar formalism (CLG: Constraint Logic Grammars).

The flexibility and modularity of the basic Eurotra framework has itself stimulated linguistic research. Experimentation with different treatments of time and modality was facilitated by the independence of the interface and transfer components from the other modules. Complementary research has been sponsored elsewhere which explores topics of concern, e.g. discourse phenomena, within a somewhat looser, but still compatible, conceptual framework. The simplicity and perspicuity of the Eurotra basic design makes it an ideal 'communication medium' for linguists starting from different intellectual backgrounds.

There are limitations, of course. A major shortcoming is the too simplistic approach to semantics. In the Eurotra framework semantics is treated primarily by features attached to nodes in essentially syntax-based structures. This shallow semantics combined with deep and broad coverage of syntax has resulted in over-generation in analysis, and insufficient filtering by disambiguation. More constrained parsing and production might reduce over-generation, but possibly at the cost of damaging the stratificational design. There are alternatives to the stratificational design available with recent advances in cognitive science and in Artificial Intelligence, and it has always been accepted that Eurotra should be flexible enough to adopt new techniques, provided that they are well founded and adequately tested.

Some of this insufficiency of semantics could be minimised in a practical system by the incorporation of an interactive facility, and this has been recommended in reports to the Commission. The reports have also stressed that priority should be given to improvements in semantic representations and a greater urgency must be given to terminological and dictionary work.

Certain design questions remain unanswered. It would seem that in principle translators could be reversible, and that consequently whole modules could be used for both analysis and generation. Some Eurotra researchers are investigating the possibilities, but whether this will become part of the 'official' design is as yet unknown.

The theoretical activity of Eurotra researchers has contributed substantially to the theoretical foundations of MT. However, it remains an explicitly 'linguistic' system; it does not attempt to incorporate any knowledge bases or cognitive modelling of the AI kind. It has been criticised by some observers for its concentration on abstract formalism, for neglecting the construction of lexicons, for its insufficient empirical testing, and for what is seen as a 'narrow' exclusion of discourse phenomena and advances in knowledge-based approaches to natural language processing.

The disappointment of many external observers of Eurotra lies predominantly in the failure to produce practical results. The Danzin report in 1990 urged the Council to permit researchers to demonstrate specific applications, not to be constrained by the full multilingual requirements of the original proposals. There could then be tangible products, monolingual in some cases, not just as spin-offs of Eurotra research but as agreed objectives: the recommendation recognises the substantial contribution to European computational linguistics of the project, and seeks to promote its potential commercial benefits.

Eurotra has successfully broadened the research base of European computational linguistics (in part by the training of manpower), it has heightened awareness amongst linguists of the need for inter-European collaboration and it has promoted awareness in governmental bodies of the growing economic and cultural importance of basic and applied research in natural language processing.

14.6 Sources and further reading

The development of Eurotra has been marked by various stages, reflected in the availability of published material on the project. Early references are very general in nature, reflecting more the political and administrative needs of the Commission, though some early reports do give an insight into the way these considerations affected the design (e.g. Johnson *et al.* 1985, Arnold 1986). The project then had perhaps three phases of scientific development, the first being now only of historical interest (and in any case only sketchily reported). The second, centring on the <C,A>,T formalism is relevant in that much of the E-framework is rooted in that formalism. Reports within the <C,A>,T framework include a special issue of *Multilingua* (Sager and Somers 1986), Arnold and des Tombe (1987), King and Perschke (1987), Raw *et al.* (1988) and Steiner *et al.* (1988).

The most up-to-date descriptions of Eurotra, from which much of the material in this chapter is adapted, are in the special issue of the journal *Machine Translation* (Allegranza *et al.* 1991). Other relevant reports include Bech and Nygaard (1988) and Varile and Lau (1988).

The Pannenborg and Danzin reports (CEC 1988, 1990) are available from the Commission of the European Communities in Luxembourg. The description in this chapter of the E-framework is specifically based on Bech *et al.* (1991), while the example of German analysis is adapted from Kirchmeier-Andersen (1991), with the assistance of members of the British Eurotra groups at UMIST and Essex. The CAT project is described in Sharp (1988), MiMo in Arnold and Sadler (1990) and van Noord *et al.* (1990), CLG in Damas and Varile (1989).

As already indicated, the writing of this chapter has benefited from the close association of one of the authors (HLS) with the project and its developers. However, it should be stressed that he left the Eurotra project in 1986 and up until the time of writing had no active involvement with it in any way. We would like to acknowledge the assistance in writing this chapter given to us by Paul Bennett, Jeanette Pugh, Nancy Underwood and Andy Way; we are of course responsible for any errors which remain.

UNIX and Yap are trademarks of AT&T Laboratories.

15
METAL

In 1989 the METAL system for German–English translation was introduced to the commercial market by the German electronics company Siemens of Munich. The product of many years of research stretching back to the mid 1960s, the METAL system is essentially based on the transfer approach; it is written in the Lisp programming language, and it represents one of the most advanced operational MT systems at the present time.

15.1 Historical background

The origins of the MT research for METAL go back to the establishment of the Linguistics Research Center (LRC) at the University of Texas (Austin, Texas) under the direction of Winfred Lehmann in 1961. Research on an MT system for German to English had already begun in 1959 with a contract from the US Army; but the major funder was the US Air Force Rome Air Development Center until 1979. Unlike many other MT groups at the time, the emphasis at LRC was long-term fundamental linguistic research. Basic research on English and German syntax led to the proposed development of a bidirectional transfer system, with reversibility of the syntactic transfer rules. This initial research phase ended in 1968.

A second phase of LRC research extended from 1970 to 1975 with the exploration of an interlingua-based approach, still concentrating on German and English. At an early stage, the LRC group convened a conference to assess the direction of MT after the ALPAC report of a few years earlier (section 1.3) and concluded that current linguistic research gave encouragement to the pursuit of deeper levels of analysis and to efforts towards interlingual representations. Like the contemporary CETA system at the University of Grenoble (section 13.1), the LRC interlingua design was interlingual only with respect to syntactic representations: translation of lexical items was handled by rules of lexical transfer.

In 1978 a new phase began with financial support from the Munich-based company Siemens, who became sole supporters from 1980. Siemens' motivation was both the need to increase the productivity of its own translation service and the desire to produce a translation system for others. The METAL system (the name originally comes from the acronym 'Mechanical Translation and Analysis of Language') changed from an interlingua design to an essentially transfer-based approach, not intended to operate fully automatically but to be augmented by sophisticated text-editing facilities and access to large terminology databanks, in particular Siemens' own TEAM database. In 1989 the first METAL system appeared on the market, for German–English translation, and is now installed at a number of large corporate users. Like Systran (Chapter 10), it is a system for mainframe computers; METAL runs on Symbolics™ 36-series Lisp machines, with batch processing and post-editing on workstations (Siemens SINIX™-based machines MX-2, MX-300 or MX-500), linked to printing facilities. There are as yet no plans for microcomputer-based versions.

The German–English version is to be followed by one for English into German and by systems for Dutch–French, French–Dutch, German–Spanish, German–French and German–Danish. Research on METAL is coordinated in Munich, with research on the English–German system conducted at LRC, on Dutch and French at the University of Leuven (Belgium), on German–Spanish at the University of Barcelona, and at the Handelshøjskole Syd in Kolding (Denmark) on German–Danish.

15.2 The basic system

METAL is intended to deal with high volumes of technical documentation, which is typically full of tables, diagrams, flow charts, etc. For economic operation a system has to be able to extract the material to be translated and to put it back in the correct locations. The basic METAL translation system has therefore been integrated into a chain of pre-translation processes, text acquisition and automatic deformatting, and post-translation processes, automatic reformatting, post-editing and transfer to typesetting and printing. These pre- and post-translation stages are performed at present on Siemens SINIX™ equipment, while the core translation system operates on a Symbolics™ Lisp machine.

The core processes of the METAL system are illustrated in Figure 15.1.

1. Text acquisition is from telecommunication links and various input facilities, e.g. magnetic tapes, floppy disks, OCRs, etc.

2. Deformatting programs separate textual data from diagrams, tables, charts, etc. and mark the latter for later re-insertion (stage 6 below); this stage includes identification and marking of 'translation units' (from single word headlines to complete sentences).

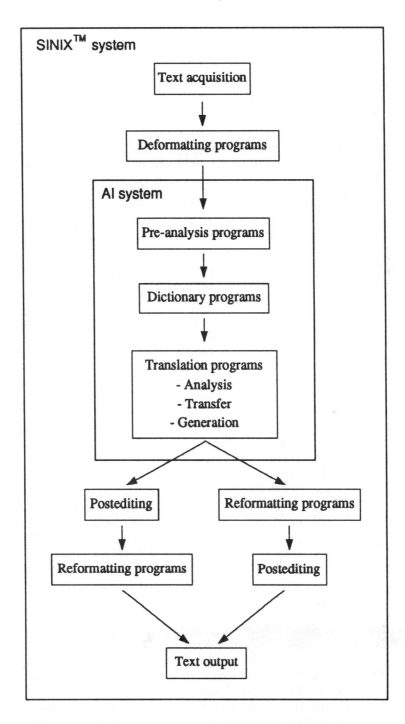

Figure 15.1 METAL core processes

3. Pre-analysis: search of the dictionary database, producing three lists: (a) unknown words listed alphabetically; (b) unknown compounds (likely to be frequent for German), with suggested possible English translations on the basis of components already present in the dictionary, e.g. for *Prüfangaben* it could suggest *testing specification*; and (c) a list of already known technical words, for the user to check for accuracy and appropriateness for the text in hand.

4. Dictionary programs: monolingual dictionaries for source and target languages contain morphological, syntactic and semantic information; the bilingual transfer dictionaries specify translational equivalences and include contextual information.

5. The METAL translation programs (described in section 15.3 below)

6. Reformatting: merging of textual and non-linguistic data

7. Post-editing: revision of translation can be performed either sentence by sentence (interlinearly) or with longer segments, and either with or without sight of the original text (on a split screen); revision can be done either before or after re-insertion of non-linguistic data (stage 6).

8. Output: word processing system, printer output, typesetting, transfer to other text processing and/or publishing systems.

The following description is based essentially on detailed accounts of the German–English system in the mid-1980s. In recent years, the METAL researchers have been introducing a number of modifications, largely in order to extend the system to more languages. These developments will be treated mainly in section 15.6 after descriptions of the databases and translation programs in the German–English version.

15.3 The linguistic databases

In the METAL system there is a clear separation between the operations of translation (analysis, transfer, generation) and the data which are called upon during operations. These data comprise monolingual lexical information for source and target languages, bilingual lexical information for a specific language pair, and sets of grammatical rules. The latter embrace rules applied at all stages of translation, to various kinds of linguistic objects (morphemes, words, phrases, clauses, sentences), and involving morphological, syntactic, and semantic features.

15.3.1 Dictionaries

The monolingual source and target dictionaries of METAL contain the basic morphological, syntactic and semantic information. METAL provides a hierarchy of vocabularies: the basic modules are the three lowest levels (function words, general vocabulary, and common technical vocabulary), which apply whatever the subject matter. To these standard modules users can add as many specialised glossaries as they wish and specify the order(s) in which they should be consulted. As well as subject-specific glossaries users can define country-specific glossaries (e.g. in order that German *Lastwagen* translates as *truck* in the United States and as *lorry* in Britain.)

Lexical entries in monolingual dictionaries are lists of features with values, e.g. root form, grammatical category, morphological variants, number, person, etc. Dictionaries include not only stem forms (typically word-initial elements) but also affixes (typically word-final elements); entries also include a 'preference' value (PRF) to enable selection between alternative analyses, indications of any lexical collocations (e.g. for discontinuous verb forms: *look up, zurückgeben*), and an indication of subject areas (TAG). Entries for nouns indicate their inflectional classes and add a semantic feature ('entity', 'living', 'commodity', etc.) used for co-occurrence restrictions; entries for verbs include case-frame specifications (in terms of 'deep case' relations: agent, target, benefactive, etc.), with attached features restricting the semantic values of arguments (e.g. *murder* requires the agent to be +RSP ('responsible')), the constituent type of arguments (e.g. noun phrase, prepositional phrase, clause, etc.), and the surface syntactic function of arguments (e.g. subject, object, *that*-complement, infinitival complement, etc.); entries for verbs include, finally, a specification of their valency pattern ('transitivity type'): intransitive with a single argument (agent), intransitive with two arguments (agent and location), transitive with two arguments (agent and target), etc.

The input of lexical entries is facilitated by the 'Intercoder' which interactively prompts the user for grammatical and translational information. The Intercoder includes a 'lexical default' program which accepts minimal information (e.g. root form and grammatical category) and automatically generates morphological variants and encodes syntactic features and values. Information in bilingual dictionaries can include the specification of particular frames, the presence of arguments of a certain semantic type, changing active phrases into impersonal constructions, adding and deleting elements, etc. The Intercoder maintains lexicon consistency and integrity with automatic validation programs which identify errors of form or syntax. This tool can be used both by system developers and, if desired, by end-users developing their own dictionaries. (Reproductions of Intercoder screens are shown in Figures 15.2 and 15.3.)

The monolingual dictionaries are designed to be neutral and independent, employed for either source language analysis or target language generation and whatever other language may be involved. The bilingual transfer dictionaries, by contrast, are designed for a specific pair in one translation direction.

Typical monolingual entries for the German *Ausgabe* and English *output* are given (somewhat simplified) in (1).

```
(1) (Ausgabe   CAT  (NST)        (output  CAT  (NST)
              ALO  (Ausgabe)              ALO  (output)
              PLC  (WI)                   PLC  (WI)
              TAG  (DP)                    TAG  (DP)
              CL   (P-N S-0)              CL   (P-S S-01)
              GD   (F)                    ON   (VC)
              SX   (N)                    SX   (N)
              TY   (ABS DUR)
```

In both cases, the entries for these 'noun stems' (NST) give a single variant (ALO = 'allomorph'), which must be word initial (WI), specify a data processing (DP) subject field, and state that they are N[eutral] in sex (SX). The other

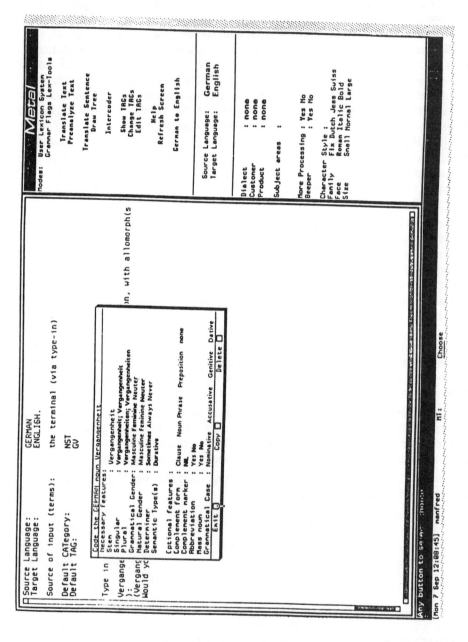

Figure 15.2 Intercoder screen: coding the German noun *Vergangenheit*

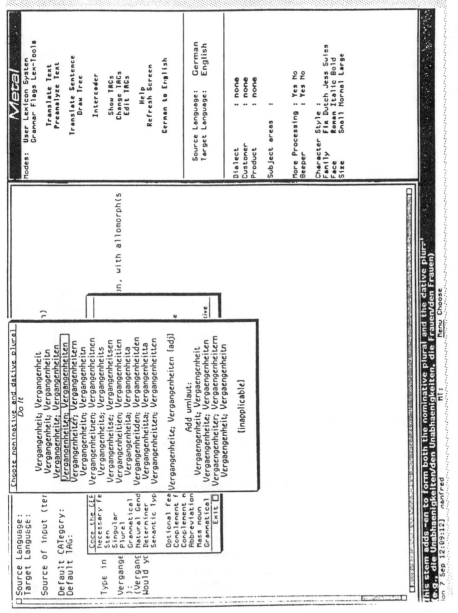

Figure 15.3 Intercoder screen with pop-up window showing possible inflection paradigms

specifications are, of course, language-dependent: the inflectional CL[asses], the grammatical gender (GD) in the German entry and the noun type (ON) in the English entry. The semantic features (TY) attached to the German entry are ABS[tract] and DUR[ative].

The entry in the bilingual dictionary which links the two items is straightforward (2).

(2) (Ausgabe (NST DP) 0   output (NST DP) 0)

The only condition attached is the restriction to the data processing field. More complex entries are found when there is more than one possible target form, e.g. (3) for the preposition *vor*.

```
(3) (vor (PREP ALL) 30 in front of (PREP ALL) 0
         OPT TY * ABS DUR PNT)
    (vor (PREP ALL) 20 before      (PREP ALL) 0
         GC D
         TY ABS PNT)
    (vor (PREP ALL) 10 ago         (PREP ALL) 0
         GC D
         TY DUR)
    (vor (PREP ALL) 0  in front of (PREP ALL) 0)
```

The English target form is determined by restrictions on semantic features (TY) or grammatical cases (GC) of following German nouns: *in front of* is produced if nouns are not (*) ABS[tract], DUR[ative] or 'punctual' (PNT); *before* if nouns are abstract or punctual and in the D[ative] case; and *ago* if nouns are durative and in the dative, the position of *ago* is later moved after the English noun. If none of these conditions apply, then the default translation is *in front of*. There are no subject field restrictions, and the order in which the options are examined is given by the PRF values (30, 20, 10, 0).

15.3.2 Grammatical rules

The grammars of METAL consist of unordered sets of context free phrase structure rules augmented by tests and conditions and by specifications of the structures to be output. All rules are formulated as Lisp functions. They include rules for inflectional morphology as well as syntactic structures; and they combine operations to be performed during analysis with operations to be performed during transfer.

Just as the lexicographers' task of building up the lexical databases is facilitated by the use of the Intercoder, there is a sophisticated software support to help grammar writers, namely the Metalshop syntax development tool. This enables linguists to see the structures being built at the various stages in the translation process, and to locate quickly the relevant rules which have applied for a given part of the structure, for example by clicking with a mouse on the appropriate node in a tree structure (Figures 15.4 and 15.5). Although this facility is not available (or even particularly useful) to the end user, it certainly supports a more controlled

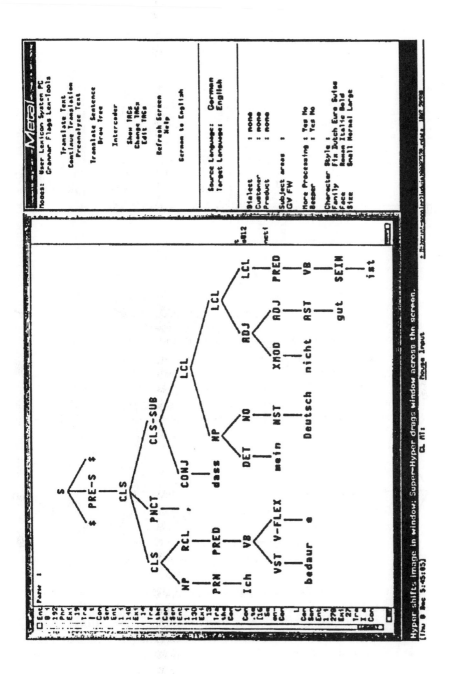

Figure 15.4 Metalshop screen showing result of parse

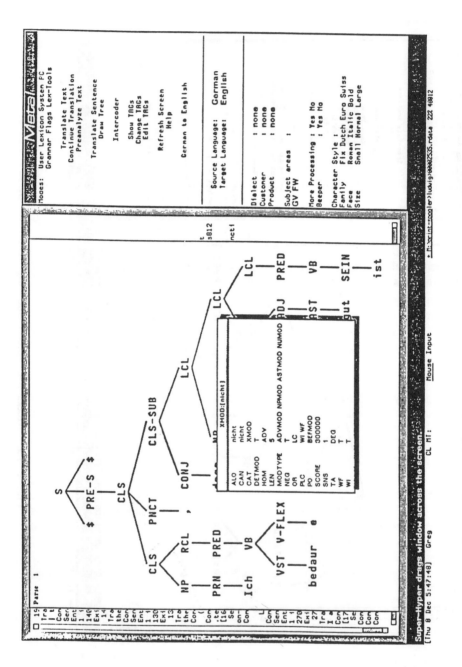

Figure 15.5 Pop-up window showing full specification of XMOD node

grammar development environment, making METAL as a whole less prone to some of the degradation problems encountered in systems like Systran (Chapter 10).

The context free rules are in the familiar rewrite form. There are two types of test. The first specifies morphological and syntactic conditions, e.g. (4).

```
(4)  VB      GE-VB      VST            V-FLEX
     0       1          2              3
             (REQ WI)   (NRQ WI)       (NRQ WI)
             --         (OPT PX NIL)   (REQ PF PAPL)
```

This rule specifies the well-formedness of a German past participle, e.g. *gemacht*. It states that a verb (VB) may consist of a past-participle marker (GE-VB) *ge*, followed by a verb stem (VST) *mach*, followed by a verb ending (V-FLEX) *t*; the GE-VB is REQuired to be word initial (WI), the VST must not be (NRQ) word initial, and nor must the V-FLEX; although the VST element may OPTionally have a 'prefix' feature (PX), it must not be present (NIL) in this construction (i.e. the rule prohibits **geausmacht* from *ausmachen*); and V-FLEX must bear the paradigmatic form (PF) for the past participle (PAPL).

The second test specifies the features required of elements having a particular constituency relation to the item in question; it operates by examining the results of intersections and unions of feature sets (5).

```
(5) ADJ ADJ PP
    0   1   2

    TEST  (COND ((INT 1 FC PP) (INT 1 MC 2 PR = X1))
                (T NIL))
```

If an ADJ[ective] permits as its complement (FC) a prepositional phrase (PP) then the feature (MC) of the adjective specifying the permissible syntactic functions of complements should be compared ('INT[ersected]') with the values of the PR[eposition] feature on the prepositional phrase which is actually present. The result of this comparison ('intersection') is recorded in a variable (X1) for later use.

Following the tests come the specifications of the structures to be built by rules during analysis. The CONSTR parts of rules specify the features and values to be attached to the governing nodes, and may also modify trees by applying transformational rules. In the familiar fashion, the (non-terminal) category on the left-hand side is the governing node and the categories on the right-hand side are its dependents. The basic processes are those of adding features and values, copying features and values, and assigning preference (PRF) values: for example, a noun phrase comprising an adjective and a noun (6).

```
(6) NO      ADJ                NO
    0       1                  2
            (REQ PO ATR)       --

    TEST    (INT 1 NU 2 NU = X1)
            (INT 1 CA 2 CA = X2)
            (INT 1 GD 2 GD = X3)
```

```
CONSTR (ADX X1)
       (ADX X2)
       (ADX X3)
       (CPX 2 IN NU CA GD)
       (CPY 1 IN DG WI)
       (ADD PNM)
       (AND (INT O CA G) (ADD GEN))
```

The TEST function identifies the values for NU[mber], CA[se] and gender (GD) shared by the adjective and the noun, as variables X1, X2 and X3 respectively. The first three lines of CONSTR add these values (ADX) to the governing node. Then, from the subordinate node (2) it copies all features and values except (CPX) those for IN[flection], number, case and gender. It then copies (CPY) to the governing node the features inflection, degree (DG) and word-initial (WI) from the adjective (node 1), and adds the feature PNM ('prenominal modifier'). Finally if the CA[se] of the governing node is specified as being G[enitive] then the feature GEN[itive] is also added.

For verb structures, the CONSTR part of the rule defines the case-frames which must be satisfied and the construction which should be formed. For example, the structure for intransitive verbs with two arguments (I2AL, e.g. *gehen*) is given as in (7).

```
(7) (DEXPR I2AL (VC MD)
         (COND ((SYNTAX)
               (COND ((AND (ACTIVE)
                           (NON-COMMAND)
                           (FRAME N NP AGT)
                           (FRAME NIL NIL LOC)
                      T)
                     ((AND (ACTIVE)
                           (COMMAND)
                           (FRAME NIL NIL LOC))
                      T))))
```

The first frame is activated if the verb is active and declarative (NON-COMMAND). It has two arguments, AGT and LOC: the AGT must be a noun phrase (NP) in the N[ominative] case, the form and features of LOC are specific to the particular verb (i.e. NIL indicates that these values have to be derived from the dictionary entries). The second frame applies if the verb is active and imperative (COMMAND); the only argument is LOC, with features again specific to the particular verb.

Transformational rules apply generally to the CONSTR parts of rules involving non-terminal categories, for example (8), where RCL indicates 'right-branching clause':

```
(8) XFM (RCL:1 ((RCL:2 ((PRED:3(-:4))-:5)) PRFX:6))
        (RCL:2 ((PRED:3 (-:4) (CPY 6 CAN)
                        (ADD VC A))
               (-:5) (ADD CLF) (ADD SPX)))
```

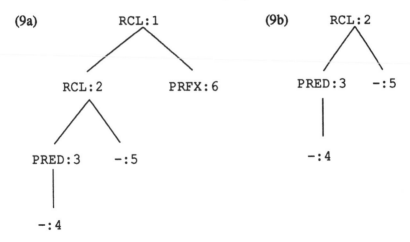

Rule (8) has the effect of transforming (9a) into (9b).

At the same time, the feature CAN[onical form] is copied from PRFX ('prefix') to PRED; the feature VC ('voice') with value A is added to PRED; and the features CLF ('clause final') and SPX ('separable prefix') are added to RCL:2.

The final sections of grammatical rules specify the operations to be performed during transfer. These embrace both lexical transfer and structural transfer. A rule such as (10) applies to verbs.

> (10) (TLX (PF NU TN PS) (V-FLEX CL PF NU TN PS))

Rule (10) takes from the V-FLEX node of the source verb the values attached to the features PF ('paradigmatic form'), NU[mber], TN ('tense') and PS ('person') and copies these onto the target verb form. As an example of structural transfer, the entry for intransitive verbs given in (7) continues as in (11).

> (11) ...
> ```
>         ((AND (ACTIVE) (NON-COMMAND) (PRED AGT LOC))
>          (ROL-ORDER (AGT) (PRED) (LOC))
>         ((AND (ACTIVE) (COMMAND) (PRED LOC))
>          (ROL-ORDER (PRED) (LOC))))
> ```

The first line applies if the structure identified during analysis has been active and declarative; the second if it has been active and imperative. In the first case, the target language order of predicates and arguments is specified (by ROL-ORDER) as the sequence AGT PRED LOC; and in the second case as PRED LOC.

15.4 The translation programs

As a transfer-based system, METAL has three basic phases: Analysis, Transfer and Generation. In some accounts a fourth phase of 'Integration' appears between Analysis and Transfer, which has the task of resolving problems of inter- and extra-sentential anaphora. As we shall see, however, the divisions between these components do not conform to the 'pure' form described in earlier chapters. Hence, METAL is usually characterised as a 'modified transfer' system.

The first stage of analysis (invoked by the function PARSE) is lexical and morphological analysis (USER-WORD): the extraction of potential roots (stems) and endings or inflections (affixes) for every word in a sentence, and the production of constructs of stems and affixes, e.g. (12).

(12)

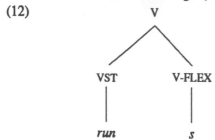

It is followed by two subsidiary functions: USER-ADD is invoked if the item is a number or a literal found on a special list, and USER-ERROR attempts to interpret words not found in dictionaries (e.g. assuming something is a proper noun).

Morphological analysis is followed by the application of a phrase structure grammar to produce alternative parsings ranked according to 'scores' assigned to particular rules or constituents. It operates on the CONSTR parts of grammatical rules (as described above), with constraints on rule application determined by the various tests included in rules. These constraints are defined in the familiar way by syntactic features. There is no use of semantic features at this stage. Syntactic analysis involves the invocation of various procedures specified in grammatical rules, e.g. the identification of case-frames (the FIND-FRAME function), the carrying out of transformations, as illustrated above in (7) and (9a,b). The scores used for choosing between potential interpretations are based on the PRF ('preference') values attached to lexical items and grammatical configurations. Most cases of homograph ambiguity are resolved by lexical preferences. For syntactic analyses the highest scoring tree is selected.

The METAL parser operates in the familiar parallel bottom-up fashion, but producing only some of the potential analyses, i.e. neither all possible interpretations nor only the single first or 'best' analysis. It uses a prioritised chart parser, with unlikely paths eliminated via preferential weightings. Grammar rules are grouped into 'levels'; the parser attempts to apply all rules at a lower level before going to rules at a higher level, and it stops as soon as one or more interpretations are found; if surface structure can be interpreted using lower level rules then the more complex and less likely rules are disregarded, if lower level rules are unsuccessful then progressively higher level rules are attempted. Thus, the system does not produce all possible interpretations. This 'some paths' approach has been extensively tested and investigated: producing faster processing times with no exponential explosions or degradation of quality. It permits also the implementation of 'fail-soft' routines: even if a complete analysis has not been achieved, transfer can still proceed with partial analyses of sentence fragments. The parser's chart is examined for the shortest path, representing the fewest and longest spanning phrases constructed during analysis, and in cases of doubt selecting the highest scoring interpretations. Often the results of such 'phrasal analyses' are in fact grammatically correct. Partial parsing is also applied when the input is itself incomplete, e.g. parenthetical expressions and chapter headings.

Transfer procedures are invoked by the next function TRANSFER. There is no central control, the process being determined by the TRANSF parts of grammatical rules. During analysis, these have been attached to appropriate nodes of structural representations, but are in effect 'suspended'. During transfer, these parts of grammatical rules are carried out (or 'evaluated' in Lisp terminology). Whereas analysis proceeds in a bottom-up fashion, transfer operates from the head nodes of trees and subtrees, working downwards to all dependent nodes.

Transfer involves complex interactions of lexical transfer rules (from the bilingual dictionary) and structural transfer rules (from the TRANSF parts of grammatical rules). Both types of rules can affect the operation of the other. The inputs to transfer in METAL are relatively shallow phrase structure representations with case role assignments and some semantic features. Outputs are surface representations with full specification of word order (e.g. the rule in (11) for *go*) and morphological constituents. As a consequence, the final generation stage (invoked by the function GENERATE) is concerned solely with producing morphologically correct target language strings.

In later versions of METAL, generation has a greater role. Some of the transformations previously applied during transfer are now invoked by GENERATE. For example, in the English–German system under development, analysis of (13) might be the (somewhat simplified) shallow representation (14).

(13) It will have been tested.

(14)

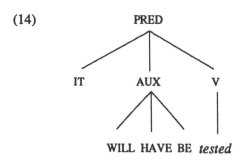

Transfer rules would produce a German structure such as (15).

Lexical transfer rules replace the future auxiliary *WILL* in (14) by the left *WERDEN* in (15), the passive auxiliary *BE* by the right *WERDEN*, and the perfective *HAVE* by the perfective *SEIN*, where selection of the latter is determined by features attached to the second *WERDEN*. In the generation phase this is transformed first into (16a) and then (16b).

(15)

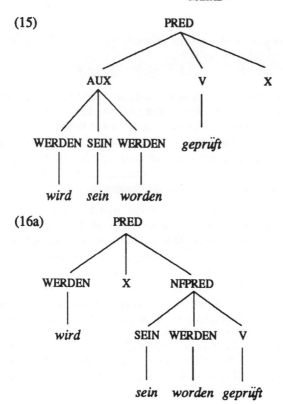

(16a)

(16b)

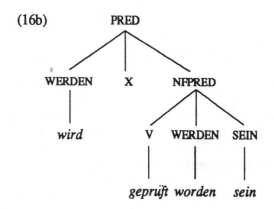

From (16b) is produced the correct German sentence (17) corresponding to (13).

(17) *Es wird geprüft worden sein.*

Details of recent developments in the design of transfer and generation components for the new METAL language pairs are not as well documented as the earlier German–English version. It is a system which is still evolving towards a multilingual design (section 15.6).

15.5 Characteristics of the German–English system

The METAL system is generally described as a 'modified transfer' system. Its transfer features are clear in a number of respects: the separation of source, target and transfer dictionaries, the separation of linguistic data (dictionaries and grammar rules) and computational methods (the Lisp evaluations and the chart parser), the completion of all stages of analysis before transfer and generation. Unlike most direct systems (including Systran, Chapter 10), there are full interpreted representations of source language sentences as output from analysis and as input to transfer.

On the other hand, some features of the German–English system, as described above, show divergence from the 'pure' form of transfer-based MT. As already pointed out, there is no clear separation of transfer and generation processes: much of the target language production is contained within the transfer phase, with generation limited to morphology. The most serious objection to the characterisation of the prototype as a true transfer-based system is, however, the mixture and close inter-relationship of analysis and transfer–generation rules in the linguistic database. There is doubt about the independence of the stages of analysis and transfer–generation; there is no doubt that all analytical procedures are completed before transfer begins and that there is an identifiable intermediate representation; what is in doubt is the independence of the rules themselves. To what extent are the analysis rules (the CONSTR parts) autonomous? And to what extent are the forms of transfer rules (the TRANSF parts) determined by source language characteristics?

Transfer operations in the German–English system are not formulated as general procedures which search representations for matching elements and structures. Transfer rules are directly tied to the rules which have been applied in analysis. Instead of one set of general rules transforming, for example, German case-frame patterns into English case-frame patterns, there are specific transformational rules for the case-frames of each German verb type. In other words, the generation of the English structures is not independent of the German-specific classification of case-frame patterns. More generally, the order in which transfer–generation rules are applied is determined by analysis structures and since these structures are relatively shallow (phrase structures with surface case relations) generation itself is determined by source-language-oriented phenomena.

There are computational advantages in tying transfer rules to analysis. There is no need for transfer to incorporate in effect a fresh 'analysis' of the intermediate representations; there do not have to be decision procedures to determine which transfer rules are applicable; there need be no wasteful application of rules which lead to dead ends. Instead, the process is expedited because it is already known which specific transfer rules must be activated. This computational advantage outweighs the relatively low level of duplication in the transfer rules present in the database. The question remains, however, whether these practical benefits may not damage the extendibility of the system.

Despite some reservations, the METAL German–English system represents the most linguistically and computationally advanced MT system available at present on the commercial market. Particularly attractive for potential purchasers is the sophistication of the text acquisition, preparation, reformatting and postediting facilities. To these should be added the excellent interactive 'expert system' for inputting and changing dictionary entries (the Intercoder) and the capacity to produce reasonable translations even when the linguistic data is deficient or absent (the phrasal analysis procedure).

15.6 Recent developments towards a multilingual system

The METAL researchers began work on new language pairs in the mid 1980s, first English–German, then Dutch and French (in both directions), German to French, and English and German to Spanish. With these additions, and various others as future possibilities also envisaged, it became evident that changes had to be made to the basic 'demonstrator' system architecture.

The German–English system, as we have seen, relies to a large extent on similarities of English and German. This is seen in the analysis and generation of case-frames, the treatment of verbal aspect and tense, and the relatively shallow structural representations. The need to develop new modules to generate from analysis representations of German meant that transfer and generation could not continue to be mixed in the same way: distinctive transfer and generation programs had to be developed. A further consequence was that the rule-based design in which transfer–generation rules were closely tied to analysis rules could not continue: there had to be completely independent analysis and generation components.

As a result, METAL can now be characterised as a 'true' transfer-based system: language-specific analysis and generation with bilingual transfer modules. Generation modules for the languages are now quite independent of source language analysis rules. METAL does not use the same grammatical database for analysis and generation, i.e. there is no reversibility of components. It is argued that the coverage of generation grammars can be narrower than those for analysis; whereas the latter must be capable of dealing with all stylistic variants, for generation it is sufficient to default to single acceptable forms.

The need for more explicit intermediate representations in multilingual systems than in bilingual ones has led the METAL researchers to the design of common 'METAL Interface Representation' (MIR) for transfer components. In contrast to representations in the German–English system, structures are simpler and more abstract. Rather than the structural representation of, for example, a complex of finite, modal and auxiliary verbs there is now a single node with features, i.e. aspect, voice, determiners, case particles, adverbs of time, etc. are now represented as feature–values on noun and verb nodes. There is a conscious move towards the kind of abstract interface representations found in the multilingual Eurotra system (Chapter 14). The implication in some accounts is that MIRs could become interlingual representations of structure for the languages in question (but not 'universal' for all languages in any sense); but lexical transfer will remain definitely bilingual and will continue to have effects on structure, i.e. there will still be lexically-conditioned structural transfer.

METAL continues to be somewhat cautious about the use of semantic features. Lexical transfer is generally determined as far as possible by syntactic information (e.g. German *Schuld* is English *guilt* if singular, or *debt(s)* if plural; English *allow* is German *erlauben* if in the active voice, or *dürfen* if in the passive) or by reference to lexical items, e.g. (18).

(18)   German *bestehen*   English   *consist of* (prep-obj = *aus*)
insist on (prep-obj = *auf*)
consist in (prep-obj = *in*)
pass (dobj-lu = *Examen*)
exist (dobj = nil)

There has always been some use of semantic features (TY), as we have seen in (3) above. In recent years there have been more intensive investigations (the 'Semantics Control Project') on the use of features to aid anaphora resolution, to represent verbal aspect and to classify semantic properties of verbs. The position of METAL researchers continues to be somewhat 'minimalist' in this regard by comparison with those other MT projects which aim for full semantic representations. Just as the approach of METAL to grammatical methods is eclectic, the application of semantic features is pragmatic. Nevertheless, it is recognised that multilinguality demands deeper (semantic) treatment than required for the bilingual uni-directional German–English METAL system.

The detailed analysis of technical terminology in terms of semantic features is not in any case considered to be feasible for a practical operational system. The basic motivation for a large MT system such as METAL is the treatment of massive corpora of technical documentation. Semantic analysis on this scale is impractical. More pertinently, most terminology is sufficiently standardised for lexical transfer to be based on easily formulated equivalences and contexts. The large dictionaries of METAL are derived mainly from the relatively simply structured TEAM term bank of Siemens. As we have seen, users are encouraged to develop more specific microglossaries (e.g. reflecting company practice) on similar lines. The accent so far has been on the technological, and one of the basic METAL dictionaries represents common technical vocabulary. With more users wishing to translate administrative and economic documentation, there is now under development a common social vocabulary.

15.7 Evaluations, users and performance

Detailed evaluations of the METAL prototype were undertaken in the mid 1980s, which demonstrated a satisfactory improvement of translation quality, both in terms of the increase in the number of 'correct' sentences (from 45% to 75% over a five-year period) and in increases in the rate of post-editing (from 15–20 pages a day to over 40 pages a day). Experience of METAL in practice is relatively short as yet, but a number of users have indicated reduced costs of up to 40% as a result of faster through-put. Raw METAL output text can be produced at a rate of one word per second, an estimated 200 pages a day. In addition, translation quality is good enough for 20% or more of text to be passed without post-editing.

The main applications of METAL have been in the fields of data processing and telecommunications, not only at Siemens, but also at a Swiss translation company Compulex and at the Philips Kommunikations-Industrie AG, a major supplier for the German PTT. Some twenty organisations have installed METAL. The vendors are commendably cautious about raising expectations. They warn that in the first few months of installation the productivity of a translation service may decrease. Translators need to be trained in new methods and acquire new skills, the dictionaries have to be augmented and revised to suit local circumstances, and administrative practices have to change. After this initial period (which may last up to a year), users of METAL have reported considerable gains in productivity and decreases in turn-around times, by factors of two to three in most cases, and an overall improvement in the quality of their translations through the greater consistency of terminology.

In coming years, practical experience with METAL will permit valid comparisons with systems which have been in longer operational use, particularly Systran (Chapter 10) and Logos. And as a system founded on clearly articulated linguistic principles, METAL will also represent a benchmark against which the performance of newer experimental systems may be assessed.

15.8 Sources and further reading

The basic description of the METAL system is to be found in Bennett and Slocum (1985) and Slocum (1987). Summaries are given in Whitelock and Kilby (1983) and Hutchins (1986), where details of earlier LRC systems are recorded. For recent information see Schneider (1989), Thurmair (1990) and Alonso (1990); and for the views of large users, Compulex and Philips, see Shah (1989) and Little (1990) respectively.

We are grateful to Tom Schneider and Siemens Nixdorf AG for permission to reproduce the Intercoder and Metalshop screens in this chapter.

Symbolics is a trademark of Symbolics, Inc. SINIX is a trademark of Siemens Nixdorf AG.

16
Rosetta

The MT project at the Philips Research Laboratories in Eindhoven (Netherlands) is one of the most innovative experimental systems at the present time. Its essential feature is the attempt to devise interlingual representations based on the principles of Montague grammar, a theory which directly links syntax and semantics. Important theses are being explored: the reversibility of grammars, the compositionality of meaning, and the potential isomorphism of grammars.

16.1 Background

The project has its roots in earlier research at Philips on a question-answering system, PHLIQA. The task was to convert a question expressed in English into the logical representation language of the database. It was undertaken by a parser based on a context-free grammar where every grammar rule was coupled to a translation rule into the logical language. In other words, the logical interpretation of the question was based on the structural relations among its elements. However, the translation was not direct: the context-free representations were transformed first into a hybrid 'logical'-cum-'deep' syntactic structure before the truly logical representation was obtained. The unsatisfactory nature of this hybrid approach led to the design of a new grammar which would be fully compositional and in which the rules were more powerful than those of context-free grammars. It was concluded that the grammars described by the philosopher Richard Montague offered an attractive model for this approach.

Jan Landsbergen decided to explore the possibilities in the Rosetta project, which began in 1980. Initially two small experimental systems were built: Rosetta1 and Rosetta2. A larger project began in 1985, to be in two phases. The first phase has concentrated on the essential linguistic and computational framework and the building of a research system (Rosetta3) for the translation of short simple sentences from Dutch into English and Spanish and from English or Spanish into Dutch. Dictionaries are small and the system generates all possible translations. No corpus of actual texts has been tested. The second phase, which began in 1989, is devoted to the development of a more robust version of Rosetta3 and then the construction of a prototype system for a real application (Rosetta4). The eventual aim is a system for users not knowing target languages; it is to include monolingual interactive disambiguation during analysis, and to produce output not requiring post-editing. These practical requirements have not yet been addressed. All research has concentrated on the theoretical and linguistic foundations.

16.2 Montague grammar

The main characteristic of Montague grammar is the binding of semantic interpretations to structural relations. Montague grammars obey the principle of **compositionality**, namely that the meaning of an expression is a function of the meaning of its parts. Since the parts are defined by the syntax, there is a close relation between syntax and semantics.

A Montague grammar specifies a set of 'basic expressions' and a set of syntactic rules. The basic expressions are the smallest meaningful units and the rules prescribe how larger expressions (and ultimately sentences) can be constructed from these basic expressions. The rules are applied bottom-up.

We may illustrate with a simple example grammar, containing two basic expressions *car* and *pass*, and two rules (1a,b) for English.

> (1a) ER1 = a rule applied to a noun which produces an indefinite singular noun phrase (by adding an article *a*).
>
> (1b) ER2 = a rule applied to a noun phrase and an intransitive verb which produces a sentence, with the noun phrase as subject, in the past tense.

From these two basic expressions and these two rules can be generated (2).

> (2) A car passed.

The process of deriving the sentence can be made explicit in a **syntactic derivation tree** (3).

The semantic component of a Montague grammar assigns a semantic interpretation to an expression by relating it to the semantic domain of a 'possible world'. Semantic values can be assigned either directly or indirectly. In direct interpretation (the method adopted in the Rosetta project), each basic expression is associated directly with an 'object' in the domain (e.g. an individual) and each rule is associated with an operation on objects in the domain (e.g. a function). There are thus 'basic meanings' corresponding to basic expressions and 'meaning operations' corresponding to syntactic rules. The semantic value (meaning) of an expression is thus defined with the help of the syntactic derivation tree, i.e. in parallel with the application of the syntactic rules the meaning operations corresponding to these

(3) S (*a car passed*) ———————————▶ ER2

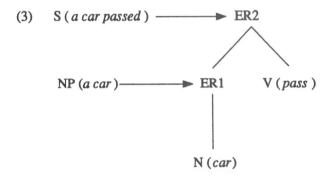

NP (*a car*)———————▶ ER1 V (*pass*)

N (*car*)

rules are applied to the meanings of their arguments (constituents), starting with the basic expressions and again working bottom-up. The process of deriving the meaning parallels the process of deriving a syntactic representation. It can be represented in a **semantic derivation tree** which has the same geometry as its corresponding syntactic derivation tree but is labelled with the names of basic meanings and meaning operations (or 'rule meanings'). The semantic derivation tree for (3) would be as in (4), where the basic meanings <CAR> (= the property 'being a car') and <PASS> (= the property 'passing') correspond to the basic expressions N(*car*) and V(*pass*), and rule meanings M1 and M2 correspond to syntactic rules R1 and R2. The semantic well-formedness of a sentence is thus determined by the truth-values of the meaning rules which have been applied.

(4)   M2

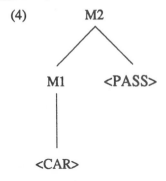

M1   <PASS>

<CAR>

It is evident that from semantic derivation trees may be derived logical expressions, and this is frequently the preferred option by Montague grammarians (employing intensional logic formalisms, which can be interpreted with respect to a model of 'possible world semantics', i.e. in a model-theoretic semantics.) One possibility in an MT system would be to use these logical expressions as interlingua representations. However, it is argued that this would entail the loss of information about the surface forms of sentences (texts), and this information can be vital for producing satisfactory translations. In addition, there would be the difficulty of devising a single logical formalism for a wide variety of languages. Consequently, the Rosetta project has taken a different approach: it uses the semantic derivation trees themselves as interlingua representations. The logical interpretation of sentences is not considered to be necessary for the purposes of translation; the semantic derivation tree contains exactly the relevant information that has to be preserved during translation.

16.3 Reversibility and isomorphism

As well as the principles of compositionality and interlinguality, the Rosetta grammars conform to three other principles. The first is **explicitness**: not only are the grammars of both source and target languages to be defined independently but all linguistic and translation processes are precisely expressed in the grammars. No procedures are to be implicit in the programming implementation.

The second is the **one grammar** principle: the same grammar is used for generation and for analysis of sentences, i.e. the grammars are intended to be reversible. The most important requirement is the reversibility of the syntactic rules. For example, the reverse rules for the example grammar in (1) above would be as in (5).

(5a) ER'1: a rule applied to an expression of the form NP (α) which produces an expression of the form N (α)

(5b) ER'2: a rule applied to an expression of the form S (α βed) which produces two expressions, one of the form NP (α), the other of the form V (β).

If ER'2 is applied to the sentence S (*a car passed*), the result is the pair NP (*a car*) and V (*pass*), where the latter is a basic expression. The application of ER'1 to NP (*a car*) yields the basic expression N (*car*). Analysis is thus successful if it reduces a sentence to its basic expressions. The analysis process itself is made explicit in a derivation tree, which is identical to (3).

The third principle, **isomorphism**, follows from the decision to adopt the compositionality principle and makes possible the use of semantic derivation trees as interlingual representations. Two sentences are considered translations of each other if they have the same semantic derivation trees, and hence corresponding syntactic derivation trees. As a consequence, the grammars of two languages have to be attuned to each other, so that for each basic expression in one grammar there is at least one corresponding basic expression in the other with the same meaning, and so that for each rule in one grammar there is at least one corresponding rule in the other. For example, a Dutch grammar which is isomorphic to the English grammar in (1) and (5) would contain two basic expressions N (*auto*) and V (*passeer*) with the meanings <CAR> and <PASS> respectively, thus corresponding to N (*car*) and V (*pass*) in the English grammar, and two rules (6a,b)

(6a) NR1: a rule applied to an expression of the form N (α) which produces an indefinite noun phrase of the form NP (*een* α)

(6b) NR2: a rule applied to a noun phrase of the form NP (*een* α) and an intransitive verb of the form V (β) which produces a sentence of the form S (*er* βde *een* α)

The application of these rules to the two basic expressions would generate (7) with the syntactic derivation tree (8).

(7) *Er passeerde een auto.*

(8) S (*er passeerde een auto*) ⟶ NR2

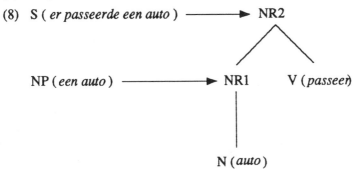

This tree would have the same semantic derivation tree as (4) thanks to the correspondences between the Dutch rule NR1 and the meaning rule M1, between NR2 and M2, between *auto* and the basic meaning <CAR> and between *passeer* and <PASS>. As a consequence, the Dutch and English grammars would be isomorphic, with corresponding basic expressions (*auto* and *car*, *passeer* and *pass*) and corresponding syntactic rules (NR1 and ER1, NR2 and ER2).

It is stressed by Rosetta researchers that isomorphism and not interlinguality is the primary characteristic of the framework. The essential condition for two sentences being translations of each other is, therefore, that they have isomorphic syntactic derivation trees: they have corresponding sets of rules, relating to the same meaning rule, and corresponding sets of basic expressions, relating to the same basic meaning. Not only are the grammars of the languages of the system designed in parallel and for the specific purpose of translation but the interlingua is also constructed specifically for the particular languages concerned. The isomorphism principle expresses the essence of the Rosetta compositional theory of translation.

16.4 Translation processes

We can now describe the Rosetta translation processes. The system has eight stages as illustrated in Figure 16.1.

The Rosetta grammars, called 'M-grammars' showing their affinity to Montague grammars, have three basic components each of which is reversible: a morphology component, a syntactic component and a semantic component. The syntactic component is divided into a part which deals with surface syntactic structures and a part which mediates between these structures and syntactic derivation trees. The semantic component deals with the interfaces between syntactic derivation trees and semantic derivation trees.

The stages are illustrated by working through the translation of the English interrogative sentence (9) into its Dutch equivalent (10).

(9) Does he love flowers?

(10) *Houdt hij van bloemen?*

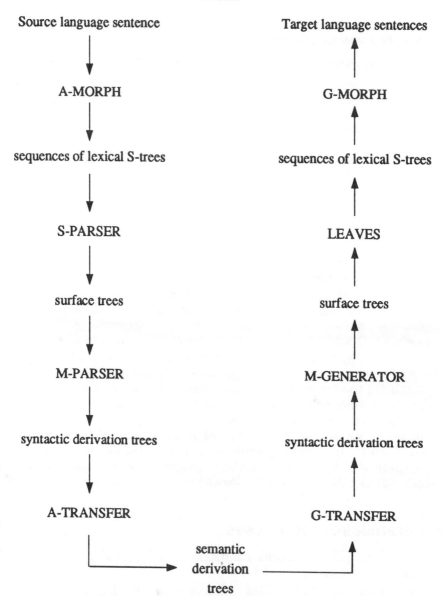

Figure 16.1 Rosetta translation process

In the first stage, **morphological analysis** (A-MORPH), input strings are decomposed into stems (*do*, *love*, *flower*) and affixes (*-es*, *-s*) to produce sequences of 'lexical S-trees'. Whereas in Montague grammar basic expressions are simple lexical items, in Rosetta they are defined as ordered trees ('S-trees' = surface trees) comprising one or more labelled elements. They may therefore be 'idiomatic' expressions of several lexical items in particular relationships, as we shall see below (section 16.8.)

The second stage is the first part of a two-step **syntactic analysis**, in which the S-PARSER produces sets of tentative analyses. Categorial homography is resolved (e.g. *love* is here not a noun but a verb) but no lexical or syntactic ambiguity. For sentence (9) the resultant surface tree is as in (11).

(11)

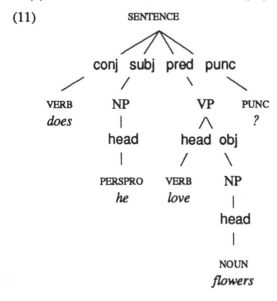

In the second part of syntactic analysis, the M-PARSER selects the syntactically correct tree structures and lays the foundation for representing the meaning of the sentence, i.e. it produces a syntactic derivation tree (in the case of (11) the tree illustrated in (12) below). The M-PARSER includes rules which may change nodes and relations in trees or modify the attributes of specific nodes. A distinction is made between rules and transformations. **Rules** (in the strict sense) are operations which have meaning or convey information relevant for translation; **transformations** are 'meaningless' and serve only to adjust structures for a particular language, they are language-specific operations which do not convey translationally relevant information. Both types are applied top-down to input surface trees under the control of the M-PARSER.

First, the sentence as a whole is considered: in the case of (11) an interrogative structure is recognised and consequently a rule RQuestion is applied which removes the question mark and which now permits the operation of a transformation TInvert to produce a statement (*He does love flowers*). Note that the inversion transformation itself is not relevant for translation (it is language-specific), only the identification of the question status is required.

Next, the identification of the tense involves the application of the rule RPresent1 (i.e. in this case 'present'), which requires also a check that subject and verb agree in person and number, a requirement specific to English, which is accomplished by the transformation TAgree (*He do love flowers*). It is followed by the recognition that the auxiliary *do* has been used, another 'meaningless'

(12)

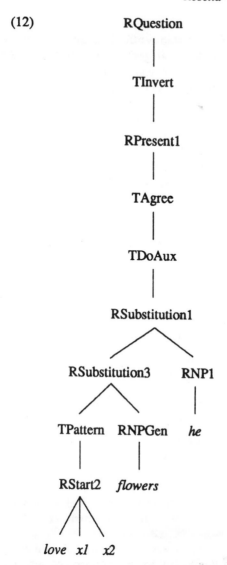

element in the context of English question structures, and so it is removed by the transformation TDoAux. We now have the basic elements *He love flowers*.

The subject and object are now replaced by abstract variables; this is done by two substitution rules (RSubstitution1 and RSubstitution3). The two extracted noun phrases are further reduced by noun phrase rules: the first RNP1 applies to noun phrases consisting of bare person pronouns, the second RNPGen applies to generic noun phrases (e.g. in English, nouns without articles). The final stage checks that the remaining structure (a verb with two abstract variables as subject and object) is acceptable by confirming the valency pattern for this specific verb, i.e. a language-specific operation and thus a transformation. The rule TPattern confirms that *love* can have a direct object, and renames the relation 'obj' by the more neutral term 'argument'. Finally, RStart2 checks that the verb can have a subject and one other argument. The result of all these operations is the syntactic derivation tree (12).

The syntactic derivation tree (12) is used to determine the meaning representation, a semantic derivation tree (13), by mapping each ('meaningful') rule onto a corresponding 'meaning operation' of the interlingua and by substituting interlingual basic expressions for source language basic expressions. This is performed by the next stage, **analytic transfer** (A-TRANSFER). Transformations in the syntactic derivation tree have no representation since they are language-specific; thus certain function words, such as the auxiliary *do*, have no corresponding basic expressions in the interlingual representation.

(13)

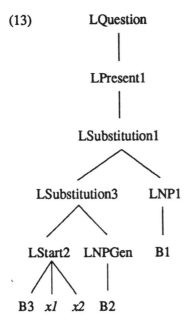

This semantic derivation tree is the source for a syntactic derivation tree in Dutch (14), which in conformity with the principle of isomorphism has the same meaning as the English tree (12). It is produced by the **generative transfer** (G-TRANSFER) module.

Generative transfer operates bottom-up producing a number of potential trees; only during the application of M-GENERATOR can the particular one for (13) be identified. In other words, M-GENERATOR has two functions (similar to those of M-PARSER): to validate syntactic derivation trees and select the correct ones, and to convert such trees into surface structures. (Obviously there can always be more than one output for a given meaning representation, see also 16.6 below.) It should be noted that the selection of *houden* as translation of basic expression B3 (i.e. *love*) entails a different pattern type in Dutch, one in which the object is preceded by a preposition (TPrepPattern). A further language-specific feature in (14) is

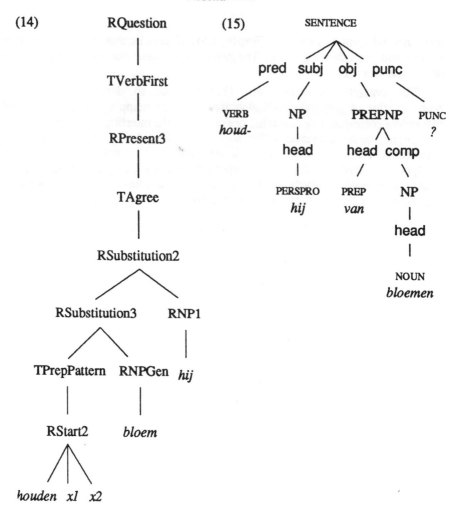

(14) RQuestion (15) SENTENCE

the placing of the verb at the beginning of Dutch questions (transformation rule TVerbFirst). The result of M-GENERATOR might be the surface structure (15).

The final generation stages are the production of a sequence of lexical S-trees by the LEAVES module, which picks off the words from the surface tree (15), and then the generation of correct morphological forms (G-MORPH), which in this case would determine the spelling of *houden* in the third person (i.e. *houdt*).

16.5 Structural correspondences

Since Rosetta does not preserve syntactic structures, it is able to change grammatical categories and to produce target structures which differ markedly from source structures. As an example of category change consider the generic noun rule (RNPGen) above. In English (and Dutch) the genericity of objects is expressed frequently without an article (*flowers*); in Spanish, however, the rule for generic nouns would have to trigger the production of a definite article (*las flores*). An example of structure change has already been given: while *love* has a direct object, *houden* requires a prepositional object (*houden van*).

More complex relations are exhibited by correspondences such as those between Dutch sentences containing the adverb *graag* and English sentences containing *like*, as in (16), similar to the *like/gern* examples seen in Chapter 6.

(16a) *Ik zwem graag.*

(16b) I like to swim.

In Rosetta, the isomorphism of the two grammars is maintained by proposing syntactic and semantic derivation trees as in (17).

(17)

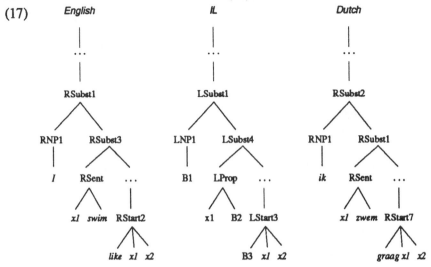

The English rules are quite straightforward: RSubst3 replaces a predicate with an infinitive (*like to swim*) by a sentential complement (*x1 swim*) and a variable (*like x1 x2*). These are mapped directly onto the interlingual rules. On the Dutch side there are a number of possible correspondences for LSubst4, one of which (RSubst1) takes a propositional structure with *graag* as its main element and by a series of transformation rules places it as an adverbial modifier of *x1 zwem*. It is assumed that *graag* is a two-place function. Apart from the motivation to maintain isomorphy with the English two-place function *like*, it is argued that the adverb *graag* imposes selection restrictions on the subjects of sentences which parallel those for *like*. Just as (18a) and (19a) are odd, the Dutch equivalents (18b) and (19b) are equally odd.

(18a) *It likes to rain.

(18b) *Het regent graag.*

(19a) *The stone likes to fall.

(19b) *De steen valt graag.*

In other words the conditions attached to the variable *x1* in Dutch correspond to those attached to the variable *x1* in English.

16.6 Subgrammars

Problems of categorial difference which this example demonstrates are handled in Rosetta by dividing M-grammars into five 'projection subgrammars', one for each major category (verb, noun, preposition, adjective, adverb). Each consists of a number of subgrammars, e.g. to form full clauses (with finite verb), to form full sentences, to form 'small clauses' (with no finite verb). In the case of a construction containing *intelligent* it should be possible to derive each of the sentences in (20).

(20a) He seems intelligent.

(20b) He seems to be intelligent.

(20c) It seems that he is intelligent.

The derivations begin with an adjectival proposition (21a), which is turned by one subgrammar into a clause (21b) and then into either an infinitival clause (21c) or into a 'full' sentence (21d). In another subgrammar it is transformed into a 'closed' adjectival formation (21a).

(21a) he intelligent

(21b) he be intelligent

(21c) he to be intelligent

(21d) (that) he is/was intelligent

Tense and aspect are applicable in the clause and sentence subgrammars but not in the adjectival subgrammar. Each of these formations is inserted into a verbal phrase construction (*seem x2*), producing (22a-c), from which appropriate transformations moving *he* to subject position or inserting *it* yield the sentences in (20).

(22a) seem he intelligent

(22b) seem he to be intelligent

(22c) seem that he is/was intelligent

In Dutch there are parallel subgrammars for the corresponding adjectival formation (23a), and for producing an infinitival clause (23b) or a sentence (23c).

(23a) *hij intelligent*

(23b) *hij intelligent te zijn*

(23c) *dat hij intelligent is/was*

Either can be arguments of *schijnen* which thus permits the eventual production of (24b) and (24c) corresponding directly to (20b) and (20c). There is no Dutch equivalent for (20a) because *schijnen* cannot have a 'closed' adjectival complement (24a).

(24a) *Hij schijnt intelligent.

(24b) *Hij schijnt intelligent te zijn.*

(24c) *Het schijnt dat hij intelligent is.*

It should now be clear how Rosetta deals with constructional mismatches of the kind exemplified in (25) and (26).

(25a) *Hij schaamt zich ervoor.*

(25b) He is ashamed of it.

(26a) *Hij is mij 3 gulden schuldig.*

(26b) He owes me 3 guilders.

In Dutch the two-place function *schaam* generates reflexive verb forms in clauses and sentences, where in English the corresponding two-place function *ashamed* generates adjectival constructions; in Dutch the operation of a sub-grammar producing an adjectival output is blocked, and in English the verbal subgrammar is unproductive. Likewise for the three-place function *owe*: in Dutch an adjectival subgrammar is successful, in English a verbal subgrammar.

The division of M-grammars into subgrammars is motivated by the need (particularly in a project involving a team of researchers) for transparent modularity. The modular approach implies the explicit definition for each subgrammar of what is used from other subgrammars (import) and what is to be used by other subgrammars (export). In addition, the rules of any one subgrammar are local to that subgrammar. In Rosetta, the subdivision was inspired by the notion of 'projection' from the $\overline{X}$ formalism (section 2.9.4). As we have seen, for every grammatical category there are tensed and tenseless propositional constructions — these are projections of the categories; hence, in the relevant subgrammars, the imports are S-trees with these categories as heads and the exports are S-trees with their projections.

There is a further argument for modularity in Rosetta. In the M-grammar formalism the explicit ordering of rules is not possible. Rules may be ordered implicitly by splitting a single syntactic category (e.g. NP) into several arbitrary categories (e.g. NP1, NP2, NP3, etc.) and by giving the rules applicability conditions which ensure the desired ordering (e.g. a rule transforming NP1 into NP2 must precede one transforming NP2 into NP3.) It is argued that the subgrammar approach to modularity provides a 'natural' way of expressing the application order of rules.

16.7 Rule classes

In addition to the division of M-grammars into subgrammars, there is also the distinction already mentioned between 'meaningful' syntactic rules and transformation rules. The latter are those rules which are specific to a particular language and serve only a syntactic function. In the earlier Rosetta2 the strict application of the isomorphism principle entailed the inclusion of such rules in grammars of other languages where they served no function. But in Rosetta3 only the meaningful 'translationally relevant' syntactic rules are subject to the isomorphy condition. These meaningful rules are formed into classes of rules handling types of linguistic phenomena, e.g. valency relations, scope, time, voice, negation. Further structure is introduced by restricting translation relations to correspondences between rule classes; only those rules of different languages which belong to the same meaningful rule class may correspond to each other, and hence rules not belonging to the same meaningful rule class cannot be translations of each other.

This classification into rule classes cuts across the division into subgrammars. In the *graag/like* example (16), the different structures are handled by different types of subgrammars (adverb and verb), but they involve the same meaningful rule class. It is proposed in Rosetta, therefore, to divide the rules of subgrammars into 'rule subclasses' and to define the application sequences of rules in terms of these rule subclasses. There are many similarities among rule classes in different subgrammars. For example, all subgrammars contain rule classes for valency and negation. Furthermore, as example (20) above showed, the subgrammars for the same head category are broadly equivalent in meaning. It is suggested that subgrammars may also be isomorphic within a language, in the sense that they correspond with respect to their meaningful rules. As a consequence, the derivation trees for (27a) and (27b) include the same sequence of meaningful rules, while being produced by different subgrammars; in the former (28a) by a subgrammar for the projection of adjective to 'adjectival phrase' (ADJPPROP), and in the latter (28b) by a subgrammar for the projection of adjective to clause.

(27a) the intelligent girl

(27b) The girl that is intelligent.

(28a)   ADJPROP   (28b)   CLAUSE

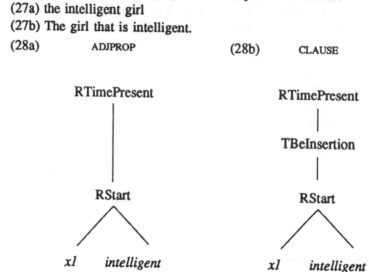

It is assumed that the time reference is needed in both, although not realised in (27a), not just for isomorphy reasons but also with a view to model-theoretic semantic interpretation (cf. section 16.2 above).

The notion of attuning subgrammars to each other applies also to subgrammars with different head categories. We have seen it already in example (16). However, the situation is rather more complex than in (27)–(28). The two subgrammars for clause projections of ADV and VERB cannot be completely isomorphic, but parts of them can be: those concerned with verb valency (*x1 swim/zwem*), with tense, and with the insertion of subject (RSubst1 and RSubst2). There can thus be partial isomorphy of subgrammars of different languages, and perhaps (it is claimed) complete isomorphy between sets of subgrammars.

16.8 Lexical transfer

The isomorphic requirement would appear to present intractable problems for translational equivalences where there can be no correspondence of component lexical items. The most obvious examples are idiomatic expressions. Consider the equivalent pair of idioms (29) in English and Dutch.

(29a) spill the beans

(29b) *zijn mond voorbij praten*
> lit. 'one's mouth past talk' ('to talk past one's mouth')

The problem is that the non-literal meanings of these expressions cannot be derived compositionally from their elements, and yet the expressions have to be translated as wholes. However, it will be recalled that basic expressions in Rosetta do not necessarily have to be single lexical items. Thus, fixed idioms such as *red herring, by and large, kant en klaar* ('ready-made') can be treated as units. Most idioms, however, cannot be treated as strings: they are structures which vary according to context (30).

(30a) Peter broke Mary's heart.

(30b) Peter was breaking his sister's heart.

(30c) Mary's heart was broken by Peter.

It is argued that idioms should be represented in Rosetta as normal syntactic structures, but at the same time as single 'basic expressions'. As a consequence, Rosetta dictionaries will contain both basic expressions with no internal structures (i.e. a primitive meaning) and also complex basic expressions that do have internal structures, defined perhaps by a subset of the grammar. In those cases where a particular expression has a literal as well as an idiomatic meaning ((29a) and *kick the bucket*), then the grammar will derive meanings compositionally in addition.

This approach is believed to be capable of dealing with problems of lexical transfer such as equivalences between simple verbs such as Spanish *madrugar* and the phrases *get up early* and (Dutch) *vroeg opstaan*. The apparent implication is that the Dutch and English phrases will be assigned a 'basic meaning' corresponding to that of the Spanish verb, i.e. they are treated as 'translation idioms'. The approach is clearly motivated by the desirability of maintaining isomorphism. In a similar vein, the translational equivalences of (31) and similar constructions are tentatively handled by the positing of an 'abstract preposition' in Spanish with the same meaning as *across/over*.

(31a) He ran across the square.

(31b) *Hij rende het plein over.*

(31c) *Cruzó la plaza corriendo.*

In the generation of Spanish there would be transformation rules (i.e. specific to Spanish) which change structures containing this preposition into structures with *cruzar* and a gerund form of the movement verb.

16.9 Comments and conclusions

In the last two sections we have seen some of the 'contortions' into which adherence to the isomorphism principle has led the Rosetta researchers. It has meant the acceptance of partial and overlapping subgrammars to deal with similar but not identical structures within and between languages, and it has meant the creation of elements or structures which cannot be motivated monolingually. What has happened is that as the Rosetta grammars have been extended to deal with larger ranges of language phenomena, and the strict isomorphy of the earlier Rosetta2 design has given way to a looser conception. There are now, as we have seen, two types of rules in M-grammars, meaningful rules and meaningless rules. The former are interlingual, in the sense that they correspond to 'rule meanings' in semantic derivation trees; the latter are language-specific, they correspond with nothing in intermediate representations and they are not isomorphic with rules in grammars of other languages.

Although compositionality and isomorphism are clearly the bedrock of Rosetta, and mutually support each other, they seem sometimes to be in conflict. Consider further the *madrugar/get up early/vroeg opstaan* examples: isomorphism demands that the Dutch and English phrases receive a 'basic meaning' corresponding to that of Spanish *madrugar*; compositionality requires the meanings of the Dutch and English phrases to be derived from the meanings of constituent 'basic expressions' (*get up* and *early*, and *opstaan* and *vroeg*) together with the meaning of the structural relation involved. It would appear to an outside observer that the only way that the Dutch/English semantic derivation trees can be made isomorphic with the Spanish semantic derivation tree is by the elimination (in some manner) of the basic meanings for *get up/opstaan* and for *early/vroeg* from the trees and retaining only the composite meaning for the phrases as wholes. But this option would not be valid for other *get up* constructions (e.g. *get up at noon*) where there must be correspondence between the basic meanings of *get up* and the Spanish equivalent *levantarse*.

The Rosetta interlingua representation is defined by the isomorphic grammars of the languages of the system. Interlingual elements are explicitly denied universal status. It is easily conceivable that the semantic derivation trees for isomorphic grammars of, say, Japanese and Chinese would differ substantially from the semantic derivation trees for the isomorphic grammars of Dutch and English. The apparatus of Montague semantics appears to have no relevance; Rosetta makes no use of any 'model-theoretic' logical interpretations, which might provide independent justification for semantic derivation trees. Indeed, in most respects the Rosetta design is like any other linguistic-based MT system: morphological analysis, surface syntactic structures, semantic analysis in terms of deep structure relations (valency, tense, voice, predicate–argument structures, etc.). The only essential difference is that whereas other systems equate dissimilar items and structures (by lexical and structural transfer), Rosetta equates the derivational histories of items and structures.

As an interlingua system, Rosetta departs from the usual assumption that source language analysis and target language generation should be completely independent (section 6.7) The isomorphism principle requires that the grammars and the procedures are explicitly oriented towards translation into particular languages. In this respect, Rosetta could quite legitimately be considered a type of direct MT system. The treatment of category mismatches and the postulation of translation idioms would lend support to this characterization.

It may be noted that the definition of isomorphism (section 16.3) appears to leave open the possibility of more than one 'basic meaning' for an expression or more than one 'meaning rule' for a syntactic operation. This would allow English *wall* to have two meanings if the grammar is to be isomorphic with, say, a German grammar. But if grammars are to be interchangeable in a multilingual system, then the meanings would have to be distinguished in both analysis and generation even when translating from or into a language where this distinction is not made. It is the familiar problem for all interlingua-based systems (section 6.7.2) The transfer-based answer is, of course, ruled out by the isomorphism principle.

Reversibility itself raises difficult problems of control. Some control of rule application is introduced by subgrammar modularization (section 16.6), but there is still the question whether all rules should be optional. The M-grammars are free production systems but computational efficiency favours the inclusion of obligatory rules. Unfortunately a rule which should be obligatory during generation may have to be optional during analysis, and it is unclear how this can be handled in reversible grammars. However, it is not a problem unique to Rosetta.

There are particular problems in trying to evaluate the Rosetta system. On the conceptual level it is difficult to grasp the potential advantages or disadvantages of the approach because of the interaction of innovative theoretical principles, most of which have not been adopted previously in MT research (only a weak form of compositionality in Eurotra, see Chapter 14). So far only small demonstration grammars have been developed and the success of their computational implementation is not known. Indeed, there have been few internal reports from Rosetta on computational aspects, and these are concerned mainly with the formalization of reversible parsers and generators — it is even unclear which programming language is to be employed, although the obvious candidate would seem to be Prolog.

In a practical implementation Rosetta is intended to operate interactively with users. It would seem that at present interaction is envisaged only during analysis, as an aid to disambiguation. There would appear to be no intention of restricting generation to a single output, e.g. the 'best' translation according to some internally specified criterion. In the present experimental phase it seems that, for example, both the legitimate sentences in (24) would be produced for any one of the input sentences in (20), and vice versa. What has been suggested for a later phase of development is the addition of a generation module which would convert 'unnatural' output into more natural 'paraphrases' — although the consequence would be asymmetry of analysis and generation processes and a loss of isomorphism.

Despite any reservations there may be about the practicality of the Rosetta approach, and the project is at too early a stage for realistic evaluation, the major contribution of Rosetta has been and will remain the solidly based exploration of a highly principled approach to translation and the consequential expansion and enrichment of MT theory. It has stimulated many MT researchers to consider more thoroughly the foundations of their own approaches to MT, which must surely be to the benefit of future research.

16.10 Sources and further reading

The theoretical content of this chapter is based on the descriptions by Appelo and
Landsbergen (1986), Landsbergen (1987a,b), all of which provide the substantial
formalism which underpins the foundations of Rosetta and which for space reasons
has been omitted in this account. For somewhat simplified descriptions of the
linguistic basis readers may consult Leermakers and Rous (1986), Sanders (1988)
and Landsbergen *et al.* (1989). The description of Rosetta subgrammars is derived
from Appelo *et al.*(1987) and Odijk (1989); and the treatment of idioms is covered
by Schenk (1989) and by Landsbergen *et al.* (1989)

17
DLT

17.1 Background

Distributed Language Translation (DLT) is the name of an MT project at the Utrecht software company Buro voor Systemontwikkeling (BSO). Preliminary investigations by A.P.M. (Toon) Witkam began in 1979, a feasibility study was supported during 1982–83 by a grant from the Commission of the European Communities, and in 1985 the project received a six-year contract from the Netherlands Ministry of Economic Affairs, with the initial task of producing a prototype English to French system in 1987 and a commercial version in 1993. The long-term aim of the DLT project is to build a system for translating between European languages of the Community (French, German, English, Italian) with eventual extensions to other languages. The prototype, written in Prolog, is designed to translate from a restricted form of English (Simplified English) into French, and it was demonstrated on schedule in December 1987. Since that date, the DLT group has been working towards a commercial system based on somewhat different principles than those in the prototype.

DLT is intended as an interactive multilingual system for use on personal computers in data communication networks, not as a tool for translators but primarily as a tool for monolingual users in the interlingual communication of 'informative' literature (abstracts, reports, manuals) or commercial messages. Translation is 'distributed' in the sense that processes of analysis and generation take place at different terminals. A monolingual user will enter a text (in English, for example) at one terminal where it is immediately translated into an interlingua, (or 'intermediate language'), which is based on Esperanto. Analysis and translation take place in 'real time'; the system attempts to translate text as it is entered, whether sentences are complete or not. Problems which the system itself cannot resolve are submitted in interactive dialogue to the user, who does not need to know the interlingua or any target language or even to know which languages the text is going to be translated into. In some cases, monolingual interactions may lead to rephrasings of original texts in order to simplify and remove translation problems. The text (in the interlingua) is then transmitted to another terminal where another user initiates translation from the interlingua into the language required (e.g. French). No dialogue with the system is possible by the recipient, and no post-editing of texts is expected.

DLT is a modular system in that source and target language modules can in principle be created for analysis into and generation from the interlingua without affecting existing modules. It is intended to be easily extendible to any other languages, whether typologically similar or not. The requirements presuppose a fully expressive interlingua which is clear and unambiguous enough to enable fully automatic translation into any target language.

17.2 The interlingua

In most interlingua-based MT systems, intermediate representations are not genuinely interlingual. Usually the structural representation is language-independent, e.g. a predicate–argument structure, but lexical items are not. In most cases, lexical transfer is based on bilingual dictionaries; there are no interlingual (language-independent) lexical items. In DLT, by contrast, the Esperanto interlingua is more like a 'natural language' with its own independent structures and lexical items.

It is usually argued that an interlingua has to be more explicit than any individual human language; it must be capable of representing all linguistic relationships (including implicit relations) within texts and within the language system. It is assumed that this means (quasi) logical representations involving semantic primitives which are universally valid (see section 6.7). The DLT researchers argue that this assumption is mistaken. Analysis into primitives, even if practically feasible, would lead to 'unimaginably huge dictionaries and a never-ending, but largely useless disambiguating process'. They contend that no artificial language can be more explicit than the human language(s) on which it is based and with which it is defined; it cannot go beyond the capabilities of human language. Thus, while an artificial language can always be translated into a human language, they argue that it is not always possible to translate fully from a human language into an artificial one. Thus, in the opinion of the DLT researchers, an interlingua can be as explicit and expressive as a human language only if it has the character of a 'human language'.

For its interlingua DLT adopted Esperanto, which it is argued combines the expressiveness of 'natural' languages and the desired regularity and consistency. Esperanto is an 'a posteriori' planned language, taking elements from existing languages and arranging them in its own (autonomous) way. But it is a language with its own speech community, it has developed into a genuine 'natural' language, which can be said to be no more 'artificial' than standardised, normalised, official languages. It has had a 'test phase' of over a hundred years, acquiring the expressivity of a human language not from the designer's drawingboard but from actual usage.

The advantages of Esperanto as an interlingua are, therefore, claimed to be: (a) as a (semi) 'natural' language it has an expressiveness, richness and flexibility which surpass constructed logical interlinguas, (b) it provides a ready-made standardised vocabulary based on common Indo-European roots, (c) it is regular and consistent, (d) it is autonomous and independent of other languages, and (e) it can be learned and understood like any other human language. Learnability is of practical importance for an interlingua, since it has to be used consistently by those working on the system, not only consistently with each other but also consistently as individuals. This consistency is difficult to achieve with an artificially constructed vocabulary of primitives and abstract structure rules. The 'naturalness' of interlingua representations (as linear strings) means also that developers of the system can more easily check whether analyses and interpretations are performing as expected; more easily than checking complex formal–linguistic tree-structure representations with multiple labels and features.

Esperanto does have some disadvantages as an MT interlingua. In use for over a hundred years, it has acquired 'naturally' some homographs, structural imprecisions and lexical ambiguities. It has no standard procedures for creating new terminology, and there are known weaknesses in technical and scientific vocabulary. DLT has sought to make modifications as necessary and to expand the lexical base.

17.3 System design

Since the interlingua (modified Esperanto) is not an abstract representation but a regularised language, the analysis of source texts and the generation of target texts represent in effect two 'translation systems': from source to Esperanto and from Esperanto to target. As a result, the DLT system may be regarded as a network of bilingual MT systems with modified Esperanto at its centre.

In the DLT system developed until 1988 for the prototype, these two halves were not fully independent bilingual translation systems; as we shall see, all semantic and pragmatic processing takes place in the kernel interlingual component whether translation is to the interlingua or from the interlingua. Since 1988, the project has been working on a different conception (involving the Bilingual Knowledge Bank) where the two halves operate in the same way.

In this section and in the following descriptions of syntactic and semantic processing (sections 17.4 to 17.6) we shall outline the basic model of the prototype, which was developed for translation of manuals from English (in fact 'Simplified English') into French. The later Bilingual Knowledge Bank approach proposed for the commercial system represents in effect a new system and for this reason will be described separately in section 18.2. This chapter is therefore devoted to the original Esperanto-based model.

The basic processing stages of the prototype English–French system are as follows:

1. Source language parsing. The parser, an Augmented Transition Network (ATN), recognises English words, their morphological and syntactic features, identifies dependency relations (subject, object, attribute, etc.) and produces a dependency tree, delivering alternatives where there is syntactic ambiguity. No semantics are involved; it generates all possible analyses regardless of semantic plausibility or statistical probability.

2. Monolingual (source language) tree transformations. At this stage, monolingual variants are reduced to common forms, e.g. *can not, cannot* and *can't* all become *can not*; and auxiliary–verb constructions are reduced to single verbs with labelled features, e.g. *has been eaten* becomes *eat* [present perfect, passive].

3. Bilingual tree transformations. This is the task of the Metataxor (section 17.4), which replaces English words by Esperanto equivalents and replaces English syntactic dependency labels by Esperanto ones. It may entail rearrangements of the tree and the insertion of function words (as explicit indicators of relationships). Because there are usually several translation alternatives for each single English item (i.e. because of the lexical ambiguities of English and the lexical transfer ambiguities of English to Esperanto), there will be a large number of alternative Esperanto trees. As in the first stage, no semantic or pragmatic selection is performed; all possibilities are produced.

4. Semantic–pragmatic word choice. From the alternative interlingual trees presented, the most likely in the given context is selected on the basis of Esperanto word patterns encoded in the 'Lexical Knowledge Bank' (LKB). This is the operation of the SWESIL component (Semantic Word Expert System for the Intermediate Language), which is described in 17.5 below. The result is a plausibility ranking of alternative interpretations.

5. Disambiguation dialogue. If no clear preference can be determined by SWESIL, the problems of interpretation are presented to the operator (normally the original author) in an interactive computer-initiated dialogue. For this dialogue the fragments of interlingua representations requiring disambiguation are expressed in the source language. After this stage there should be only a single interlingual representation of the input sentence.

6. Monolingual (interlingua) tree transformations. This involves the regularisation and determination of the morphological features for 'correct' interlingua representations, including government and agreement indicators.

7. Tree linearisation of the interlingua. The transformation of interlingua tree into the linear form of Esperanto involves the determination of the correct word order and the removal of labels and feature lists. The result is a plain Esperanto text which can be read by humans.

8. Correctness check. For security, each sentence is passed through a parser to check for syntactic well-formedness; any rejected sentences are sent back to step 6.

9. Coding and network transmission. Accepted sentences are converted for electronic transmission.

10. Decoding. Esperanto text is received at another terminal.

11. Esperanto parser. The decoded string is transformed into a dependency tree; because input is relatively unambiguous this process is fast.

12. Monolingual (interlingua) tree transformations. This stage mirrors stage 2, this time for Esperanto.

13. Bilingual tree transformations. The Metataxor generates from the single Esperanto tree a set of alternative French dependency trees; e.g. lexical transfer may indicate more than one French equivalent for a single Esperanto word.

14. Semantic–pragmatic word choice. In this stage, the correct French words are selected on the basis of word pattern information in the LKB (i.e. based on interlingua information), as illustrated in section 17.6 below. As there can be no interaction with users (they are passive receivers of the information with no knowledge of the source language), selection must be fully automatic.

15. Monolingual (target) tree transformations. This involves adjustments of incorrect French dependency trees and the insertion of government and agreement relations and features.

16. Tree linearisation of the target language. The French tree is linearised, with any necessary contractions and elisions, e.g. *de le → du, je ai → j'ai.*

The two halves of the translation process are distinct but not congruent 'translation systems': the conversion of source text into interlingua text (stages 1 to 8) is not the same as the conversion of interlingua text into target text (stages 11 to 16). As far as morphological and syntactic aspects are concerned, there are close parallels: (a) dependency parsing (1 and 11), (b) source tree transformations (2 and 12), (c) bilingual tree transformations (3 and 13), (d) target tree transformations (6 and 15), and (e) tree linearisation (7 and 16). The major differences lie in the stages of semantic–pragmatic interpretation and disambiguation; no processes are carried out in the source and target languages but all are performed in the Esperanto kernel of the system. In the first half, the heavy load of semantic processing is performed at the target language end (stage 4); in the second half, the processing takes place at the source language end (stage 14). As a result the modules which are specific to source and target languages can concentrate on language-specific manipulations of morphological and syntactic forms and structures. All the content (meaning) analysis and transfer takes place in the interlingua component of the overall system.

The basic processes, the modules and the data used at each stage may be illustrated schematically as in Figure 17.1, where SL is 'source language', IL is 'intermediate language' or 'interlingua', and TL is 'target language'.

It is evident from the description and from the diagram that simplification could be introduced by omitting the stages of generating the Esperanto string, its coding and decoding and the reanalysis as a tree (stages 7 to 12); and it is in fact accepted as a variant of the basic design that intermediate representations could be distributed over the network as Esperanto trees. However, this option would have the disadvantage that developers of the system would not have easy access to Esperanto texts in order to check the validity of interlingual interpretations, which, as we have seen, was claimed to be one of the primary benefits of a 'natural' language interlingua.

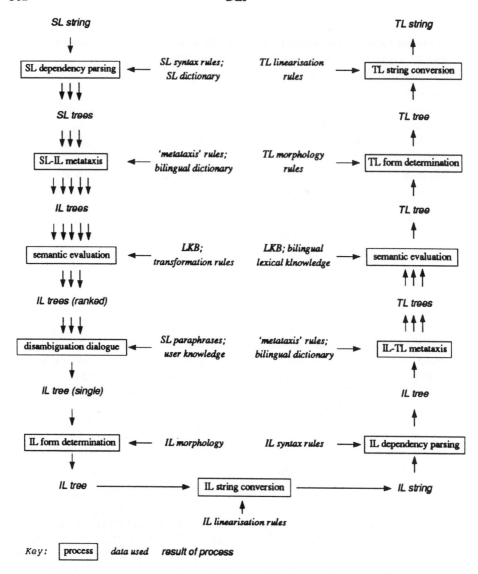

Figure 17.1 DLT basic processes

17.4 Dependency parsing

The formalism used in DLT for the representation of structures at all stages is based on dependency syntax (section 2.8.1) The basic arguments for using dependency trees are that structural relations (subject, object, attribute, etc.) are more central to analysis and transfer than constituency structures (noun phrase, prepositional phrase) and that dependency analyses are more suitable for languages with 'free' word orders than most constituency analyses. In DLT, the syntax of each language is developed with no reference to meanings (i.e. purely on distributional grounds) and quite independent of all other languages in the system. Thus, even for similar structures in closely related languages there are differences of structure and labelling; compare the representations of English (1) and German (2).

(1a) He gives it to her.

(2a) *Er gibt es ihr.*

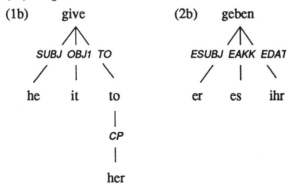

The DLT parser is based on a version of the ATN parser. In the analysis of source strings, the parser operates on information located in the 'syntactic dictionary' entries of the source language lexical items. These entries are in uninflected root forms; therefore, as in most MT systems morphological analysis precedes syntactic (dependency) analysis. Multiple parses are passed to the next stage of structural transfer.

17.5 Metataxis

Metataxis is the name given in DLT for the rule systems which link the dependency syntaxes of two languages, and the mechanism which transforms structures is called the 'Metataxor'. Rule systems are specific to one pair of languages and in one translation direction only. Thus, for the English to French prototype two metataxis rule systems have been developed: from English to Esperanto and from Esperanto to French. (Outlines of metataxis systems have also been described for other languages, including German, Danish, Polish, Bangla, Finnish, Hungarian and Japanese, and several others not published.)

The 'Metataxor' transforms dependency trees of source texts into dependency trees of target texts. Rules are effective at all levels: word, sentence and text. Metataxis rules may (a) change the syntactic category of a word, (b) change its morphological form, (c) change its syntactic function, (d) change a configuration of dependency relations, (e) add or remove words or items, and (f) merge or split dependency trees. Constraints on metataxis are imposed by the well-formedness conditions of the syntaxes of the source and target languages.

Metataxis operates on both lexical items and on trees, in two closely interlinked processes: the replacement of source words by one or more target language equivalents taken from bilingual dictionary, and the formation of tentative, syntactically correct target trees. Choices of different equivalents trigger changes in tree structures, and some tree transformations necessitate changes in lexical items. It follows that conditions on lexical items are also formulated as tree fragments, e.g. (3) for English.

(3) sell — to — [ ]

Metataxis is not concerned with resolving ambiguities: if the bilingual dictionary contains more than one translation, metataxis will produce more than one structural representation. The objective of metataxis is to ensure that the representations are syntactically valid. Choice between alternative representations is made on semantic and pragmatic grounds by the 'expert system' SWESIL (section 17.6 below).

To illustrate metataxis from English into Esperanto (stage 3), consider the translation of (4a), with the dependency parse (4b), into the Esperanto (5), where the English subject has been transformed into a prepositional complement (with the preposition *al* 'to') and the English direct object into a subject. The theme–rheme word order can be preserved because the nominative case of *subvencioj* indicates it is a subject.

(4a) Multinationals were allocated grants.

(4b)

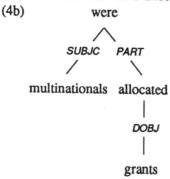

(5) *Al multnaciaj entreprenoj asignajtis subvencioj.*

The relevant metataxis rule is shown in (6), transforming the English passive subtree (6a) into the Esperanto tree (6b).

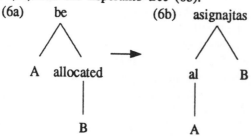

A similar metataxis rule would apply in the second half of the prototype (stage 13) to convert Esperanto trees into French trees. For example, to produce the French equivalent of (4a) and (5), namely (7), the rule might be as in (8).

(7) *Les multinationales se sont vu allouer des subventions.*

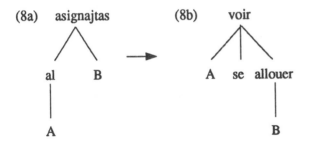

Such rules are clearly specific to particular structure types and particular sets of lexical items. In addition, the Metataxor has available general default rules in order to ensure that everything gets converted if no specific rules have applied. One would be that a source subject dependency becomes a target subject dependency.

17.6 Interlingual data and SWESIL

Originally conceived simply as a means of compact intermediate representation, Esperanto acquired greater importance as the project developed. By concentrating routines for semantic interpretation in the intermediate stages of the system, so that they do not have to be repeated for every additional language, the interlingua represents a linguistic 'knowledge bank' which is referred to in semantic and pragmatic processing. In the prototype system there were two databases: the LKB of Esperanto texts and the bilingual Esperanto–French dictionary. The LKB comprised pairs of 'content' words linked by a function or relator (e.g. Table 17.1), extracted from a dependency analysis of a 500,000-word corpus of Esperanto texts. The frequency of each pair was, however, not recorded, for reasons of computational simplicity. A typical example is given in Table 17.1 for the Esperanto word *ĉambro* ('room'), where *a* is the attribute relator.

ĉambro a apuda	'adjoining room'
ĉambro a bela	'beautiful room'
ĉambro a granda	'large room'
ĉambro a hela	'light room'
ĉambro a komforta	'comfortable room'
ĉambro a komuna	'common room'
ĉambro a nuda	'bare room'
etc.	

Table 17.1 Word pairs for *ĉambro*

In the bilingual dictionary the pairing of Esperanto and French lexical items was accompanied by contextual clues indicating the circumstances in which choices were to be made during lexical transfer. These clues were also given in Esperanto, e.g. Table 17.2 for the word *akra*.

akra a (doloro, malvarmo, vortoj, ...)	→	*vif*
akra a (nazo, oreloj, turo)	→	*pointu*
akra a (spico, pipro, brando)	→	*fort*
akra a (disputo, batalo, krizo, ...)	→	*violent*
akra a (ironio)	→	*mordant*

Table 17.2 Contextual clues for bilingual pairings

The table shows that Esperanto *akra* should be translated as *vif* if it is an attribute of *doloro* ('pain'), *malvarmo* ('cold'), *vortoj* ('words'); as *pointu* if an attribute of 'nose', 'ears' or 'tower'; as *fort* in the context of 'spice', 'pepper' and 'brandy'; etc.

The two databases have been the sources for the 'expert system' SWESIL at two stages of semantic processing: during translation from English into the interlingua and during translation of the interlingua representation into French.

17.6.1 English to Esperanto semantic processing

Tables such as 17.1 have been employed in the prototype for checking the acceptability of Esperanto lexical relationships. Checks (obviously performed on root forms) would confirm, for example, that *hela* is the correct translation of English *light* when modifying *ĉambro* and that *malpeza* ('light in weight') is incorrect. The problem comes, of course, when the database (the LKB) does not contain the sought pattern.

In the initial phase of the prototype design new and unknown combinations were dealt with by reference to hierarchies of words (i.e. in a thesaurus structure). For example, English *wood* can be either *ligno* ('wood as material') or *arbaro* ('wood as group of trees'); in translating (9) the Metataxor (stage 3; section 17.5) would present both as possibilities (10).

(9) The wood has been ordered.

(10a) *La ligno menditas.*

(10b) *La arbaro menditas.*

On consulting the hierarchies for these two possibilities, SWESIL would find *materialo* and *vegetaĵo* as their respective superordinates. It would then find that 'order' (Esperanto *mendi*) can have 'material' objects but not 'vegetable' ones. Thus *wood* must be translated as *ligno*.

However, the building of large and consistent hierarchies of Esperanto words proved to be extremely time-consuming and yet still insufficient for some types of contextual analysis; e.g. *eat* and *cook* are related not hierarchically but procedurally (as in an AI-type 'script' of event sequences). It was decided, therefore, to check the plausibilities of unknown patterns on the basis of word-pair comparisons alone. (In all cases, SWESIL worked with word pairs rather than triples or larger groups — again for reasons of computational simplicity.)

For every pair of words the comparison is done in two stages, an examination of the known contexts of the first word and an examination the known contexts of the second word. The process may again be illustrated with sentence (9). From the two possibilities generated by the Metataxor (10a) and (10b) are derived two standardised pairs of content words plus relator (11), where *n* indicates an 'object' relation.

(11a) *mendi n ligno* ('to order wood')

(11b) *mendi n arbaro* ('to order a wood')

SWESIL first calculates the 'semantic proximities' of *ligno* and *arbaro* to each of the words given in the database as objects of *mendi*. The semantic proximity of two words is a simple calculation of the number of their identical word-pair contexts as a proportion of the total word-pairs in which the two occur. Thus *nigra* ('black') occurs in 50 word-pairs, *blanka* ('white') in 51 word-pairs, and on 7 occasions the word context is the same ('hair', 'skin', 'colour', etc.); their semantic proximity is calculated as 0.829; by contrast, *lando* ('country') occurring in 346 word-pairs and *filo* ('son') in 109 word-pairs have only 7 in common, and a lower proximity score of 0.202.

In the database (LKB) SWESIL would find the following words occurring as objects of *mendi*: *armilo* ('weapon'), *automobilo* ('car'), *bileto* ('ticket'), *glaso* ('glass'), *materialo* ('material'), *servo* ('service'), *telefono* ('telephone'), *varo* ('ware'). The proximity scores for each of these and *ligno* or *arbaro* are given in Table 17.3 (next page).

The results show that the best available analogy for *ligno* is *materialo* (0.752) and for *arbaro* it is *varo* (0.137); and that, therefore, the clear preference is for the interpretation in (10a) and (11a), with *ligno*.

In the second stage, SWESIL calculates the plausibility of *mendi* ('order') as an action applied to both *ligno* and *arbaro*. For the *ligno* ('material') the LKB lists as actions: *bori* ('drill'), *eksporti* ('export'), *konsumi* ('consume'), *poluri* ('polish'), *rompi* ('break'), *vendi* ('sell'), etc.; for *arbaro* it lists: *ataki* ('attack') and *planti* ('plant'). The highest values for semantic proximities were *mendi* and *vendi* (0.817) and *mendi* and *konsumi* (0.777) — both found with *ligno* as object; whereas the highest proximity scores for *mendi* with *ataki* and *planti* are 0.379 and −0.078 respectively. The clear preference is again for the 'material' translation (*ligno*) of *wood*.

The same procedure is applied to relational words. For example *with* can be translated in (at least) two ways: *kun* (association) and *per* (instrument). Either are possible with the verb *look at* (12).

(12a) to look at with love

(12b) to look at with a microscope

The Metataxor generates two alternatives, *kun* and *per*, in both cases. SWESIL would calculate the word-pair match scores as in Table 17.4. and therefore accept (13) as preferred translations.

ligno	materialo	→	0.752
ligno	armilo	→	0.542
ligno	bileto	→	0.537
ligno	varo	→	0.526
ligno	automobilo	→	0.495
ligno	servo	→	0.242
arbaro	varo	→	0.137
arbaro	materialo	→	-0.047
arbaro	armilo	→	-0.089
arbaro	glaso	→	-0.096
arbaro	telefono	→	-0.154
arbaro	bileto	→	-0.181
arbaro	automobilo	→	-0.210
arbaro	servo	→	-0.249
ligno	glaso	→	-0.290
ligno	telefono	→	-0.411

Table 17.3 Proximity scores for *ligno* and *arbaro*

rigardi	amo	mikroskopo
kun	0.570	-0.116
per	0.015	0.732

Table 17.4 Word-pair match scores

(13a) *rigardi kun amo*

(13b) *rigardi per mikroskopo*

Not all source language (English) ambiguities can be solved by SWESIL and so the DLT prototype includes a stage of 'Dialogue disambiguation' (stage 5). Essentially this involves the presentation to the user of translation choices in English. For example, SWESIL might not have been able to decide between *devii disde* and *foriri de* as translations of *depart from*. It would consequently select two paraphrases for the user to choose between: *deviate from* and *leave*, respectively. The selection of appropriate paraphrases remains, however, a major difficulty (as it is in any MT system with interactive disambiguation, section 8.3.3) and is not fully solved in the prototype.

17.6.2 Esperanto to French semantic processing

Whereas in the first half of translation (from source to interlingua, stage 4), disambiguation involves only monolingual knowledge of word-pair matches in the interlingua LKB, in the second half (from interlingua to target, stage 13) disambiguation involves bilingual knowledge and a different type of matching procedure is applied. Lexical choice in the target language (French) is determined, not by the monolingual plausibility of the possible combinations of the French words but by matching contextual clues against the input (Esperanto) context.

We illustrate this with the problem of translating Esperanto *fako*. This may appear in French as *branche, case, compartiment, division, discipline, section, spécialité,* etc. according to context. The possibilities are listed in the dictionary as Esperanto pairs (with relators) and their French translations (Table 17.5).

fako a blanka ('empty square')	*case*
fako a libera ('free square')	*case*
fako de dungitaro ('personnel')	*division*
fako de ekonomio	*branche*
fako de financo	*section*
fako de matematico	*section*
fako de medicino	*spécialité*
fako de industrio	*branche*
fako de scienco	*spécialité*
fako de sporto	*discipline*
fako en bretaro ('shelving')	*rayon*
fako en dokumentujo ('filing cabinet')	*compartiment*
fako en ekonomio	*branche*
fako en kofro ('case')	*compartiment*
fako en magazeno ('store')	*rayon*
fako en medicino	*spécialité*
fako en scienco	*spécialité*

Table 17.5 Translation into French of *fako*

If there is a straight match, as in (14a), there is no problem with the translation (14b); but if the particular pair does not occur, e.g. (15a), then proximity scores of *industrio* and the known conjuncts of *fako* must be calculated. The closest analogy is *ekonomio*, based on such examples in LKB as: *industrio en lando* ('industry in a country'), *ekonomio en lando* ('economy in a country'), *industrio de agrikultura* ('industry of agriculture'), *ekonomio de agrikulturo* ('economy of agriculture'), *kreski as industrio* ('industry grows'), *kreski as ekonomio* ('economy grows'), etc. As a result the French output is (15b).

(14a) *fako de medicino*

(14b) *spécialité de la médecine*

(15a) *fako de industrio*

(15b) *branche d'industrie*

As in the first half of translation (stage 4, section 17.6.1 above), the same method is applied also to relational ambiguity. The Esperanto *ĉirkaŭ* could be *autour de, vers* or *aux environs de*. The highest word-pair match scores for each French version in the contexts of phrases (16a,b) are given in Table 17.6.

(16a) *flugi ĉirkaŭ planedo* ('fly around a planet')

(16b) *veni ĉirkaŭ tempo* ('come around a time')

	autour de	*vers*	*aux environs de*
flugi	*rotacii* 'rotate'	*alveni* 'arrive'	*viziti* 'visit'
Score	0.604	-0.218	-0.293
planedo	*tero* 'earth'	*dato* 'date'	*dato* 'date'
Score	0.761	0.320	0.320
Average	0.683	0.051	0.014
veni	*instali* 'install'	*alveni* 'arrive'	*okazii* 'happen'
Score	0.530	0.820	0.789
tempo	*jaro* 'year'	*horo* 'time of day'	*dato* 'date'
Score	0.677	0.801	0.753
Average	0.604	0.811	0.771

Table 17.6 Word-pair scores for *ĉirkaŭ*

The clear preference in the case of (16a) is *autour de* (17a), and the preference (but by not so great a margin) in the case of (16b) is *vers* (17b).

(17a) *voler autour d'une planète*

(17b) *venir vers le temps [de la vendage]*

17.6.3 Evaluation of SWESIL

In early 1988 an evaluation was made of the effectiveness of SWESIL in lexical transfer, with test passages amounting to some 600 words restricted to the vocabulary of 'Simplified English.' The conclusion was that performance suffered from (a) the lack of frequency information in the LKB, both of lexical collocations and of structural plausibilities (i.e. neither the Metataxor nor SWESIL gave probability rankings to different analyses); (b) the lack of source language information in the first (English–Esperanto) stage, in particular the relational contexts of any pairs of words being examined; and (c) the deficiencies and inconsistencies of the databases. In addition, the model took no account of morphological structure (e.g. it did not know that the suffix *-isto* refers to agentive nouns); it had no access to phrase-level relations; it handled structural ambiguity poorly; and it could not handle inter-sentence relations or other text grammatical features.

It was decided, therefore, in 1989 that for the commercial system to be developed by 1993 a new translation model should be adopted by DLT based on the concept of the Bilingual Knowledge Bank (BKB). A major motive was the recognition that the large databases required could not be constructed in the way they were in the prototype; lexical information was henceforth to be derived from actual texts, not built by human effort in dictionaries largely subjectively. In general, rule-driven processing was to be reduced and replaced by example-based processing using data from structured corpora of parallel bilingual texts. There would be no rigid distinction between syntactic and semantic analysis, disambiguation and transfer would be based on comparative bilingual examples, frequency information and dynamic updating would be provided, and in particular texts themselves would be the actual databases.

17.7 Conclusions

The BKB concept represents the final stage of a gradual move in DLT from the traditional rule-based approach to MT to an example-based approach. It is also a departure from the initial Esperanto-centred model: there is no longer an Esperanto 'knowledge base' (LKB) as the sole source of information for source language disambiguation. Esperanto is effectively seen as just one of the languages which may be present in BKBs. In theory, the new DLT model (described in section 18.2) need not involve translation from and into Esperanto at all, although it is argued that an intermediate language is still essential in the kind of multilingual configuration envisaged at the outset, namely a system for monolingual users to communicate in a communications network (section 17.1 above).

The main points of interest in the DLT prototype project can be summarized, then, as: the thorough exploration of a 'natural language' interlingua as the basis for an MT system; the full commitment to autonomous dependency syntax (i.e. not attuned as in Rosetta, cf. Chapter 16); and the use of text-based information in disambiguation and transfer (as opposed to rule-based dictionaries with semantic features, etc.). Although Esperanto may be more regular and consistent lexically and structurally than 'unplanned' natural languages such as English, French, Russian and Japanese, it presents similar problems of lexical and structural transfer, as we saw in the *akra*, *fako* and *ĉirkaŭ* examples above, and it is probably the distinctive approach to these problems which gives the DLT investigations significance beyond this particular project. However, it may well be the later example-based BKB model which, from a future prespective, proves more influential than the Esperanto-based prototype design.

17.8 Sources and further reading

The overall conception of the basic DLT prototype is discussed in the report of the feasibilty study by Witkam (1983) and in later accounts by Schubert (1986, 1988). The primary source for details of the metataxis is Schubert (1987) and Maxwell and Schubert (1989), and for the prototype version of SWESIL the source is Papegaaij *et al.* (1986). SWESIL is also described in Sadler (1989), which is devoted primarily, however, to an outline of the BKB model (see section 18.2).

18

Some other systems and directions of research

In this chapter we attempt to indicate major current lines of MT research and to predict some future directions. In doing so we shall be describing briefly some MT projects which have not been given the full treatment dedicated to systems in the last eight chapters. This chapter will necessarily be more suggestive and speculative than preceding ones and readers should regard it as a gateway into the somewhat confusing picture of contemporary MT research activity.

18.1 AI and Knowledge-based MT at CMU

For many observers of MT development it has been the conventional wisdom that the most likely source of techniques for improving MT quality is the research on natural language processing within the context of **Artificial Intelligence (AI)**. The involvement of AI researchers in MT-related projects began in the early 1970s with Yorick Wilks' work at Stanford University and the research of Roger Schank and his colleagues at Yale University. This was after the ALPAC report had highlighted the inadequacies of current approaches to MT. A major deficiency, obvious to many at the time, was their impotence in face of what was called the 'semantic barrier'.

The basic justification for AI approaches is the argument that since translation is concerned primarily with conveying the content or 'meaning' of a text in one language into a text in another language any MT system must be able to 'understand' the meanings of texts, as Bar-Hillel, Yngve and others were arguing already in the early 1960s. Without understanding, it is contended, no system can be expected to be able to decide which of possible target language expressions correspond most closely to the meaning of the original text. AI research claims to tackle this problem directly and is thus seen as likely to improve the quality of MT output. Characteristic of AI approaches is the adoption of primarily semantics-oriented parsing, the interpretation of texts by reference to knowledge bases and the use of inference mechanisms, and language-independent representations of the 'meaning' of texts.

The 1980s saw continued and increasing activity in research on AI approaches to translation, in Europe (some in relation to the Eurotra project), in Japan (notably at the Electro-Technical Laboratory), and in particular in North America. Much of this AI-inspired research has been on a small-scale, but a major centre has for some years been located at the Carnegie-Mellon University (CMU) in Pittsburgh.

The research at the CMU Center for Machine Translation under Jaime Carbonell and Sergei Nirenburg continues work which began initially in 1983 at Colgate University. The experimental systems are based on a methodology described as 'meaning-oriented MT in an interlingua paradigm'. Most attention is paid to the creation of appropriate and efficient software and the acquisition of the knowledge bases, giving the research theme its name **Knowledge-based MT** (KBMT). The systems developed are seen as gradual approximations of an ideal interlingua-based MT system. Some parts of the system are relatively complete, others are still experimental, including domain knowledge and lexicons and many areas of linguistic processing.

The working prototype for English and Japanese in both directions is designed for translation of personal computer manuals. It has a small 'domain model' of 1,500 concepts, and analysis and generation lexicons for both languages, each of nearly 900 items. The system is written in CommonLisp, and the grammar formalism is based on Lexical Functional Grammar (LFG). The basic modules are (Figure 18.1): syntactic parser with semantic constraints, a semantic mapper (for semantic interpretation), an interactive 'augmentor' for remaining ambiguities, a semantic generator producing syntactic structures with lexical selection, and a syntactic generator for producing target strings. The language-specific databases are analysis and generation grammars, and analysis and generation lexicons providing syntactic information. The concept lexicon and the semantic information in the analysis and generation lexicons (i.e. defining some semantic constraints) are language-independent but specific to the subject domain. The mapping rules, which convert f-structures into interlingua texts are both language- and domain-dependent. The CMU system is supported by software for creating concept lexicons (the 'knowledge acquisition tool' ONTOS), for compiling grammars and for testing modules and components.

The Analyzer consists of two components, a syntactic parser and a semantic interpreter, the 'mapping rule interpreter'. The syntactic parser uses an LFG-type grammar and produces an LFG-type 'f-structure' (see section 2.10.1). For example, the sentence (1) is represented as in (2).

   (1) Remove the diskette from the drive.

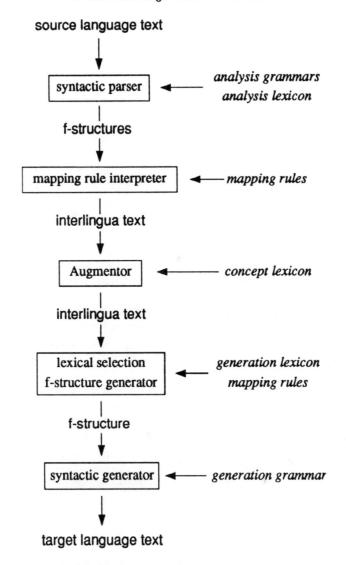

Figure 18.1 KBMT basic modules

```
(2) ((OBJ ((CASE ACC) (REF DEFINITE)
          (DET ((ROOT THE) (REF DEFINITE)))
          (ROOT DISKETTE) (PERSON 3) (NUMBER SINGULAR)
          (COUNT YES) (PROPER NO))
      (PPADJUNCT ((PREP FROM) (REF DEFINITE)
          (DET ((ROOT THE) (REF DEFINITE)))
          (ROOT DRIVE) (PERSON 3) (NUMBER SINGULAR)
          (COUNT YES) (PROPER NO)))
      (VALENCY TRANS)
      (MOOD IMPERATIVE)
```

```
(TENSE PRESENT)
(FORM INF)
(COMP-TYPE NO)
(ROOT REMOVE))
```

The semantic interpreter tests any f-structure component for ambiguities and substitutes interlingual units for source language lexical items and constructions, e.g. surface subject–predicate structures are replaced by case frames ('agent', 'theme', 'experiencer', etc.)

The central core of the system is the representation of interlingua texts. These are representations of 'actual events' as reported in the source texts. They are in the form of networks of propositions, i.e. events or states with their arguments and causal, temporal, spatial, etc. links to other events or states. The representations are produced as instantiations of concepts (events, individuals, etc.) from the 'concept lexicon'. The latter is a database of knowledge about the events and entities in the domain (subject field of the system). There is thus a clear distinction between the static knowledge database (network of relations independent of particular texts) and the dynamic interlingua text representations. It is argued that to ensure adequate understanding of input texts, the knowledge required must go beyond propositional knowledge, it must cover pragmatic and discourse meaning, i.e. the attitudes of speakers and hearers to the propositions expressed, speech acts, thematic structures, and the ways in which separate utterances are combined as coherent texts (cf. section 2.7).

The interlingua text is represented as a non-linear network of frames with slot values. Typically the values correspond to those listed in the concept lexicon; e.g. a textual *rose* will have as its 'color' value one of the list '(white red yellow blue ...)' attached to the concept 'flower' (of which *rose* is identified as an instance). The representation of non-propositional information from input texts is regarded as an innovative feature of the CMU project. The same knowledge structure is used in the concept lexicon and in interlingua texts as for propositional information. Thus, the lexicon indicates the potential values for speech acts ('statement', 'definition', 'request-info', 'request-action'), one of which is relevant for a particular sentence (or clause) in a text. Similarly, the lexicon offers sets of values for markers of text cohesion: 'expansion', 'similar', 'generalization', 'contrastive', 'digression', etc.

The result of a mapping rule application on the f-structure above (2) is a candidate interlingua text (3).

```
(3) [*REMOVE
       (THEME (*DISKETTE (NUMBER SINGULAR)
                         (REFERENCE DEFINITE))))
       (SOURCE (*DISKETTE-DRIVE (NUMBER SINGULAR)
                               (REFERENCE DEFINITE))))
       (TENSE PRESENT)
       (MOOD IMPERATIVE)]
```

As the example shows, the knowledge base has enabled the identification of *drive* as referring in this subject domain to a 'diskette drive'.

The task of the Augmentor is to produce a single unambiguous interlingua text for input to the Generator. Since the output from the Analyzer still reflects to some extent the syntactic configurations of the source language it must first be reformatted by the Augmentor into a language-independent form. Secondly, the Augmentor has to disambiguate genuinely ambiguous candidate interlingua texts. For example, *tape* might refer to 'adhesive tape' or 'magnetic tape' in this domain, and the semantic processing of the Analyzer is unable to resolve the ambiguity in a sentence such as (4).

(4) Remove the tape from the diskette drive.

It is here that the 'knowledge' of the subject matter as embodied in the concept lexicon is to be called upon. As yet, however, the CMU project has automated only one part of the Augmentor's disambiguation operations, namely the task of identifying referents of pronominal anaphors across sentences; consequently, most of the Augmentor tasks are at present performed interactively with users.

The Generator produces first a target language f-structure by the selection of lexical items and the application of mapping rules similar to those in the Analyzer; and then produces a surface structure and output text. Whereas the result of analysis is multiple output of possible interpretations, generation stops as soon as one valid target string has been produced (i.e. the first and not necessarily either the 'best' or even one expressing the complete input text). The same grammars are used for both analysis and generation, but only in the case of Japanese is there some partial reversibility of rule application.

As this brief description indicates, the development of the CMU system is still at an early stage. Its importance lies in the investigation of MT via representations in a conceptual ('meaning') interlingua, specific to a domain but independent of particular languages. It remains to be seen whether the CMU project will confound the arguments of those sceptical about interlingual representations (section 6.8) or indeed about the need for 'understanding' of the AI-type in translation at all. It is pointed out that human translators often do not need to fully understand what they are translating (in fact it would be unusual if they understood scientific reports as well as the researchers themselves). A secondary objection that AI-type meaning-oriented systems produce 'paraphrases' rather than translations (because the surface presentation of the content in the source is lost) may be answered in the CMU project by the incorporation of textual (pragmatic) information in 'interlingua texts'. The main reservations, however, are practical: whether the construction of language-independent knowledge bases is feasible for other than highly restricted subject domains — although this is a question for any system designed for a particular sublanguage which is intended to be applicable in general — and whether the potential improvements in quality will be commensurate with the greatly increased computation involved.

18.2 Example-based MT at BSO

In section 6.9 we briefly described **example-based** methods as alternatives to knowledge-based approaches and as supplementary to traditional rule-based methods. Various researchers have been investigating their potential, including members of the Japanese ATR project (see section 18.6 below). To illustrate what is involved we describe a proposal from the DLT project to use a 'Bilingual

Knowledge Bank' (BKB) as a translation tool. The earlier DLT research is described in Chapter 17.

The purpose of the BKB is to serve as the primary source of linguistic 'knowledge' for all modules in the translation process. It consists of a corpus of equivalent texts in two languages which have been structurally analysed (by the same type of parser) into 'translation units' and which have been aligned to each other. Translation units are fragments of text in the two languages, which a translator would consider equivalent and mutually substitutable, and as far as possible structurally autonomous. Such aligned 'bitexts' have previously been proposed as aids for professional translators, giving them access to their own or others' previous practice in translation. The DLT researchers intend to use the structured bilingual corpus for the automatic resolution of source language ambiguities, problems of lexical and structural transfer and difficulties in target language selection.

As an illustration of alignment, the sentences (5a) and (5b) in an English–French BKB might be analysed, by a dependency parser, as (6a) and (6b).

(5a) The board unanimously confirms the mandate.

(5b) *Le conseil est unanime dans sa confirmation du mandat.*

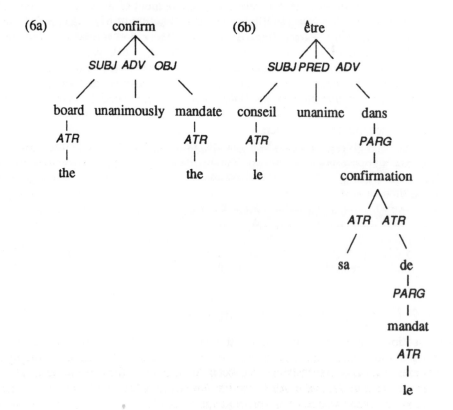

The aligned translation units for the structure would be derived by rules relating bilingual structural equivalents (7).

(7) the board ↔ *le conseil*
the ↔ *le*
unanimously confirm ↔ *être unanime dans sa confirmation de*
unanimously ↔ *unanime*
the mandate ↔ *le mandat*

As a result of the full comparative analysis and alignment of translation units in a large bilingual corpus, the data in (8) might be available for English expressions of the form *have... effect on....*

(8) have a direct effect on ↔ *ont une influence directe à*
have a direct effect on ↔ *intéressent directement*
had a direct effect on ↔ *ont eu une répercussion directe sur*
has had a marked effect on ↔ *a largement influencé*
had a positive effect on ↔ *s'est avérée positive dans*
had a highly negative effect on ↔ *en auraient été gravement affectés*
will have a decisive effect on ↔ *influencera de façon déterminante*

The stages of transfer from source to target remain as in the earlier DLT model (Figure 17.1). The difference lies in the type of information applied at each stage. Modules operate on a common data structure, rather than passing on tree structures sequentially. The various databases (dictionaries and other knowledge bases) are integrated into the BKB. There are four mechanisms which operate interactively: Parser, Text Expert, Metataxor and Examiner. The Parser and Metataxor correspond roughly to the mechanisms for syntactic analysis and transformation described in sections 17.4 and 17.5, except that neither is now restricted to rule-based analyses and to unordered (uninterpreted) output; they can use frequency information in the BKB about which structural patterns are most likely, and the Metataxor can also assess potential target structures with evidence from aligned bilingual subtrees.

The Text Expert is a new module which is proposed to deal with referential relations across sentences. Given, for example, the sentence sequence (9), the Text Expert would seek potential antecedents of the pronoun *it*: in this case, either *translation* or *screen* but not *translator* because of semantic incompatibilities.

(9) The translator may see the translation on his screen. It will be
displayed in a special format.

A decision is needed when translating into French or German: *il* or *er* would refer to the screen (*écran* or *Bildschirm*), *elle* or *sie* to the translation (*traduction* or *Übersetzung*).

It is the task of the Examiner (which replaces SWESIL of the earlier DLT model, section 17.6) to select the best analyses from the Parser, to choose the best transformations from the Metataxor and to resolve text–grammatical uncertainties from the Text Expert. It assesses the semantic and pragmatic plausibility of interpretations and proposed translations by reference to the BKB. Thus, to test whether in a particular instance, *around* is to be translated as *autour de* or as *vers*, *sharp* as *aigu, pointu, vif* or *aigre*, the Examiner would look for examples of similar contexts in either source or target language texts (or both). The procedure should be able to tackle problems of lexical transfer often characterised as 'stylistic' (cf. section 7.4), such as the choice between *big* and *large* (as translations of French *grand* and German *gross*), the subtle differences between *fast, swift, rapid* and *quick* when translating French *rapide*, and so forth. The procedure potentially identifies implicit relations, e.g. that in *radiation protection* something is being protected against radiation, while in *wildlife protection* it is the wildlife which is being protected against something or someone. Relevant texts might include phrases such as: *steps taken to protect the inhabitants against radiation hazards* and *reservations for the protection of wild birds and animals* (plus other fragments linking *birds* and *animals* to *wildlife*). The approach could also in principle tackle the inter-sentential problems illustrated in (9), e.g. by finding examples linking *translation* and *text* and fragments such as *the text was displayed....* In all these cases, it should be stressed the examples could come from either texts in the source language or texts in the target language; the bilingual corpus as a whole represents a database of extra-linguistic knowledge, as well as a source of linguistic knowledge about the two languages concerned.

The advantages of the BKB approach are claimed to be: (a) the system is in principle reversible; the same procedures and textual information are applied in both translation directions; (b) no dictionaries and no knowledge bases have to be compiled with great expenditure of specialist effort: the dangers of inconsistency and insufficiency are avoided; (c) analysis can be as deep or as shallow as desired and can be adjusted with experience; with a full-text database no information is lost; (d) text corpora (and thus lexical coverage) can be selected to suit the needs of specific users; (e) decisions about homography and polysemy are superfluous; the 'sublanguages' of text corpora determine correspondences and differences between languages; (f) databases can be easily updated to deal with neologisms by adding new texts and by 'learning' from texts while the system is translating; (g) translation expertise is acquired by 'imitating' the best human translators, i.e. using the wealth of complex contextual information usually absent from dictionaries.

The concept of example-based MT is also found in the UMIST–ATR project, described below (18.5).

18.3 Statistics-based MT at IBM

Most of the systems and methods described in this book involve linguistic analysis and generation of sentences and texts. This is true not only for the traditional 'linguistics-based' systems (Systran, Susy, Ariane, Eurotra, METAL) but also for the less typical Météo, Rosetta and DLT systems and for the knowledge-based and example-based approaches in the last two sections. A more radical departure from the assumptions which have dominated MT research since the early 1960s is represented by the investigation at the IBM Research Laboratories at Yorktown Heights, NY, of a translation system based almost exclusively on statistical techniques.

The use of statistical analysis was not uncommon in the early years of MT research. It was employed primarily as a tool for the automatic classification of linguistic data, on the assumption that contemporary knowledge about language was insufficient for computational processing. This application has continued to the present time: many research projects make use of statistical data to guide rule writing and the formulation of routines; some go further, as we have seen (Chapter 17), and use statistical information in lexical selection and disambiguation. What is unique about the IBM project is the use of statistical techniques as the sole tool for analysis and generation. It has been made possible by the increasingly sophisticated application of statistics-based approaches in speech recognition and parsing.

The IBM research is based on a large corpus of the Canadian *Hansard*, which records parliamentary debates in both English and French. The corpus for the experiment was 40,000 pairs of sentences (totalling some 800,000 words) in each language. The essence of the method is the alignment of sentences in the two languages and the calculation of the probabilities that any one word in a sentence of one language corresponds to two, one or zero words in the translated sentence in the other language. Alignment was established by a technique widely used in speech recognition. The probabilities were estimated by matching bigrams (two consecutive words) in each English sentence against bigrams in 'equivalent' French sentences.

Two sets of probabilities were calculated. First, for each individual English word the probabilities of its correspondences to a set of French words; e.g. *the* corresponds to French *le* with probability .610, to *la* with .178, to *l'* with .083, to *les* with .023, to *ce* with .013, to *il* with .012, etc. Second, the probabilities that two, one or zero French words correspond to a single English word, e.g. *the* corresponds to one French word with .871 probability, to zero with .124, and to two with .004. In the case of *not* there is a .758 probability of correspondence with two French words, and these are most likely to be *ne* (.460) and *pas* (.469), with *plus* (.002) and *jamais* (.002) much less likely; other correspondences of *not* are *non* (.024), *pas du tout* (.003), and *faux* (.003), etc.

The effectiveness of the approach was evaluated by translating from French into English. The vocabulary was limited to the 1,000 most frequent English words and their corresponding most frequent 1,700 French words. The translation model was tested on 73 new French sentences from elsewhere in the *Hansard* corpus. The results were classified as: (a) exact (same as *Hansard* translation), (b) alternative (same meaning but in slightly different words), (c) different (legitimate translation but not conveying the same meaning as the *Hansard* translation), (d) wrong (intelligible result but not a translation of the French), and (e) ungrammatical (no sense conveyed). Some examples are shown in Table 18.1.

Although only 5% came into the 'exact' category, translations were considered 'reasonable' if they came into any of the first three categories (exact, alternate, different). On this criterion, the system performed with 48% success. Improvements are expected with a larger corpus (only 10% of the *Hansard* was used), by probabilistic segmentation of sentences into phrases, by using trigrams as well as bigrams, and by including data on inflectional morphology to group together, for example *tall, taller, tallest* and *va, vais, vont*.

The proposed incorporation of segmentation and morphology data suggests that statistical approaches have inherent limitations that even their advocates

exact	*Ces amendements sont certainement nécessaires*
Hansard	These amendments are certainly necessary
IBM	These amendments are certainly necessary
alternative	*C'est pourtant très simple*
Hansard	Yet it is very simple
IBM	It is still very simple
different	*J'ai reçu cette demande en effet*
Hansard	Such a request was made
IBM	I have received this request in effect
wrong	*Permettez que je donne un exemple à la Chambre*
Hansard	Let me give the House one example
IBM	Let me give an example in the House
ungrammatical	*Vous avez besoin de toute l'aide disponible*
Hansard	You need all the help you can get
IBM	You need of the whole benefits available

Table 18.1 Examples of translations

acknowledge. Nevertheless, the importance of this research is that it demonstrates how far it is possible to go in bilingual uni-directional MT without recourse to linguistic analysis. However, it must be remembered that the results are biased to a particular corpus. For example, in these texts the translation of *hear* would invariably be *bravo* (a probability of .992) — i.e. in the Canadian parliament *Hear, hear!* corresponds to *Bravo!* — while the 'normal' translation *entendre* has a very low probability of just .005.

There is little doubt that statistics-based techniques will be a feature of many future MT projects, although whether many will follow the exclusivity of the IBM team is uncertain. At the present time, the assumption is that linguistic data and methodology will remain at the centre of any practical MT system.

18.4 Sublanguage translation: TITUS

The restriction of an MT system to one particular text corpus may be regarded as an extreme variant of the **sublanguage** approach (section 8.4). It is justifiable only if the corpus is particularly large. This was certainly the case with the aviation manuals for which the TAUM team were asked to develop an MT system. However, as we have already mentioned (Chapter 12), their success with the sublanguage system Météo could not be repeated.

In practice, nearly all MT systems, whether experimental or commercial, are limited to particular subject fields. This can be seen in many implementations of Systran, in the Pan American Health Organization systems (medical and public health documents), in the Eurotra prototype (information technology), in METAL (technical documents), in the CMU system (personal computer manuals), and in many microcomputer-based systems from Japanese computer companies, which have concentrated on translations of computer technology and electronic engineering. Some further examples come later in this chapter. However, these systems are not classifiable as 'sublanguage systems' as such, because they are neither designed for nor intended to be restricted to particular subjects. Their present limitations are regarded as temporary: extension to other subject areas is anticipated. By contrast, sublanguage MT systems are developed specifically for one particular subject or text type, in order to minimise problems of homography, translational ambiguity and structural variety (section 8.4). The archetypal system, as we have seen, is Météo (Chapter 12); another example is TITUS.

The TITUS system was designed by the Institut Textile de France for the multilingual treatment of abstracts in an on-line database for the textile industry. First installed in 1970, the system is now in its fourth version. Abstracts are stored in representations from which texts can be generated in any one of four languages: English, French, German, and Spanish. Abstracts can be entered in any of the languages; they are formulated in a controlled syntax, in a controlled basic vocabulary, and in the standardised terminology of the textile industry sublanguage. The controlled syntax determines the order of basic phrase types: subject NP, circumstantial NP, verb phrase, complement NP, prepositional NP (where some of these NP types may be coordinate phrases, and the VP and the complement NP are optional). The syntax defines also the structure of noun phrases and of verb phrases, in terms of the order and optionality of constituents. At a pre-editing stage, words which are potentially ambiguous are distinguished, e.g. the French verb form *a* is distinguished from the preposition *a* (not entered with the grave accent) by a following slash. Furthermore, structural ambiguities (e.g. antecedents of prepositional phrases) are eliminated by the insertion of punctuation marks. Abstracts are entered interactively; the system requests reformulations of phrases and sentences not conforming to the controlled syntax and asks for clarification of homographs and structural ambiguities. Despite the constraints, the range of permitted structures is nevertheless impressive, for example (10).

> (10) *L'analyse du fluage des fibres de polyéthylène après irridiation sous vide montre ; qu'un processus de pontage survient dans la région amorphe ; tandis qu'une coupure de la chaîne moléculaire de la région cristalline est observée.*

After entry, the system produces a version in the input language to check that analysis is correct, and then generates versions in each of the other languages. For example, the English entry corresponding to (10) would be (11).

> (11) The polyethylene fibre creep analysis after irridiation under vacuum shows that a cross-linking process occurs in the amorphous region whereas a molecular chain scission of crystalline region is observed.

The quality of the translations is ensured by combining control of the input, extensive pre-editing, interactive feedback during and after analysis, and restriction to a regulated sublanguage. With such constraints, some may doubt whether TITUS should be considered a real MT system at all; what is clear is that it illustrates, as well as Météo, what can be achieved in well-defined environments.

It is perhaps surprising that there have not been more sublanguage systems. It does appear, however, that there must be very few situations where translation can be restricted to a relatively self-contained lexical and syntactic domain. Since Météo, researchers from the TAUM group have been searching for an ideal area for applying sublanguage methods, and at present some are working on MT for livestock market reports (see 18.7 below). As we shall see, other sublanguages under investigation include business correspondence, hotel and conference reservations and police communication.

18.5 MT for monolingual users

As discussed already, most MT systems are intended (explicitly or implicitly) for users knowing both source and target languages, who are able to make good the deficiencies of current MT systems in various ways (Chapter 9). However, the use of MT by monolinguals not familiar with one of the source or target languages is also possible. The output from batch systems, such as Systran, can be valuable unrevised to specialists expert in the subject field, but since these experts do not necessarily know the source language, they could not be expected to be of assistance in the translation process itself. But when we consider users at the other end of the process, at the input of text, there are a number of interesting possibilities, as we have already mentioned (section 8.3.4). Some of these are now under active investigation; in particular, systems for the interactive composition of texts to be translated into a language that the user does not know.

At UMIST (University of Manchester Institute of Science and Technology), pioneering work on MT systems for **monolingual users** was undertaken in the development of Ntran. This was an English–Japanese system which involved interactive disambiguation of the English source text and, where further ambiguities arose during lexical transfer, a stage of interaction involving choices that a user with no knowledge of Japanese could nevertheless be expected to make (i.e. based on English paraphrases of the target language distinctions). The Japanese generation was entirely automatic. Inspired by the relative success of this prototype system, researchers at UMIST have become involved in several further projects having as a common theme the development of MT for the monolingual user.

One such project, funded by British Telecom, aims at developing an MT system which will help users to compose business letters in an unfamiliar foreign language, by guiding them through a menu of choices. The system is based on the idea of 'pro-forma' texts corresponding to certain types of business letter, e.g. complaint, offer, enquiry, and so on. The pro-forma texts are templates with slots for set phrases, names, dates, addresses, etc., which have to be entered by users in their own language. Once the pro-forma is complete, the system is able to generate multilingual equivalents of the text by comparing the information provided by the user with a database of 'pre-translated' text fragments. The attraction of the system is that, because the target langauge templates are based on stylistically appropriate texts written by human translators (rather than built up by largely literal translation), high quality output can be guaranteed, as long as the text remains strictly within the given domain. A similar approach is found in a system being developed in Malaysia which helps writers draft official letters in Malay language.

Another system, also being developed at UMIST, takes the idea of system–user interaction in place of a 'source text' a little further. In a project being carried out together with the Japanese ATR (Advanced Telecommunications Research) Laboratories, a **dialogue translation** system is being developed. The domain is that of an on-line conversation (ultimately, by telephone, but keyboard conversation is the medium) between a conference office in Japan and an English-speaking enquirer. The idea is that the system works as an intermediary between the two conversation partners, translating their dialogue between English and Japanese. Dialogue translation is a particularly difficult task because of the high frequency of elliptical, partial or ill-formed utterances, as well as the use of anaphora and deictic reference (cf. section 2.7). Furthermore, in comparison with the kinds of texts normally translated by MT systems, dialogue contains a much larger proportion of language where literal translation is inappropriate: identical utterances can have completely different discourse functions — and hence translations — from one moment to the next. For example, *OK* in a dialogue might mean any of the paraphrases in (12).

(12a) I agree with you.

(12b) I can still hear you.

(12c) Let's change the subject now.

(12d) That is good.

As in the UMIST–British Telecom research, the system has some expectations of the kinds of things the user might want to say: the system has a bilingual 'dialogue model', and interacts with the user to try to match the user's input to the range of possible utterances in the model, which of course the system can be confident of translating correctly. There are two possible scenarios. In one, the user takes the initiative, typing in proposed utterances. In the other, the system might take the intiative, making proposals about what the next utterance might be, on the basis of its dialogue model.

In so far as these systems attempt to match input phrases against pre-translated text segments in a database, they belong to the genre of Example-based MT systems (cf. 18.2 above). A rather more ambitious project, known as LIDIA ('Large Internationalisation of Documents through Interaction with Authors'), has been proposed from the University of Grenoble. For its linguistic techniques it is founded on GETA's well tested Ariane system (described in Chapter 13). The aim is an interactive system enabling researchers to translate their own texts from their own language (French in this case) into another unknown language (German or Russian), providing also as a check a translation of the target text back into the original. Unlike the UMIST projects it will not be based on pre-translated text fragments but will translate in the familiar MT manner from largely already written texts.

18.6 Speech translation: British Telecom and ATR

Advances in speech technology in recent years have encouraged a number of researchers to investigate the integration of translation systems with **speech recognition and synthesis**. We have seen already (section 18.3 above) the application of methods from speech research in a statistics-based translation system. Here, we describe briefly two projects where input and output is spoken but where translation itself is based on more traditional linguistics-based approaches.

The experiment at the British Telecom Research Laboratories was based on the matching of spoken words against standard phrases in the highly restricted domain of telephonic business communication. The restriction was necessitated by the severe performance limitations of current speech recognisers. The researchers isolated the distinctive words which uniquely identified phrases. For example, given the three phrases in (13), the recognition of the three keywords *you, speak* and *I* would be sufficient to ensure unique identification.

(13a) Whom do you want to speak to?

(13b) I cannot hear you.

(13c) May I speak to Mr Smith please?

With a phrasebook of 400 sentences it was found that the ten most useful English keywords were *the, a, I, you, to, room, is, hotel, for, of.* Similar sets were found for French, German and Spanish. Obviously, variable elements such as times and prices could not be treated in the same way; these had to be identified and translated individually. The system involved three stages: the telephone caller input a phrase to the speech recogniser, enunciating each word clearly and pausing between each word; the computer selected a phrase and processed any variables; the chosen phrase was displayed on a screen; if acceptable as a paraphrase, the stored translation was transmitted; and the final message was output in synthetic speech (and/or displayed on a screen) at the receiver's end. The BT researchers are now investigating a bilingual spoken communication system for use by the French and British police forces, involving research on the sublanguage of police messages ('Policespeak').

A much more ambitious project for telephone translation is underway, at the ATR Laboratories in Japan. The long-term aim is a system for translating unrestrained spoken dialogue between English and Japanese. It involves basic research on speech recognition, speech synthesis and automatic translation of dialogue. Current speech recognisers usually require pauses between words and are adapted to particular individuals. Speaker-independent recognition of continuous conversation presents considerable challenges, involving the incorporation of prosodic information such as pitch, stress and duration, the recognition of syllable boundaries, the integration with a parser for identifying phonemes and word boundaries, the use of semantic and pragmatic information to narrow down potential interpretations, and much else. The requirements for automatic speech synthesis are almost equally challenging: in comparison with current synthesisers the demand is for higher quality, more 'natural' output which takes account of prosody and inflexion and which is more 'personalised'.

As for the translation of dialogue, this is itself a new area for MT (cf. 18.5 above): spoken dialogue differs from written text in vocabulary and grammar, while incomplete utterances, false starts, ellipses, unstated implications, etc. are commonplace. The ATR project is undertaking fundamental linguistic research on speech acts, dialogue switching, Japanese honorifics, inferring function words and omitted subjects, and producing idiomatic output (including use of example-based methods). As stated above, the research focus at present is the communication environment of an international conference office. Whether an operational prototype emerges or not, the basic research at ATR has been contributing substantially to MT in general and will continue to do so in the future.

18.7 Reversible grammars

The linguistic foundations of MT continue to be explored in a number of directions. There is much attention to the application and implementation of recent developments in theoretical linguistics, such as LFG, GPSG, GB, Systemic–Functional grammar, Categorial grammar, Situation Semantics, Logic grammars (some of which have been mentioned in passing). Other prominent topics at present include compositionality and reversibility, as we saw in Chapter 16 on Rosetta. **Reversibility** of grammars, in particular, has been an objective of a number of projects; just one fairly typical example is given here: the CRITTER project in Canada. (See also Chapter 7 for further references.)

CRITTER is a transfer-based system for translating between English and French. It has been developed at the Centre Canadien de Recherche sur l'Informatisation du Travail (CCRIT), the Canadian Workplace Automation Research Centre, by researchers originally attached to the TAUM project in Montreal. It is designed as a general experimental MT model applied at present to the specific sublanguage of the weekly reports produced by the Canadian Department of Agriculture which describe the situation in the livestock and meat trade markets of Canadian provinces. The principal consequence is that the lexicon is restricted to the vocabulary of the reports, although the grammatical formalism and the computational implementation are not constrained.

CRITTER exemplifies many typical features of the current philosophy in linguistics-oriented MT. Syntactic representations are fairly standard surface structure dependency trees, labelled with syntactic and semantic features, reflecting $\overline{X}$ conventions, and marking gaps and traces in the normal way. For (14a) the syntactic tree is (14b).

(14a) Last week hog prices in Saskatchewan increased 5% at $69.

In this particular tree, the only feature reflecting the sublanguage type is the inclusion of an idiosyncratic 'meas_p' as a subcategorisation of the verb *increase*. The intermediate semantic representation for the same sentence (14c) is an abstract dependency tree with branches labelled by argument numbers and with lexical items as nodes. The treatment of *last week* as an unanalysed unit is justified by its status as a fixed 'idiom' in the sublanguage.

(14b)

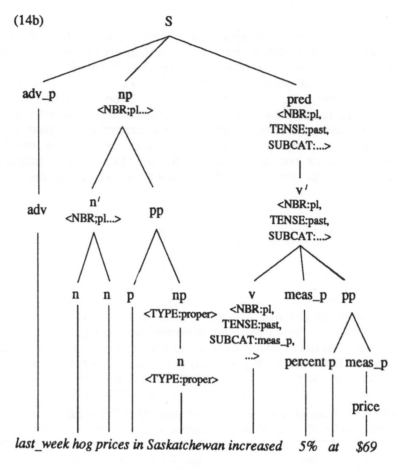

last_week hog prices in Saskatchewan increased 5% at $69

(14c)

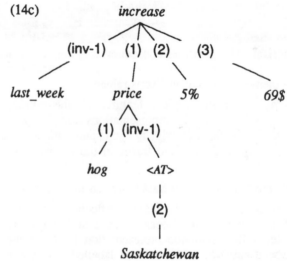

The use of 'inverted' argument numbers ('inv-1') enables the indication of two types of relationship: predicate–argument relations and syntactic dependency. Thus the dependent *last week* is a predicate with *increase* as argument, and *prices* is in first argument position relative to the 'abstract' item <AT> (the second argument being *Saskatchewan*).

Before transfer, the semantic structure is checked for consistency of predicate and argument nodes. A semantic lexicon associates semantic 'types' to nodes (e.g. MOVEMENT to *increase*, MEASURE-FUNCTION to *price*, INCREMENT to 5%, etc.) and validates predicate–argument structures against 'schemas' of semantic types, such as (15).

(15) MOVEMENT(MEASURE-FUNCTION,INCREMENT,MEASURE)

Transfer rules are all associated with lexical entries. They are mostly straightforward, as in (16a), but may deal with 'structural' differences, such as argument conversion (16b), or more complex transfer (16c).

(16a) eat ↔ *manger*

(16b) miss(1:X,2:Y) ↔ *manquer*(1:Y',2:X')

(16c) walk(inv-1:across(2:X)) ↔ *traverser*(2:X',inv-1:$manner(2:à_pied))

CRITTER's grammars are the same for both analysis and generation, and are written in a Definite Clause Grammar formalism suitable for implementation in Prolog. From them are derived the parsers and generators, which differ primarily in the order in which rules are applied. In so far as the grammars used for syntactic analysis are also used for generation, and as the transfer rules are reversible, CRITTER exemplifies the reversibility methodology. In fact, its developers argue that CRITTER is as yet the only MT system with fully reversible grammars; Rosetta, for example (Chapter 16), includes a surface syntactic component in analysis which is absent on the generation side. On the other hand, CRITTER is itself, in one respect, not a truly symmetric system, since the semantic checking that is part of the analysis is not necessary for generation.

18.8 Computational developments

One of the most significant advances in the computational modelling of cognition, perception and learning has been research on parallel computation, neural networks and connectionist models. There is a widespread belief that the higher mental functions of language understanding, logical inferencing, and memory can only be modelled with brain-like mechanisms which compute massive amounts of information in parallel. The representation of knowledge demands likewise highly complex networks of interrelated 'concepts'. The neural network of the brain is assumed, with much experimental evidence, to be able to access and activate nodes simultaneously. The 'spreading activation' model of neural networks can be computationally modelled by the connectionist approach to computer design.

The relevance of the **connectionist** model to natural language processing is clear enough. The traditional stratificational approach to parsing and generation (morphology, syntax, semantics), while conceptually and computationally tractable, is not seriously accepted by linguists or computer scientists as a psychologically real model of how humans understand and communicate. The frequently expressed aspiration to integrate syntactic, semantic and pragmatic operations is an acknowledgement of the intrinsic attraction of connectionist processing. It is indeed difficult to envisage how the ambitious ATR speech translation system can possibly be realistically implemented without massively parallel computation. From a 'lower level' perspective it is obvious that parallel parsing of syntactic structures could bring marked improvements in present speeds of computer processing.

Speculation about the impact of parallel computation is complicated by the dearth of programming experience with neural networks, most of which have to be simulated on existing sequential computers. Evidence so far, however, suggests that connectionist networks can successfully 'learn' (or be 'trained') to parse previously unseen sentences with a high degree of accuracy. The idea of an MT system learning from past mistakes and from the corrections of post-editors has been put forward frequently. Indeed 'learning' routines have been implemented (e.g. on the Japanese MAPTRAN system and on the commercial Tovna system), but what is meant usually is that changes are suggested by the system on the basis of statistics about errors and corrections, and confirmed or rejected by developers or users. In a true learning system, changes would be initiated automatically by a complex feedback mechanism and constantly tested against new input. The connectionist model arguably offers the prospect of MT systems which really learn.

Less speculative developments are the possible integration of MT with other natural language processes. There have already been successful links with **information retrieval** systems, i.e. systems which enable users to search for titles and abstracts of documents on subjects of interest. Users are able to search remote databases containing abstracts in unknown languages and request translations of the abstracts or the full documents into their own language. Either the queries are translated and searches carried out in the other language, or the titles (or abstracts) have been already translated (e.g. by an MT system) and are searched in the user's language. At present the information retrieval systems and the MT systems are separated, but it is not difficult to envisage a future integrated multilingual information retrieval system.

A further step would be the automatic production of **abstracts** or summaries of texts for users unfamiliar with the original language. Summaries of foreign language documents would certainly be more attractive to most administrators, business people and scientists than even the roughest translations of full texts. However, it is evident from small-scale experiments on summarisation in restricted domains that the complexities of the task are at least equal to those of MT itself.

18.9 Concluding comments

The focus of this book has been the problems and difficulties of programming computers to translate and the methods which have been developed to tackle and overcome them. Except in two chapters (8 and 9), we have not discussed the practical aspects of MT operations, for reasons stated in the Preface. However, research on MT is not 'pure' research: it is directed towards the provision of tools for practical use, and it should be motivated by clearly defined objectives.

This has often been forgotten or ignored. Until the late 1970s most MT research activity was undertaken in academic environments with relatively little regard for immediate or even potential long-term applications. During the 1980s much basic research has been undertaken by independent companies, mainly in the electronics and computer business, for short- or long-term commercial interests. The impact has been two-fold: on the range of languages covered and on the types of systems developed.

For the first two decades of the history of MT, systems were developed primarily for the use of scientists to keep abreast of technological activity. Research concentrated on translation from Russian, or — in the case of Soviet MT research — from English. In the 1970s systems were designed for the pressing needs of bilingual Canada and the multilingual European Communities. The emphasis was on systems producing translations in bulk for post-editing by translators. In the 1980s the demand has been for systems covering the major commercial languages of the world (chiefly English, French, German, Spanish, and Japanese), and the need was for high-quality output: systems where the input could be controlled or systems involving considerable intervention by translators. Now, additional demands are emerging: systems translating other commercially important languages (e.g. Arabic, Chinese, Korean), systems for translating documents, textbooks and manuals from the 'major' languages of the developed world into the languages of the less developed countries, and systems for business people and researchers to translate messages and documents into languages they do not know. At the same time, the traditional expectations remain: there is a growing demand for rough translations for information-gathering and review purposes; users want improved translation aids (not just automatic dictionaries, multilingual word-processing and the like, but provisional pre-translations produced automatically); and companies are looking for systems to tackle multilingual documentation of various kinds and levels of quality (correspondence, technical manuals, marketing literature, etc.)

What can be safely predicted is that in the future we will see MT systems serving many varieties of purposes and users: systems for free unedited text input, for guided input, for texts in controlled languages, for pre-edited texts; systems for spoken communication, for on-line dialogue, for access to databases; systems for specific sublanguages, for specific text types (e.g. patents, abstracts), for broad subject areas (technical documents), even for 'any' subject; systems producing rough translations, good quality translations, preliminary drafts for translators; systems demanding human interaction during analysis, transfer or generation and systems operating in batch modes; systems for monolingual users, for professional translators, for occasional translators, for users ignorant of the source language, for users not knowing the target language; systems for scientists, for business people, for travellers, for administrators, for diplomats, for language learners, etc.; expensive systems for large multinational companies, systems for freelance translators, cheap desktop systems, hand-held systems. The permutations begin to seem endless, but what we can also predict is that there will not, in the foreseeable future, be an 'ideal' system capable of accepting all types of texts in all or most subjects producing output to the standard of the best human translators, and that there will not be MT systems capable of literary translation.

As for future methods and techniques, we can predict an equal variety of permutations: linguistics-based, knowledge-based, example-based, and statistics-based methods; direct, transfer and interlingua systems, and hybrids of various types; bilingual and multilingual configurations; facilities for non-interactive text input, dialogue-based composition of texts, spoken input; reversible grammars, rule-based systems, learning systems; and no doubt many others. Approaches and methods will be developed in response to purposes and goals, and in response to developments in linguistics, in computer science and technology, in cognitive science, in telecommunications, and no doubt elsewhere. Which approaches and techniques (or rather combinations of techniques) will lead to substantial improvements in the quality of MT output cannot be foreseen.

Machine Translation is one of the most challenging research activities, involving the application of complex theoretical knowledge to the building of systems whose successes and failures can be judged by laymen in the simplest of terms. We hope that this book has shown the nature and difficulties of the task and will inspire others to take up the challenge.

18.10 Sources and further reading

Surveys of current research appear regularly; recent ones by the authors include Hutchins (1988, 1990) and Somers (1990, 1991);

The most complete description of the CMU system is found in a special issue of *Machine Translation* edited by Goodman (1989); see especially Nirenburg (1989). The theoretical arguments for the CMU approach are given by Nirenburg and Goodman (1990). For details of earlier AI approaches, see Chapter 15 of Hutchins (1986).

The Bilingual Knowledge Bank of the DLT project is described most fully by Sadler (1989). The notion of 'bitext' corpora as aids for translators was proposed by Harris (1988). References to other experiments in Example-based MT are given in Chapter 6.

The statistical methods employed by the IBM system are described by Brown *et al.* (1990). For TITUS see Ducrot (1989).

The Ntran system is described in Whitelock *et al.* (1986) and in Wood and Chandler (1988). For the UMIST–British Telecom research see Jones and Tsujii (1990); the Malaysian work is described in Zaki and Muhayat (1991). For the UMIST–ATR work see Somers *et al.* (1990). The LIDIA project is described in Boitet (1990).

The discussion of CRITTER is based on Isabelle *et al.* (1988)

The BT 'phrasebook' project is described by Steer and Stentiford (1990), and the plans for Policespeak by Jackson (1990). There are numerous papers describing the ATR speech project, including Kakigahara and Aizawa (1988), Yoshimoto (1988), Kume *et al.* (1989), Kogure *et al.* (1990).

The 'learning' mechanism (PECOF) for the English–Japanese MAPTRAN system is described by Nishida and Takamatsu (1990). The investigation of the use of various Japanese–English MT systems in conjunction with Japanese databases of scientific and technical abstracts has been described by Sigurdson and Greatrex (1987).

For those readers who want to keep up to date with MT research, the proceedings of conferences are essential, notably the MT Summit conferences, the series of International Conferences on Theoretical and Methodological Issues in Machine Translation of Natural Language and the series of biennial Coling conferences. The main journal in the field is *Machine Translation* published by Kluwer (Dordrecht, The Netherlands), but articles on this topic appear in a wide range of other journals.

Bibliography

Abbou, A. (1989) (ed.) *Traduction assistée par ordinateur: perspectives technologiques, industrielles et économiques envisageables à l'horizon 1990: l'offre, la demande, les marchés et les évolutions en cours*, Editions Daicadif, Paris.

Allegranza, V., S. Krauwer and E. Steiner (1991) (eds) Eurotra Special Issue. *Machine Translation* 6, Nos.2/3.

Allerton, D.J. (1979) *Essentials of grammatical theory: a consensus view of syntax and morphology*. Routledge & Kegan Paul, London.

Alonso, J.A. (1990) Transfer InterStructure: designing an 'interlingua' for transfer-based MT systems. Third International Conference on Theoretical and Methodological Issues in Machine Translation of Natural Languages (Austin, TX), pp.189–201.

ALPAC (1966) *Language and machines: computers in translation and linguistics* A report by the Automatic Language Processing Advisory Committee, Division of Behavioral Sciences, National Research Council. National Academy of Sciences, Washington DC.

Appelo, L. and J. Landsbergen (1986) The machine translation project Rosetta. In Gerhardt (1986), pp.34–51.

Appelo, L., C. Fellinger and J. Landsbergen (1987) Subgrammars, rule classes and control in the Rosetta translation system. 3rd Conference of the European Chapter of the Association for Computational Linguistics (Copenhagen). Proceedings, pp.118–133.

Arnold, D. (1986) Eurotra: a European perspective on MT, *Proceedings of the IEEE*, 74, 979–992.

Arnold, D. and L. des Tombe (1987) Basic theory and methodology in EUROTRA. In Nirenburg (1987a), pp.114–135.

Arnold, D. and L. Sadler (1990) The theoretical basis of MiMo, *Machine Translation* **5**, 195–222.

Bar-Hillel, Y. (1953) A quasi-arithmetical notation for syntactic description, *Language* **29**, 47–58.

Bar-Hillel, Y. (1960) The present status of automatic translation of languages, *Advances in Computers* **1**, 91–163.

Barwise, J. and R. Cooper (1981) Generalized quantifiers and natural language, *Linguistics and Philosophy* **4**, 159–219.

Barwise, J. and J. Perry (1983) *Situations and attitudes.* MIT Press, Cambridge, Mass.

Bateman, R. (1985) Introduction to interactive translation. In Lawson (1985), pp.193–197.

Bátori, I. and H.J. Weber (1986) (eds) *Neue Ansätze in maschineller Sprachübersetzung: Wissensrepräsentation und Textbezug* (Sprache und Information 13). Niemeyer, Tübingen.

Bauer, L. (1988) *Introducing linguistic morphology.* Edinburgh University Press.

Bech, A. and A. Nygaard (1988) The E-framework: a formalism for natural language processing. In Coling (1988), pp.36–39.

Bech, A., B. Maegaard and A. Nygaard (1991) The Eurotra MT formalism, *Machine Translation* **6**, 83–101.

Becker, J.D. (1984) Multilingual word processing, *Scientific American* **251**, 82–93.

Bédard, C. (1990) Qu'est-ce que la prétraduction automatique (PTA)? *Circuit* **30**, Cahier spécial, hors série n° 1, p. Q11.

Bennett, P.A., R.L. Johnson, J. McNaught, J.M. Pugh, J.C. Sager and H.L. Somers (1986) *Multilingual aspects of information technology.* Gower, Aldershot.

Bennett, W.S. and J. Slocum (1985) The LRC machine translation system, *Computational Linguistics* **11**, 111–121; reprinted in Slocum (1988), pp.111–140.

Biewer, A., C. Feynerol, J. Ritzke and E. Stegentritt (1985) Ascof — A modular multilevel system for French–German translation, *Computational Linguistics* **11**, 137–154; reprinted in Slocum (1988), pp.49–84.

Blatt, A., K.-H. Freigang, K.-D. Schmitz and G. Thome (1985) *Computer und Übersetzen, eine Einführung* (Hildesheimer Beiträge zu den Erziehungs- und Sozialwissenschaften: Studien – Texte – Entwürfe 21). Olms, Hildesheim.

Boitet, C. (1987) Research and development on MT and related techniques at Grenoble University. In King (1987), pp.133–153.

Boitet, C. (1988) Pros and cons of the pivot and transfer approaches in multilingual machine translation. In Maxwell *et al.* (1988), pp.93–106.

Boitet, C. (1989a) GETA Project. In Nagao (1989), pp.54–65.

Boitet, C. (1989b) Speech synthesis and dialogue based machine translation. ATR Symposium on Basic Research for Telephone Interpretation (Kyoto), pp.6.18–25.

Boitet, C. (1990) Towards personal MT: general design, dialogue structure, potential role of speech. In Coling (1990), Vol. 3, pp.30–35.

Boitet, C. and R. Gerber (1986) Expert systems and other new techniques in M(a)T. In Bátori and Weber (1986), pp.103–119.

Boitet, C. and N. Nédobejkine (1981) Recent developments in Russian–French machine translation at Grenoble, *Linguistics* **19**, 199–271.

Booth, A.D. (1967) *Machine translation.* North-Holland, Amsterdam.

Bostad, D.A. (1986) Machine translation in the USAF, *Terminologie et Traduction* 1986/**1**, 68–72.

Bostad, D.A. (1988) Machine translation: the USAF experience. In K. Kummer (ed.) *American Translators Association Conference 1987: Across the language gap*, Learned Information, Medford, NJ, pp.435–443

Bresnan, J. (1982) (ed.) *The mental representation of grammatical relations.* MIT Press, Cambridge, Mass.

Brown, P., J. Cocke, S. Della Pietra, V.J. Della Pietra, F. Jelinek, J.D. Lafferty, R.L. Mercer and P.S. Roossin (1990) A statistical approach to machine translation, *Computational Linguistics* **16**, 79–85.

Bruderer, H.E. (1982) (ed.) *Automatische Sprachübersetzung.* Wissenschaftliche Buchgesellschaft, Darmstadt.

Brunner, P. (1985) Le projet national français Traduction Assistée par Ordinateur (TAO). Actes I.T.A. du Premier Colloque "La Traduction Automatique: Mythe ou Réalité", Ensealangues, Cergy, pp.7–15.

Canisius, P. (1977) Automatic partial translation in a multilingual information system. In CEC (1977), Vol. 1, pp.259–269.

CEC (Commission of the European Communities) (1977) *Overcoming the language barrier* (Third European Congress on Information Systems and Networks, Luxembourg). Verlag Dokumentation, München.

CEC (Commission of the European Communities) (1988) Eurotra assessment panel. Final report, October 1987. Comm(88) 270 final SYN 137, Annexe 1. Commission of the European Communities, Luxembourg.

CEC (Commission of the European Communities) (1990) EUROTRA Programme assessment report, March 1990. Comm(89) 603. Commission of the European Communities, Luxembourg.

Chandioux, J. (1976) MÉTÉO: un système opérationnel pour la traduction automatique des bulletins météorologiques destinés au grand public, *META* **21**, 127–133.

Chandioux, J. (1989a) 10 ans de Météo (MD). In Abbou (1989), pp.169–172.

Chandioux, J. (1989b) Météo: 100 million words later. In D.L. Hammond (ed.) *American Translators Association Conference 1989: Coming of Age.* Learned Information, Medford, NJ, pp.449–453.

Chevalier, M., J. Dansereau and G. Poulin (1978) TAUM-MÉTÉO: Description du système, janvier 1978. Publication interne, TAUM, Université de Montréal.

Chomsky, N. (1982) *Lectures on Government and Binding.* Foris, Dordrecht.

Coling (1980) *Proceedings of the 8th International Conference on Computational Linguistics*, Tokyo.

Coling (1982) J. Horecký (ed.) *COLING 82: Proceedings of the Ninth International Conference on Computational Linguistics* (North-Holland Linguistic Series 47) North-Holland, Amsterdam.

Coling (1984) *10th International Conference on Computational Linguistics*, 22nd Annual Meeting of the Association for Computational Linguistics: Proceedings of Coling84, Stanford, California.

Coling (1986) *11th International Conference on Computational Linguistics*: Proceedings of Coling '86 (Universität Bonn).

Coling (1988) D. Vargha (ed.) COLING *Budapest: Proceedings of the 12th International Conference on Computational Linguistics*. John von Neumann Society for Computing Sciences, Budapest.

Coling (1990) H. Karlgren (ed.) COLING-90: *Papers presented to the 13th International Conference on Computational Linguistics*. Yliopistopaino, Helsinki.

Colmerauer, A. (1970) Les systèmes Q, ou un formalisme pour analyser et synthétiser des phrases sur ordinateur. Publication interne No. 43. TAUM, Université de Montréal.

Damas, L. and G.B. Varile (1989) CLG: a grammar formalism based on constraint resolution. In E.M. Morgado and J.P. Martins (eds) *Proceedings of EPIA 1989* (Lecture Notes in Artificial Intelligence 390), Springer, Berlin, pp.175–186.

Davis, R. and J. King (1977) An overview of production systems. In E.W. Elcock and D. Michie (eds) *Machine Intelligence 8*, Edinburgh University Press, pp.300–304.

de Roeck, A. (1983) An underview of parsing. In King (1983), pp.3–17.

DiMarco, C. and G. Hirst (1988) Stylistic grammars in language translation. In Coling (1988), pp.148–153.

DiMarco, C. and G. Hirst (1990) Accounting for style in machine translation. Third International Conference on Theoretical and Methodological Issues in Machine Translation of Natural Languages (Austin, TX), pp.65–73.

Dowty, D.R., L. Karttunen and A.M. Zwicky (1985) (eds) *Natural language parsing: psychological, computational and theoretical perspectives*. Cambridge University Press.

Dowty, D.R., R.E. Wall and S. Peters (1981) *Introduction to Montague semantics*. Reidel, Dordrecht.

Ducrot, J.M. (1989) Le système TITUS IV: système de traduction automatique et simultanée en quatre langues. In Abbou (1989), pp.55–75.

Dyson, M.C. and J. Hannah (1987) Toward a methodology for the evaluation of machine-assisted translation systems, *Computers and Translation* 2, 163–176.

Elliston, J.S.G. (1979) Computer aided translation: a business viewpoint. In Snell (1979), pp.149–158.

Emele, M., W. Kehl and D. Rösner. Generating natural language from semantic representations — an AI approach to a Japanese/German machine translation project. In Gerhardt (1986), pp.67–78.

Farwell, D. and Y. Wilks (1991) Ultra: a multilingual machine translator. MT Summit III (Washington), Proceedings, pp.19–24.

Frazier, L. (1985) Syntactic complexity. In Dowty *et al.* (1985), pp.129–189.

Gachot, D.A. (1989) The SYSTRAN renaissance. MT Summit II (Munich), Final Programme, Exhibition, Papers, pp.60–65.

Gal, A., G. Lapalme, P. Saint-Dizier and H. Somers (1991) *Prolog for natural language processing*. John Wiley, Chichester.

Gavare, R. (1988) Alphabetical ordering in a lexicological perspective (a computational model for exacting alphabetization of dictionary and encyclopedic material). In Språkdata (University of Göteborg) *Studies in computer-aided lexicology* (Data linguistica 18). Almqvist & Wiksell International, Stockholm, pp.63–102.

Gazdar, G. and C. Mellish (1989) *Natural language processing in PROLOG: an introduction to computational linguistics*. Addison-Wesley, Reading, MA.

Gazdar, G., E. Klein, G. Pullum and I. Sag (1985) *Generalized phrase structure grammar*. Blackwell, Oxford

Gerhardt, T.C. (1986) (ed.) *I. International Conference on the State of the Art in Machine Translation in America, Asia and Europe: Proceedings of IAI-MT86*, IAI/EUROTRA-D, Saarbrücken.

Goetschalckx, J. and L. Rolling (1982) (eds) *Lexicography in the electronic age*. North-Holland, Amsterdam.

Goodman, K. (1989) (ed.) Special issue on Knowledge-Based Machine Translation, I and II, *Machine Translation* 4, Nos.1/2.

Grosz, B., B.L. Webber and K. Sparck Jones (1986) (eds) *Readings in natural language processing*. Morgan Kaufmann, Los Altos CA.

Guilbaud, J.-P. (1987) Principles and results of a German to French MT system at Grenoble University (GETA). In King (1987), pp.278–318.

Habermann, F.W.A. (1986) Provision and use of raw machine translation, *Terminologie et Traduction* 1986/1, 29–42.

Halliday, M.A.K. and R. Hasan (1976) *Cohesion in English*. Longman, London.

Harada, T. (1986) NEC's machine translation system "PIVOT", *Japan Computer Quarterly*, 64 24–31.

Harris, B. (1988) Bi-text: a new concept in translation theory, *Language Monthly* 54, 8–10.

Hartmann, R.K.K. (1984) (ed.) *LEXeter '83 Proceedings: papers from the International Conference on Lexicography*. Niemeyer, Tübingen.

Herbst, T., D. Heath and H.-M. Dedering (1979) *Grimm's grandchildren: current topics in German linguistics*. Longman, London.

Hirst, G. (1987) *Semantic interpretation and the resolution of ambiguity*. Cambridge University Press.

Hobbs, J.R. (1983) An improper treatment of quantification in ordinary English. 21st Annual Meeting of the Association for Computational Linguistics (Cambridge, MA.). Proceedings, pp.464–467.

Hobbs, J.R. and M. Kameyama (1990) Translation by abduction. In Coling (1990), Vol. 3, pp.155–161.

Hobbs, J.R. and S.M. Shieber (1987) An algorithm for generating quantifier scopings, *Comptational Linguistics* 13, 47–63.

Horrocks, G. (1987) *Generative grammar*. Longman, London.

Huang, X. (1988) Semantic analysis in XTRA, an English–Chinese machine translation system, *Computers and Translation* **3**, 101–120.

Hutchins, W.J. (1986) *Machine translation: past, present, future.* Ellis Horwood, Chichester.

Hutchins, W.J. (1988) Recent developments in machine translation: a review of the last five years. In Maxwell *et al.* (1988), pp.7–62.

Hutchins, W.J. (1990) Out of the shadows: a retrospect of machine translation in the eighties, *Teminologie et Traduction* 1990/3, 275–292.

Ikegami, Y. (1978) *How universal is a localist hypothesis? A linguistic contribution to the study of "semantic styles" of language* (Series A, No. 49). Linguistic Agency University of Trier.

Isabelle, P., M. Dymetman and E. Macklovitch (1988) CRITTER: a translation system for agricultural market reports. In Coling (1988), pp.261–266.

Jackson, T. (1990) Less is more, *Electric Word* **19**, 42–45.

Johnson, R.L. (1983) Parsing — an MT perspective. In Sparck Jones and Wilks (1983), pp.32–38.

Johnson, R.L. (1984) Contemporary perspectives in machine translation. *Contrastes* (Revue de l'Association pour le Développement des Etudes Contrastives) hors série A4 "Traduction Automatique — Aspects Européens", janvier 1984, pp.141–155.

Johnson, R.L. and P. Whitelock (1987) Machine translation as an expert task. In Nirenburg (1987a), pp.136–144.

Johnson, R.L., M. King and L. des Tombe (1985) EUROTRA: a multilingual system under development, *Computational Linguistics* **11**, 155–169.

Jones, D. and J. Tsujii (1990) High quality machine-driven text translation. Third International Conference on Theoretical and Methodological Issues in Machine Translation of Natural Languages (Austin, TX), pp.43–46.

Joscelyne, A. (1987) Calliope and other pipe dreams, *Language Technology* **4**, 20–21.

Kakigahara, K. and T. Aizawa (1988) Completion of Japanese sentences by inferring function words from content words. In Coling (1988), pp.291–296.

Kaplan, R.M. (1973) A general syntactic processor. In Rustin (1973), pp.193–241.

Kaplan, R.M., K. Netter, J. Wedekind and A. Zaenen. (1989) Translation by structural correspondences. 4th Conference of the European Chapter of the Association for Computational Linguistics (Manchester). Proceedings, pp.272–281.

Karlgren, H. (1987) Good use of poor translations, *International Forum on Information and Documentation* **12**.4, 23–29.

Kay, M. (1973) The MIND system. In Rustin (1973), pp.155–188.

Kay, M. (1976) Experiments with a powerful parser, *American Journal of Computational Linguistics* **3**, microfiche 43.

Kay, M. (1980) The proper place of men and machines in language translation. Research Report CSL–80–11. Xerox Palo Alto Research Center, Palo Alto, California.

King, M. (1982) Eurotra: an attempt to achieve multilingual MT. In Lawson (1982), pp.139–148.

King, M. (1983) (ed.) *Parsing natural language*. Academic Press, London.

King, M. (1987) (ed.) *Machine translation today: the state of the art* (Edinburgh Information Technology Series 2), Edinburgh University Press.

King, M. and K. Falkedal (1990) Using test suites in evaluation of machine translation systems. In Coling (1990), Vol. 2, pp.211–216.

King, M. and S. Perschke (1987) EUROTRA. In King (1987), pp.373–391.

Kirchmeier-Andersen, S. (1991) Implementing monolingual grammars and transfer components in the Eurotra formalism, *Machine Translation* **6**, 149–170.

Kittredge, R.I. (1987) The significance of sublanguage for automatic translation. In Nirenburg (1987a), pp.59–67.

Kittredge, R.I. and J. Lehrberger (1982) (eds). *Sublanguage: studies of language in restricted semantic domains*. De Gruyter, Berlin.

Kittredge, R.I., A. Polguère and E. Goldberg (1986) Synthesizing weather forecasts from formatted data. In Coling (1986), pp.563–565.

Knowles, F. (1979) Error analysis of Systran output: a suggested criterion for 'internal' evaluation of translation quality and a possible corrective for system design. In Snell (1979), pp.109–134.

Kogure, K., M. Kume and H. Iida (1990) Illocutionary act based translation of dialogues. Third International Conference on Theoretical and Methodological Issues in Machine Translation of Natural Languages (Austin, TX), pp.47–55.

Krauwer, S. and L. des Tombe. (1984) Transfer in a multilingual MT system. In Coling (1984), pp.464–467.

Kroupa, E. and H.H. Zimmermann (1987) Multilinguale Anwendungen der Sprach-datenverarbeitung in Referenz–Informationssysteme. In Wilss and Schmitz (1987), pp.33–48.

Kume, M., G.K. Sato and K. Yoshimoto (1989) A descriptive framework for translating speaker's meaning: towards a dialogue translation system between Japanese and English. 4th Conference of the European Chapter of the Association for Computational Linguistics (Manchester). Proceedings, pp.264–271.

Kurtzman, H.S. (1984) Ambiguity resolution in the human syntactic parser: an experimental study. In Coling (1984), pp.481–484.

Landsbergen, J. (1987a) Isomorphic grammars and their use in the ROSETTA translation system. In King (1987), pp.351–372.

Landsbergen, J. (1987b) Montague grammar and machine translation. In Whitelock *et al.* (1987), pp.113–147.

Landsbergen, J., J. Odijk and A. Schenk (1989) The power of compositional translation, *Literary & Linguistic Computing* **4**, 191–199.

Laubsch, J., D. Roesner, K. Hanakata and A. Lesniewski (1984) Language generation from conceptual structure: synthesis of German in a Japanese/German MT project. In Coling (1984), pp.491–494.

Lawson, V. (1982) (ed.) *Practical experience of machine translation.* North-Holland, Amsterdam.

Lawson, V. (1985) (ed.) *Tools for the trade: Translating and the Computer 5.* North-Holland, Amsterdam.

Leech, G. (1974) *Semantics.* Penguin, Harmondsworth.

Leermakers, R. and J. Rous (1986) The translation method of Rosetta, *Computers and Translation* 1, 169–183.

Lehrberger, J. and L. Bourbeau (1988) *Machine translation: linguistic characteristics of MT systems and general methodology of evaluation* (Lingvisticæ Investigationes: Supplementa, Volume 15). John Benjamins, Amsterdam.

Lieber, R. (1983) Argument linking and compounds in English, *Linguistic Inquiry* 14, 251–285.

Lippmann, E.O. (1971) An approach to computer-aided translation, *IEEE Transactions on Engineering Writing and Speech* 14, 10–33.

Little, P. (1990) METAL — machine translation in practice. In Picken (1990), pp.94–107.

Locke, W.N. and A.D. Booth (1955) *Machine translation of languages.* MIT Press, Cambridge, Mass.

Luckhardt, H.-D. (1976) Technische Beschreibung des Saarbrücker Übersetzungssystems SUSY, Teil i: Programmablauf und Dateibeschreibung. Linguistische Arbeiten 21, Universität des Saarlandes, Saarbrücken.

Luckhardt, H.-D. (1982) SUSY: capabilities and range of application, *Multilingua* 1, 213–220.

Luckhardt, H.-D. (1985) Parsing mit SUSY und SUSY-II: Strategien, Software und linguistisches Wissen. Linguistische Arbeiten Neue Folge 12, Universität des Saarlandes, Saarbrücken.

Luckhardt, H.-D. (1987) *Der Transfer in der maschinellen Sprachübersetzung* (Sprache und Information 18). Niemeyer, Tübingen.

Luckhardt, H.-D. and H.-D. Maas (1983) SUSY — Handbuch für Transfer und Synthese: Die Erzeugung deutscher, englischer oder französischer Sätze aus SATAN-Analyseergebnissen. Linguistische Arbeiten Neue Folge 7, Universität des Saarlandes, Saarbrücken.

Lyons, J. (1981a) *Language and linguistics: an introduction.* Cambridge University Press.

Lyons, J. (1981b) *Language, meaning and context.* Fontana, London.

Maas, H.-D. (1977) The Saarbrücken automatic translation system (SUSY). In CEC (1977), Vol. 1, pp.585–592.

Maas, H.-D. (1978) Das Saarbrücker Übersetzungssystem SUSY, *Sprache und Datenverarbeitung* 2, 43–62.

Maas, H.-D. (1980) Zur Analyse deutscher Komposita und Derivationen. Linguistische Arbeiten Neue Folge 3.1, Universität des Saarlandes, Saarbrücken.

Maas, H.-D. (1981) SUSY I und SUSY II: verschiedene Analysestrategien in der maschinellen Übersetzung, *Sprache und Datenverarbeitung* 5, 9–15.

Maas, H.-D. (1984) Susy-II-Handbuch. Linguistische Arbeiten Neue Folge 14, Universität des Saarlandes, Saarbrücken.

Maas, H.-D. (1987) The MT system Susy. In King (1987), pp.209–246.

Magnusson Murray, U. (1988) Are you being served? User-friendliness of CAT systems. In Picken (1988), pp.80–90.

Martin, L. (1986) "Eskimo words for snow": a case study in the genesis and decay of an anthropological example, *Amercian Anthropologist* **88**, 418–423.

Maxwell, D. and K. Schubert (1989) (eds) *Metataxis in practice: dependency syntax for multilingual machine translation* (Distributed Language Translation 6). Foris, Dordrecht.

Maxwell, D., K. Schubert and T. Witkam (1988) (eds) *New directions in machine translation* (Distributed Language Translation 4). Foris, Dordrecht.

Mayorcas, P. (1990) (ed.) *Translating and the Computer 10: The translation environment 10 years on.* Aslib, London.

McDonald, D.D. (1987) Natural language generation: complexities and techniques. In Nirenburg (1987a), pp.192–224.

McElhaney, T. and M. Vasconcellos (1988) The translator and the postediting experience. In Vasconcellos (1988), pp.140–148.

Melby, A.K. (1982) Multi-level translation aids in a distributed system. In Coling (1982), pp.215–220.

Melby, A.K. (1983) Computer-assisted translation systems: the standard design and a multi-level design. Conference on Applied Natural Language Processing (Santa Monica, California). Proceedings, pp.174–177.

Melby, A.K. (1987) On human-machine interaction in translation. In Nirenburg (1987a), pp.145–154.

Melby, A.K. (1988) Lexical transfer: between a source rock and a hard target. In Coling (1988), pp.411–419.

Nagao, M. (1986) *Machine translation: how far can it go?*. Oxford University Press, 1989; translation by N.D. Cook of *Kikai hon'yaku wa doko made kano ka*, Iwanami Shoten, Tokyo.

Nagao, M. (1989) (ed.-in-chief) *Machine Translation Summit*. Ohmsha, Tokyo.

Newell, A. (1973) Production systems, models of control structures. In W.G. Chase (ed.) *Visual information processing*, Academic Press, New York, pp.463–526.

Nirenburg, S. (1987a) (ed.) *Machine translation: theoretical and methodological issues.* Cambridge University Press.

Nirenburg, S. (1987b) Knowledge and choices in machine translation. In Nirenburg (1987a), pp.1–21.

Nirenburg, S. (1989) Knowledge-based machine translation, *Machine Translation* **4**, 5–24.

Nirenburg, S. and K. Goodman (1990) Treatment of meaning in MT systems. Third International Conference on Theoretical and Methodological Issues in Machine Translation of Natural Languages (Austin, TX), pp.171–188.

Nishida, F. and S. Takamatsu (1990) Automated procedures for the improvement of a machine translation system by feedback from postediting, *Machine Translation* **5**, 223–246.

Nishida, F., S. Takamatsu and H. Kuroki (1980) English–Japanese translation through case-structure conversion. In Coling (1980), pp.447–454.

Odijk, J. (1989) The organization of the Rosetta grammars. 4th Conference of the European Chapter of the Association for Computational Linguistics (Manchester). Proceedings, pp.80–87.

Oehrle, R.T., E. Bach and D. Wheeler (1988) (eds) *Categorial grammars and natural language structures.* Reidel, Dordrecht.

Panov, D.Y. (1960) Machine translation and the human being, *Impact of Science on Society* **10**, 16–25.

Papegaaij, B.C., V. Sadler and A.P.M. Witkam (1986) (eds) *Word expert semantics: an interlingual knowledge-based approach* (Distributed Language Translation 1). Foris, Dordrecht.

Pereira, F.C.N. and S.M. Shieber (1987) *Prolog and natural language analysis* (CSLI Lecture Notes 10). Center for the Study of Language and Information, Stanford.

Picken, C. (1985) (ed.) *Translation and Communication: Translating and the Computer 6.* Aslib, London.

Picken, C. (1986) (ed.) *Translating and the Computer 7.* Aslib, London.

Picken, C. (1987) (ed.) *Translating and the Computer 8: a profession on the move.* Aslib, London.

Picken, C. (1988) (ed.) *Translating and the Computer 9: potential and practice.* Aslib, London.

Picken, C. (1990) (ed.) *Translating and the Computer 11: preparing for the next decade.* Aslib, London.

Pigott, I.M. (1989) Systran at the Commission of the European Communities. International Forum for Translation Technology '89, Tokyo. Manuscripts and Program, pp.29–31.

Pullum, G.K. (1989) The great Eskimo vocabulary hoax, *Natural Language & Linguistic Theory* **7**, 275–281.

Pulman, S.G. (1987) Computational models of parsing. In A.W. Ellis (ed.) *Progress in the psychology of language*, Lawrence Erlbaum, Hillsdale, NJ., Vol. 3, pp.159–231.

Radford, A. (1988) *Transformational grammar.* Cambridge University Press.

Raskin, V. (1974) On the feasibility of fully automatic high quality machine translation, *American Journal of Computational Linguistics* **1**, microfiche 9.

Raw, A., B. Vandecapelle and F. van Eynde (1988) Eurotra: an overview, *Interface* **3**, 5–32.

Reinhart, T. (1983) *Anaphora and semantic resolution.* Croom Helm, London.

Richardson, S.D. and L.C. Braden-Harder (1988) The experience of developing a large-scale natural language text processing system: CRITIQUE. 2nd Conference on Applied Natural Language Processing (Austin, Texas). Proceedings, pp.195–202.

Rohrer, C. (1986) Maschinelle Übersetzung mit Unifikationsgrammatiken. In Bátori and Weber (1986), pp.75–99.

Rösner, D. (1986a) When Mariko talks to Siegfried: experiences from a Japanese/German machine translation project. In Coling (1986), pp.652–654.

Rösner, D. (1986b) SEMSYN — Wissensquellen und Strategien bei der Generierung von Deutsch aus einer semantischen Repräsentation. In Bátori and Weber (1986), pp.121–137.

Rosner, M. (1983) Production systems. In King (1983), pp.35–58.

Ruffino, J.R. (1982) Coping with machine translation. In Lawson (1982), pp.57–60.

Rupp, C.J. (1989) Situation semantics and machine translation. 4th Conference of the European Chapter of the Association for Computational Linguistics (Manchester). Proceedings, pp.308–318.

Rustin, R. (1973) (ed.) *Natural language processing* (Courant Computer Science Symposium 8), Algorithmic Press, New York.

Sadler, L., I. Crookston, D. Arnold and A. Way (1990) LFG and translation. Third International Conference on Theoretical and Methodological Issues in Machine Translation of Natural Languages (Austin, TX), pp.121–130.

Sadler, V. (1989) *Working with analogical semantics: disambiguation techniques in DLT* (Distributed Language Translation 5). Foris, Dordrecht.

Sager, J.C. (1986) Conclusions. In World Systran Conference (1986), pp.161–166.

Sager J.C. and H.L. Somers (1986) (eds) EUROTRA Special Issue, *Multilingua* 5, No. 3.

Saito, H. and M. Tomita (1986) On automatic composition of stereotypic documents in foreign languages. Presented at 1st International Conference on Applications of Artificial Intelligence to Engineering Problems (Southampton). Research Report CMU–CS–86–107, Department of Computer Science, Carnegie-Mellon University, Pittsburgh.

Sanders, M.J. (1988) The Rosetta translation system. Technical Report, Philips Research Laboratories, Eindhoven.

Sato, S. and M. Nagao (1990) Toward memory-based translation. In Coling (1990), Vol. 3, pp.247–252.

Schenk, A. (1989) The formation of idiomatic structures. Technical Report, Philips Research Laboratories, Eindhoven.

Schneider, T. (1989) The METAL system. Status 1989. MT Summit II (Munich), Final Programme, Exhibition, Papers, pp.128–136.

Schubert, K. (1986) Linguistic and extra-linguistic knowledge, *Computers and Translation* 1, 125–152.

Schubert, K. (1987) *Metataxis: contrastive dependency syntax for machine translation* (Distributed Language Translation 2). Foris, Dordrecht.

Schubert, K. (1988) The architecture of DLT — interlingual or double direct? In Maxwell *et al.* (1988), pp.131–144.

Scott, M. (1990) The automated translation of software, particularly the computer user interface and user manuals. In Mayorcas (1990), pp.109–118.

Selkirk, E. (1982) *The syntax of words*. MIT Press, Cambridge, Mass.

Sells, P. (1985) *Lectures on contemporary syntactic theories: an introduction to government-binding theory, generalized phrase-structure grammar, and lexical-functional grammar* (CSLI Lecture Notes 3). Stanford, CA, Center for the Study of Languauge and Information.

Shah, R. (1989) Translation of engineering documentation with METAL. In Nagao (1989), pp.152–159.

Sharp, R. (1988) CAT2 — Implementing a formalism for multi-lingual MT. Second International Conference on Theoretical and Methodological Issues in Machine Translation of Natural Languages, (Pittsburgh). Paper 3.2.

Shieber, S.M. (1986) *An introduction to unification-based approaches to grammar* (CSLI Lecture Notes 4). Stanford, CA, Center for the Study of Languauge and Information.

Sigurd, B. (1988) Translating to and from Swedish by SWETRA — a multilanguage translation system. In Maxwell *et al.* (1988), pp.205–217.

Sigurdson, J. and R. Greatrex (1987) *Machine translation of on-line searches in Japanese databases: a way to facilitate access to Japanese techno-economic information?* Research Policy Unit, Lund University.

Sinaiko, H.W. and G.R. Klare (1972) Further experiments in language translation: readability of computer translations, *ITL* **15**, 1–29.

Sinaiko, H.W. and G.R. Klare (1973) Further experiments in language translation: a second evaluation of the readability of computer translations, *ITL* **19** 29–52.

Slocum, J. (1987) METAL: the LRC machine translation system. In King (1987), pp.319–350.

Slocum, J. (1988) (ed.) *Machine translation systems*. Cambridge University Press.

Snell, B.M. (1979) (ed.) *Translating and the computer*. North-Holland, Amsterdam.

Snell, B.M. (1983) (ed.) *Term banks for tomorrow's world: Translating and the Computer 4*. Aslib, London.

Somers, H.L. (1983) Investigating the possibility of a microprocessor-based machine translation system. Conference on Applied Natural Language Processing (Santa Monica, California). Proceedings, pp.149–155.

Somers, H.L. (1987a) *Valency and case in computational linguistics* (Edinburgh Information Technology Series 3). Edinburgh University Press.

Somers, H.L. (1987b) Some thoughts on interface structure(s). In Wilss and Schmitz (1987), pp.81–99.

Somers, H.L. (1990) Current research in machine translation. Third International Conference on Theoretical and Methodological Issues in Machine Translation of Natural Languages (Austin, TX), pp.1–12.

Somers, H.L. (1991) Current research in machine translation. To appear in J. Newton (ed.) *Computers in translation — a practical appraisal*, Routledge, London.

Somers, H.L. and J. McNaught (1980) The translator as a computer user, *The Incorporated Linguist* **19**, 49–53.

Somers, H.L., H. Hirakawa, S. Miike and S. Amano (1988) The treatment of complex English nominalizations in machine translation, *Computers and Translation* **3**, 3–21.

Somers, H.L., J-I. Tsujii and D. Jones (1990) Machine Translation without a source text. In Coling (1990), Vol. 3, pp.271–276.

Sparck Jones, K. and Y. Wilks (1983) (eds). *Automatic natural language parsing.* Ellis Horwood, Chichester.

Stefik, M., J. Aikins, R. Balzer, J. Benoit, L. Birnbaum, F. Hayes-Roth and E. Sacerdoti (1982) The organization of expert systems: a tutorial, *Artificial Intelligence* **18**, 135–173.

Steiner, E.H., P. Schmidt and C. Zelinsky-Wibbelt (1988) (eds) *From syntax to semantics: insights from machine translation.* Pinter, London.

Stentiford, F.W.M. and M.G. Steer (1990) Machine translation of speech. In C. Wheddon and R. Linggard (eds) *Speech and language processing*, Chapman and Hall, London, pp.183–196.

Stoll, C.-H. (1988) Translation tools on PC. In Picken (1988), pp.11–26.

Sumita, E., H. Iida and H. Kohyama (1990) Translating with examples: a new approach to machine translation. Third International Conference on Theoretical and Methodological Issues in Machine Translation of Natural Languages (Austin, TX), pp.203–212.

Tenney, M.D. (1985) Machine translation, machine-aided translation, and machine-impeded translation. In Lawson (1985), pp.105–114.

Thompson, H. and G. Ritchie (1984) Implementing natural language parsers. In T. O'Shea and M. Eisenstadt (eds) *Artificial intelligence: tools, techniques and applications*, Harper & Row, New York, Chapter 9.

Thurmair, G. (1990) Complex lexical transfer in METAL. Third International Conference on Theoretical and Methodological Issues in Machine Translation of Natural Languages (Austin, TX), pp.91–107.

Toma, P. (1976) An operational machine translation system. In R.W. Brislin (ed.) *Translation: applications and research*, Gardner Press, New York, pp.247–259.

Toma, P. (1977) Systran as a multilingual machine translation system. In CEC (1977), pp.569–581.

Tong, L-C. (1987) The engineering of a translator workstation, *Computers and Translation* **2**, 263–273.

Trabulsi, S. (1989) Le système SYSTRAN. In Abbou (1989), pp.15–34.

Tsujii, J-I. (1986) Future directions of machine translation. In Coling (1986), pp.655–668.

Tsujii, J-I. (1988) What is a cross-linguistically valid interpretation of discourse? In Maxwell *et al.* (1988), pp.157–166.

Tucker, A.B. (1987) Current strategies in machine translation research and development. In Nirenburg (1987a), pp.22–41.

Uchida, H. (1988) ATLAS: A MT system by interlingua [*sic*]. Second International Conference on Theoretical and Methodological Issues in Machine Translation of Natural Languages, Carnegie Mellon University, Pittsburgh, Paper 5.2.

Uchida, H. (1989) ATLAS II: a machine translation system using conceptual structure as an interlingua. In Nagao (1989), pp.93–100.

van Noord, G., J. Dorrepaal, P. van der Eijk, M. Florenza and L. des Tombe (1990) The MiMo2 research system. Third International Conference on Theoretical and Methodological Issues in Machine Translation of Natural Languages (Austin, TX), pp.213–233.

van Slype, G. (1979) Systran: evaluation of the 1978 version of the Systran English–French automatic system of the Commisssion of the European Communities, *The Incorporated Linguist* **18**, 86–89.

van Slype, G. (1982) Economic aspects of machine translation. In Lawson (1982), pp.79–93.

van Slype, G. and I. Pigott (1979) Description du système de traduction automatique SYSTRAN de la Commission des Communautés Européennes, *Documentaliste* **16**, 150–159.

Varile, G.B. (1983) Charts: a data structure for parsing. In King (1983), pp.73–87.

Varile, G.B. and P. Lau (1988) Eurotra: practical experience with a multilingual machine translation system under development. 2nd Conference on Applied Natural Language Processing (Austin, Texas). Proceedings, pp.160–167.

Vasconcellos, M. (1987) Post-editing on-screen: machine translation from Spanish into English. In Picken (1987), pp.133–146.

Vasconcellos, M. (1988) (ed.) *Technology as translation strategy*(American Translators Association Scholarly Monograph Series, Volume II). State University of New York at Binghamton.

Vauquois, B. (1968) A survey of formal grammars and algorithms for recognition and transformation in machine translation. IFIP Congress-68, (Edinburgh), pp.254–260; reprinted in Vauquois (1988), pp.201–213.

Vauquois, B. (1975) *La traduction automatique à Grenoble* (Documents de Linguistique Quantitative 24). Dunod, Paris.

Vauquois, B. (1988) *Bernard Vauquois et la TAO: vingt-cinq ans de traduction automatique — analectes; Bernard Vauquois and MT: twenty-five years of machine translation — selected writings* édité par Ch. Boitet. Association Champollion, Grenoble.

Vauquois, B. and C. Boitet (1985) Automated translation at Grenoble University, *Computational Linguistics* **11**, 28–36; reprinted in Slocum (1988), pp.85–110.

Vauquois, B. and S. Chappuy (1985) Static grammars: a formalism for the description of linguistic model. Proceedings of the Conference on Theoretical and Methodological Issues in Machine Translation of Natural Languages (Colgate University, Hamilton NY), pp.298–322; reprinted in Vauquois (1988), pp.687–712.

von Ammon, R. and R. Wessoly (1984/5) Das Evaluationskonzept des automatischen Übersetzungsprojekts SUSY-DJT (Deutsch–Japanisch Titelübersetzung), *Multilingua* **3**, 189–1195, **4**, 27–33.

Wagner, E. (1985) Rapid post-editing of Systran. In Lawson (1985), pp.199–214.

Waterman, D. and F. Hayes-Roth (1978) *Pattern-directed inference systems*. Academic Press, London.

Weaver, A. (1988) Two aspects of interactive machine translation. In Vasconcellos (1988), pp.116–123.

Weaver, W. (1949) Translation. Reprinted in Locke and Booth (1955), pp.15–23.

Wheeler, P.J. (1987) SYSTRAN. In King (1987), pp.192–208.

Whitelock, P.J. and K.J. Kilby (1983) Linguistic and computational techniques in machine translation system design. CCL/UMIST Report 84/2, Centre for Computational Linguistics, UMIST, Manchester.

Whitelock, P.J., M. McGee Wood, B.J. Chandler, N. Holden and H.J. Horsfall (1986) Strategies for interactive machine translation: the experience and implications of the UMIST Japanese project. In Coling (1986), pp.329–334.

Whitelock, P.J., M.M. Wood, H.L. Somers, R. Johnson and P. Bennett (1987) (eds) *Linguistic theory and computer applications*. Academic Press, London.

Wilks, Y. (1989) More advanced machine translation. International Forum for Translation Technology IFTT '89 "Harmonizing Human Beings and Computers in Translation" (Oiso), Manuscripts and Program, p.59.

Wilks, Y., X. Huang and D. Fass (1985) Syntax, preference and right attachment. International Joint Conference on Artificial Intelligence, Los Angeles. Proceedings, vol. 2, pp.779–784.

Wilms, F.J.M. (1981) Von SUSY zu SUSY-BSA: Forderungen an eine anwenderbezogenes MÜ-Systems, *Sprache und Datenverarbeitung* 5, 38–43.

Wilss, W. und K.-D. Schmitz (1987) (eds) *Maschinelle Übersetzung — Methoden und Werkzeuge* (Sprache und Information 16). Niemeyer, Tübingen.

Winograd, T. (1983) *Language as a cognitive process, Volume I: Syntax*. Addison-Wesley, Reading, MA.

Witkam, A.P.M. (1983) *Distributed language translation: feasibility study of a multilingual facility for videotex information networks*. BSO, Utrecht.

World Systran Conference (1986) *Terminologie et Traduction*, 1986/1, special issue.

Wood, M.M. and B.J. Chandler (1988) Machine translation for monolinguals. In Coling (1988), pp.760–763.

Yoshimoto, K. (1988) Identifying zero pronouns in Japanese dialogue. In Coling (1988), pp.779–784.

Zajac, R. (1988) Interactive translation: a new approach. In Coling (1988), pp.785–790.

Zajac, R. (1989) A transfer model using a typed feature structure rewriting system with inheritance. 27th Annual Meeting of the Association for Computational Linguistics (Vancouver, BC). Proceedings, pp.1–6.

Zajac, R. (1990) A relational approach to translation. Third International Conference on Theoretical and Methodological Issues in Machine Translation of Natural Languages (Austin, TX), pp.235–254.

Zaki Abu Bakar, A. and N.H. Muhayat (1991) Malay official letters translation. International Conference on Current Issues in Computational Linguistics (Penang), Proceedings, pp.413–420.

Index

Page references in *italics* refer to 'Further reading' sections.